THE SONGS OF A

By the same author

*The Message of the Psalter:
An Eschatological Programme in the Book of Psalms*

Messiah ben Joseph

www.brightmorningstar.org

The Songs of Ascents

*Psalms 120 to 134 in the Worship
of Jerusalem's Temples*

DAVID C. MITCHELL

CAMPBELL
PUBLISHERS

CAMPBELL PUBLISHERS
GLASGOW SCOTLAND

Copyright © 2015 David C. Mitchell

The author has asserted his moral right under the
Copyright, Designs and Patents Act, 1988, to be identified
as the author of this work

First Edition

All rights reserved. No part of this publication may be reproduced, copied, stored in a retrieval system, or transmitted, in any form or by any means, without the prior written consent of the copyright holder, nor be otherwise circulated in any form of binding or cover other than that in which it is published and without a similar condition being imposed on the subsequent purchaser

Cover illustration: Levites singing on the *dukhan*. (Courtesy of the Temple Institute, Jerusalem.)

ISBN 978-1-916619-03-6

CampbellPublishers.com

Cover design and layout by Claroprint.co.uk

Brightmorningstar.org

Contents

Figures, Tables, and Musical Examples	ix
Foreword	xi
Preface	xii
Abbreviations	xv

Proem. In the Garden of God	1

1. Books Within Books	3
One Name	4
One Mood	5
One Lord	6
One City	7
One King	8
One Tongue	9
One Story	11
…and a Multitude of Patterns	12
Summary	14

2. Words Within Words	15
Numerology and *gematria*	15
Encoded numeric messages	17
More encoded messages	20
The name *yedid* encoded in the central psalm	21
Gypsy rose	23
The value of numerology	24

3. Steps Within Steps	27
The 'Ascents' as pilgrim ways to Jerusalem	27
The 'Ascents' and the Feast of Sukkot	31
The 'Ascents' as steps of the temple	32
Summary	34

4. Who Lies Behind Them?	36
1. The tribes of Israel united	36
2. Under one king of David's line	37
3. In Jerusalem	37
4. In a polity called Israel	38

5. With a temple	38
6. With Aaronite *kohanim*	39
7. With the Ark	40
8. In a peaceful kingdom	40
Weighing up the evidence	41
Solomon's reign	43

5. The Lodgings of the Holy Ark — 45

The ark of the covenant	45
What did the ark represent?	47
From tabernacle to Zion tent	51
The ark in Solomon's temple	52
What didn't happen to the ark?	54
What did happen to the ark?	56
What the rabbi saw	61

6. For What Event Were They Composed? — 63

The summons of Psalm 132	63
The Ascents at the temple's dedication	65
When did the ark enter the temple?	66

7. Who Wrote Them? — 70

The author headings of the Psalms	70
Authorship of Psalms 122, 124, 131, and 133	75
Who wrote the other Songs of Ascents?	78
Summary	80

8. The Temple Orchestra: Origins and Instruments — 82

Origins of the temple orchestra	82
Névél and kinnor	85
Pipes and flutes	86
Magrefah	88
Trumpets	89
Percussion instruments	92
Musical style of temple worship	95

9. The Temple Orchestra: The Levite Singers — 97

The Director of Music	97
the Levite chorus	105
Deployment of forces	107
Singing in parts	109
Rehearsal and public appearance	110
Privileges and status	112

10. Moonlight on Moriah — **114**

Simḥat beth ha-sho'evah — 114
Fifteen steps to the holy house — 115
Back down the steps — 117
The downward procession mirrors the upward — 118
From Herod's Temple to Solomon's — 120

11. Temple Song, Where Are You Now? — **122**

Where did the temple psalmody go? — 122
The Masoretes and their work — 126
The dissemination of the Masoretic Text — 131
The Aleppo Codex today — 133
Antiquity of the Masoretic punctillation — 134
What traces remain? — 136

12. Restoring the Temple Song — **138**

Gregorian and synagogue psalmody — 139
Decoding the Masoretic te'amim — 140
Was Haïk-Vantoura right? — 142
Was Haïk-Vantoura totally right? — 151
Deciphering the psalms — 154

13. The Songs of Zion — **159**

14. In the Latter Days — **211**

The prophetic Book of Psalms — 211
The timetable of the Book of Psalms — 212
The ascents of Zechariah — 213
The Songs of Ascents in the Psalter — 215

15. I Will Proclaim Your Name to My Brethren — **217**

The power of music — 218
Music and the word of God — 221
Will the real Director of Music please stand up? — 226

Appendix I. Singing the Sacred Name — **229**

Difficulties in the 'Yahweh' construct — 231
The plausibility of the Masoretic vocalization — 233
Does 'Yehovah' explain the anomalies? — 235
The meaning of the Name — 238
The sacred name in this book — 238

Appendix II. Temple Where and When — **240**
    Existence of Solomon's Temple — 241
    Date, location, and layout of Solomon's Temple — 245

Appendix II. The Hebrew Calendar — **249**
    The rabbinic luni-solar calendar — 249
    A lost lunar calendar? — 251

Appendix IV. *Revia mugrash* and *oleh ve-yored* — **255**
    Revia mugrash — 255
    Revia mugrash as read by Haïk-Vantoura — 256
    Evidence for Haïk-Vantoura's view — 257
    Rethinking Haïk-Vantoura's view — 259
    Oleh ve-yored — 261
    Oleh ve-yored in Haïk-Vantoura and the cantors — 262

Appendix V. Pietro Santi Bartoli's Arch of Titus — **264**

Glossary — 265
Bibliography — 267
Index of Extra-Biblical Names — 289

Figures, Tables, and Musical Examples

Figures

Figure 1. Edinburgh Coat of Arms 4
Figure 2. Fifteen Steps from the Court of Women to the Court of Israel. 35
Figure 3. The King of Megiddo on *keruvim* throne 46
Figure 4. Ramses III on sphinx palanquin, from Medinet Habu 47
Figure 5. Atarsuhis on keruvim chariot. 50
Figure 6. The *sh'tiyah* Foundation Stone within the Dome of the Rock. 59
Figure 7. The *al-maghara* cavern beneath the *sh'tiyah* Foundation Stone.... 60
Figure 8. The Taanach cult stand 69
Figure 9. Khirbet Qeiyafa ostracon 72
Figure 10. Temple lyre on Bar Kokhba coin 85
Figure 11. Lyre-playing Semite from the tomb of Khnumhotep 85
Figure 12. Assyrian harps 86
Figure 13. Playing *ḥalil* with one hand on each pipe 87
Figure 14. Temple *hatsotserot* in the Arch of Titus 90
Figure 15. Kudu horn *shofar*. 91
Figure 16. Small clapper cymbals and Assyrian hand-held cymbals. 93
Figure 17. Bearded Levite with *tof*. 94
Figure 18. Egyptian cheironomers of the 3rd millennium BC 99
Figure 19. Sumerian cheironomers (c. 3200 BC). 100
Figure 20. Egyptian cheironomer (3rd from left) covering left ear. 102
Figure 21. The *dukhan* 111
Figure 22. The Ascents in Herod's Temple 119
Figure 23. The Ascents in Solomon's Temple 121
Figure 24. Egyptian cheironomers and musicians (2700 BC). 122
Figure 25. Medieval Jewish cheironomer and singers sing Psalm 149 126
Figure 26. Aleppo Codex text of Psalm 123. 127
Figure 27. The Masoretic *te'amim* 128
Figure 28. Shasu of Yhw 229

Tables

Table 1. Two heptades in the Songs of Ascents 12
Table 2. The numerology of the Hebrew alphabet 16
Table 3. Occurences of YHVH in each Song of Ascents 17
Table 4. In him, YHVH, is prosperity 18
Table 5. YHVH encoded before Yedid 18
Table 6. YHVH, he is my father 19
Table 7. In him is life, in him is prosperity 19

Table 8. YHVH loves Yedid-Yah 20
Table 9. His beloved prospers 21
Table 10. Three times seventeen 21
Table 11. Yedid encoded around *yedid-ô* 22
Table 12. Fifteen for Yah, fourteen for David 23
Table 13. Which period do the Songs of Ascents reflect? 44
Table 14. Babylonian and Greek modes compared 145

Musical examples

Example 1. Trumpet fanfares 92
Example 2. Ashkenazi and Gregorian chants to Psalm 114 139
Example 3. The scale of the sublinear *te'amim* of the prosodic books 141
Example 4. The scale of the sublinear *te'amim* of the poetic books 141
Example 5. The nine-note scales of Mesopotamian lyres 144
Example 6. Sephardi form of the *tonus peregrinus* to Psalm 114 146
Example 7. Psalm 114.2–6 after Haïk-Vantoura 147
Example 8. Psalm 114.7 after Haïk-Vantoura 147
Example 9. Syrian cantillational system compared with Haïk-Vantoura ... 149
Example 10. Sephardi tradition for the prophets 149
Example 11. Maronite liturgy for Holy Week 150
Example 12. Syncopation in Psalm 122? 155
Example 13. *Revia mugrash* in Haïk-Vantoura's conception 256
Example 14. The rhythmic execution of *revia mugrash* 257
Example 15. Bowing *revia mugrash* in Psalm 95.6 257
Example 16. Bowing *revia mugrash* in Psalm 132.7 258
Example 17. Bowing *revia mugrash* in Psalm 29.2 258
Example 18. Bowing *revia mugrash* in Psalm 72.9 258
Example 19. *Tifha* versus *revia mugrash* in Psalm 91:13 259
Example 20. *Tifha* versus *revia mugrash* in Psalm 131.2 259
Example 21. Trilled *revia mugrash* 260
Example 22. Three readings of *revia mugrash* 260
Example 23. *Revia mugrash* as a lower shake 261
Example 24. *Oleh ve-yored* as leap to the sixth above 262
Example 25. *Oleh ve-yored* as leap to the fourth above (Haïk-Vantoura) .. 262
Example 26. Three readings of *oleh ve-yored* 263
Example 27. *Oleh ve-yored* in Syrian cantoral tradition 263
Example 28. *Oleh ve-yored* in Finzi's tradition 263
Example 29. *Oleh ve-yored* of a rising sixth 263

Foreword

David Mitchell's *Songs of Ascents* is a fresh direction in the study of the Psalms. In the twentieth century, scholars tended to regard the Psalms as 'early' (stemming from Solomon's temple), against the older idea that they belonged to second temple Judaism, and there were many reconstructions of the kind of liturgy they belonged to. More recently, interest has shifted to the Psalter as a book, a compilation showing signs of deliberate design. Mitchell is the first scholar to combine these interests. The Psalms of Ascents, he argues, were composed not only for Solomon's temple but actually for its dedication; yet they represent also a coherent collection, with shared themes and a progression of thought. Drawing on his musical knowledge, he also shows how they may have been sung, drawing on recent archaeomusicological insights into the meaning of the Masoretic cantillation signs.

This is a novel and stimulating study, which should engage all who are interested in the origins of the Psalms. It depends on very detailed study by one who knows the Hebrew Psalter well, and who has access not only to technical musical knowledge not shared by many, but also to rabbinic sources and to modern scholarship. This ground-breaking study will have to be taken into account by future students of the most enigmatic Book of Psalms.

John Barton, FBA
Oriel & Laing Professor of the Interpretation of Holy Scripture
University of Oxford

Preface

This is a commentary on a short group of Psalms, 120 to 134. Together, they make up 101 verses, 810 words, some four percent of the Book of Psalms. Yet the book in your hand runs to over 115,000 words. And should anyone ask, 'Why so much?', one must reply that much was to find. For, truly, more could have been said.

In fact, much has been left unsaid. For this commentary does not set out to recount what has already been said about the Psalms. Instead, it seeks to open new areas of understanding and interpretation which follow from looking at the Psalms in temple worship. These are as follows.

First, it seeks to recover the ancient music of the Songs of Ascents. The music of the Psalms is less lost than is often supposed. It is preserved in the cantillation marks of the Masoretic text. Recent archaeomusicological insights, combined with fragments of temple psalmody preserved by church and synagogue, allow us to reconstruct the lost music of the Psalms with increasing confidence. This is the first Psalms commentary to attempt a printed version of the ancient music of the Psalms.

Second, this book seeks to reconstruct the ritual and liturgical context in which the Songs of Ascents were first sung. The basis of this approach is the conviction that the Psalms should be studied according to the genera of their ancient 'headings' rather than according to any modern category. Gone, then, are twentieth-century disciplines such as Form Criticism, which classified the Psalms according to their literary forms with no reference to their headings. It is in the 'Song of Ascents' heading that their ancient liturgical role will be found. Understanding this liturgical context gives us insight into when the Songs of Ascents were first composed and first performed. I propose an exact date and time for when they were first sung.

Next, we are concerned not only with their first liturgical context, but also with their historical 'strata'. For instance, parts of Psalm 132 seem to pre-date that psalm's inclusion in the Songs of Ascents collection. And later, after the Ascents collection was first sung liturgically, it took on a second liturgical role, a role that lasted for a thousand years, in Israel's greatest annual festival. And more than halfway through these thousand years, the Songs of Ascents gained a new role, when they joined the Book of Psalms, forming a book about the Messiah's coming kingdom. In this form, they were treasured as prophecy by Synagogue and Church, interpreted according to the lights of each. And today they are part of our Bible, Jewish or Christian, and we apply them to the issues of our day and the struggles and hopes of our daily lives. I have recognized all these strata, which grew out of the Songs of Ascents first liturgical role.

Next, this commentary visits the world of numerology or *gematria*. Modern biblical scholarship has tended to avoid numerology. One understands why. It can be hard to pin down. And, if concerned simply with numerical patterns for their own sake, it is dull. But it has always been intrinsic to rabbinic interpretation, and when rightly applied, it can provide evidence for textual origins and open unseen depths in the holographic text.

Amidst these new approaches, I have had an eye to the ancient Jewish and Christian traditions of fourfold interpretation, seeking the literal, allegorical, tropological, and anagogical sense of a text. With this approach, we seek not only a text's ancient origin, date, and use, but equally how it may apply to our daily hopes, our ethical conduct, our knowledge of the divine, or the messianic kingdom. Therefore the reader should be aware that this book is not only a work of academic biblical study, but also of Christian theology.

A word is due on methodology. Within Biblical Studies, opposing camps contest the reliability of the Hebrew Bible. One camp – sometimes called 'minimalist' – holds that the Bible is historically valueless unless verified by the assured results of archaeology and critical scholarship. The other camp – whom minimalists call 'maximalist' – holds that the scriptural texts are themselves primary historical sources for understanding ancient Israel. The first camp deny that David's kingdom and Solomon's temple ever existed as described in the Bible because, they say, there is no evidence. For them, the books of Samuel, Kings, and Chronicles are fictional accounts, written by dream-spinners, of a kingdom and temple that never existed. The other camp are less concerned by the purported lack of material evidence, for the testimony of the historical books is self-consistent and consistent with ancient eastern custom. They therefore take the historical books at face value as official state chronicles, issuing from the highest authorities of the Kingdom of Judah. Although questions about the dating of archaeological evidence are involved, yet, overall, the two camps hold contrasting basic dispositions to approach the Israelite historians in bad faith or in good, with distrust or with respect. The minimalists give no more credence to the biblical writers than one would to a proven liar or cheat. But, since there is no basis for these suspicions, I incline to good faith. Yet, in answer to the minimalists, I present evidence for David's kingdom and Solomon's temple in Chapter Seven and Appendix I respectively.

Good and bad faith issues arise with rabbinic sources too. These days one can hardly cite the Talmud without someone objecting to 'uncritical' use of rabbinic sources. But, while rabbinic literature does not always mirror biblical-period ways and uses, it certainly does reflect rabbinic opinion. And on many subjects, including temple ritual, that opinion is valuable. Nor is the current extreme scepticism about rabbinic tradition valid. The respect in which the rabbis held their teachers, the care which rabbinic works give to attaching sayings to certain teachers, and the consistency with which these sayings are attributed to the same teachers in different documents, suggest that the rabbis were doing their best to record a true tradition, not invent a false one.

Given the importance of the Masoretic cantillation to this commentary, I have followed the online Aleppo Codex throughout. Although much of the Codex was lost in 1947, the Songs of Ascents are entire. When citing Bible texts, I have given chapters and verses as they occur in English Bibles. The verse-numbering of the Songs of Ascents is identical in English and Hebrew Bibles, but in other Bible passages the numbering may diverge. Where the Hebrew is important, I have given divergent Hebrew numeration in square brackets.

Hebrew transliteration is a challenge. I have been influenced by the most recent standard of the Hebrew Academy (2006), adopted by the UN (2007), which discourages double letters, silent letters, and diacritics. Overall, its ease in reading outweighs its lack of detail. Yet the Hebrew Academy helpfully adds that the standard should be followed only as far as possible, a necessary concession, unless we are to write 'Rabi' and 'Tora'. I have availed myself of this liberty.

I am grateful to John Barton, Matt Candler, Richard Dumbrill, Gershon Galil, Susan Gillingham, Nehemia Gordon, Joshua Jacobson, Yigal Levin, Nidaa Abou Mrad, Yosef Ofer, Edwin Seroussi, Leen Ritmeyer, and John Wheeler who have been generous with their insights.

I warmly thank my family for their support in these labours. To them this book is dedicated with love.

David C. Mitchell
Brussels
Sukkot 2014

Abbreviations

Bible texts

| MT | Masoretic Text | LXX | Septuagint |

Apocrypha and Pseudepigrapha

1 Macc.	1 Maccabees	4 Macc.	4 Maccabees
2 Macc.	2 Maccabees	4 Ezra	4 Ezra (2 Esdras 3-14)
3 Macc.	3 Maccabees		

Dead Sea Scrolls (omitting those referred to by reference number only)

1QpHab	Habakkuk pesher
1QIsa	Isaiah Scroll
1QM	*Milhamah* (War Scroll)
11QPs[a]	The Psalms Scroll. Also 11QPs[b], Ps[c], etc.

Mishnaic and talmudic tractates

Ber.	Berakhoth	Git.	Gittin
Bik.	Bikkurim	Kid.	Kiddushin
Shab.	Shabbat	BK	Baba Kamma
Erub.	Erubin	BM	Baba Mezia
Pes.	Pesahim	BB	Baba Batra
Shek.	Shekalim	Sanh.	Sanhedrin
Yoma	Yoma	Shebu.	Shebuot
Suk.	Sukkah	Edu.	Eduyot
RH	Rosh ha-Shanah	AZ	Abodah Zarah
Ta'an.	Ta'anit	Abot	Abot
Meg.	Megillah	Zeb.	Zebahim
MK	Moed Katan	Hul.	Hullin
Hag.	Hagigah	Arak.	Arakhin
Yeb.	Yebamot	Tam.	Tamid
Ket.	Ketubot	Mid.	Middot
Ned.	Nedarim	Nid.	Niddah
Sot.	Sotah		

Other rabbinic texts

B.	Babylonian Talmud
Gen. R.	Midrash Rabbah to Genesis
M.	Mishnah
Midr. Pss.	Midrash on Psalms (Midrash Tehillim)
Pes. de-Rav Kah.	Pesikta de Rav Kahana
R.	Rav, Rabbi
Song R.	Midrash Rabbah to the Song of Songs
T.	Tosefta
Y.	Jerusalem Talmud

Ancient Greek and Latin texts

Ant.	Josephus, *Antiquities*
Con. Ap.	Josephus, *Contra Apion*
Eusebius, *Hist.*	Eusebius, *Historia Ecclesiae*
Lib. Ant. Bib.	Pseudo-Philo, *Liber Antiquitatum Biblicarum*
Tacitus, *Hist.*	Tacitus, *Historiae*
Vit. Con.	Philo, *De Vita Contemplativa*
War	Josephus, *Jewish War*

Periodicals, reference works, serials, and other

ANET	*Ancient Near Eastern Texts,* (ed.) Pritchard
ARANE	Archaeomusicological Review of the Ancient Near East
BAR	*Biblical Archaeology Review*
EJ	*Encyclopaedia Judaica,* (ed.) Roth
ET	English Translation
GKC	Gesenius, Kautzsch, Cowley, *Gesenius' Hebrew Grammar.*
IEJ	*Israel Exploration Journal*
JBL	*Journal of Biblical Literature*
JBQ	*Jewish Bible Quarterly*
JSOT	*Journal for the Study of the Old Testament*
JSOTS	*JSOT Supplement Series*
OTE	*Old Testament Essays*
PG	*Patrologia Graeca* (ed.) Migne
PL	*Patrologia Latina* (ed.) Migne
PTR	*Princeton Theological Review*
RevExp	*Review and Expositor*
VT	*Vetus Testamentum*
ZAW	*Zeitschrift für die alttestamentliche Wissenschaft*

*Turn it over and turn it over again,
for everything is in it.*

R. ben Bag-bag

Proem

In the Garden of God

Fragrant and fair are the flowers in the garden of God.
Five ever-living redwoods there support the sky:
These are the books of Moses upholding the world.
A grove of yews makes fearsome bows:
The death-dealing books of Joshua and Judges.
There spread the cedars, fair in form and grace:
Samuel, Kings, and Chronicles with two houses of Lebanon.
There stand oaks of truth no wind can shake:
These are the great prophets.
There twelve poplars point up to the sky:
These are the minor prophets.
An arbour of jessamine and every healing herb,
Where one who sits is filled with wisdom's store:
These are the proverbs of Solomon.
There is the quince, first bitter, later sweet:
This is Job, whose age surpassed his youth.
The little flowers appear on earth in spring:
This is the Song of Solomon.
There golden fields are ripe for harvest songs:
This is Ruth, ingathered from the nations.
There is the fragrant, starry myrtle bush:
Hidden Esther, appearing like the dawn.
Four sweet trees give life to all:
The gospels of the apple tree among the trees of the wood.
There is the olive tree, the fount of joy:
The Acts of Apostles filled with the Holy Spirit.
The vine, whose blood makes glad the harvest feast:
This is the Apocalypse of John.
And there, amidst of all, five flower-beds:
The book of Psalms, all redolent with praises.

One bed is purple roses none dare touch:
These are the Psalms of David, the unconquerable king.
Then the fragrant Lily of the Valley,
Blooms in springtime like the risen dead:
These are the Psalms of the Sons of Korah.
The Rose of Sharon is red for blood and war:
These are the Psalms of Asaph, the *mazkir*.
The fourth bed holds the desert saxifrage:
The songs of the wilderness wanderings.
From fourth to fifth bed grow chrysanthemums,
Golden with their high and victory head:
Halleluyah psalms to hail the king.
And there, amidst the final flower bed,
Is crocus *cancellatus*.
Sprung from the Beloved Land,
It blooms at the autumnal Feast,
Fragrant, like the sacred oil,
Azure, like the robe of the ephod
Of Israel's chief *Kohen* at hour of sacrifice.
Within the blue, its golden crown shines bright,
Like King Messiah on the lion throne,
Gazing east toward the smiling sun,
Upon Mount Zion in the glorious morn:
And these are the Songs of Ascents.

1

Books Within Books

Ten men wrote the Book of Psalms. So say the Rabbis.[1] For, while many Bible books present themselves as the work of a single author, the Book of Psalms never pretends to be anything other than a work of many hands. Some psalms bear the name of David, others the name of Asaph or the sons of Korah, still others the names of Moses, Solomon, Jeduthun, and Heman. Someone collected all these different groups of psalms together. Perhaps it was Nehemiah the governor, when he founded the library in the second temple and gathered together 'the books about the kings and prophets, and the writings of David, and letters of kings about votive offerings'.[2] And, sometime in the early second temple period, someone edited them into a single Book of Psalms.[3] Perhaps it was Ezra the scribe, to whom Jewish tradition credits the compilation of the Hebrew scriptures.[4] Yet before our Book of Psalms was compiled, the different lyrics existed in separate collections according to their headings: a collection, or possibly several, of David psalms; a collection of Asaph psalms; another of Korah psalms; and a collection of fifteen psalms called the Songs of Ascents, which form the subject of this book.

The Songs of Ascents have always been popular. Together with Psalms 135 and 136, they form the Great Hallel, sung at the Passover meal.[5] In medieval Christendom they were sung at the great feast of Easter, and formed part of the

---

[1] *Song R.* IV.4.1, cf. IV.19; B. *B.B.* 14b/15a; cf. Y. *Pes.* 1c.

[2] 2 Macc. 2.13.

[3] This redaction was the result not of a gradual process of accretion, but of a single creative impulse. For no partial section of the Psalter reads like a purposeful literary composition (Mitchell 1997: 66–78, 88–89; 2006c: 530–532). The current view that the 'accretion' continued to the mid-1st century AD, ignores the fact that the Greek translation of the Psalms existed before the mid-2nd century BC (Mitchell 2006c: 546–547). I am glad that Klaus Seybold (2013: 168–181) recently restated the case for a Hebrew text of the whole Book of Psalms, kept in the Jerusalem temple, by at least the 3rd century BC.

[4] 4 Ezra (2 Esdras) 14.42–46 tells how Ezra dictated the 24 books of the Hebrew scriptures; *Song R.* IV.4.1 names Ezra among the ten men who wrote the Book of Psalms.

[5] 'From where the Great Hallel? From *A Song of Ascents* to the *Rivers of Babylon*' (B. *Pes.* 118a). Cf. Booij 2010: 248.

daily rite of the Rule of Benedict.[6] To this day, observant Jews recite all fifteen Songs every Shabbat afternoon.[7] Psalm 130 is part of synagogue daily prayer and Psalm 126 part of the *Birkat ha-mazon*, the Grace after Meals. In the second century AD, when Jerusalem became Aelia Capitolina and Hadrian built a temple to Jupiter on the Temple Mount, Christians sang Psalm 122's *In domum domine ibimus* – 'Let us go to the house of the Lord' – beneath Jupiter's foundations.[8] In later centuries, the same psalm featured in the Marian Vespers of Monteverdi and Vivaldi, and was sung at the coronation of every British monarch since Tudor times, in settings by Purcell, Boyce, and, magnificently, Parry. Psalm 130 was set by Josquin, Lassus, Purcell, Zelenka, Bach, Handel, Mozart, Mendelssohn, and others. Outside the world of music, Psalm 127 can be traced from the *Nisi Dominus Frustra* of Edinburgh's coat of arms to Khalil Gibran's *The Prophet* to the Gye-Nyame symbol that adorns the market-stalls of Ghana, proclaiming that 'Except God' there is no helper.

Figure 1. Edinburgh Coat of Arms

Their line has gone out into all the earth, their words to the ends of the world.

But the Songs of Ascents are special not only because of their enduring popularity. They are unique also because, more than any other Psalms, they bear evidence of having been a collection in their own right before they were ever included in the Psalter.[9]

ONE NAME

First, they share a common title or heading, namely, *A Song of the Ascents*. (The title of Psalm 121 differs by one Hebrew letter, making it *A song* for *the Ascents*.) Now, while this may seem obvious, it is worth mentioning. It shows, for a start, that these fifteen songs share a common background. But it shows more. Other psalms – the David, Asaph, and Sons of Korah psalms – also share a common background, yet they are divided within the Book of Psalms. The Songs of Ascents, on the other hand, are the only group of psalms with a common heading that are undivided. Evidently, the compiler of the Psalms

---

[6] Gillingham 2008: 103.

[7] In some communities, only on the Sabbaths from Sukkot to Passover. Klein 1992: 70; Sawyer 2013: 140.

[8] In the 1970s, restorations to St Helena's chapel in the Church of the Holy Sepulchre revealed an eastern room (now St Varta's Chapel), extending under the temple area, illustrated with a picture of a 2nd-century boat and the words *Domine ivimus* (Lord, we have come) from the Latin of Psalm 122.

[9] This is widely recognized. But views vary on how far the Songs were written as, or redacted into, a book: Allen 1983: 193–97; Auffret 1982: 439–531; Beaucamp 1979: 73–90; Crow 1996; Goldingay 2008: III.752; Grossberg 1989: 15–54; Liebreich 1955: 33–36; Mannati 1979: 85–100; Seybold 1979: 247–268; Viviers 1994: 275–89; Zenger 1998: 77–102 (92).

thought they belonged together in such a way they should not be split up and spread around, as other psalm-groups are.

ONE MOOD

The Songs of Ascents exhale a quiet bliss, like a warm evening in late harvest. Yet this serene mood is rare in the Book of Psalms. Many psalms are shot through with dark threads of fear, war, trouble, and pain. King David cries out for deliverance from deadly enemies: *Save me, O God... for merciless men seek my life* (Ps. 54.1, 3). The Asaph Psalms tell how foreign invaders have laid Israel waste, and cry out for judgement: *O God, the nations have invaded your inheritance; they have defiled your holy temple, they have reduced Jerusalem to rubble...Pour out your wrath on the nations* (Ps. 79.1, 6). The Korah collection tell of one slain and cast into the underworld: *Loose among the dead, like the slain lying in the grave...you have put me in the lowest pit, the darkness, the depths* (Ps. 88.5–6); *You have rejected, you have been very angry with your Anointed...you have pierced his crown to the dust* (Ps. 89.38–39). The 'Moses' psalms describe the Israelites perishing in the desert through unbelief in the divine promise: *All our days pass away under your wrath* (Ps. 90.9).[10] And when other psalms speak of Israel's joy, it often follows bloody victory. The Holy One, like a lion, is majestic from the mountains of prey where the plundered enemy sleep their last sleep (Ps. 76.4–5). The king of Israel is a mighty conqueror who will burn his enemies with fire, pierce their hearts with arrows, and crush heads all over the earth (Pss. 21, 45 and 110).

The Songs of Ascents have none of this. They have no present sorrows to speak of, no hot rage against enemies. There are distant memories of foreign aggression in Psalms 123, 124, and 129. But their overall mood is one of Israel emerging into a happy present after a troubled past. Of Jerusalem they say, *May they prosper who love you! Peace be within your walls, security within your fortresses...Peace within you;* of Israel they say, *Peace upon Israel...How good and pleasant it is when brothers dwell as one;* of the king they say that *the LORD gives his beloved rest* and *upon him his crown will shine.*[11]

---

[10] Following the heading of Ps. 90, Pss. 90–99 are ascribed to Moses by *Midr. Pss.* 90.3, and by the Christian Hebraists Jerome (*Ep.*140 *ad Cypr.*) and Origen, the latter citing as a Jewish tradition, 'Those psalms which have no title, or which have a title but not the name of the writer, belong to the author whose name stands at the head of the last preceding Psalm that has a title' (Tollinton 1929: 96–97). Origen's view is borne out by other Semitic hymnic texts (Wilson 1985: 199). Of course, Moses did not write all ten psalms (cf. 97.8; 99.6), but their 'desert' theme makes the Moses heading appropriate.

[11] Pss. 122.6–8; 125.5; 128.6; 133.1; 127.2; 132.18.

ONE LORD

Related to their common serene mood, the Songs of Ascents share a common theology. This is seen, first, in the names they use for God. Most common by far is the sacred personal name, YHVH, often rendered the LORD or the ETERNAL.[12] This name occurs fifty-one times in the collection, while its short form, Yah, appears twice more. On the other hand, *elohim*, that is, 'God', occurs only twice, and both times it is in conjunction with YHVH.[13] This is in striking contrast to the other groups of psalms, which use *elohim* frequently and freely. There is an old Hebrew tradition which associates *elohim* with God's judgment and YHVH with his mercy.[14] So, when YHVH appears often and *elohim* rarely, and appears only as 'YHVH *elohim*', as if to speak of the merciful judge, we may conclude that the Holy One is smiling in the Songs of Ascents.

The Ascents also use the title *Maker of heaven and earth* three times, a title which occurs only twice elsewhere in the Bible.[15] However, they completely avoid divine names which are characteristic of other psalm-groups. They do not mention the Korahite titles, 'Most High God (*El Elyon*)', 'Living God (*El Ḥai*)' and the martial 'LORD of hosts (YHVH *ts'vaot*)'. Likewise, they avoid the majestic agglomerated titles of the Asaph Psalms, like '*El elohim* YHVH' or 'YHVH *elohim ts'vaot*'.[16] Simply the merciful name YHVH is enough for the Songs of Ascents.

The overall theology of the Ascents might be summed up as 'YHVH blesses and keeps faithful Israel.' This idea appears over and over again in the words of happiness, security, and peace which mark these psalms. For instance, the Hebrew word *barakh*, 'bless', occurs eleven times in these fifteen short psalms, while another word, *ashre*, also meaning 'blessed' or 'happy' occurs three times.[17] The word *shamar*, meaning 'protect', 'keep', or 'guard' occurs eleven times.[18] And the key word *shalom* – 'peace' or 'well-being' – occurs seven times.[19]

---

[12] In this book, it is generally rendered the LORD, except when accuracy demands YHVH. For more on the Tetragrammaton and its pronunciation, see Appendix I.

[13] Pss. 122.9; 123.2.

[14] Cf. *Sifre* § 27; *Pes. de-Rav Kah.*149a; *Midr. Pss.* 74.2; Zohar, *Shemot* 173b–174a. Hayman (1976: 465) says, 'The doctrine of the two divine attributes, Justice and Mercy, runs like a thread through all the rabbinic writings. It is the basis of a fundamental exegetical rule, namely that the divine name *Yahweh* denotes the attribute of Mercy, the name *Elohim,* the attribute of Justice.' Cf. Mitchell 1997: 179–183.

[15] Ascents Pss. 121.2, 124.8, 134.3. In Ps. 115.15 it is also a closing phrase, but in 146.6 an opening phrase. The related expression, *You have* (or *who has*) *made the heavens and the earth* occurs at Isa 37.16; 2 Kgs 19.15; and 2 Chr. 2.12 [2.11].

[16] Pss. 50.1; 80.4, 19.

[17] 'Bless' (*barakh*) is at Pss. 124.6; 128.4, 5; 129.8a, 8b; 132.15 [twice]; 133.3; 134.1, 2, 3. 'Happy' (*ashre*) is at 127.5; 128.1, 2.

[18] Pss. 121.3, 4, 5, 7 [twice], 8; 127.1 [twice]; 130.6 [twice]; 132.12.

[19] Pss. 120.6, 7; 122.6, 7, 8; 125.5; 128.6.

The Songs of Ascents also share a range of 'blessing responses' not found in other psalms. These include:

Psalms	121, 124, 134	Maker of heaven and earth.
Psalms	121, 125, 131	From now until forever.
Psalms	124, 129	Let Israel now say.
Psalms	125, 128	Shalom on Israel.
Psalms	128, 134	The LORD bless you from Zion.
Psalm	129	We bless you in the name of the Lord.
Psalms	130, 131	Hope, Israel, in the Lord.

In fact, of the fifteen songs, all but two, Psalms 120 and 123, close with some kind of blessing. But this kind of language is rare in the psalms. The Asaph Psalms do not mention blessing at all. They mention *shalom* only once and it is the wicked, not Israel, who enjoy it; and as for 'keeping' and 'guarding', it is not the LORD who keeps Israel, but Israel who do *not* keep the LORD's commandments.[20] In fact, if the Songs of Ascents are about YHVH blessing the faithful, then the Psalms of Asaph are about God judging the faithless.

All this talk about 'blessing' and 'keeping' and *shalom* in the Songs of Ascents comes from one source, namely, the *Birkat Kohanim* or 'Priestly Blessing' in the book of Numbers 6.24–26.[21] Moses received this blessing from on high so that the *kohanim*, the Aaronite priests, might bless Israel in the holy name. The blessing proceeds, in crescendo, from blessing and protection, through favour and kindness, to love and *shalom*.[22] In Hebrew it has only fifteen words: three in the first line, five in the second, and seven in the third. English, however, is less concise, and we must translate it as follows:

> The LORD bless you and keep you
> The LORD smile upon you and be kind to you
> The LORD look lovingly upon you and give you *shalom*

Since the Songs of Ascents repeatedly echo the words of the *Birkat Kohanim* in this way, and since these words could lawfully be spoken only by the *kohanim,* it looks like the Songs of Ascents are linked with the temple ministry.

ONE CITY

The Songs of Ascents share a common love and longing for Jerusalem, its temple, and its fortified Zion hill. Everything revolves around this geographical centre. For instance:

---

[20] Pss. 73.3; 78.10, 56.
[21] The links between the Ascents and the *Birkat Kohanim* were noted by Liebreich 1955.
[22] In Assyrian, 'lift up the face' expresses love and affection (Delitzsch 1903: 29–30).

Psalm 122. I rejoiced when they said to me, Let us go to the house of the LORD. Our feet are standing in your gates, Jerusalem! Jerusalem, built like a city well put together!

Psalm 125. Those who trust in the Lord are like Mount Zion… As the mountains surround Jerusalem, so the Lord surrounds his people.

Psalm 126. When the LORD brought back the captives to Zion, we were like men who dreamed.

Psalm 127. Unless the LORD builds the house [the temple], the builders labour in vain.

Psalm 128. The LORD bless you from Zion! May you see the prosperity of Jerusalem all the days of your life.

Psalm 129. May all who hate Zion be turned back in shame.

Psalm 132. The Lord has chosen Zion, he has desired it for his dwelling. 'This is my resting place for ever and ever; here I will sit enthroned for I have desired it.'

Psalm 133 describes the anointed *kohen ha-gadol* ministering in Zion: Like precious oil poured on the head, running down on the beard, running down on Aaron's beard, down upon the collar of his robes…like the dew of Hermon falling on Mount Zion.

Psalm 134. Praise the LORD, you servants of the LORD, who minister by night in the house of the LORD.

And these are only the most obvious references. We shall see, as we proceed, that every one of the Songs of Ascents revolves around life and worship in the holy city.

But this Jerusalem location is absent from many other Psalms. The ten 'Moses' Psalms and many Psalms of David have as their backdrop the desert, *a dry and weary land where no water is*.[23] And while the Psalms of Asaph mention Jerusalem, it is a city invaded, pillaged, and burned. The only other psalm-group which depicts a peaceful Jerusalem in anything like the same way is the Korah Psalms; but, even then, the end of the Korah Psalms shows Israel's king and Jerusalem in dire distress.[24] The picture of Jerusalem happy and untroubled throughout is unique to the Songs of Ascents.

ONE KING

The Songs of Ascents have a common interest in the kingship of the house of David. Psalm 122 tells how the throne of David's house administers justice in Jerusalem. Psalms 132 recites the LORD's covenant with David and prays for

---

[23] Ps. 63.1.
[24] Jerusalem strong and free is the theme of Korah Pss. 46, 48, and 87. But in Korah Ps. 86.6–12, the king has fallen into Sheol; Ps. 89, the Korah *coda* (Mitchell 2006a: 366; Hengstenberg 1845-48: II. 484–85), is a lament for the king and his ravaged city (89.40-44).

the blessings of eternal sovereignty on David's house. Four Songs bear the heading *Of David* and one *Of Solomon*.

Such an interest in the house of David is not standard throughout the Psalms. Of course, the 'David' Psalms are about David; they record his trials and bear his name in the headings. But they differ from the Songs of Ascents as the king's view differs from the courtier's. The David Psalms relate David's struggles in coming to the throne, while the Songs of Ascents admire and bless the reigning house of David. Meanwhile, in other psalms-groups, David is rather under-represented. He is absent from the Moses Psalms and the Haleluyah Psalms, he is not named in the Korah Psalms, and features in only one Asaph Psalm.[25]

ONE TONGUE

Not only do the Songs of Ascents tell one story, but they tell it, so to speak, with one tongue. That is, they share elements of language, vocabulary, style, and poetic technique not found in other psalms.

Let us begin with language. One writer has said that the Songs of Ascents 'teem with dialectical elements'.[26] Their many unusual words and phrases, found nowhere else in the Bible, show the influence of Aramaic, the language of ancient Syria to the north-east of Israel. The influence of Aramaic on Hebrew is a complex matter.[27] But it is fair to say that, in this case, Aramaized Hebrew probably reflects the speech of Israelites from the eastern, Transjordan area.[28]

Next, the Songs of Ascents share details of literary style. For a start, they tend to be short. Three of them have only three verses, eleven others have between four and nine. Even the longest one, Psalm 132, has only a modest eighteen verses. And so, while fifteen psalms in a collection of 150 psalms might be expected to make up ten per cent of the whole, the Songs of Ascents actually make up less than four per cent of the Book of Psalms because of their brevity. Their 110 verses contrast strikingly with the 176 verses of the preceding massive Psalm 119. This gives the Songs of Ascents the air of finely-crafted lyrical gems, like Japanese *haiku*, where less is more.

---

[25] David does appear in the Korah 'Coda' Ps. 89.3, 20, 35, 49; and in Asaph Ps. 78.70, 72.
[26] Dahood 1965–70: III.196.
[27] As Wilson, 1925: 234–66, amply demonstrated long ago. For more, see chapter 7.
[28] In the 10th and 9th centuries BC, Aramaic's influence on Hebrew was a matter of ancestral memory (Abraham, Rebecca, Leah, and Rachel spoke Aramaic; cf. Gen. 31.47) and contact with Aramean tribes east of the Jordan. After Assyrian expansion, from the late 10th century BC, Aramaic became the lingua franca of the east, well known in Israel (2 Kgs 18.26; Isa. 36.11) and used in the Bible (Ezra 4.8–6.18; 7.12–26; Dan. 2.4–7.28). Since the Songs of Ascents were written in the early 10th century BC (see chapters 2–7), their Aramaized tongue points to an origin in Transjordanian Israel (chapter 7).

They also share poetic techniques not found in other psalms. We have already spoken about the 'blessing phrases' that occur throughout the collection, but there are other techniques as well. They repeat single words or phrases twice in succession. For instance, Psalm 121:

> There go up the tribes, the tribes of Yah (v. 4).
>
> There are set up thrones, thrones of the house of David (v. 5).

And Psalm 126:

> Then said they among the nations,
>   'Great things the LORD has done for them!'
>   Great things the LORD has done for us. We are glad.

Or Psalm 130:

> My soul waits for the Lord more than watchmen for the morning,
>   watchmen for the morning.

Or Psalm 131:

> Like a little child on its mother,
>   like that little child is my soul on me.

A related repetition technique is anadiplosis, sometimes called 'step parallelism' or 'terrace parallelism', where a word from the end of one line repeats at the beginning of the next line.[29] For instance, Psalm 120:

> Too long has dwelt my soul with the hater of *peace*
>   I [am] *peace*, but when I speak, they [are] for war.

Or Psalm 121:

> I lift my eyes to the hills. From where comes *my help*?
> *My help* is from the LORD, Maker of heaven and earth.

And Psalm 122:

> Our feet are standing in your gates, *Jerusalem*.
> *Jerusalem*, built as a city that is compact together.

Such shared features of language and style show that certain poems or songs have a similar origin. Just as the poems of Robert Burns stand out from English poetry because of their Scots dialect, or as the poems of Walt Whitman stand out by their repeated beginnings of lines, or as Browning cuts out his little words, so the shared language of the Songs of Ascents suggests they come from a common source.

---

[29] Pss. 120.5–7; 121.1–2, 3–5, 7–8; 122.2–3; 4a–b; 5a–b; 123.2d–3a; 124.4–5, 7a–b.

ONE STORY

The Songs of Ascents share a narrative or story-line running from the first psalm through to the last. It goes something like this:

Psalm 120 begins the story with an Israelite living in exile in a pagan society. He is a man of peace, but his neighbours are cruel and hostile. His heart longs for a place of *shalom*.

Psalm 121 depicts his journey to Jerusalem, the city of *shalom*. His eyes fixed on the Jerusalem hills ahead, he looks for heavenly protection on his journey.

Psalm 122 describes his arrival with his friends in Jerusalem. They stand in the gates and admire the beautiful, well-built city and the palaces of David's house. They sing a blessing for the city's *shalom*.

Psalm 123 turns to worship, as they raise their eyes to the One enthroned in the temple to pray for mercy on Israel.

Psalm 124 offers thanksgiving for national deliverance in the past.

Psalm 125 affirms that the Holy One will always protect and deliver his people.

Psalm 126 compares national restoration with harvest. Weary sowing leads to reaping in due course.

Psalm 127 affirms that no house – whether human or divine, physical or dynastic, personal or national – can be built without the help of heaven. Dynasties and palaces depend on his favour.

Psalm 128 confesses that the foundation of national prosperity is family and children; it speaks a fertility blessing on Israel in harvest imagery.

Psalm 129 pronounces a non-blessing against Israel's past oppressors in harvest imagery.

Psalm 130 is a confession of past help and ongoing mercy and forgiveness.

Psalm 131 breathes the tranquility that follows forgiveness. Eyes turned down, Israel is no longer praying, but is forgiven and accepted.

Psalm 132 celebrates celebrates the ark's entry to Zion and prays for the continuity of David's dynasty.

Psalm 133 tells how the unity of the tribes of Israel will make divine blessing flow into all the land with the departing pilgrims.

Psalm 134 is a farewell blessing to the *kohanim* ministering in the temple, to which they respond with the blessing in the sacred name.

This story-line in the Songs of Ascents has long been recognized. In the third century, Origen had a version of it which resembles the one above, but begins with the Jerusalemites triumphing over their enemies in battle.[30] But here it is enough to notice that there is a story running through the Songs of Ascents, with a beginning, a middle, and an end.

---

[30] Origen's version is cited in Mitchell 1997: 125.

...AND A MULTITUDE OF PATTERNS

Jean-Luc Vesco records some eight different structural patterns to be found in the Songs of Ascents, to which he adds a ninth, his own tripartite structure: (1) From adversity to the house of YHVH (Pss. 120-124); The house of YHVH (Pss. 125-129); For the sake of David (Pss. 130-135).[31] To these, we can add a couple more which even Professor Vesco missed.[32] Ernst Hengstenberg of Bonn pointed out, more than 150 years ago, that if the Songs of Ascents are divided into two heptades, or groups of seven, on each side of the central Psalm 127, then each group contains the holy name 24 times. And, if each heptade is further divided into four and three, that is, a tetrad and a triad, then each sub-group contains the holy name 12 times. 'This,' Hengstenberg rightly observed, 'cannot be accidental.'[33] Further investigation shows that the third psalm of each heptade contains the name *Yah*.[34] In addition, the name of David occurs in one psalm-heading in each of the four groups, while the central psalm is headed by the name of David's son Solomon.[35] We can represent this pattern as follows.

Table 1. Two heptades in the Songs of Ascents

\multicolumn{15}{c}{The 15 Songs of Ascents}

120	121	122 Of David	123	124 Of David	125	126	127 Of Solomon	128	129	130	131 Of David	132	133 Of David	134
\multicolumn{6}{c	}{First heptade: 24 × YHVH 3rd psalm mentions David (122.5) Two David headings (122, 124)}	\multicolumn{3}{c	}{The central Solomon psalm 3 × YHVH}	\multicolumn{6}{c}{Second heptade: 24 × YHVH 3rd last psalm (132) mentions David × 4 Two David headings (131, 133)}
\multicolumn{3}{c	}{1st tetrad 12 × YHVH 3rd psalm (122.4): *Yah*}	\multicolumn{3}{c	}{1st triad 12 × YHVH}			\multicolumn{3}{c	}{2nd tetrad 12 × YHVH 3rd psalm (130.3): *Yah*}	\multicolumn{3}{c}{2nd triad 12 × YHVH}

This pattern embraces the entire Song of Ascents collection. If we take one song away from the collection, then the pattern would be incomplete. The same would happen if we added one psalm to it. The pattern resists any improvements because the collection is complete as it stands.

Yet another pattern can be formed with a series of thematic cross-linkages between the first and last psalm (120, 134), the second psalm and second-last (121, 133), the third and third-last (122, 132) and so on, with Psalm 127, as

---

[31] Those of Seybold 1978, Mannati 1979, Beaucamp 1979, Auffret 1982, Seidel 1982, Viviers 1994, Crow 1996, Zenger 1998; Vesco 2006: 1167–69.

[32] In addition to the structural patterns of Hengstenberg and Prinsloo, which follow, see also the logotechnical analysis of C. Labuschagne, whose study of Ps. 127 also emphasizes its structural centrality to the Ascents collection (http://www.labuschagne.nl/ps127.pdf).

[33] Hengstenberg 1845–48: III.409.

[34] 122.4; 130.3; as noted by Forbes 1888: 190. English Bibles tend to render Yah as 'the Lord', making it indistinguishable from YHVH.

[35] We are dealing here only with the MT. 11QPs[a] adds a David heading for Ps. 123; Codex Vaticanus lacks the David headings of Pss. 122 and 124.

the capstone of it all. Such a structure – called a *chiasm* – is quite common in Hebrew literature.[36] Like a Russian doll, it encloses all the elements in a single unit and concentrates attention on the middle element, that is, Psalm 127.

A   Ps. 120. Surrounded by heathen in Meshekh and Kedar; departing for Zion.
   B   Ps. 121. Up, up, up to Zion for blessing.
      C   Ps. 122. Pilgrims enter Jerusalem; David's thrones bestow justice.
         D   **Ps. 123. Eyes lifted up: humility not pride; servant to master.**
            E   **Ps. 124. Hostile waters; deep trouble; redeemed by the LORD.**
               F   **Ps. 125. Delivered from foreign domination.**
                  G   Ps. 126. Fertility (agrarian); fruitful labour.
                     H   Ps. 127. Solomon. Building temple and nation.
                  G   Ps. 128. Fertility (human: agrarian imagery); fruitful labour.
               F   **Ps. 129. Delivered from foreign domination.**
            E   **Ps. 130. Hostile waters; deep trouble; redeemed by the LORD.**
         D   **Ps. 131. Eyes not lifted up: humility not pride; child to mother.**
      C   Ps. 132. Ark enters temple; king of David's line sits crowned.
   B   Ps. 133. Down, down, down: blessing from Zion to Israel.
A   Ps. 134. Surrounded by the holy in the Jerusalem Temple.

Professor Prinsloo notes that the chiastic structure is reinforced by a series of happy and sad or 'light' and 'dark' bands that run through the collection. The 'dark' bands are shown above in bold typeface.[37] The first three songs, Psalms 120 to 122, deal with the pilgrim's departure, journey, and happy arrival in Jerusalem. The next three, Psalms 123 to 125, are a 'dark' band, the middle Psalm 124 being the darkest of all. They turn to prayer, recounting memories of sore oppression and deliverance. The three central songs, Psalms 126 to 128, are 'lighter' and happier again in mood, the middle Psalm 127 being the capstone of the collection. They describe the daily human round of sowing and reaping, building homes and raising families, working and reaping the fruit of work and family life. Yet, at the same time, the same three psalms mirror the fortunes of Israel and the house of David. Israel has sown in tears and now reaps with joy (126); Solomon has built a house for the LORD and is a son who brings credit to his father in the gate (127); he is a father of sons who will continue the dynasty into the future (128). Then follows another dark band: Psalm 129 leads down into the vale of recollection, Psalm 130 leads to repentance and return, and Psalm 131 completes the journey back up to peace. Then three strong, happy songs, focussed on the present, Psalms 132 to 134, bring the collection to a joyful end. The ark enters the temple and the Holy One blesses Jerusalem, temple ministers, and the house of David (132); through the Aaronite *kohanim* the united twelve tribes of Israel obtain the heavenly blessing, which descends to all the land (133); the blessing is spoken by the mouth of the *kohen ha-gadol* (134).

---

[36] *Chiasm* from Greek χ (*chi*). In such a structure, the first item pairs with the fourth and the second with the third, giving a form ABBA. If this is written on two lines, AB and BA, a line drawn between the matching letters forms a χ-shape.

[37] Prinsloo 2005: 457–477.

SUMMARY

The Songs of Ascents share one name, one serene mood, one theology of blessing, one heart for Jerusalem and the king of David's line, one common language, and one single story. Shot through all this are complex overlapping structures of divine names, words, and themes, as multifariously patterned as any magic carpet, whose colours and cross-motifs converge from clearly-defined borders to a single central medallion, which is Psalm 127. These features bind the fifteen Songs of Ascents into one, marking them as an independent collection which existed in its own right before it was included in the big Book of Psalms. Just as the Psalms themselves are now preserved as a book within the Bible, so the Songs of Ascents are preserved within the Psalms, a book within a book within a book.

2

Words Within Words

The old Hebrew method of fourfold interpretation is represented by the letters of the Hebrew word PaRDeS, the Paradise Garden.[1]

P	Peshat	'Plain'
R	Remez	'Hint'
D	Derash	'Investigation'
S	Sod	'Mystery'

And so, before ascending the Ascents, we descend to uncover mysteries. A closer study of the patterns we saw in the last chapter will reveal more encoded messages, which will not only leave us wondering at the intricacy of this little collection of Psalms, but provide further evidence for its unity and shed light on its date of composition.

NUMEROLOGY AND *GEMATRIA*

The Spanish kabbalist, Joseph ben Abraham Gikatilla (1248–1305), said that the name of God was woven throughout the Bible like gold thread through a garment, bearing secret messages. He was speaking of the cryptic world of numerology. To enter this world and read, we must understand a little about the Hebrew alphabet.

The Hebrews, like the Romans and Greeks, represented numbers by letters of the alphabet. Now, it follows that, where each letter represents a number, every word will have a numerical value. For instance, the Hebrew word for a hand, *yad*, is composed of two letters – *yod* and *daleth* (יד) – that have a value

---

[1] The PRDS mnemonic is Jewish, but it is unclear whether fourfold exegesis was Jewish or Christian in origin. The first mention of the Christian model – literal, tropological, allegorical, and anagogical – from the 8th century Englishman Bede, predates by five centuries the earliest use of the PRDS mnemonic in the *Zohar* (1280–90) and the Pentateuch commentary of Baḥya ben Asher of Saragossa (1291). Fourfold exegesis may have entered Spanish Judaism during the Jewish–Christian debates of the 13th century. But those who accept Moses de Leon's claims for the antiquity of the *Zohar* will give Judaism the priority.

of ten and four, and so the numerical value of *yad* is fourteen. The rabbis called this kind of number symbolism *gematria*.² Here are the twenty-two letters of the Hebrew alphabet with their numerical values:

Table 2. The numerology of the Hebrew alphabet

Letter	Name	Value	Letter	Name	Value
א	Aleph	1	ל	Lamed	30
ב	Bet	2	מ	Mem	40
ג	Gimel	3	נ	Nun	50
ד	Daleth	4	ס	Samekh	60
ה	Heh	5	ע	Ayin	70
ו	Vav	6	פ	Peh	80
ז	Zayin	7	צ	Tsade	90
ח	Het	8	ק	Qof	100
ט	Tet	9	ר	Resh	200
י	Yodh	10	ש	Shin	300
כ	Kaf	20	ת	Tav	400

Since every word has a numerical value, it follows that certain numbers will be important because they represent important words. And there are two numbers that we must pay particular attention to. The first of these is the number of the sacred name, YHVH. The first letter, *yodh*, equivalent to English *Y*, has a value of ten. The second letter, *heh*, equivalent to English *H*, has a value of five. The third letter, *vav*, equivalent to English *V*, has a value of six. The fourth letter is *heh* again, with a value of five. So altogether the name YHVH has a *gematria* value of 26. In Hebrew, reading from right to left, it looks like this:

The name YHVH and the sacred 26

ה = 5   ו = 6   ה = 5   י = 10

יהוה

The second important number is the one which represents the shorter form of the holy name, that is, Yah. This name is itself very ancient, occurring in some of the oldest strata of the Bible.³ It is made up of two Hebrew letters, equal to English YH (no vowel). The first one is *yodh* with a value of ten. The second is *heh* with a value of five. Together they add up to fifteen.

---

² Pronounced *gᵉmátriya*, it derives from Greek *grammatia*, 'accounts, calculations'.
³ For the relationship between YHVH and Yah, see Appendix I.

The name Yah and the sacred 15

ה = 5   י = 10

יה

So the numbers 15 and 26 are sacred because they represent the revealed names of God. They also happen to represent the Hebrew words for 'splendour' (*hod* הוד) and 'glory' (*kavod* כבד) – ideas closely associated with the names of God – which also have numerical values of 15 and 26 respectively. And we find that these names and numbers underlie the whole structure of the Songs of Ascents.

ENCODED NUMERIC MESSAGES

There are fifteen Songs of Ascents, and these represent the name Yah. In fact, as we shall see, there are many fifteens around the Songs of Ascents. For the fifteen songs, of the number of the name of Yah, were built upon the fifteen words of the *Birkat Kohanim* or 'Priestly Blessing', and were sung on fifteen steps on the fifteenth day of the month.

Now, as we saw in the last chapter, the name Yah occurs twice in the Ascents, in Psalms 122.4 and 130.3, the third psalm of each heptade. Between these two occurrences of the name Yah, the name YHVH occurs 26 times. Since 26 is the number of YHVH, these 26 occurrences of the name represent the name itself encoded numerically in the middle of the Ascents. A diagram may help. The number of occurrences of the name YHVH in each psalm is given in the third row, beneath the number of the Psalm.

Table 3. Occurences of YHVH in each Song of Ascents

The 15 Songs of Ascents 15 = Yah (יה) = splendour (הוד)															
120	121	122	123	124	125	126	127	128	129	130	131	132	133	134
2	5	1 Yah 2	2	4	4	4	3	3	3	1 Yah 3	2	6	1	5
8 × YHVH		26 × YHVH = YHVH encoded										17 × YHVH			

The two occurrences of Yah form two pillars, so to speak, like the pillars of Solomon's temple, upholding the whole collection, with the glory of YHVH, the invisible God, invisibly present between them. Outside the Yah pillars, the name occurs eight times before and seventeen after. Eight represents Hebrew *bo* (בו), meaning 'in him'. And seventeen represents Hebrew *tov* or *tuv*, two related words, an adjective and a noun, spelt the same way (טוב), meaning 'good' or 'goodness' or 'prosperity'. With such meanings, an encoded message appears: *Bo YHVH tuv*, 'In him, YHVH, is prosperity.'

Table 4. In him, YHVH, is prosperity

The 15 Songs of Ascents 15 = Yah (יה) = splendour (הוד)														
120	121	122	123	124	125	126	127	128	129	130	131	132	133	134
2	5	1 Yah	2	2	4	4	4	3	3	3 1 Yah	3	2	6	1	5
8 × YHVH 8 = בו in him			26 × YHVH = YHVH encoded								17 × YHVH 17 = טוב Prosperity			

Next, the absolute centre-point of the Ascents collection, the central word of the central psalm, is the word *Yedid-ô* or 'his Beloved' in Psalm 127: *He gives prosperity to his Beloved* (v. 2). King David's crown prince had two names. There was the name given him by his father: Solomon, Man of Peace (2 Sam. 12.24; 1 Chr. 22.9). And there was the name given him by the Holy One, because he loved him: Yedid-Yah – Jedidiah in English – meaning Beloved of Yah (2 Sam. 12.24–25). So 'his Beloved' in the centre of Psalm 127 is the Beloved of Yah, that is, Yedid-Yah. It refers to King Solomon, whose name stands at the head of the psalm and who built the temple or 'house' which the psalm talks about. Now, from the beginning of the collection to the central Yedid-name in Psalm 127.2, the sacred name YHVH occurs another 26 times. And so, once again, the name YHVH is encoded beneath the written text.

Table 5. YHVH encoded before Yedid

The 15 Songs of Ascents														
120	121	122	123	124	125	126	127	128	129	130	131	132	133	134
2	5	1 Yah	2	2	4	4	4	2 Yedid	1	3	3	1 Yah	3	2	6	1	5
		26 × YHVH = YHVH encoded													

Astute readers will already have calculated the number of times YHVH appears after Yedid, and will have found that there are 25. What are we to make of this? It would be easy to argue that the text is corrupt and one YHVH has simply got lost. It would be easy to change an *Adonai* to YHVH in Psalm 130 and – *voilà!* – the sacred 26 appears on each side of Yedid. But any such fix is foiled by Hengstenberg's pattern of four twelve-groups of YHVH. So, since Hengstenberg's pattern also looks deliberate, let us accept the text as it stands, and look for a rationale in the number 25.

Although several options might be proposed, 25 should perhaps be taken as the numerical representation of the Hebrew *avi-hu*, 'He is my father.'[4] Taken with the preceding YHVH it makes perfect sense in Hebrew: 'YHVH – he is my father.' Such a statement would be fully true of King Solomon, at whose birth the Holy One said, *I shall be his father and he shall be my son* (2 Sam. 7.14).

Table 6. YHVH, he is my father

The 15 Songs of Ascents															
120	121	122	123	124	125	126	127	128	129	130	131	132	133	134
2	5	1 Yah 2	2	4	4	4	2 Yedid 1	3	3	1 Yah 3	2	6	1	5
26 × YHVH = YHVH encoded								25 × YHVH = אביהוא (avi-hu) He is my father						

But there is more. Note that the psalm is now divided by three pillars: namely, Yah-Yedid-Yah, reflecting the name of God and of King Solomon, Yedid-Yah. Now let us look at the pattern in relation to these three pillars. YHVH occurs eight times before the first Yah-pillar, eighteen times before the central Yedid-pillar, eight times again before the second Yah-pillar, then seventeen times to the end. Each of these numbers represents a word by *gematria*. Eight, as we saw, represents Hebrew *bo* (בו), 'in him', while seventeen represents *tov* or *tuv* (טוב), meaning 'good' or 'prosperity'. Eighteen represents Hebrew *ḥai* (חי), which is 'life'. Here is a diagram.

Table 7. In him is life, in him is prosperity

The 15 Songs of Ascents															
120	121	122	123	124	125	126	127	128	129	130	131	132	133	134
2	5	1 Yah	2	2	4	4	4	2 Yedid 1	3	3	1 Yah	3	2	6	1	5
8 × YHVH 8 = בו in him		18 × YHVH 18 = חי Life					8 × YHVH 8 = בו in him			17 × YHVH 17 = טוב prosperity			

---

[4] That is, *avihu*, אביהוא = 25. Other options might include *hava-yah* (חביה = 25), meaning 'He whom Yah protects'. Clearly, that would be true of Solomon, and would give the message, 'Yehovah (and) he whom Yah protects' Or another option might be *yeḥubah* (יחבה = 25), meaning 'hidden'. For, clearly, being encoded in this way, the message 'YHVH is hidden' is manifestly true, as it is said, *Surely you are a God who hides himself* (Isa. 45.15).

In Hebrew, which does not require a verb, a message emerges which makes perfectly good sense. It says: *bo ḥai, bo tuv* – 'In him is life. In him is prosperity', 'him' being, of course, the One whose name encodes the message. It reminds us, in fact, of the name *Bo-az* – 'In him is strength' – the name not only of Solomon's great-great-grandfather but also of the great bronze pillar which supported the northern end of the great portico to Solomon's temple.[5]

MORE ENCODED MESSAGES

Next, we can see that from the beginning of the collection to the first Yah-pillar, the sacred name occurs eight times, and thereafter it occurs another 43 times to the end of the collection. Now 43 is the number of Yedid-Yah, composed of 28 for Yedid and 15 for Yah.[6] And eight is the number of *ahav*, the Hebrew word meaning 'he loves' or 'he loved'.[7] So another encoded message appears: 'He loves/loved Yedid-Yah.' It recalls the description of Solomon's birth in 2 Samuel 12.24–25: *And YHVH loved him. And he sent by the hand of Nathan the prophet and he called his name Yedid-Yah because of YHVH.* We see too that the encoded name of Yedid-Yah begins immediately after the first Yah-pillar in Psalm 122.4, where the psalmist speaks of the thrones of the house of David (122.5). These thrones are the thrones of Yedid-Yah which will continue to the end.

Table 8. YHVH loves Yedid-Yah

The 15 Songs of Ascents															
120	121	122		123	124	125	126	127		128	129	130		131	132	133	134
2	5	1	2	2	4	4	4	2	Y e d i d	1	3	3	1	Y a h	3	2	6	1	5
8 × YHVH 8 = אהב *ahav* he loves	Y a h	43 × YHVH 43 = YDYDYH (ידידיה) Yedid-Yah													

Or again, if we take only the last Yah-pillar, the sacred name occurs 34 times before it, and 17 times after it. Now 34 is the gematric number of *Yedid-ô*, 'his Beloved', which, as we saw, is the central word of the central Song of Ascents.[8] And 17, as we saw above, means 'good' or 'prosperity' as a noun. But it can

---

[5] Ruth 4.21–22; 2 Chr. 3.17.
[6] The Hebrew of Yedid-Yah omits most of the vowels. That is *ydyd-yh*, ידיד־יה = 43.
[7] That is, *ahav*, אהב = 8.
[8] That is, *yedid-ô*, ידידו.

also be an adjective – 'good, well, prosperous' – or a verb, 'to do well, prosper'. So once again a hidden message appears: 'His Beloved prospers' or 'It is well with his Beloved.'

Table 9. His beloved prospers

\multicolumn{15}{c	}{The 15 Songs of Ascents}
120	121	122	123	124	125	126	127	128	129	130	131	132	133	134
2	5	1 Yah	2	2	4	4	4	2 Yedid	1	3	3	1 Yah	3	2	6	1	5
\multicolumn{7}{c	}{34 × YHVH}	\multicolumn{4}{c	}{}	\multicolumn{4}{c	}{17 × YHVH}
\multicolumn{7}{c	}{34 = YDYDV (ידידו)}	\multicolumn{4}{c	}{}	\multicolumn{4}{c	}{17 = טוב}
\multicolumn{7}{c	}{his beloved}	\multicolumn{4}{c	}{}	\multicolumn{4}{c	}{prospers}

Then, again, we can see that YHVH occurs 51 times in the whole collection. This equals three times seventeen. In biblical literature, a threefold repetition expresses completeness. *Holy, holy, holy!* say the cherubim, for the One on the throne is all holy (Isa. 6.3). *I will overturn, overturn, overturn,* writes Ezekiel, for the destruction will be complete (Ezek. 21.27). And so, since 17 – *tov* – is goodness or prosperity, three times seventeen represents the perfect goodness of the LORD, as the Levites cried, *Give thanks to YHVH, for he is good!*[9] And it shows the perfect prosperity which he gives his beloved Solomon and Israel.

Table 10. Three times seventeen

\multicolumn{15}{c	}{The 15 Songs of Ascents}
120	121	122	123	124	125	126	127	128	129	130	131	132	133	134
2	5	1 Yah	2	2	4	4	4	2 Yedid	1	3	3	1 Yah	3	2	6	1	5
\multicolumn{15}{c	}{51 × YHVH = Good! Good! Good!}
\multicolumn{15}{c	}{Prosperity! Prosperity! Prosperity!}

THE NAME *YEDID* ENCODED IN THE CENTRAL PSALM

Now let us return to the central psalm, Psalm 127. It is about Solomon. It bears the name *Of Solomon* at the top. It is about building the house of the LORD, which was Solomon's great achievement. And the central word of the psalm

---

[9] *Hodu li-yhovah ki tov* was a Levite acclamation, as much as the more familiar *Halelu Yah!* It occurs at 2 Chr 5.13; 7.3; 20.21; Pss. 106.1; 107.1; 118.1, 29; 136.1; and, contracted, at Pss. 100.5; 105.1; 135.3.

is *yedid-ô*, 'His Beloved', the Beloved of Yah, who is Yedid-Yah or Solomon. This psalm, omitting the heading, has fifty-seven words, and *yedid-ô* is the twenty-ninth and central word. This means that *yedid-ô* has twenty-eight words before it, and twenty-eight after it. Since twenty-eight is the number of Yedid, it follows that the name *yedid* appears in *gematria* on each side of the central *yedid-ô*.[10]

Table 11. Yedid encoded around *yedid-ô*

28 words before	Middle word	28 words after
= Yedid	*yedid-ô* his beloved	= Yedid

So the name *Yedid* or Beloved, Solomon's birth-name, Yedid-Yah, actually appears three times in this psalm. It appears once explicitly in the middle word (*yedid-ô*), and twice encoded in *gematria* in the twenty-eight words on each side of it. Now, someone might say, 'Very well, I see Yedid, but where is Yah?' But, remember, the name of Yah appears twice in the Songs of Ascents, in Psalms 122 and 130. And, more, the fifteen Songs of Ascents represent Yah numerologically. Like the hidden God himself, the number of his name surrounds the king, invisible to the casual observer, but seen by the wise. And the reason why Yah surrounds the king is because the king is Yedid-Yah, Yah's beloved (2 Sam. 12.25). On him Yah has conferred unbounded *tuv*, or prosperity, as on no other before. He sits at the centre of the peaceful and prosperous kingdom, guarded and kept on all sides by the invisible pillars of Yah. The hidden names Yedid and Yah depict what the Songs of Ascents are really all about. The threefold name of Yah, in the fifteen songs and in Psalms 122.4 and 130.3, encompasses 'his Beloved', whose name lies threefold in Psalm 127 at the heart of the collection. Yah's overarching protection, his encompassing wings, give his Beloved rest (Ps. 127.2).

Yet there is more. On each side of central Psalm 127, there are psalms headed with David's name, two before (Pss. 122 and 124) and two after (Pss. 131 and 133). Since the name David has a numerical value of 14 (Hebrew: *dvd* דוד), it follows that the two David-headings on each side of central Psalm 127 add up once again to 28, that is, Yedid or Beloved. So once again Yedid sits on each side of the central psalm. Moreover, since the name David also means 'Beloved' – it comes from the same Hebrew verb as Yedid – David is incorporated within Solomon in every way, numerically, grammatically, and semantically. David is embodied in his son Solomon, Solomon has inherited twice David's number, just as he inherited the double portion of his father's spirit, the right of the firstborn, and David's descendants are beloved by Yah.[11]

---

[10] That is *ydyd* or ידיד = 28.

[11] As Elisha inherited the double portion of Elijah's spirit (2 Kgs 2.9). The double portion was the right of the firstborn (Deut. 21.16–17). Solomon, although not a firstborn, received the firstborn's portion in falling heir to the throne.

In the same way, there are seven non-Solomonic psalms on each side of the central psalm, again making fourteen, the number of David. But the number fourteen, as we saw, represents the word 'hand' by *gematria*, and rabbinic interpretation takes this as representing the controlling royal hand of David. And so we have fifteen psalms in total, representing invisible Yah above, and fourteen non-Solomonic psalms, representing David's kingly hand below.

Table 12. Fifteen for Yah, fourteen for David

							The 15 Songs of Ascents (=Yah)							
120	121	122 דוד David Yah 122.4	123	124 דוד David	125	126	127 שלמה Solomon (Yedid) Yedidô (Yedid)	128	129	130 Yah 130.3	131 דוד David	132	133 דוד David	134
		2 × Dvd (14) = Yedid (28)								2 × Dvd (14) = Yedid (28)				
							14 non-Solomon psalms = David							

So the Yedid name appears three times in the central psalm, once written and twice shy, so to speak, by *gematria*. It is balanced by three names of Yah in the wider collection, twice written, once encoded, overarching the whole collection. And the headings of the psalms refer once to Solomon, and four times to David, these last four references being numerically equivalent to two further names of Yedid, who is Solomon, and showing that David's seed and dynasty continue in his son, who has received the firstborn's right of the double portion. The fifteen songs show Yah setting Solomon on the throne from above, and the fourteen non-Solomon psalms show David raising his son to the throne by his royal hand.

GYPSY ROSE

I am suggesting that there is a complex series of codes and patterns permeating the whole of the Songs of Ascents. Is this correct or am I dreaming? Clearly, some of the patterns are evident enough and cannot be dismissed. But what about the hidden messages, like 'He loves Yedid-Yah' or 'In him is life. In him is prosperity.' Are they really there? Or am I like Gypsy Rose prognosticating over tea-leaves?

In reply, we need to address the question of whether there can be more than one word for each number, and, if so, whether one cannot find any message one wants through numerology. The first answer is, yes, there are several words for each number. For instance, I already took the number eight to mean both 'in him' (*bo*) and 'he loves' (*ahav*). But, on the other hand, one cannot make simply any message at all. For instance, leaving aside some proper names, the number twenty-six (the number of YHVH) can represent the Hebrew words for 'glory', for a 'hook', for a 'peak', and for the verbs, 'to cut', 'to deceive', and 'to be sad'.[12] But it cannot represent an unlimited range of words. Likewise, the number fifteen (Yah) can represent the Hebrew for 'splendour', 'praise' and 'majesty', all words related to the character of Yah, as well as 'springtime', 'bullrush', and even such negative words as 'faithless', 'ruin', and 'contempt'.[13] But that is the range of words for fifteen. So there is a limited number of messages that could be made from the numbers I have identified above. For instance, the numbers forty-three and eight, which I identified as saying 'He loves Yedid-Yah' could be taken as saying 'He chews fish' or 'He removes fish' or even 'Big fish'.[14] One might find one or two other messages. But these messages employ rare words and variant spellings, and the options are still few rather than many. One cannot make numerology say simply anything one chooses.

A degree of ambiguity is intrinsic to most codes. Decoding them requires not only knowledge of the code, but knowledge of the subject matter, and willingness to understand. In Tolstoy's *Anna Karenina*, Levin proposes to his beloved Kitty by a code game, in which they write down only the first letter of each word. If Kitty had been slow-witted or obdurate, Levin could not have communicated with her. Luckily for him, she was neither; she understood and accepted his proposal. So with numerology. One must sort through the likeliest possibilities of likeliest words to make the likeliest messages. For instance, 'YHVH' is a central Bible word, and should be considered first choice for the number 26, while the words for 'hook', 'cut', 'lie', and 'sad' are rare words, little-used. Likewise, the message 'He loves Yedid-Yah' is appropriate to the Songs of Ascents, while other possible messages are not.

THE VALUE OF NUMEROLOGY

Some may fail to see the value of this approach, thinking it an intellectual pursuit far from a 'plain words' approach to the Bible. Surely one's time can be better spent than counting Jehovahs! However, numerology, like any scientific research, should not require too swift a justification. Some pursue cancer research – reproducing, measuring, testing and examining cells – for years on end, to advance the field of knowledge by one small step. Without careful research there would be no scientific advance.

---

[12] That is: 'he is glorious' (*kavad* כבד) or 'glory' (*kavod* כבד); also 'ring, hook' (*ḥaḥi* חחי); 'peak' (*hᵉdid* חדיד); 'to cut' (*ḥaṭaṭ* חטט); 'to deceive' (*kadab* כדב); 'to be sad' (*ka'ah* כאה).

[13] That is: 'splendour' (*hod* הוד); 'praise' (*yada* ידא); and 'majesty' (*ga'avah* גאוה); 'sprout-springtime' (*aviv* אביב); 'bullrush' (*aḥu* אחו); 'faithless' (*begud* בגוד); 'ruin' (*id* איד); and 'contempt' (*buz* בוז).

[14] The number 43 can equal 'he chews' (*lahah* להה), 'he removes' (*zul* זול), 'big' (*gadol* גדול). The number 8 can equal an uncommon variant spelling of the word 'fish' (*dag* דאג: Neh. 13.16). The standard spelling of 'fish', as in Jonah 1.17, is *dg* דג.

Yet biblical numerology yields visible fruit quicker than many sciences. First, it can provide evidence for the reliability of the Bible text. Numerological patterns and messages confirm that the text we have is the correct text. We need no additions, subtractions, or amendments, which would erase these very patterns and messages. With the Songs of Ascents, we can be encouraged that the text we have today is much the same as it was when it left the hand of the compiler.

Second, numerology can provide important information about the background to Bible texts. In our present case, since the names Yedid, Yah, and Yedid-Yah permeate the whole collection, weaving the name and claims of Solomon the whole way through from beginning to end, they show that King Solomon is central to the Songs of Ascents.

Third, numerology does contain its own perfectly plain and simple messages. The encoded messages, 'YHVH is my father', 'In him is life. In him is prosperity', or 'He loves Yedid-Yah', and so on, may not be easy to spot, but once found, they are both plain and relevant to the main text.

Fourth, numerology is a symbolic message in its own right. For instance, the 26's encoding the sacred name underneath the written text reinforce the message that 'YHVH is hidden.' They symbolize the fact that the Holy One, who speaks to Israel in psalms and prophecies, is also the unseen, hidden presence behind all their doings. Or again, the central psalm, with its threefold 'Yedid' sitting amidst threefold 'Yah' and fifty-one fold YHVH depicts King Solomon, enthroned on Mount Zion, supported and surrounded on all sides by invisible Yah, who set him on the throne, amidst the unbounded favour and prosperity of YHVH.

Fifth, numerology allows us to see into the minds that put the Bible together. For such complex patterns do not arise by accident. One does not find them in the newspaper. One may occasionally find them in complex literature. But even then, the patterns in the Bible are of the highest order of complexity. How did they get there? Clearly, they arose from a cultivated civilization whose literati had the intelligence and leisure to plan and compose works of this nature. So we must imagine a time when Israel was living in peace, free from the pressing threat of war, a time like Solomon's.

But one wonders about the mind behind this. In the city of Edinburgh, in Princes Street Gardens, there is a floral clock with turning hands. Every year the gardeners lay it out in new and beautiful patterns. But take a flower from the clock and put it under a magnifying glass and a level of patterning and complexity will be seen – in petals, stylae, and stamens – that had nothing to do with the gardener. So too, in dealing with the Bible, we are sometimes left wondering which minds impressed which patterns upon it.

We have not exhausted this subject of numerology. Further examples of words within words will appear on our journey. But this is a study of a bouquet of crocuses from the Paradise Garden. We have examined them through a magnifying glass. We might produce an electron microscope and pass from botany to chemistry to atomic physics. But then we might lose sight of the crocuses. Our numerological study confirms what we saw in the last chapter, that our Songs of Ascents are a self-contained group of psalms. It also shows that they had something to do with King Solomon. Our task now is to discover who put this collection together, why they did it, and what it had to do with Solomon.

3

Steps Within Steps

We turn now to the heading, 'A Song of the Ascents'. The English word 'Ascents', represents the Hebrew *ma'alot*. This word has two meanings. First, it is the normal classical Hebrew word for steps: steps to an altar, steps to a throne, steps to a temple or palace or ordinary house.[1] So we could translate the heading as 'A Song of the Steps.' This is what the first translators of the word did, rendering *ma'alot* in the Greek Septuagint Bible as *anabathmōn*, that is, 'steps'.

The second meaning of *ma'alot* is 'ascents' in the more general sense of 'roads going up'. The temples and shrines of the ancient east were built on hills. So people would 'go up' or 'ascend' to worship, perhaps to the calf-idol in Bethel, as the urchins of Bethel urged Elisha to do (2 Kgs 2.23), or, of course, to Jerusalem. 'There is no doubt,' said R.D. Wilson of Princeton, 'that "go up" was the ordinary term in use for the yearly, or other, ascents to the house of the Lord at Jerusalem.'[2] And so the roads leading up to Jerusalem, and the whole idea of pilgrimage there, were called the 'ascents' or *ma'alot*. In this sense, we could translate the heading as 'A Song of the Pilgrim Ways'.[3]

Now the question is: Which of these two meanings of *ma'alot* or 'ascents' do we have in these psalms? Are they 'Songs of the Steps'? Or are they 'Songs of the Pilgrim Ways'? Let's look at the two options in reverse order.

THE 'ASCENTS' AS PILGRIM WAYS TO JERUSALEM

There is evidence within the Songs of Ascents that they were connected with pilgrimage to Jerusalem. For a start, since their language is not entirely classical Hebrew, they do not derive from Jerusalem or central Israel. Yet Jerusalem is their great theme. So it seems they were written by provincial

---

[1] Exod. 20.26; 1 Kgs 10.19–20; 2 Kgs 9.13; 20.9–11; 2 Chr. 9.18–19; Neh. 3.15; 12.37; Isa. 38.8; Ezek. 40.6, 22, 26, 31, 34, 37, 49.
[2] Wilson 1926b: 367.
[3] So, *e.g.*, Keet 1969: 1–17.

Israelites who loved Jerusalem and who would visit their beloved city at the feasts. That alone suggests that pilgrimage to Jerusalem is a theme of these psalms.

But more, the Songs of Ascents actually paint a picture of such a pilgrimage. In Psalm 120, the psalmist is living in foreign lands, in Meshekh and Kedar, far away from Jerusalem. The people there are cruel and he longs for a place of peace, a city whose name is Peace. In Psalm 121, the psalmist is on the road, lifting his eyes to the Judean hills to claim protection from Zion's deity, as he ascends. In Psalm 122, he has attained his goal; he is standing in the gates of Jerusalem. Then, in Psalm 123, he lifts his eyes to the temple and directs his prayer to the God whom he has come so far to worship. The next nine songs describe aspects of worship in the city: psalms of remembrance and praise. Then Psalm 133, near the end of the collection, speaks of holy oil dropping down, down, as the returning pilgrims take the blessing of God home. In the last psalm, Psalm 134, the *kohanim* and the people bestow parting blessings on one another. So the collection paints a picture of a pilgrimage to and from Jerusalem.

Again, Psalm 122.4 uses the word 'ascend' or 'go up' – the same Hebrew word as in the Ascents heading – to describe pilgrimage to Jerusalem:

> Jerusalem…where the tribes ascend – the tribes of Yah –
> a statute of Israel
> to give thanks to the name of the LORD.

This recalls the legislation which required the tribes of Israel to make pilgrimage to worship together three times a year. So central was this to Israel's life that it is legislated in four out of five of the books of Moses. Deuteronomy, for instance, says, *Three times a year all your men must appear before the LORD your God at the place he will choose: at the Feast of Unleavened Bread, the Feast of Weeks and the Feast of Sukkot.*[4]

Ancient Israel had three feasts every year. The Feast of Unleavened Bread or Passover – *Pesaḥ* in Hebrew – was held in the spring. It celebrated the beginning of the new agricultural year. But most of all it recalled the beginning of the Israelite nation, when the angel slew Egypt's firstborn and passed over the Hebrews.

The second feast was the Feast of Weeks or *Shavuot*, a Hebrew word meaning both 'weeks' and 'sevens'. It was held seven sevens, that is, seven weeks, after Passover, from which came its Greek name, *Pentecost,* 'fiftieth day'. It was also called the Feast of Firstfruits or Reaping (*bikkurim* or *qatsir*: Exod. 23.16). If Passover was a feast of beginnings, then Weeks was a feast of middles. Held in the early summer, it gave thanks for the first fruits of the

---

[4] Deut. 16.16. Attendance at the three feasts is a requirement at Exod. 23.14–17; 34.18–26; Lev. 23.1-44; Num. 28.16–29.40; Deut. 16.1–17. The feasts are, of course, absent from Genesis, whose events take place before the time of Moses' law. But Abraham's offering to the priest-king Melchizedek in Salem (Jerusalem) is held up as an example (Gen. 14).

harvest, prayed for the latter rain, and looked to the final harvest. It was also understood symbolically as a thanksgiving for Israel's redemption and a looking-forward to the gathering of all nations. The Book of Ruth became the liturgy for this feast. Its bucolic narrative, running from early to late harvest, tells how Ruth the Moabitess left her people to become a believer in Israel's God.

The third feast was really a season of feasts and fasts, running from the beginning till almost the end of the seventh month, Ethanim. It began on the first day of the month with *Yom teruah* or the Feast of Trumpets, marking the New Year day of Rosh Hashanah, and summoning Israel to repentance. Then, on the tenth day of the month, came *Yom Kippur,* the Day of Atonement, when the nation's sins were atoned for. Finally, the Israelites went up to Jerusalem to celebrate the Feast of Sukkot, which began on the fifteenth of the month. The Feast lasted seven days and was followed by a solemn assembly on the eighth day of 'tarrying', *Shemini Atzeret*, the twenty-second day of the month.[5]

The Feast of Sukkot – sometimes translated as the Feast of Tabernacles or Booths – was the greatest of all Israel's feasts. This can be seen from the other names by which it was called: the Feast of Ingathering, the Feast of the LORD, or simply *the* Feast.[6] Its sacrifices exceeded those of every other feast, both in quantity and in symbolism. The week of Sukkot saw 182 sacrifices – 70 bullocks, 14 rams, 98 lambs – equalling 26 multiplied by seven, the number of the sacred Name multiplied by completion. The feast gave thanks for the end of harvest, the gathering of corn and grapes, the first new wine, and the general autumnal abundance. It looked back to the past, when Israel first left Egypt and camped in the desert in booths at the place they called Sukkot.[7] Yet, from early times, it was also understood to look to the future, to the time of the end, when earth's golden age would come. Zechariah saw it as a time when all nations would come to worship the God of Israel (Zech. 14.16-19). So too the Book of Revelation, with its palm-waving hosts from every nation, sees it as the time of God's triumph over global evil (Rev. 7.9-17). Indeed, the redemption of the nations was such a central theme of the Feast that its seventy bullocks were regarded by the rabbis as offerings for the world.[8]

> God arranged for the feast of Sukkot when seventy offerings are made in behalf of the seventy nations of the world (B. *Suk.* 55b).

> At the Feast of Sukkot we offer up seventy bullocks for the seventy nations, and we pray that rain will come down for them (*Midr. Pss.* 109.4).

---

[5] Lev. 23.23–36; Num. 29.1–38; 1 Kings 8.2; Ezek. 45.25; Ezra 3.1–6; Neh. 8.17.

[6] Sukkot: Lev. 23.42-43; Deut. 16.13,16; 31.10; 2 Chr. 8.13; Ezra 3.4; Ingathering (*Asif*): Exod. 23.16; 34.22; the Feast of YHVH (Lev 23.39); the Feast (1 Kings 8.2; 2 Chron 5.3; 7.8,9).

[7] Exod. 12.37. Such huts were made as required for livestock (Gen. 33.17; again giving a name to the place), military on campaign (2 Sam. 11.11), or watchmen (Isa. 1.8).

[8] These traditions, though post-biblical, were of ancient origin. The Maccabees, in the 2nd century BC, told the Spartans how they offered sacrifice and prayed for them (1 Macc. 12.11).

Sukkot looked to the time when the Holy One would harvest the whole earth, crush his enemies like grapes in a winepress, gather the nations to himself like wheat into a granary, and lay a table for them at the Messiah's banquet.[9] As Edersheim says:

> That these are not ideal comparisons, but the very design of the Feast of Tabernacles, appears not only from the language of the prophets and the peculiar services of the feast, but also from its position in the Calendar, and even from the names by which it is designated in Scripture. Thus in its reference to the harvest it is called 'the feast of ingathering' (Exo 23.16; 34.22); in that to the history of Israel in the past, 'the Feast of Tabernacles' (Lev 23.34; and specially v 43; Deut 16.13,16; 31.10; 2 Chron 8.13; Ezra 3.4); while its symbolical bearing on the future is brought out in its designation as emphatically 'the feast' (1 Kings 8.2; 2 Chron 5.3; 7.8,9); and 'the Feast of Jehovah' (Lev 23.39).[10]

The law appointed these three feasts for Israel, and so they were called the 'appointed feasts'. Yet, for all their importance in the law of Moses, it appears that the Feast of Sukkot was the only one celebrated regularly throughout most of the kingdom period.[11] After Joshua's time, there is little mention of Passover (Josh. 5.10-11). Solomon fulfilled its sacrifical obligations, along with those of the Feast of Weeks, but there is no mention of the people attending (2 Chr. 8.13). Passover was then neglected until the reign of Hezekiah more than two hundred years later (2 Chr. 30.26), and then for another hundred years until Josiah's time (2 Chr. 35.18). Since Passover was neglected in this way, the lesser Feast of Weeks would have been more neglected still: apart from Solomon's sacrifices, it is not mentioned during kingdom times.

While the law required all Israelite men to attend the feasts, they were not all-male affairs. Women and children went along too, as Hannah went with Elkanah to the feast in Shiloh, or, more than a thousand years later, Mary and Joseph went with all their family (1 Sam. 1.3–8; Lk. 2.41). And they were essentially happy occasions, with coming and going, eating and drinking, singing and dancing.

So, all in all, Psalm 122's description of the tribes of Israel going up according to the statute, taken together with the pilgrimage depicted in Psalms 120 to 123, and the general importance of Jerusalem in these psalms, makes a good case for saying that the Songs of Ascents had something to do with the 'ascents' or 'pilgrim ways' to Israel's appointed feasts.

---

[9] The 'ultimate' quality of the Feast may well go back to Israel's earliest days. In the Ugaritic literature of the second millennium BC, the autumn feast is the time when Ba'al, rising from the underworld, sets up his throne on the holy mountain.

[10] Edersheim 1874: 176.

[11] Neh. 8.17–18 tells how the returnees from Babylon celebrated the Feast of Sukkot. The comment that they had not celebrated the Feast like this from the days of Joshua until that day refers to their building and living in booths rather than to the observation of the Feast itself.

THE 'ASCENTS' AND THE FEAST OF SUKKOT

Yet we can be more precise still. There are good reasons for thinking that the Songs of Ascents were particularly associated with the Feast of Sukkot.

First, since the Feast of Sukkot was the only feast celebrated regularly by the people throughout most of the kingdom period, any festal liturgy from kingdom times is likely to belong to this feast.

Second, the Chronicler cites a song sung at the Feast of Sukkot in Solomon's time: *Arise, LORD God, to your resting place, you and the ark of your power* (2 Chron. 6.41–42) Since these words come from Ascents Psalm 132.8, it looks like this Song of Ascents was sung at that Feast of Sukkot.

Third, the Songs of Ascents abound in images of harvest-time. Psalm 126 has autumn rains in the Negev desert and joyful reaping after tearful sowing. Psalm 128 has the happy man eating the fruit of his labour amidst a family of fruitful vines and olive shoots. Psalm 129 has ploughmen and reapers. Psalm 132 has the LORD bless his people with abundant food. Psalm 133 has extra-virgin olive oil running copiously from the head of the *kohen* to his beard and robes. Such pictures suit Sukkot, the autumn feast, better than the spring and summer feasts of Passover and Pentecost.

Finally, Psalm 134, the last Songs of Ascents, addresses the *kohanim* who stand ministering by night in the temple. We know of only one night service in the temple, and it happened during the Feast of Sukkot. It is described in Mishnah *Sukkah* 5.2–3.

> 2. At sundown of the first festival day of Sukkot they descended to the Court of Women where they had made a great enactment. Great golden candlebras were there with four golden bowls on the top of each of them and four ladders to each and four youths drawn from the priestly stock in whose hands were held jars of oil containing 120 *log*. 3. From the worn-out under-garments and girdles of the *kohanim* they made wicks and with them they kindled the lamps. And there was not a courtyard in Jerusalem that was not illumined by the light of the place of the water drawing.[12]

In fact, the Mishnah goes on to make an explicit link between the Songs of Ascents and the Feast of Sukkot. It tells how, at the feast,

> Countless Levites [played] on harps, lyres, cymbals, and trumpets, and musical instruments on the fifteen steps which descend from the Court of Israel to the Court of Women, and which correspond to the fifteen Songs of Ascents in the Psalms. On these steps the Levites stood with musical instruments and played melodies. (M. *Suk.* 5.4)

---

[12] The events described in this Mishnah date from between AD 55 and 65 (Mitchell 2005). The 'great enactment' was the building of a women's gallery in the Court of Women. A jar of 120 *log* held about ten litres.

So there is a clear link between the Songs of Ascents and the Feast of Sukkot. Because of this, some have suggested that the Songs of Ascents were a *vademecum* or travelling song-book for pilgrims going to that Feast. But while this looks feasible for the first two psalms, it fails thereafter. For Psalm 122 speaks of Jerusalem as an observer looking at the city from within; Psalm 123 raises eyes to the temple; Psalm 133 speaks of the anointed *kohen*; and Psalm 134 addresses the *kohanim* directly. Moreover, the collection is suffused with the language of the *Birkat kohanim* and with the imagery of temple worship. Most of these songs are for singing inside the city, not on the road.

THE 'ASCENTS' AS STEPS OF THE TEMPLE

A strong case can also be made for seeing the Songs of Ascents as 'Songs of the Steps'. We return to the Mishnah passage above, which describes the Levites standing on the fifteen steps which 'correspond' to the fifteen Songs of Ascents.[13] We should not imagine, as some do, that the sages are pointing out a merely numerical correspondence of two diverse things, like a bumpkin saying, 'Hey guys, I just realized, a horse has four legs and so has a chair!' Fine sages they would be! No, the fifteen songs must have a pertinent relation with the fifteen steps, and, since the Levites sing on the steps, we may deduce that the fifteen songs were sung on the fifteen steps. The Tosefta, commenting on the Mishnah passage above, confirms exactly this point.

> What did they [the Levites] sing [on the steps]? [They sang:] A Song of Ascents. Come bless the Lord, all you servants of the Lord, who stand by nights in the house of the Lord [Ps. 134.1]. Some of them sang: Lift up your hands to the holy place and bless the Lord [Ps. 134.2]. And when they parted, what did they sing? The Lord bless you from Zion who made heaven and earth [Ps. 134.3]. (T. *Suk.* 4.7–9)

In faraway Rome, Hippolytus (170–235) knew of this correspondence between the steps and the Songs: 'There are certain Songs of Ascents, fifteen in number, the same number as the steps of the temple.'[14] The Talmud confirms the same view. Its commentary on the Mishnaic passage is as follows:

---

[13] Josephus, an eye-witness of Herod's temple, testifies to fifteen steps leading from the Court of Women to the Court of Israel (*War* V.v.2–3). The presence of fifteen steps in Solomon's temple is confirmed by Ezekiel, an eye-witness of Solomon's temple, whose ideal temple has fifteen steps, arranged in flights of seven and eight, on the east-west ascent to the temple portico (Ezek. 40.6, 22, 32–34).

[14] Πάλιν τε αὐτοῦ εἰσι τινὲς τῶν ἀναβαθμῶν ᾠδαί, τὸν ἀριθμόν πεντεκαίδεκα, ὅσοι καὶ οἱ ἀναβαθμοὶ τοῦ ναοῦ. Lagarde 1858: 190.

[Mishnah] *Fifteen steps.* [Talmud] R. Hisda said to a certain Rabbi who was arranging his Aggadas before him, 'Have you heard in correspondence to what David composed his fifteen Songs of Ascent?' (B. *Suk* 53a).

But one may go further. The Mishnah's word 'correspond' – Hebrew *k'neged* – really indicates an exact, one-on-one correspondence, as Adam corresponded to Eve (Gen. 2.20; *k'negdo*), or as a glove corresponds to the hand; not vaguely, like a mitten, but particularly, finger to finger. The implication is that each of the fifteen songs corresponded to one of the fifteen steps. That is why the Tosefta has the Levites greet the ministering *kohanim* in the last Song of Ascents. For the last song would have been sung from the top of the stairway, from where the Levites would see the *kohanim* in the temple *ulam* or portico.

Ancient writers confirm this same point. In Bethlehem, the Hebraist Jerome (c. 347–420) was aware that the Levites used to ascend the steps singing the fifteen Songs: 'Just as there are fifteen songs in the Psalter, so there were also fifteen steps on which they would ascend to God singing.'[15] The medieval rabbi, David Kimḥi (c.1160-1235), states the same thing quite unequivocally.[16]

> These Songs of Ascents are fifteen [in number], and they say that the Levites used to recite them on the fifteen steps which were on the Temple Mount, and which separated the Court of Israel from the Court of Women. For they used to ascend by these steps from the Court of Women to the Court of Israel, singing one song on each step.

In addition to these written testimonies linking the fifteen Songs and the fifteen steps, their poetic technique of anadiplosis or 'step parallelism' forms, as it were, visual steps on the page. Indeed, the step pattern would even be audible, as the singers' repetition of a word from one line to the next gave the feeling of upward climbing, as here in Psalm 120:

		7. I *peace* indeed do speak;	they, war.
	6. Too long has *dwelt* my soul	with the hater of *peace*	
5. Woe is me that I sojourn in Meshekh	that I *dwell* with tents of Kedar		

---

[15] Siquidem quindecim sunt carmina in Psalterio, et quindecim gradus per quod ad canendum ascendunt Deo (*Comm. in Epis. ad Galatas*, I, cap. 1, *PL* XXVI, col. 354).

[16] On Ps 120. He is followed by Lyra, *Postillae* on Ps. 120 (Vg Ps. 119) and Leonitius 1650. Delitzsch 1887: III.266, Kirkpatrick 1902: xxviii, Briggs 1906: I.lxxix, Baker and Nicholson 1973: 3, thought Kimhi was making too much of a merely numerical correspondence; none of them mentions the Tosefta.

Or in Psalm 121:

		5. YHVH is your **guardian**	YHVH is your shade on the right hand
	4. Behold, he neither **slumbers** nor sleeps,	the **guardian** of Israel	
3. He will not let your foot slip,	he will not **slumber**, your guardian.		

So striking is this feature of 'step-parallelism' that some have suggested it was the origin of the Ascents heading.[17] But, although step-parallelism is prominent in those Songs that deal with pilgrimage to the Feast, that is, Psalms 120 to 122, it is absent from the others, and is unlikely to have given its name to the whole collection. Rather, it looks like the Songs were associated with the steps from their first conception and the poets included step-parallelism to depict the ascent up the steps where the Songs were sung.

SUMMARY

To ask whether the Songs of Ascents are 'Songs of the Steps' or 'Songs of the Pilgrim Ways' is a false dichotomy. They are both. They are deeply associated with pilgrimage to the Feast of Sukkot and with the fifteen steps in the temple. The Hebrew language lends itself readily to word-plays and *double-entendres*, and Bible writers make the most of them. Tournay remarks that the wise men of Israel readily sought out expressions which were ambiguous or capable of carrying multiple meanings, in order to stimulate the curiosity of the reader.[18] Asaph the psalmist was a temple Levite (1 Chr. 25), but *asaph* is also the Hebrew word for *gather*, and so Asaph begins his psalms with a decree to gather Israel (Psalm 50.5).[19] Likewise, the Songs of Ascents title is another word-play. At the Feast of Sukkot, the Levites ascended the fifteen steps of the temple, singing one Song of Ascents on each step. But these songs also describe a pilgrim going up to worship at that same feast. And so the Levites, in their singing ascent from the lower to the upper court, enacted the very story they sang. Singing in the persona of pilgrims ascending to worship, they played out the double meaning of the 'Ascents' on the fifteen temple steps.

---

[17] Step-parallelism was advanced as the basis for the *ma'alot* heading by Gesenius 1812, 1834 (מעלות); De Wette 1811 on Ps. 120; Winer 1833–38: II.317; Delitzsch 1887: III.267.

[18] Tournay 1982: 116–19, 122, n. 34.

[19] Word-plays upon names (*midrash shem*) was standard in Hebrew literature from early biblical times. See Garsiel 1991; Raabe 1991: 213–227; Glück 1970: 50–78

Steps Within Steps

Figure 2. Fifteen Steps from the Court of Women to the Court of Israel. The doors to the singers' chambers are visible on each side.

4

Who Lies Behind Them?

The Songs of Ascents, then, are a single liturgy, sung at the Feast of Sukkot by Levites enacting a ritual pilgrimage upon the temple steps. But when does this liturgy date from? Is it from the period of the monarchy?[1] Or was it written, or compiled, in the time of the return of the exiles, when Zerubbabel built the second temple?[2] Or is it from later still, perhaps from the time of the Maccabees, as others have argued?[3] Let us see if there are enough clues within the text to lead us to a particular period in Israelite history.[4]

1. THE TRIBES OF ISRAEL UNITED

The Songs of Ascents paint a picture of the tribes of Israel united. We see this in Psalm 122, which says, *Jerusalem, where the tribes go up, the tribes of Yah*. Clearly, this means not just one or two, but many tribes of Israel. Psalm 133 gives a similar picture, exclaiming, *Behold! How good and how lovely, brothers dwelling together as one*. Given the national flavour of these psalms, this refers not simply to happy family life, but to the tribes of Israel living in unity. This brotherly co-existence, the psalm continues, is *like the dew of Hermon falling on Mount Zion*. This is a picture of the tribes from the far north – Asher, Naphtali, and Dan, from the foothills of Mount Hermon in upper Galilee – coming down to worship in Jerusalem.

But for most of their history the tribes of Israel were divided. After becoming a nation under Moses, they stayed together until the death of Joshua. Then they clashed intermittently throughout the Judges period. Samuel reunited them, and they remained together for a century under Saul, David, and Solomon. But after Solomon's death, they divided into the rival kingdoms

---

[1] Dahood 1965–1970: III.194

[2] So *e.g.* Seidel 1982: 26-40; Allen 1983: 220; Goulder 1997: 43; Goldingay 2008: 470, 473–74, 488, 538; Hossfeld and Steiner 2013: 255.

[3] So *e.g.* Briggs 1906-07: lxxx.

[4] In defence of the biblical history outlined here, see Kitchen 2003, Provan, Long, Longman 2003; Hoffmeier 1996, 2005, and older works like Bright 1959 and Bruce 1997.

of Judah and Ephraim and resumed their internecine warfare with fresh vigour. In a single encounter in the late tenth century BC, the Judahites – and the Chronicler's astounding figure is endorsed by the Septuagint – inflicted 500,000 casualties on the men of Ephraim (2 Chr. 13.17). In the eighth century, the Ephramites killed 120,000 Judahites and took 200,000 women and children as slaves (2 Chr. 28.6–8). After the Assyrian captivity of the Ephraimites in 722 BC, their remnant, the Samaritans, were spurned by the Judeans in the time of Nehemiah and Ezra, cruelly subjugated by the Maccabees, and reviled by the Sanhedrin, until the Roman destruction of Jerusalem. The twelve tribes of Israel were united only for a short period in the 11th and 10th centuries BC.

2. UNDER ONE KING OF DAVID'S LINE

These tribes of Israel are united under one king of David's line. In Psalm 122 they go up to the city where *the thrones of judgment are established, the thrones of the house of David.* Psalm 132 celebrates the covenant of eternal kingship which the Holy One swore to David and his sons (vv. 11-12) and beseeches divine favour on the regnant son of David (v. 10).

The house of David ruled over the twelve tribes for just over seventy years, from David's accession to the death of Solomon (c. 1004–930 BC), after which the kingdom was torn in two by the Ephraimite revolt under Jeroboam (1 Kgs 12.1–20).

3. IN JERUSALEM

The Songs of Ascents depict a society centred around Jerusalem and its Zion citadel.[5] It is to Jerusalem that Israel goes up, and in Jerusalem that David's house dispenses justice (Pss. 120-122). It is Jerusalem that the Israelites love; it is there they come and go; it is for Jerusalem's peace they pray (Ps. 122). It is Jerusalem and her people that the Holy One protects and sustains (Ps. 125.1; 132.15). It is Zion's fortunes that he restores (Ps. 126.1), Zion's enemies that he turns back (Ps. 129.5). Zion is his chosen dwelling-place where he will establish David's line (Ps. 132.13-17). To Zion the northern tribes – the dew of Hermon – come for his blessings (Ps. 133.3). From Zion he blesses his people (Pss. 128.5; 134.3).

Yet the twelve tribes looked to Jerusalem and Zion as their capital only during the time of David and Solomon. No earlier Israelite leader was able to hold the city. But David conquered it and made it Israel's capital by bringing the ark of the covenant there in 1004 BC. After the division of the kingdom in

---

[5] In David's day, the Jebusite-built Zion citadel, with its ready water supply, was the only fortified part of the city. It lay north of the city and south of David's palace. See Mazar 2009.

930 BC, Jeroboam set up shrines at Dan and Bethel for the calf-idols, and it was to these places that the ten tribes under his control came and went, leaving Jerusalem to the Judahites and their confederation, including the Aaronite *kohanim* and Levites who forsook Jeroboam's kingdom for the south.[6]

Yet the Jerusalem of which Psalm 122 speaks is a fine city *well-built together*. This is not the Jerusalem of Nehemiah's time, barely rising from the rubble of the Babylonian desolation. It sounds more like Solomon's city, with silver as common as stones and cedar like sycamore-fig trees (2 Chr. 9.27).

4. IN A POLITY CALLED ISRAEL

The twelve tribes are united in a polity called Israel. Psalms 125 and 128 have the blessing, *Peace on Israel*. The tribes who go up in Psalm 122 do so because of *a statute of Israel* (v. 4). In Psalm 124 it is Israel who confess, *Had the* LORD *not been on our side*. In Psalm 129 it is Israel who recall, *Much have they troubled me since my youth*. In Psalm 130 it is Israel whom the Lord will redeem from all their sins.

This nation called Israel are evidently dwelling in the Holy Land. Apart from the repeated references to Jerusalem and Zion, we read in Psalm 132 of Ephrathah, that is Bethlehem, and of Sa'ade Ya'ar – the fields of Ya'ar – which is the territory of Kiryat Ye'arim in Benjamin.[7] Psalm 126 speaks of Judah's Negev desert and Psalm 133 of Mount Hermon above Galilee.

Again, such a situation was far from standard. When the Hebrews lived in Egypt and the Sinai wilderness, they called themselves Israel, but when they entered the Promised Land – in the time of the Judges – they mostly identified as opposing tribal groups. After the division of the kingdom in 925 BC, the Ephraimites continued to call themselves Israel, but they were only ten tribes, without access to Jerusalem. It was only in the united monarchy, from Saul to Solomon, that the twelve tribes lived in the Holy Land in a kingdom called Israel, and only under David and Solomon that they had access to Jerusalem.

5. WITH A TEMPLE

The Songs of Ascents speak of a temple in Jerusalem. Psalm 122 begins, *I rejoiced when they said to me, Let us go to the house of the* LORD. And it ends: *For the sake of the house of the* LORD *our God, I will seek your prosperity*. Psalm 132 recalls David's determination to build a house for the Holy One, and records the latter's pleasure on settling into this new home.[8] Psalm 134

---

[6] 2 Chr. 11.13–17; 13.9.
[7] For Ephrat or Ephrathah as Bethlehem, see Gen. 35.16; Ruth 4.11; 1 Chr. 4.4.
[8] Ps. 132.1–5, 13–14; cf. 2 Sam. 7.2; 1 Kgs 8.17; 1 Chr. 22.1–19.

speaks of the servants of the LORD who stand by nights in the house of the LORD.

In Bible times there were two temples in Jerusalem. But before either of them existed, David set up a tent for the ark in Jerusalem and the ark was placed inside it.[9] Some of the psalms recall this time. Psalm 15.1 says, *LORD, who may stay in your tent?* and Psalm 27.5–6 says, *He will hide me in his tent* and *I will sacrifice in his tent.* David wanted to build a temple, but was told in prophecy that the work was to be done by his son.[10] So David took 'great pains' and made preparations on a vast scale for the building work, and Solomon built the temple after his father's death. It was completed in the eleventh year of Solomon's reign, 959 BC, and stood until 586 BC, when the Babylonians razed it to the ground.[11] The second temple was built by the returnees from the Babylonian exile and completed in 515 BC. When it was first built in the time of Ezra and Nehemiah, it was thought to be poor in comparison to Solomon's temple.[12] Yet it later became quite splendid, after being augmented by the Maccabees and then by the huge and magnificent enlargements of Herod the Great.

The Songs of Ascents refer to the first temple. For the opening verses of Psalm 132, recalling David's laborious preparations for the building work, naturally suggest that David's labours were the foundation of the new temple which the psalm celebrates.

6. WITH AARONITE *KOHANIM*

The Songs of Ascents come from a society where Aaronite *kohanim* ministered in the temple. Psalm 133 compares the united tribes of Israel to Aaron, the *kohen ha-gadol* (v. 2). The phrase *The LORD bless you* (Pss. 128.5; 134.3) is a citation from the Aaronic blessing, which was lawful only for the sons of Aaron to speak (Num. 6.22–27).

Once again, such a situation was far from common in Israel. In the Judges period, sacrifice was carried out by non-Aaronites, including the Korahite Samuel, who seems to have demanded a unique right to do so.[13] In David's time, his own Judahite sons were *kohanim*, presumably at the Zion tent, as was Ira the Jairite, a Manassite.[14] And after the division of the kingdom, the *kohanim* at the Ephraimite shrines of Dan and Bethel were not Aaronites (2 Chr. 13.4-12). Only the temple in Jerusalem was under the exclusive oversight of Aaronite *kohanim*.

---

[9] 2 Sam 6.17; 1 Chr. 15.1; 16.1.
[10] 2 Sam. 7.5, 13; 1 Kgs 8.17–19; 1 Chr. 22.6–10.
[11] For the dating of Solomon's temple, See Appendix II.
[12] Haggai 2.3–9; Ezra 3.12.
[13] 1 Sam. 7.9; 9.13; 13.8–14.
[14] 2 Sam. 8.18; 20.26; cf. Judg. 10.3–5.

7. WITH THE ARK

Psalm 132 contains the summons that the LORD should arise to his resting-place with his ark. The implication is that the psalm describes the ark being borne to its resting-place.

After being made by Moses in the desert, the ark continued in Israelite life until it disappeared in King Josiah's time, as Jeremiah records (Jer. 3.16; cf. 3.6). This is a matter we shall investigate in greater detail in the following chapter. But, for now, it is enough to say that the Songs of Ascents reflect a time when the ark played a central role in Israel's cultic life.

8. IN A PEACEFUL KINGDOM

The Songs of Ascents' sevenfold *shalom* suggests a peaceful kingdom.[15] Although there are distant memories of past oppression and hostility, there is no mention of any present threat nor any prayer for deliverance from enemies. Israel is at peace, free from threat of invasion.

Once again, such a situation was far from normal. Under Moses, Joshua, the Judges, Samuel, and Saul, Israel had constant hardship and warfare. David came to the throne when Israel was beset by enemies and waged war against them for many years. Civil war broke out in the last years of his reign, with the rebellions of Absalom and Sheba ben Bicri.[16] But finally, at the end of his reign, David could say to Israel, *Is not the LORD your God with you? And has he not granted you rest on every side? For he has handed the inhabitants of the earth over to me, and the earth is subject to the LORD and to his people* (1 Chr. 22.18). Then Solomon came to the throne and Israel enjoyed peace throughout his reign. Immediately upon Solomon's death, the Ephraimite rebellion divided the nation into two kingdoms which were never again reunited. Five years later, both kingdoms were almost obliterated by the massive invasion of Pharaoh Shishak in 925 BC.

Excursus. The attack of the Libyan Pharaoh Shishak (Shoshenq I; 945-924 BC) in 925 BC was one of the most devastating Israel ever suffered. Shishak overran Judah with twelve hundred chariots, sixty thousand cavalry, and infantry beyond number. Judah's newly-fortified cities were swept away: Bethlehem, Etam, Tekoa, Beth Zur, Soco, Adullam, Gath, Mareshah, Ziph, Adoraim, Lachish, Azekah, Zorah, Aijalon, and Hebron. Jerusalem and the temple were plundered. Without Solomon's gold, they were so impoverished that the substitute bronze shields were kept under guard (1 Kgs 14.25–28; 2 Chr. 12.1-12).

Although the Chronicler dwells on the destruction of Judah, the archaeological evidence shows that Shishaq swept up into the Kingdom of Ephraim, ravaging the fortified cities of Gibeah, Bethel, Gilgal, Shechem, and Samaria. Egyptian records

---

[15] 'Peace' (*shalom*) is at 120.6, 7; 122.6, 7, 8; 125.5; 128.6.
[16] 2 Sam. 7.1; 15.1–20.25.

confirm that Shishak invaded Ephraim to punish his rebellious vassal, Jeroboam I. The unfortunate populace of both Israelite kingdoms were violated, enslaved, and slaughtered, the houses were looted, the fields consumed. The remnant left in the land, under Egyptian overlords, were subject to heavy tribute.

Yet, amid the devastation, the temple and David's dynasty remained, permitting Israel's survival. Rehoboam lived to reflect that his intransigence, which handed Ephraim to Shishak's protegé, Jeroboam, gave Shishak ground for invasion and divided Israel in the face of his attack. Meanwhile, Shishak, on his return to Egypt, set a monumental frieze depicting his conquest of the Levant on the wall of the temple of Karnak, where he is shown receiving captive kings from Amun. Over 150 in number, each king bears a cartouche stating the name of his conquered city.[17]

After the division of the kingdom and Shishak's attack, there was almost constant war, either between Judah and Ephraim, or with the hostile nations round about. In 722 BC, the Assyrians swept the Ephraimites into a dispersion from which few returned. In 587 BC, The Judahites went into captivity in Babylon, then returned to Jerusalem under Persian and Greek domination. They briefly regained national sovereignty under the Aaronite Maccabees, but, from the mid-first century BC, they were gradually subjugated by the Romans who, little more than a century later, destroyed Jerusalem and temple, and the Judahites lost sovereignty of the holy city until modern times.

WEIGHING UP THE EVIDENCE

These eight features enable us to identify the time of composition of the Songs of Ascents. It is a time when the twelve tribes of Israel are united under one Davidic king enthroned in Jerusalem, in a polity called Israel, free from internal discord and foreign threat, where the temple stands under the oversight of Aaronite *kohanim*, and the ark of the covenant plays a part in the cult. Which period of Israel's history might this be?

In the Exodus and Conquest period, the twelve tribes were united under Moses and Joshua, with an Aaronite priesthood, with the ark, and with the name Israel. But there was no Davidic king, no base in Jerusalem, no temple, and their situation was one of continual warfare.[18]

---

[17] *ANET*, 263; Sagrillo 2012: 137–146; Levin 2012: 42–52, 66; 2010: 189–215; Kitchen 2001: 38–50; 2003: 10, 31–32, 502n; 1986: 466–468; Bruce 1997: 30. Most find no reference to Jerusalem in the inscription at Karnak's Bubastite portal. The city may have been named in one of the obliterated cartouches in the fourth row of the list. Kitchen suggests Jerusalem is absent because the city surrendered and was not destroyed (2001: 45). Levin (2012) offers other reasons why Jerusalem may have been omitted, but defends the view that Shishak's inscription describes the attack in 1 Kgs 14.25–28; 2 Chr. 12.1–12.

[18] Joshua defeated the king of Jerusalem, but did not secure the city (Josh. 10.5–15; 15.63). After his death the Israelites took the city, but its inhabitants remained and appear to have regained control (Judg. 1.7–8, 21).

In the Judges period, we find few of our eight variables. The twelve tribes were divided and warring, there was no king, Jerusalem was in the hands of Jebusites who held the city as Egyptian vassals, there was no temple, and Israel had continual warfare.[19] No Aaronite *kohen* or leader is named in literature of this period. But the Israelites did have the ark. And they did call themselves Israel when speaking to outsiders, although, internally, tribal allegiance was everything.[20]

Samuel drew the twelve tribes together around the ark, and Saul ruled over a united kingdom which called itself Israel. But there was no king from David's line. Jerusalem was not under Israelite control. There was no temple. There was no peace, but continual threat from neighbouring peoples. The Aaronite priesthood of Eli and his family came to disaster through the prophetic word of Samuel.[21] Then Samuel himself, not an Aaronite but a Korahite Levite, became the *de facto* high priest, setting up and deposing kings, and performing the holy war rites and sacrifices.[22]

David conquered Jerusalem and was proclaimed king there by the twelve tribes in 1004 BC. He made Jerusalem the capital of the kingdom and the dwelling-place of the ark. Aaronite *kohanim* ministered there. But there was frequent warfare and some civil strife. And there was no temple.

In Solomon's time, the twelve tribes were united under a king of David's line. Jerusalem was the centre of national life and worship. Solomon built the temple in the city, completing it in 959 BC. Temple worship was under the exclusive oversight of Aaronites. The ark held a central role in Israel's cult. Solomon's kingdom was a kingdom of peace, as his name foretold.[23] In this period, from the completion of the temple to the death of Solomon (959–930 BC), we find all eight characteristics of the Songs of Ascents.

On Solomon's death, Rehoboam's kingdom was divided in the first days of his reign. Five years later, Shishak's onslaught shattered both kingdoms and plunged them into a century of brokenness and subjection. After that, the kingdom of Ephraim continued to be called Israel, even by the Judahites. But it had no Davidic king, no Jerusalem, no Aaronite priesthood, no ark, and its temples were the calf-shrines at Dan and Bethel. In 722 BC, its king and its foremost clans were swept away by the Assyrians. The Judahites remained, with a Davidic king, a temple, an Aaronite priesthood in Jerusalem, and the ark. But they were divided from the ten tribes and bereft of peace, and they called themselves Judah, not Israel. Although Josiah extended his rule into the

---

[19] The Amarna letters show that Jerusalem was an Egyptian vassal in this period; cf. Na'aman 2010.

[20] Judg. 11.12–26; 5.13–18; 12.1–6.

[21] 1 Sam. 1.3; 2.30–36; 3.11–14; 4.11–18.

[22] Samuel's father Elkanah is called an Ephraimite at 1 Sam. 1.1. However, the short genealogy is expanded at 1 Chr. 6.33–35 (cf. 1 Chr. 6.26–28; 1 Sam. 8.2), where he is a Korahite Levite dwelling in Ephraim, as rabbinic tradition recognizes (*Meg.* 14a; *Num. R.* 18.8). Samuel was therefore a Korahite.

[23] 1 Kgs 4.24; 1 Chr. 22.9.

southern parts of the northern kingdom, he did not unify all Israel. And nothing is said of the ark in all this period, until its disappearance in Josiah's time.

In 586 BC, the Babylonians destroyed Jerusalem and the temple and took the Judahites into captivity. During this time, all twelve tribes were divided, excluded from Jerusalem, without temple, without ark, and without peace. The royal and priestly succession continued only under foreign sway.

In the period after the return from Babylon – from Ezra to Malachi – the Davidic kingship, the Aaronite priesthood, and ultimately the temple were restored in Jerusalem. But the twelve tribes remained divided and Jerusalem, without the ark, was the cult centre only for Judahites and Levites. The nation and its king were in continual subjection to foreign powers. The kingdom was called Judah rather than Israel.

Finally, under the Maccabees, Judah enjoyed a brief period of restored self-government and peace, with Aaronite *kohanim* and a Jerusalem temple. The Judahites even began to call themselves Israel. But there was bitter war between the Judeans and the Ephraimite Samaritans. The ark was missing. And the Davidic throne had been usurped by the Aaronite Maccabees until the Maccabees themselves were subjected by the invading Romans, and non-Israelite Herod took the throne.

Therefore, in all biblical history, there is only one brief period of less than thirty years in which we find all eight clues found in the Songs of Ascents. This is the period from the completion of Solomon's temple in 959 BC to Solomon's death in 930 BC.

SOLOMON'S REIGN

Now we can understand the sense of all the references to Solomon which we have seen in the Songs of Ascents. The central Psalm 127 bears the name of Solomon at the top. It talks about building the house, for Solomon built the holy house. Then there are all those concealed, or half-concealed, references to Solomon's birth-name, Yedid-Yah – the Beloved of Yah. The word *yedidô*, 'His Beloved' sits as a signature in the central word of the central psalm. The word *yedid* – beloved – is encoded numerologically in the twenty-eight words on each side. There are messages encoded in the number of occurrences of the sacred name: 'He loves Yedid-Yah' and 'He prospers his beloved (*yedidô*).' The two David headings on each side of Psalm 127, add up numerologically to Yedid, while the fifteen songs of the collection represent numerologically the name of Yah, making the name Yedid-Yah. The names and characteristics of King Solomon are, as it were, stamped, encoded, and watermarked all through the Songs of Ascents. Now, too, we can see an added dimension to all the appearances of the word *shalom* in the Songs of Ascents. They do not simply reflect Israel's peace. They are a succession of word-plays upon the name Shlomoh or Solomon, Israel's king of peace.

The Songs of Ascents reflect the period of Solomon's reign. Therefore the king who oversees the thrones of judgment of the house of David is Solomon (Ps. 122.5). The one who builds with divine aid, whose quiverful of sons will defend him in the gate, is Solomon (Ps. 127.1, 5). The LORD's Anointed for whom the tribes of Israel pray is Solomon (Ps. 132.10, 17). It is the golden period of Solomon's reign, from the dedication of the temple to his death (959–930 BC), that the Songs of Ascents reflect.

Table 13. Which period do the Songs of Ascents reflect?

	United 12 tribes	Sovereign Davidic king	Jerusalem as capital	Polity called Israel	Temple in Jerusalem	Aaronite kohanim	Ark in cult	Peaceful kingdom
Moses & Joshua	✓	✗	✗	✓	✗	✓	✓	✗
Judges period	✗	✗	✗	✗	✗	✗	✓	✗
Samuel & Saul	✓	✗	✗	✓	✗	✗	✓	✗
David	✓	✓	✓	✓	✗	✓/✗	✓	✗
Early Solomon 970–959 BC	✓	✓	✓	✓	✗	✓/?	✓	✓
Later Solomon 959–930 BC	✓	✓	✓	✓	✓	✓	✓	✓
Kingdom of Ephraim	✗	✗	✗	✓	✗	✗	✗	✗
Kingdom of Judah	✗	✓	✓	✗	✓	✓	✓	✗
Josiah's reign	✗	✓	✓	✗	✓	✓	✓/✗	✗
Exile in Babylon	✗	✗	✗	✗	✗	✗	✗	✗
Judahite second temple period	✗	✓	✓	✗	✓	✓	✗	✗
Maccabees period	✗	✗	✓	✓	✓	✓	✗	✗

5

The Lodgings of the Holy Ark

The Songs of Ascents, then, reflect Israel's condition in the latter part of Solomon's reign, in the period from the dedication of the temple to his death, that is, from 959 to 930 BC. They are also a liturgy for the Feast of Sukkot. The next question we must ask is: What event in Solomon's reign might have occasioned the composition of these songs? To answer this, we must take a refresher course on the ark of the covenant and its dwelling-places.

THE ARK OF THE COVENANT

In the desert, after the Exodus from Egypt, Moses was instructed to make a ceremonial ark or *aron* – a wooden chest – as a sign of the covenant made at Mount Sinai.[1] The ark was made of acacia wood – a box within a box within a box – a metre long, and overlaid with gold.[2] On top was a solid-gold cover called the *kapporet*, where two golden *keruvim* or 'cherubim' faced each other, wing-tips touching.

The *keruv* or cherub is a being whose general type is well known to us from ancient eastern iconography. It was not a winged man; much less a little flying *putto* or baby boy. Rather it was a being combining human characteristics with those of fierce animals and birds, and representing a solar or stellar deity. The best-known example is the great man-headed lion the ancient Egyptians called Re-Hor-Akhty – 'Ra-Horus of the two horizons' – better known nowadays as the Great Sphinx of Giza. And while the Egyptians do not seem to have had a generic name for such creatures – 'sphinx' is a Greek word – they had many of them, winged and wingless. King Tut-ankh-amun's throne is upborne by winged sphinxes. Further eastward, the Levantine sphinx or *lamassu* is routinely a winged man-headed bull or lion. The king of 13th century BC

---

[1] Exod. 25.10–22; 37.1–9. The ark's having the same name as Noah's boat derives from Tyndale, who employed English 'arcke' – a wooden vessel – for both. But the Hebrew words are as different as the objects themselves. The cultic chest is *aron*; Noah's boat is *tebah*.

[2] For the ark's three-shell construction, see B. Yoma 72b. The *kapporet* sat upon the inner boxes, and lay within the outer one.

Megiddo sits on a throne supported by lion-bodied *lamassu*: stellar deities to attend a heavenly king. (His queen offers him wine and a life-giving lotus. A concubine sings and plays the harp. He sips, unaware that the sword of Joshua is raised to cut him from his celestial throne.[3])

The 'Ain Dara temple in northern Syria, which stood from 1300 to 740 BC, has man-headed, eagle-winged, bull-bodied *lamassu* on each side of the entrance.

Similar images were made in Assyria, to Israel's northeast. Two colossal winged man-headed lions, from the entrance to the palace of King Ashurnasirpal II (883–859 BC) at Nimrud are preserved in the British Museum. Man-headed bulls, from Ashurnasirpal's palace and from the palace of Sargon II in Khorsabad, can also be seen there.[4] Further east, Persian sphinxes had the head of King Darius on a lion body.

Figure 3. The King of Megiddo on *keruvim* throne

The Israelite *keruv* must have shared similarities with its ancient counterparts, but it had distinctive features of its own. The *keruvim* seen by Ezekiel, for instance, have the form of a man, with calves' feet, human hands, four wings, and four faces; the faces are those of a man, a lion, a bull, and an eagle; or alternately, of a man, a lion, an eagle, and, yes, a *keruv*.[5] Israelite artisans apparently knew what *keruvim* – even their faces – looked like. After all, they embroidered and carved their images throughout Moses' Tabernacle and the temple. But no image of Israelite *keruvim* has survived to this day. Yet, like sphinx or *lamassu*, Israel's *keruvim* were guardian deities, manifestations of heavenly bodies, waiting upon the divine king. Given Israel's cultural and geographical proximity to Canaan, it is likely that the *keruvim* of Moses' and Solomon's time resembled the creatures flanking the Megiddo throne.

The ark was carried by means of gold-plated acacia poles which ran along the sides of the ark, inserted in the rings attached to its feet; these poles were a permanent feature of the ark and were not removed from their rings.[6] Inside the ark, beneath the *kapporet* cover and the *keruvim*, Moses placed the two stone tablets of the ten commandments – Israel's covenant obligations to their

---

[3] Other depictions of a king on a *keruvim* throne, dating from 1200 to 800 B.C., have been found at Byblos (King Hiram) and Hamath. See Albright 1961: 96.

[4] The bull-*lamassu* are each one of a separated pair, with their original twins in the Metropolitan Museum of New York and the Oriental Institute Museum at the University of Chicago. Sargon's *lamassu* weigh over forty tons.

[5] Ezek. 1.5–10; 10.14.

[6] Exod. 25.15. For the poles being on the short sides of the ark, see Appendix II.

divine king – together with Aaron's staff and a jar of manna. The ark, borne aloft on the shoulders of the Kohathite Levites, accompanied the Israelites through the wilderness, thrice-shrouded from prying eyes beneath coverings of sanctuary curtain, dugong skins, and cloth of heavenly blue.[7]

The Israelites also made a magnificent tent, the Tent of the Tabernacle of Meeting to house the ark when resting. (This ornate tabernacle should not be confused with the simpler Tent of Meeting set outside the camp.[8]) Inside the great Tabernacle, once a year, the blood of the sacrifice of atonement was sprinkled upon the *kapporet*, so that the Holy One, looking to the commandments beneath, might see the atoning blood and pardon his people.

WHAT DID THE ARK REPRESENT?

What did this artifact represent? Some suggest that it represented a portable throne for the deity. Such an idea finds support in the ancient prototypes that lay behind Moses' ark, not only the thrones of Tut-ankh-amun and Megiddo but also the sphinx-palanquins in which the Pharaohs were borne forth.

Figure 4. Ramses III on sphinx palanquin, from Medinet Habu

---

[7] Num. 4.4–15.

[8] The first Tent of Meeting (*ohel moʻed*), outside the camp, is described in Exod. 33.7–11; 34.34–35. The ark's Tabernacle of Meeting (*mishkan moʻed*) was built after it (Exod. 36.8–38; 39.32–43) and superseded it, as is implied in the repeated use of 'Tent of Meeting' and even 'Tent of the Tabernacle of Meeting' (*ohel mishkan moʻed*) to describe the newly-built Tabernacle (cf. Exod. 40.2, 6, 29, 34, 35).

Various Bible verses in English translation initially seem to support this idea.

1 Sam. 4.4	The ark of the covenant of the LORD of hosts enthroned upon the cherubim.
2 Sam. 6.2	The ark of God which is called by the name, the name of the LORD of hosts enthroned upon the cherubim upon it.
2 Kgs 19.15	LORD God of Israel, enthroned upon the cherubim
Isa. 37.16	LORD of hosts, God of Israel, enthroned upon the cherubim.
Ps. 80.1	O One enthroned upon the cherubim, shine forth.
Ps. 99.1	He sits enthroned upon the cherubim; let the earth quake.

It was perhaps such an understanding of the ark that led the King James Bible to translate *kapporet* – the ark cover – as 'mercy seat'. But the Hebrew and Septuagint Greek terms, *kapporet* and *hilasterion*, contain no idea of a seat. They speak rather of atonement, of the place where the atoning blood was sprinkled. And indeed, the whole idea of the Holy One sitting on the ark is suspect. For why would one sprinkle blood on a seat? And while a one-metre-wide seat might be fine for a man, it suggests a smallish deity. Nor do these phrases contain any Hebrew word meaning 'on' or 'upon'. In fact, the verb *yashav*, above translated as 'sit enthroned', can also mean 'dwell'. A neutral translation would be as follows.

1 Sam. 4.4	The ark of the covenant of the LORD of hosts dwelling the cherubim.
2 Sam. 6.2	The ark of God which is called by the name, the name of the LORD of hosts dwelling the cherubim upon it.
2 Kgs 19.15	LORD God of Israel, dwelling the cherubim.
Isa. 37.16	LORD of hosts, God of Israel, dwelling the cherubim.
Ps. 80.1	O One dwelling the cherubim, shine forth.
Ps. 99.1	He dwells the cherubim; let the earth quake.

This more neutral translation allows us to see the two passages from Samuel as somehow representing the LORD 'dwelling' the *keruvim* on the ark, without being actually seated upon them. What would this mean? Well, let us begin with the last four texts. They date from temple times, and one may therefore suspect that they are not speaking of the *keruvim* upon the ark at all. Rather, they are speaking of the great *golden chariot of the keruvim that spread their wings*, which David planned and Solomon built in the holy of holies.[9]

David's golden *keruvim*-chariot was designed as the earthly counterpart of the divine chariot-throne on high, from which the Holy One rode out across his heavens. David believed that Israel's God rode forth on a chariot to his defence (Ps. 18.10). But this idea neither began nor ended with him. Its roots lay in Mesopotamian beliefs of the third millennium BC, and it flourished later in the chariot visions of Elijah, Elisha, Ezekiel, and the medieval kabbalists.[10]

---

[9] 1 Chr. 28.18; cf. 1 Kgs 6.23–28; 2 Chr. 3.10–13.
[10] Chilton 2011: 20.

So David, under the guidance of the divine spirit, designed a *keruvim* chariot-throne for the invisible deity who would dwell in the house in Jerusalem. And beneath it, under its overspreading wings, was the place of the ark.

Therefore a likelier explanation altogether is that the ark represented the footstool of the Holy One. In this sense, he could remain or dwell upon the ark, as in the texts from Samuel, for his feet rested upon it. For the footstool, like the sceptre and crown, is a perennial symbol of royal estate. The king puts his royal feet up, while others attend him, standing in the dust. No self-respecting monarch goes without one. Tut-ankh-amun had a footstool. The king of Megiddo, shown above, has a footstool. The kings of Israel had footstools.[11] Even in 1953, Great Britain's Queen Elizabeth II was crowned with her feet on a footstool. And so the ark was the footstool of the LORD. We find this in the same passage of Chronicles that speaks of the *keruvim* chariot.

> 1 Chr. 28.2 I had it in my heart to build a house of rest for the ark of the covenant of the LORD, for the footstool of our God.

We find it also in the Psalms, including one of the Songs of Ascents:

> Ps. 99.5   Extol the LORD our God and worship at his footstool.
> Ps. 132.7 Let us go to his dwelling place and bow down at his footstool.
>   Arise, LORD, to your resting place, you and the ark of your power.

We find it too in the prophets, in Isaiah, where the Jerusalem sanctuary (where the ark sits) is the place of the Holy One's feet, and in Lamentations, where he spurns his footstool, the ark, in the day of Jerusalem's devastation.

> Isa. 60.13 The glory of Lebanon will come to you,...
>   to adorn the place of my sanctuary;
>   and I will glorify the place of my feet.
>
> Lam. 2.1   He has not remembered his footstool in the day of his anger.

The idea of the ark as a footstool is confirmed by other ancient texts which show that a covenant or treaty was placed in a chest beneath the feet of the god who served as witness to it. Ramses II, making a treaty with the Hittite king Hattusil, wrote to him as follows:[12]

> The writing of the treaty which I have made to the Great King, the king of Hattu, lies beneath the feet of the god Teshup: the great gods are witnesses of it. The writings of the oath which the Great King, the king of Hattu, has made to me, lies beneath the feet of the god Ra: the great gods are witnesses of it.

---

[11] Ps. 110.1; 2 Chr. 9.18.
[12] Text from De Vaux 1961: 301.

In the same way, the ark was a footstool, and Israel's covenant obligations – the commandments within – rested under the invisible feet of Israel's deity.

Seeing the ark as a footstool may help us better imagine what it looked like. The *keruvim* and their wings would not enclose all sides of the ark, as is sometimes depicted. Rather, the *keruvim* at the ends of the ark would have touched each other with one raised wing-tip each on one long side, while their other wing would have been lowered and not touching, so forming a periphery of *keruvim* wings and bodies on three sides of the ark, but leaving one long side of the cover open to receive the feet of the invisible king.[13] Indeed, it may be that the *keruvim* were not entirely located on top of the golden cover. It is more likely that, like the Megiddo throne, their heads, bodies and wings rose on the cover on three sides, while their legs and feet formed the feet of the ark itself (Exod. 25.12).

Finally, here is a statuette from Carchemish in Syria, dating from around the same time as Solomon's temple, which may help to give a sense of the structure of the ark and of the *keruvim* chariot in the holy of holies. The Hittite storm-god Atarsuhis rides forth to battle on a great lion-headed chariot. Between the lion-*keruvim*, his feet rest on a footstool. Thus the gods of the ancient east went forth to war. In the same way Israel's God in his throne room sat on a chariot of *keruvim*, attended head and foot by these heavenly beings, ever ready to go forth, as the prophets depict him, his footstool borne aloft by his earthly ministers, to save his people and execute judgment upon the earth.[14]

Figure 5. Atarsuhis on keruvim chariot.

---

[13] Likewise Pharaoh Amenhotep III (1386–1349 BC) is shown seated upon a throne with sphinx side-arms (see Plate 111 in G. Steindorff und W. Wolf), as is King Ahiram on a stone sarcophagus from 12th century BC Byblos. All these kings, incidentally, are drawn with footstools.

[14] Ps. 18.10; Ezek.1.4–28; 10.9–22, where the wheels of the chariot, the *ofanim*, are heavenly beings; Dan. 7.9; Hab. 3.8, 13.

FROM TABERNACLE TO ZION TENT

From the day of its construction, the ark was the central object of Israel's faith. The second commandment prohibited Israel from having images of the deity, as other nations had. Instead, Israel had the ark, the invisible deity's footstool. Where the ark went, the LORD went (Num. 10.34); its presence ensured his (1 Sam. 4.3). He spoke from between the *keruvim* on the ark, amidst a glowing cloud (Exod. 25.22; 30.6; 40.35). The honour due him was paid to the ark. When the ark appeared in public, sacrifices were offered before it, people bowed to it and cried on every side, *Yehovah Ts'vaot! Yehovah Ts'vaot!*[15] Wherever it went, it was fêted by singing and shouting, by praising and praying, by blowing of trumpets and rams' horns, by rattling of sistrums, drumming of drums, and striking of tambourines.[16] Israel's entire life and faith revolved round this most sacred object.

Since the ark equalled the presence of the Holy One, it was particularly associated with Israel's military campaigns. Like any king, the LORD took his footstool with him to war, so that he might sit in state above the field and command his hosts. At such times, Moses would send forth the ark with the words,

> Arise, O LORD! May your enemies be scattered;
> May your foes flee before you (Num. 10.35).

And when the ark returned victorious to camp, Moses would say,

> Return, O LORD, to the countless thousands of Israel (Num. 10.36).

In the desert, the ark's presence gave Israel victory in every campaign, while its absence brought defeat (Num. 15.44). It spear-headed the conquest of the promised land under Joshua. During the period of Joshua and the Judges, it rested in Joshua's town, Shiloh, from where it went briefly to Bethel in Benjamin, and then back to Shiloh again.[17] From Shiloh it went against the Philistines and, for the sin of Eli's house, was captured. But, in Philistine territory, plague broke out around it. The panic-stricken Philistines shunted it from one city to another before returning it to Israel, to the priestly town of Beth Shemesh. There the townsmen who thought they might peek inside it did not live long enough to regret their presumption. The survivors bundled it off

---

[15] 1 Sam. 6.15; 2 Sam. 6.13; 1 Kgs 8.5; 2 Sam. 6.2. *Ts'vaot* or 'hosts' is the plural of *tsava*, the standard word for Israel's army, both in Bible times and now. The plural implies that Yehovah commands many armies. The name *Yehovah Ts'vaot* first appears in the mouth of Korahite Hannah, the mother of Samuel (1 Sam. 1.11). The Korahites held that the dead would ascend from Sheol to dwell among the stars (Mitchell 2006a: 365–84). Yehovah *ts'vaot* is therefore the head, not only of Israel's army, but of the armies of heaven.

[16] 2 Sam. 6.5, 15; 1 Chr. 13.8; 15.16–22; 2 Chr. 5.12–13; 7.6.

[17] Josh. 18.1, 8–10, 21.1–2; Judg. 18.31; 20.26–28; 1 Sam. 1.3; 3.3. A sanctuary at Shechem served as a cultic centre in Joshua's time, though the ark is not mentioned (Josh. 24.1, 25–26).

to Kiryat-Ye'arim, to the house of Abinadab, where it stayed throughout Saul's reign, undisturbed.[18] Finally, David, having conquered Jerusalem, sought out the ark to bring it to his new capital. But the ark, illicitly borne and touched, asserted its power by striking the offender dead, and was hastily deposited at the house of Obed-Edom.[19] Finally, after a three-month regroup, it was carried to Jerusalem by its poles on the shoulders of the Levites, as the law prescribed. Amidst psalms and rejoicing, the gatekeepers of Zion citadel theatrically challenged the ark's approach, while the ark's Levite entourage replied that the approaching conqueror was not to be defied.

Gates:	Who is this King of Glory?
Bearers:	Yehovah, mighty and a hero;
	Yehovah, hero in battle (Psalm 24.8).[20]

The ark was brought into the city and placed in the tent which David had set up some months before.[21] There it remained throughout David's reign, going out to battle, as in former times, and quelling Israel's enemies on every side.[22]

Meanwhile, since the ark's Philistine captivity, Moses' Tabernacle and altar of burnt offering had made their own way, first to Nob, and then, after Nob's destruction, to the priestly city of Gibeon in Benjamin, where they became the focus of Israel's foremost shrine until Solomon's temple was dedicated. Thereafter, if Josephus is correct, the Gibeon ministry ceased and its artefacts and personnel were transferred to the newly-built temple.[23]

THE ARK IN SOLOMON'S TEMPLE

After the ark was installed on Zion, David conceived the idea of building a dwelling for it. However, Nathan the prophet brought word that the LORD

---

[18] 1 Sam. 4.1–7.2. The Hebrew of 1 Sam. 14.18 has Saul call for the ark in his war against the Philistines, while the Septuagint speaks of the high-priestly ephod, not the ark.

[19] Num. 4.4–15; 2 Sam. 6.3–11; 2 Sam. 6.3–12; 1 Chr. 13.7–14.

[20] Ps. 24 was certainly the liturgy of the ark's ascent to Zion. The Holy One and his ark are entering for the first time. (If it were not the first time, there would be no demand to open and no enquiry as to who was entering.) And the 'ancient doors' (vv. 7, 9) must be the gates of Zion citadel, for the gates of the temple were new not ancient, when the ark first entered. The summons for them to 'Lift your heads,' suggests that they were lifting gates, portcullises or *cataracta*.

[21] 1 Chr. 15.1; 16.1.

[22] 2 Sam. 11.11.

[23] 1 Sam. 21.4–6; 22.18–19; Gibeon: Josh. 21.17; 1 Chr. 16.39-42; 21.29; 1 Kgs 3.4; 2 Chr. 1.3–6. Josephus (*Ant.* VIII.iv.1) says that 'the tabernacle (*skēnē*) which Moses pitched', which had been in Gibeon, accompanied the ark from Zion to the temple (1 Kgs 8.4). This is confirmed by the fact that Heman and Jeduthun, who initially ministered at the Gibeon shrine, went to join Asaph in Jerusalem in the ministry of the temple (see chapter nine).

himself would build a house – an eternal dynasty – for David, but that the house of the LORD would not be built by David but by his son. David therefore did all he could to enable his successor to complete the task. He made 'extensive preparations' and went to 'great pains', working 'with all his resources' and denying himself every comfort to achieve this goal.[24]

He purchased land for the site. First, for the sum of fifty silver shekels, he bought the threshing-floor of Araunah the Jebusite, near the summit of Mount Moriah, for the site of an altar. Then, for the much greater sum of 600 shekels of gold, he bought the entire mountain.[25] He built up the Mount on all sides – a vast feat of engineering – to provide a level upper surface 500 cubits square, almost ten times the size of a soccer field.[26] And through the supporting substructures and through the limestone rock – soft to the chisel, but hardening in the air – he constructed a network of secret tunnels and chambers and galleries..

Under divine direction he drew up architectural plans for the building, its ministry, and the golden *keruvim*-chariot.[27] He amassed, we are told, unimaginable quantities of precious metals: three and a half thousand tons of gold, thirty-four thousand tons of silver, and vast quantities of bronze, iron, fragrant cedar, and noble stone; he received the plans for the building under the inspiration of the Holy Spirit; he provided craftsmen of every kind to do the work: builders, masons, carpenters, and goldsmiths.[28] He provided detailed plans for the future ministry of the *kohanim* and Levites; he set apart 4,000 Levites to support the ministry of song, with the 288 best and strongest singers selected to minister in twenty-four courses of twelve, serving in rotation a week at a time, and playing fine instruments provided by the king.[29] He provided gatekeepers, treasurers, and accountants. In short, he provided everything required for the temple and its worship, and then he committed the execution of the plan to his son Solomon at his accession.[30]

Solomon, in the fourth year of his reign, in the spring of 966 BC, began building according to the heavenly plan. The work was completed seven years later, in the late autumn month of Bul (October-November) 960 BC. Eleven months later, at the Feast of Sukkot in the month of Ethanim (September-October) 959 BC, the temple was dedicated. The books of 1 Kings and 2 Chronicles relate the event. Solomon instructed all Israel to come to Jerusalem for the great day. The ark was brought up from Zion citadel into the temple and installed in the place prepared for it, in the inner sanctuary, the Holy of

---

[24] 2 Sam. 7.2; 1 Chr. 22.5, 14; 29.2; Ps. 132.1–5.
[25] 2 Sam. 24.24; 1 Chr. 21.25.
[26] 500 cubits square is 68,906 m² (Appendix II); Old Trafford field is 7,140 m².
[27] 1 Chr. 28.2, 11–12, 19.
[28] 1 Chr. 22.3, 4, 14; 29.2–8; 28.14–19; 22.15–16. The temple and the royal palace were called the houses of Lebanon, for their quantity of cedar (Zech. 11.1; 1 Kgs 7.2; Jer. 22.23).
[29] 1 Chr. 28.13; 2 Kgs 11.5–9; 2 Chr. 23.4, 8; 1 Chr. 23.3–5; 25.7–31.
[30] 1 Chr. 22.6–23.1.

Holies, beneath the overspreading wings of the *keruvim* chariot.[31] With it went up the sacred vessels and Moses' tent, to be stored in the temple.[32] Solomon dedicated the building with solemn prayer, the divine glory filled it, and vast numbers of sacrifices were offered on the altar and in the temple courts.[33]

After its installation in the temple, the next three hundred years of the ark's comings and goings are cloaked in mystery. There is no record of it going out to battle after David's time. Solomon's reign was a time of peace. And when, after Solomon's death, Shishak looted the temple and took many of the holy things, the ark was not among them, for we hear of it in Israel some three hundred and forty years later, during King Josiah's reform, around 621 BC. At that time, Josiah instructed the Levites, *Put the sacred ark in the temple that Solomon son of David king of Israel built; it is not to be carried on your shoulders* (2 Chr. 35.3). Its whereabouts before Josiah's time can only be guessed. But, since it was under the supervision of the Levites, we may imagine that it was kept outside the temple by the Levite ark-keepers, the Elizaphanite families of Shimri and Jeiel, and had been committed to them for protection during Manasseh's reign of idolatry.[34] Then, after Josiah's Levites returned the ark to the temple, it disappeared, for Jeremiah cryptically remarks that it will not be remembered or missed and that no replacement will be made.[35] The comments suggest more than its withdrawal from public view. Rather, Jeremiah the *kohen* is writing of something known to the *kohanim*: the ark's complete disappearance.

WHAT DIDN'T HAPPEN TO THE ARK?

What became of the ark? Some imagine that the Babylonians destroyed it when they sacked Jerusalem in 586 BC. This view is found as long ago as the first-century AD Apocalypse of Ezra and is mentioned among several competing talmudic views on the subject.[36] But this is unlikely. Jeremiah speaks of the ark's disappearance during the reign of Josiah, who died in 609 BC, more than two decades before the Babylonian conquest (Jer. 3.16; cf. 3.6). Moreover, the ark is not listed among the holy things taken by the Babylonians, neither in Jeremiah's lists (27.16–28.4; 52.17–23) nor in the official record (2 Kgs 25.13-

---

[31] 1 Kgs. 8.1–7; 2 Chr. 5.7–8.

[32] 1 Kgs 8.4. Josephus says (*Ant.* VIII.iv.1) that this was Moses' tent, not David's Zion tent. It would have been brought from Gibeon, whose shrine would have ceased to function as the temple ministry began.

[33] 1 Kgs 8; 2 Chr. 5.1–7.11.

[34] Num. 3.27–31; 2 Chr. 29.13; 2 Kgs 21.1–18; 2 Chr. 33.1–9.

[35] Jer. 3.16.

[36] 4 Ezra 10.22. This pseudepigraphic vision probably dates from the years after Titus's destruction. It is debatable whether the author did think the Babylonians took the ark or whether he sought to put others off the scent. The talmudic discussion is in Yoma 52b–53b.

17). These writers would hardly have detailed the wick-trimmers, firepans and shovels and forgotten the holy ark. Nor is it listed among the temple treasures in Babylon at Belshazzar's feast (Dan. 5.2–3). Nor is its presence or absence noted in Ezra's list of temple treasures restored by Cyrus (Ezra 1.7-11).

But if the Babylonians did not take the ark, what happened to it? Clearly, its absence was taken for granted even before the building of the second temple, for it is conspicuously absent from Ezekiel's visionary restored temple (Ezek. 40–48). So we are not surprised to learn that the ancient authorities agree that no ark was seen in the second temple.[37] And although the Books of Maccabees, which represent the view of institutional Judaism in the second century BC, make the return of the glory of God dependent on the revelation of the ark, yet no replacement was ever made (2 Macc. 2.7–8). Instead, the *kohen ha-gadol* sprinkled the Yom Kippur blood on the place where the ark formerly rested.[38] And so the ark was not removed by Antiochus Epiphanes in 167 BC,[39] nor by Pompey or Crassus in their invasions in 63 and 54 BC respectively.[40] Indeed, when Pompey entered the holy of holies to see what was unlawful for men to behold, he was amazed to find nothing at all.[41] Nor was the ark among the treasures removed in the Roman destruction of 70 CE. Rome's Arch of Titus shows the spoils: the golden *menorah*, the table of showbread, the silver trumpets. But no ark.

Ethiopians claim the ark is now in their land, in the church of St Mary of Zion in Axum. They certainly do have an ancient ark. The fourteenth-century *Kebra Negast* or 'Glory of the Kings' tells how Menelik I of Ethiopia, the son of Solomon and the Queen of Sheba, broke into Solomon's temple at night with his friends, stole the ark, and left a forgery in its place. Another scenario to explain the Ethiopian ark is that it was taken from Jerusalem by invading Shishak in 925 BC and made its way to Ethiopia with Shishak's Cushites (2 Chr. 12.3). (The *Indiana Jones* movie takes a similar line, with the ark ending up in Egypt.) Another theory is that the ark arrived in Ethiopia from the Jewish temple in Elephantine, Egypt, who received it from the Judeans before the Babylonian invasion. But these claims are contradicted by the fact that the temple *kohanim* and Levites would have known the true ark from a fake, that it was still in Judah in Josiah's time, and that the Judeans would never have sent their most sacred artefact outside the Holy Land. We must conclude that the ancient Ethiopian ark is a copy, perhaps from the Elephantine temple.

And, of course, there are other views about the whereabouts of the ark. One is that the ark was stolen by Queen Athaliah and her henchmen.[42] (But Josiah

---

[37] M. *Yoma* 5.2 (B. *Yoma* 21b, 52b); B. *Sanh.* 26a; B. *Men.* 27b; Y. *Shek.* 1.1; cf. *War*, V.v.5.
[38] Sanders 1992: 141-43.
[39] *Ant.*, XII.v.4; XII.vii.6; 1 Macc. 1.21–24; 4.49–51; 2 Macc. 5.16.
[40] *War*, I.7.6; *Ant.*, XIV.iv.4; XIV.vii.1.
[41] *Ant.*, XIV.iv.4; Tacitus, *Hist.*, V.8–9.
[42] Ehrlich 2012: 175–78.

still had it two hundred years later.) Or the ark is become the remnants of a burnt-out Lemba drum, mouldering in the basement of Harare Museum.[43] Other views involve Scotland, England, Ireland, Mexico, Japan, North America, and more.

WHAT DID HAPPEN TO THE ARK?

When we ask what really became of the ark, nothing is more striking than the Bible's silence on the matter. How did the cynosure of Israel's faith simply disappear so very quietly? An eloquent silence. It suggests that the ark was removed with the full knowledge of Judah's rulers and temple authorities. If it had been otherwise, someone would surely have recorded the loss, as they did with the other artefacts, for later generations. In fact, it rather looks like Josiah's decree of 621 BC had more behind it than the centralization of worship. In the time of Josiah's great-grandfather Hezekiah, around 700 BC, the prophets Micah and Isaiah had already foretold the looting and destruction of the temple by the Babylonians.[44] In Josiah's own time, many others – Jeremiah, Uriah ben Shemaiah, Huldah, and Zephaniah – told of a coming catastrophe that would desolate city and temple.[45] Being so warned, Josiah and the temple authorities must have taken thought for the safety of the ark and concealed it quietly.[46] With this, the Talmud agrees.

> Surely it has been taught: When the ark was hidden, there was hidden with it the bottle containing the Manna, and that containing the sprinkling water, the staff of Aaron, with its almonds and blossoms, and the chest which the Philistines had sent as a gift to the God of Israel, as it is said: *And put the jewels of gold which you return to him for a guilt-offering in a coffer by the side thereof and send it away that it may go* (1 Sam. 6.8). Who hid it? Josiah hid it. (B. Yoma 52b).

It is suggestive that the final chapters of the books of Chronicles, which close the Jewish Bible, contain the last information on the ark. It has been placed 'in the temple' and the people are told to go up to Jerusalem and rebuild the temple (2 Chr. 35.3; 36.23). This is surely a sign to future generations of Judahites

---

[43] Parfitt 2008.
[44] Isa. 39.5–6; 2 Kgs 20.16–17; Mic. 3.12; 4.10; Jer. 26.18.
[45] Jeremiah (1.2–16; 25.8–14); Uriah ben Shemaiah (Jer. 26.20); Huldah (2 Kgs 22.11–20; 2 Chr. 34.22–28); Zephaniah (Zeph. 1.1–2.3). Jeremiah includes the southern Babylonians with 'tribes of the north' because the routes of the Fertile Crescent ensured that Israel's eastern enemies entered the land from the north.
[46] Rambam credits Josiah with hiding the ark (*Hilchot Beit Ha-Beḥirah*, 4.1). Meanwhile, 2 Macc. 2.4 says that Jeremiah hid it (in Mount Horeb).

that they should go up to Jerusalem – as some have now done – and find there the ark, the reason for the temple's existence, and rebuild the temple around it.

But if the ark remains hidden to this day in the same place where Josiah and his men hid it, where might this be?

When David prepared the site for the temple he turned the mountain top into a flat surface supported by a substructure, with tunnels, chambers, and cisterns running beneath the Mount itself. A cross-section of the Mount would show it to be full of secret chambers and passageways, like one of the great pyramids.[47] David had good reason for doing this. The temple was to be the most important building in all Israel. It was to be the repository of vast sums of money, the national treasury. It was to be the repository of the sacred scriptures.[48] It was to be the repository of Israel's genealogical records.[49] It was to be the stronghold of the nation's most sacred artefacts, not least the ark. And so, in order to be secure against any possible threat, it was necessary that the Mount should be amply supplied with hidden vaults. Over the two millennia since the temple's destruction in AD 70, the Mount has been by turns neglected, profaned, disputed, conquered, and built upon. But it has never been excavated. The Byzantines, in reprisal for the Judeo-Persian attack on Christian Jerusalem in AD 614, turned the Mount to a rubbish-heap. Then, after the Muslim conquest, Caliph Abd al-Malik built a shrine exactly where the temple once stood, preserving its location to this day. But throughout the ages the passages beneath the Mount remained sealed. And so the likeliest scenario by far is that the ark was hidden in the tunnels beneath the Temple Mount in Josiah's time.

Indeed, the Bible itself implies such a thing. The books of Kings say that the poles of the ark remain in the holy place to this day.[50] Since these books were compiled after the Babylonian destruction, and since the poles might not be separated from the ark, we must conclude that the ark and its poles remained

---

[47] The 19th-century explorers Warren, Wilson, Conder, and Schick discovered 45 subterranean caverns beneath the Mount, not including those under the Dome itself. These included 37 cisterns (Wilson 1866: 42-45; Warren 1871: 204–17; Conder 1884; Schick 1887: 72–87; 1896: 292–305; Ritmeyer 2006: 221–39; Gibson & Jacobson 1996). Their total capacity was some 20 million gallons of water. The largest of them, the so-called 'Great Sea', held two million gallons and was fed by a 13-mile-long aqueduct that carried water to the Mount from the spring Etam, south of Bethlehem, near Solomon's Pools. The *Letter of Aristeas* 88–91, an eye-witness account of the temple and its ministry from the 3rd or 2nd century BC, describes the copious amounts of water continually channelled around the base of the altar from the cisterns below.

[48] Nehemiah founded a library in the second temple, to which he added 'the books about the kings and prophets, and the writings of David, and letters of kings about votive offerings' (2 Macc. 2.13). Since no mention is made of the writings of Moses, which had existed in some form since Joshua's time (Josh. 8.32–35), it seems that the writings of Moses were stored in the temple before Nehemiah's time, as 2 Kgs 22.8 confirms.

[49] Josephus (*Con. Ap.* I.7) states that the second temple held priestly genealogies going back 2,000 years. The records were largely destroyed by Herod the Great to obscure the shame of his own pedigree (Eusebius, *Hist.* I.13.5; III.12.32 [3–4]).

[50] 1 Kgs 8.8; 2 Chr. 5.9. This view is cited in B. *Yoma* 53b.

in the holy place before, during, and after the Babylonian invasion, yet the Babylonians did not find it.[51]

How could this be? The Hebrew concept of sacred space sees the holiness of the temple extend vertically upward into the heavens above it and downward into the earth beneath. The area directly above and below the holy of holies is as holy as the part at ground level. (This is one reason why modern Israel allows no air traffic to fly over the Mount.) The implication, then, of the poles being in the holy place *to this day* is that the ark is hidden deep in the Temple Mount beneath the holy of holies.

Such a scenario is confirmed by the Mishnah, which tells how the families of R. Gamliel and R. Hananiah bowed toward the wood chamber as they had a tradition that the entry to the place of the ark was in there. It proceeds to tell how a *kohen*, noticing an irregularity in the paving stones, went to tell others but died before he finished speaking, from which they deduced that this was the place of the ark's concealment (M. *Shek.* 6.1).

For rabbinic literature records that, inside the temple, the ark anciently rested on top of a great flat rock – the very rock summit of Mount Moriah – called the *sh'tiyah* or 'Foundation' stone, which formed the floor of the holy place.

> Palestine is the centre of the world, Jerusalem the centre of Palestine, the temple the centre of Jerusalem, the Holy of Holies the centre of the temple, the ark the centre of the Holy of Holies; and before the ark was a stone called the *sh'tiyah* stone, the foundation stone of the world (*Midrash Tanhuma*, Kedoshim 10).

Today this same stone or rock gives its name to the Islamic *Kubbet es Sakhra* or Dome of the Rock, built over the temple's holy of holies. Upon this rock, the ark anciently rested, the tips of its poles pressing into the sanctuary curtain, to reassure the ministering *kohanim* on the other side of its presence, even when hidden from view.[52]

Beneath the *sh'tiyah* stone is 'the cavern', in Arabic *al-maghara*, which is sometimes open to visitors, who enter by the stairs leading down behind the rock.[53] Muslims believe that whoever prays in this place will be guaranteed a place in Paradise. But, despite what some may imagine, the cavern is not the result of the Rock's wish to fly heavenward with Islam's prophet. It is more ancient. For the hole in the rock, leading to the cavern below, was already there in the fourth century, when the anonymous Bordeaux Pilgrim saw the Jews lamenting over the 'pierced stone' on the Temple Mount.[54]

---

[51] 2 Kgs 24–26; Exod. 25.15.

[52] Visible in the surface of the *sh'tiyah* stone to this day is a niche which Ritmeyer (2006: 247, 264–77) maintains is the ancient emplacement of the ark; see Appendix II.

[53] Ritmeyer 2006: 262–63. A cross-section of the Mount, showing the cavern beneath the Rock, is in Ritmeyer 2006: 251.

[54] From the *Itinerarium Burdigalense* (Bordeaux Itinerary). The text is in Geyer & Kuntz 1965.

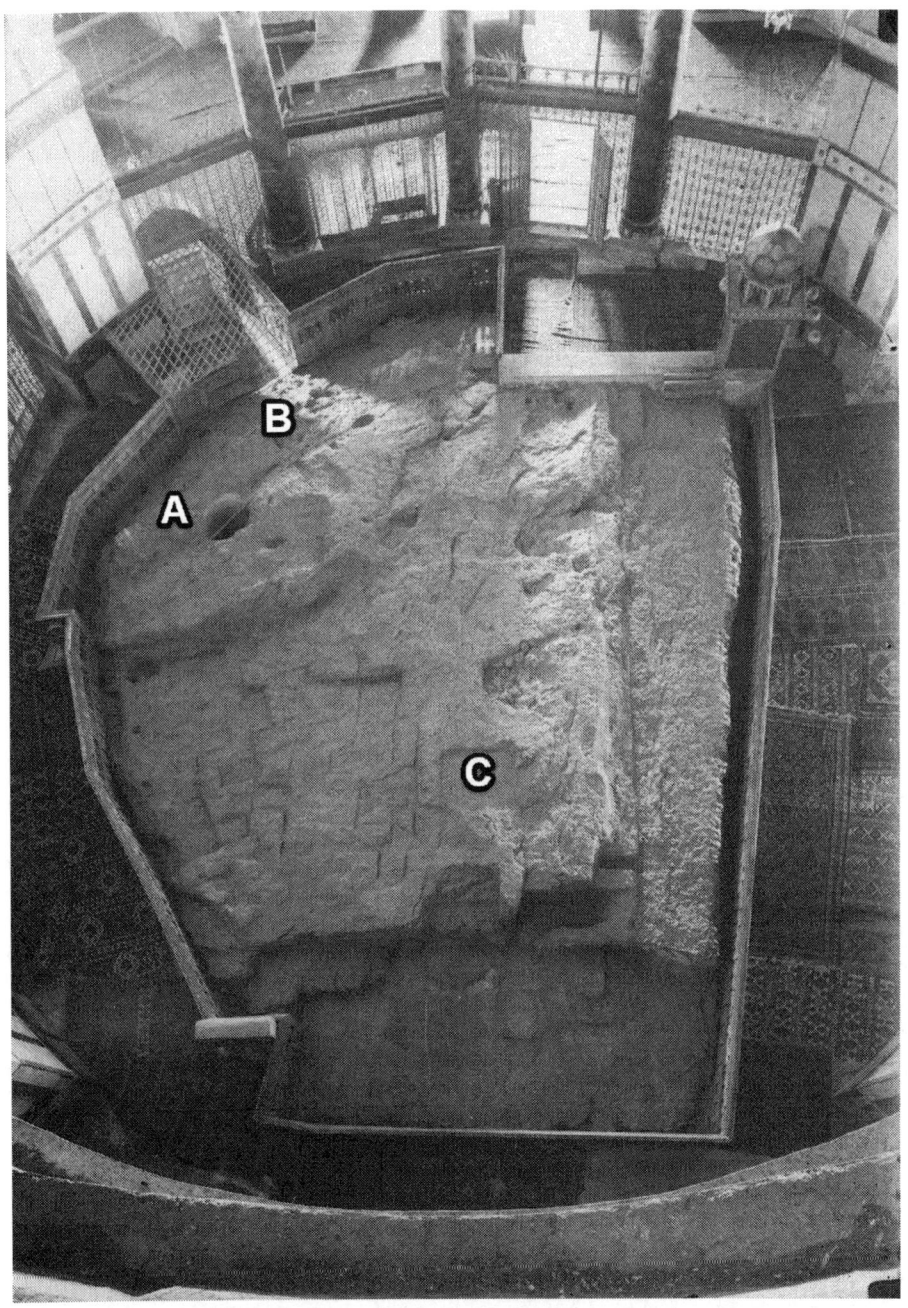

Figure 6. The *sh'tiyah* Foundation Stone within the Dome of the Rock. South is at the top. The pierced hole is visible at left (A). The entry to the cavern is by the caged stairway (B). The rectangular indentation (C) is said by Ritmeyer to be the ark's emplacement.

Beneath the Rock, the floor of the cavern features a circular marble slab of almost two metres diameter which, when knocked, produces a hollow noise. The circular slab is said to cover another chamber, the *bir el-arwah* or Well of Souls, named from the noises like the sighing of imprisoned souls which emanate from below the slab.[55] And so the Rock's Muslim caretakers regard the *bir* with dread, and the slab is not known ever to have been lifted. Lady Burton, who visited *al-maghara* with her audacious husband, Sir Richard Burton, in 1871, recorded, 'My husband did his best to procure the opening of the hollow-sounding slab in the centre, but the time has not yet come.'[56] But it is rumoured that the ark rests in the secret chambers below, undisturbed for two and a half millennia, only a stone's fall from its original place.

Figure 7. The *al-maghara* cavern beneath the *sh'tiyah* Foundation Stone. The marble slab covering the Well of Souls is directly beneath the kneeling figure on the carpet.[57]

---

[55] The carpet in the 19th-century picture above has been replaced in modern times by a fitted carpet of red and yellow rectangular pattern covering the entire cavern floor, preventing all access to the circular marble slab. It can be seen at www.islamiclandmarks.com/palestine/jerusalem/dome_of_the_rock_underneath.html.

[56] Burton 1884: 376–377.

[57] Illustration from Lane-Poole 1883.

WHAT THE RABBI SAW

Whether the ark will be seen anytime soon depends on several things, all linked with modern Middle Eastern politics.

During the six-day war of 1967, Israeli forces gained all Jerusalem, including the Temple Mount and its surrounding walls. But, ten days later, Israel's Defence Minister, Moshe Dayan, the epitome of the secular Jew, returned the whole temple area, except for the Western Wall, to the Jordanians to ensure their acquiescence over the land taken. This may have made Israel's 1967 gains more secure, but it earned Dayan everlasting opprobrium in the eyes of religious Jews. The Jordanians, with the Palestinians and other Muslim nations, set up a trust, the Jerusalem Islamic Waqf, to manage the Temple Mount. To this day, the Waqf controls the Mount, prohibiting Jewish prayer there, and any kind of archaeological activity. Any challenge to their authority provokes immediate retaliation in Jerusalem and beyond.

However, in the summer of 1981, some archaeological activity did take place without the Waqf's consent.[58] At that time, excavations of the tunnel running the length of the Western Wall were being carried out in accordance with Israeli authority over the Western Wall. The Rabbi of the Western Wall, Yehuda Getz, secretly opened a stone-sealed doorway, Warren's Gate, about 150 metres into the Wall Tunnel. This disclosed the entrance to a tunnel running perpendicular to the Western Wall, directly north-east, right under the centre of the Temple Mount. It was a huge affair – six metres wide and twenty-eight metres long – carved out of the solid rock. Getz identified it as the Tunnel of the Priests, recorded by Josephus, the Mishnah, and the Talmud, built to allow ritually-clean *kohanim* to enter the temple precincts without risk of defilement. Motivated by a desire to ascertain the location of the Holy of Holies and find the ark, Getz, together with Ashkenazi Chief Rabbi Shlomo Goren and their helpers, made a way through the tunnels, clearing the dirt and detritus that had fallen from shafts in the precincts above. But, after seven weeks of excavation, Waqf guards on the Mount heard, by one of these shafts, the sound of digging. By the same shafts, they sent youths down into the tunnel. Some fighting ensued, and worse was avoided only by the appearance of the police. The Israeli government immediately ordered the entrance to this momentous archaeological discovery to be sealed with six feet of reinforced concete, in response, it was said, to UN pressure. The excitement of the excavators had been unbounded. 'It was the greatest day of my life,' they wrote. 'I thank God that I lived to see it.' Now their disappointment was without bounds. Yet Goren announced that their excavations had allowed them to identify precisely the location of the holy of holies on the Mount above. And rumours circulated that they had discovered the whereabouts of the ark. Goren died in 1994, Getz in 1995, but their work continues in their spiritual heirs, the

---

[58] Shragai 2006.

Temple Institute, who are dedicated to rebuilding the temple in our time. They state:

> In reality, the expression "lost" ark is not an accurate description for the Jewish people's point of view - because we have always known exactly where it is. So the Ark is "Hidden," and hidden quite well, but it is not lost.... This location is recorded in our sources, and today, there are those who know exactly where this chamber is. And we know that the ark is still there, undisturbed, and waiting for the day when it will be revealed.[59]

In tacit confirmation of their claim, the Temple Institute show no sign of searching for the ark, either inside or outside Jerusalem. They have made modern replicas of all the ancient temple artefacts, but not another ark. Other Jewish authorities show the same attitude. Israel's President, its Minister of Foreign Affairs, and a Chief Rabbi of Jerusalem have all independently appealed to the Pope for the return of the *menorah*, but not for the ark, even though in medieval times St John Lateran boasted both ark and *menorah* among its treasures.[60]

But would not the ark have rotted away after twenty-six centuries of concealment? Perhaps not. The portable ark found in Tut-ankh-amun's tomb, made around the same time as Moses' ark, was found well-preserved after a longer concealment. And while some of the underground chambers of the Temple Mount were water-filled cisterns, others like the *al-maghara* cavern were dry and insulated from water, and the Holy Land had lower rainfall over the last two millennia than it has now. The ark's construction from dense, water-resistant acacia wood would also have favoured its survival.

The reinforced concrete that seals Warren's Gate is surely a matter of comfort to the State of Israel. The appearing of the ark would trigger uproar, with the Waqf violently protesting the breach of their authority and opposing any attempt to revive Israel's ancient cult. Surely it is better that the ark rest a little longer where it has rested these last twenty-six centuries, beyond the reach of the Waqf and the importunities of tourists, deep within the Temple Mount, beneath the Holy of Holies, until the time of its revealing.

---

[59] www.templeinstitute.org/ark_of_the_covenant.htm
[60] Fine 2005: 18–25, 62–63.

6

For What Event Were They Composed?

The ark, then, since its first construction, lived in a small number of dwelling-places. First, there was Moses' Tabernacle, in which it travelled through the Sinai and rested in Shiloh and Bethel. Then it stayed, for many years, without the Tabernacle, at Abinadab's house at Kiryat-Ye'arim. Then, still without Tabernacle, David brought it, via Obed-Edom's house, to Jerusalem and placed it in a new tent on Mount Zion. From there it was taken to Solomon's temple, where it was installed in 959 BC. Then, after a peripatetic period necessitated by King Manasseh's reign of idolatry, it was brought back to Solomon's temple and concealed around 621 BC in a secret place where it remains to this day.

THE SUMMONS OF PSALM 132

Now let us return to the Songs of Ascents. Psalm 132, the thirteenth song of Ascents, has this great summons:

> Arise, O LORD, to your resting-place,
> you and the ark of your power (v. 8).

Here the Holy One and his ark are entering a resting place which, as the latter part of the psalm shows, is in Jerusalem (v. 13). We may therefore exclude the possibility that this summons refers to Moses' Tabernacle, or the houses of Abinadab and Obed-Edom, or any place it was borne away from Jerusalem by the Levites.

The song also shows that the ark is entering this resting-place for the first time. It does not say, as Moses said in the Song of the Ark, *Return, O LORD, to your resting place.*[1] Rather, re-arranging Moses' words, it becomes, *Arise, O LORD, to your resting place.* The implication is that the LORD and his ark are about to enter a new resting-place which they have not entered before, somewhere permanent, befitting their presence. And the LORD, for his part,

---
[1] Num. 10.35–36.

replies through his oracle like a king entering a palace newly-built to his own specifications: *This is my resting-place for ever and ever. Here I shall dwell, for I have desired it* (v. 14).

So, again, this dwelling-place could not have been the houses of Abinadab or Obed-Edom. They were never meant to be the ark's permanent dwelling, nor was its entry there attended with any ceremony. Neither could it be the entry of the ark into David's tent, for that too was not meant to be permanent. At that time, as everyone knew, the ark was separated from its official Tabernacle, which was in Gibeon. And David had no sooner installed the ark in the Zion tent, than he began planning a permanent home for it.[2] The same Song of Ascents, Psalm 132, recalls David's promise at that time to build a house for the LORD and the LORD's reciprocal covenant with David.

> He [David] swore an oath to the LORD...I will not enter my house...till I find...a dwelling for the Might of Jacob (Ps. 132.1–5).
> The LORD swore an oath to David, a sure oath that he will not break (Ps. 132.11; cf. 2 Sam. 7.1-17).

Since both David's promise and the LORD's covenant were made after the ark came to Zion, the words of the psalm about a permanent resting-place, *This is my resting-place for ever and ever*, must date from after the ark's entry to the Zion tent. After that time, its only other dwelling places were Solomon's temple and its hidden location since Josiah's time. And, since no public ceremony or songs attended the day of its concealment, there remains only one option for the liturgical context of the words of Psalm 132: they must have been sung at the ark's first entry into Solomon's temple.

This is confirmed by details of Psalm 132 that chime with the Chronicler's account of the dedication of the temple. Just as verse 11 recounts the divine oath to David, so Solomon says in his prayer: *You have kept your oath to your servant David, my father* (2 Chr. 6.4-17). As verse 12 makes the promise conditional on the obedience of David's seed, so Solomon recites the same covenant stipulation: *If only your sons keep their way to walk in my Torah* (2 Chr. 6.16). And as verse 14 recalls the LORD's promise to dwell in this house for ever, so he tells Solomon: *I have chosen and sanctified this house so that my name will be there for ever. My eyes and my heart will always be there* (2 Chr. 7.16). There is no record of such language at the ark's entry to any other dwelling.

Finally, 2 Chronicles 6.41–42 records that Psalm 132.8-10 was actually spoken by Solomon at the dedication of the temple. Here is the text from Chronicles:

> And now, arise, LORD God, to your resting-place,
> you and the ark of your might;
> Your *kohanim*, LORD God, be clad in salvation

---

[2] 2 Sam. 7.1–2.

> and your devotees rejoice in goodness.
> LORD God, do not turn aside the face of your *mashiah*;
> Remember the devotion of David your servant (2 Chr. 6.41-42).

And here is the psalm:

> Arise, O LORD, to your resting place,
> you and the ark of your might;
> your *kohanim* be clad in righteousness
> and your devotees sing for joy.
> For the sake of David your servant
> do not turn aside the face of your *mashiah* (Ps. 132.8-10).

There are slight differences in the two citations. The change to 'LORD God', and its repeated insertion, might stem from the Chronicler's wish to magnify God's glory. If one wanted to account for the other small changes, one might imagine that the Levite choir sang the words of the psalm as the Elizaphanites bore the ark up the fifteen steps toward the sacred precincts, and then Solomon spoke the words in Chronicles as the *kohanim* carried the ark into the holy place. But, in essence, the two versions say the same thing. The Chronicles passage confirms that the words of Psalm 132 were actually spoken at the dedication of the temple. Someone might object that the Chronicler has only three verses sung at the dedication, not the whole psalm. But the whole of Psalm 132 refers to the same event. David's suffering for the holy house and his searching for the ark are recounted because his suffering has borne fruit in this event, the ark's entry to the temple (vv. 1–7). Meanwhile, the second part of the psalm is the Holy One's response to entering the new house (vv. 13-18). The Chronicler's short citation therefore alludes to the whole psalm. The conclusion must be that Psalm 132 was part of the liturgy for the entry of the ark into Solomon's temple. Yet it was not a liturgy for an annual enthronement ritual in the temple, as Mowinckel proposed; Israelite literature has no record at all of any such annual event. Psalm 132 was the liturgy for a single and unique event, the ark's entry to the new temple on the day of its dedication, on the first day of the Feast of Sukkot on the fifteenth of Ethanim, 959 BC.

THE ASCENTS AT THE TEMPLE'S DEDICATION

If Psalm 132 was sung at the entry of the ark into Solomon's temple, can we conclude that the whole Ascents collection was composed for the same event? Perhaps. Let us take a few examples and look at them in this light.

Psalm 120 depicts an Israelite, oppressed by foreigners, praying to the LORD in Jerusalem for deliverance. This echoes Solomon's prayer of dedication which speaks of just such a situation where Israelites will cry to the temple from faraway lands.[3] Psalm 121 tells how the psalmist travels to Jerusalem, just as the people travelled up for the great day of the dedication. Psalm 122 relates how he stands in the city gate, overjoyed that his friends encouraged him to come. What greater reason for this journey and this joy if not to see the new house in all its splendour for the very first time? Why do the tribes of Yah go up according to the precept given to Israel (122.4)? Because all Israel went up to Jerusalem, in response to Moses' precept and Solomon's command, for this greatest ever Feast of Sukkot. Why will he seek the good of Jerusalem for the sake of the house of God? Because the new temple is become the jewel at the centre of Israel's capital city. Why does Psalm 126 speak of joyful reaping after painful sowing? Because their years of trouble have borne fruit in this glorious new house. Why does Psalm 127 say that without heaven's help, the builders labour in vain? Because it is celebrating the successful completion of the house, which has been built with divine help. Why does the same psalm revolve around the Hebrew word-play for sons and builders, *banim* and *bonim*. Because it is looking back to 2 Samuel 7, where the LORD says he will build a house for David, and David's son will build a house for the LORD.

Finally, we may ask, if the Songs of Ascents were not written for the dedication of the temple, then what were they written for? Since, as we saw in chapter four, internal evidence points to their being composed in the period 959–930 BC, what other event in this period might have warranted the composition of such a liturgy? The dedication of the temple was one of the greatest days in Israel's history. For those attending it would have been the greatest day of their lives. It inaugurated a whole new cultic situation that demanded new liturgies. Surely it is to be expected that these liturgies would have been preserved. Where are they to be found, if not here in the Songs of Ascents?

All in all, then, the short citation of Psalm 132 in 2 Chronicles 6.41–42 is placed there to show that the Songs of Ascents were the liturgy for the dedication of Solomon's temple. To object that three verses of Psalm 132 do not prove that all the Songs were sung misses the point. As we saw in chapter two, the Ascents Psalms were a complete collection from Solomon's time on. After all, the Chronicler could hardly quote all fifteen songs: he had other things to say. And, since he was writing for the wise, he did not need to spell it out.

WHEN DID THE ARK ENTER THE TEMPLE?

The time of day the ark was installed in the Holy of Holies can be deduced. Here is the sequence of events in Kings and Chronicles.

---

[3] 1 Kgs 8.46–53; 2 Chr. 6.36–39.

The *kohanim* and the Jerusalem leaders dedicated the altar for seven days, from the eighth to fourteenth days of the month (2 Chr. 7.9; cf. 1 Kgs 8.65).

The Levites and the heads of the congregation of Israel brought up the ark, amid sacrifices, to the temple on the first 'day' of the Feast of Sukkot, which began at sunset. (1 Kgs 8.1–5; 2 Chr. 5.2–6; 7.8).

The Levites delivered the ark to the *kohanim* who placed it in the Holy of Holies. The Levites offered up songs and the glory of the Lord filled the house (1 Kgs 8.6-11; 2 Chr. 5.7-14).

The morning sacrifice was prepared and laid on the new altar, to await ignition after Solomon's prayer (2 Chr. 7.1).

Solomon spoke his prayer of dedication (1 Kgs 8.22–53; 2 Chr. 6.1–42).

The first sacrifice was ignited on the new altar in the temple. Its intended time of offering was the time of the morning sacrifice, that is, the third hour of the day, our 9 a.m. But heavenly fire pre-empted human action (2 Chr. 7.1). The writer of Kings omits the heavenly fire, but even without it, the morning sacrifice would have been offered at 9 a.m. (1 Kgs 8.62–64).

Solomon and Israel spent the entire first day of the Feast of Sukkot offering thousands of sacrifices and feasting. The sacrifices continued for one week (1 Kgs 8.62–65; 2 Chr. 7.4–8).

On the twenty-second day, *Shemini atzeret*, they held an assembly.

On the twenty-third day the people departed (2 Chr. 7.9-10; 1 Kgs 9.66).

The determining time-point is that the morning sacrifice of the first day of the Feast, the fifteenth of Sukkot, prepared for ignition at 9 a.m., was ignited before that time by heavenly fire. All the preceding events must have taken place beforehand. The Feast would have taken place within a month of the autumnal equinox, during which period the sun would have risen between 6.30 and 7.00 a.m. Allowing about thirty minutes for each event, the timetable looks like this:

8.30 a.m.	Morning sacrifice ignited by heavenly fire.
8.00 a.m.	Solomon's prayer of dedication.
7.30 a.m.	Morning sacrifice prepared and laid on the altar.
7.00 a.m.	Ark installed in the holy of holies.

Therefore the ark was installed in the temple at sunrise on the first day of the Feast. The ark's ascent to the temple, accompanied by the assembled chiefs of Israel, would therefore have commenced at sunset, the beginning of the fifteenth day of the month.[4] During the hour of twilight, they may have borne the ark from the Zion tent to the temple area. Then, during the night of the full moon, sacrifices were offered before the ark in the lower precincts, and the ark was borne up the final ascent of fifteen steps, amidst the song of the Levites, toward the temple. Finally, at dawn, the *kohanim* carried it across the *azarah*,

---

[4] See Appendix III: The Hebrew Calendar.

through the outer sanctuary into the holy of holies as the light of the risen sun streamed in through the temple's eastward-facing open door.

Several factors confirm this supposition. First, there are the opening words of Solomon's prayer.

> The LORD has set the sun in the heavens,
> but has said that he would dwell in thick darkness. (1 Kgs 8.12)

The phrase *the sun in the heavens, but* is lacking in the Hebrew but is preserved in the Septuagint. Many translations omit it, the translators no doubt seeing the significance of the *thick darkness* in the cloud of glory which filled the temple, but failing to grasp the point of *the sun in the heavens*. But the Septuagint passage bears the hallmarks of greater antiquity than the truncated Masoretic text. The contrast between the sun and the darkness of the inner temple lends Solomon's words a rhetorical and poetic force quite missing when the Septuagint phrase is removed. Likewise, the declaration that it is the LORD who set the sun in the heavens accords perfectly with the dedication of a temple to *the Maker of heaven and earth* at a time when the surrounding nations worshipped the sun as deity. The whole couplet suggests a meeting point of light and darkness, as night gives way to the risen sun. It accords perfectly with Solomon, his back turned to the risen sun (1 Kgs 8.14), speaking into the sun-illuminated temple, where the dark cloud of divine glory recedes into the windowless holy of holies at the far end.

Of course, Israel frequently saw their invisible deity as the sun coming to them in mercy like the dawn. The idea is often found in the Bible.[5]

> The LORD God is a sun and shield. (Ps. 84.11)

> The glory of the LORD has dawned upon you...
> The LORD will dawn upon you and his glory shall be seen on you (Isa. 60.1).

> God came from Teman [in the east], the Holy One from Mount Paran;
> His glory covered the heavens, and the earth was full of his praise;
> His brightness was like the light, rays flashed from his hand (Hab. 3.3–4).

> His going forth is sure as the dawn. (Hos. 6.3)

In Israelite popular religion, the identification of Israel's God with the sun was stronger still. Indeed, there was a continuous tension between the invisible deity and the sun as his symbol. The Taanach Cult Stand, dating from the tenth-century BC, portrays, in its top and third-down tiers, two images of YHVH. In the top tier is found his symbol: a winged sun-disk riding a horse; in the third is found his invisible representation: an empty space between two *keruvim*.[6]

---

[5] See also Isa. 58.8; Lam. 3.22–23; Ps. 90.14; Taylor 1993.

[6] The four-tiered cult stand was excavated in 1968 by Paul Lapp; see Taylor 1994. Thanks to Stéphane Beaulieu for his drawing.

Figure 8. Taanach cult stand

The kings of Judah dedicated horses and chariots to the sun and kept them in the entrance to the temple (2 Kgs 23.11). So widespread was veneration of the sun-disk that the prophets continually denounced its tendency to usurp the worship of the invisible god.[7] Both officially and unofficially, the sun was the image of Israel's God.

As the Holy One comes to his people like the sun, so it befits his entry to the temple to come with the sun in attendance. That is why the temple was built with a lower wall toward the east, so that the first light of the sun would shine over the Mount of Olives, over the temple's eastern wall, through the eastern gate, directly into the holy place.[8]

The first prophets took pains to make the eastern gate such that the light of sunrise would shine in it in the first moment of the [winter] solstice of Tebet and [summer] solstice of Tammuz. (Y. *Eruvin* V.22c [33a])

All the walls there were high, save only the eastern wall, because the *kohen* that burns the [Red] heifer and stands on top of the Mount of Olives should be able to look directly into the entrance of the Sanctuary when the blood is sprinkled. (M. *Middot* 2.4)

Consider the mind of David, Solomon and the heads of Israel as they foresaw the completion of their great project. They would surely not think that the ark might be brought into the new house on any date whatsoever. They would have earnestly divined which moment of the 365 days in the year would be the most auspicious. They would fix on the first day of the Feast of Sukkot not only as the nation's greatest annual gathering, but also because its mood of joy and plenty would presage a time of coming prosperity and happiness. Having chosen that day, they would decide that the best moment would be the dawn, the earthly representation of the coming of God, the time of hope and new beginnings. After the moonlit night of festivities, the ark was brought into the temple illumined by the risen sun, and the rest of the day was given over to celebration.

---

[7] Deut. 4.19; 17.3; 2 Kgs 23.5; Job 31.26–28; Jer. 8.2; Ezek. 8.16.

[8] In Herod's temple, the eastern wall was the Nicanor Gate, but an eastern gate also existed in Solomon's temple, as the Y. *Eruvin* text above confirms.

7

Who Wrote Them?

If the Songs of Ascents were first sung at the dedication of Solomon's temple on the fifteenth of Ethanim-Tishri 959 BC, then they must have been composed some time before. But who wrote them and when? There are two clues. First, the author headings, and, second, the language.

THE AUTHOR HEADINGS OF THE PSALMS

Four Songs of Ascents – Psalms 122, 124, 131, and 133 – bear the heading *Of David*, while the central Psalm 127 bears the heading *Of Solomon*. Is it possible that these psalms were written by these two kings?

In the nineteenth century, there arose a tendency to dismiss the headings of the Psalms. This tendency reached its flower in the New English Bible (1970), which simply omitted all the headings of all the Psalms. G.R. Driver, Professor of Semitic Philology at Oxford, and Joint Director of the translation project, explained why in his introduction. The Psalm headings, he said, 'are almost certainly not original'. On the basis of this assertion, some sixty verses of the canonical Book of Psalms were confidently excised. Yet Driver offered neither any explanation as to what he meant by 'original' nor any evidence of any kind to show that the headings were not accurate.

In fact, there is solid evidence in favour of the antiquity of the headings. They exist in all the most ancient Psalms' texts which we possess. If they were later additions, we would expect the oldest texts to lack them. But no Psalms text without headings has ever been found. The Psalms texts of the Dead Sea Scrolls have headings. Among their 39 scrolls or fragments of the Psalms, there are only two minor divergences from the Masoretic psalms headings: a David heading to Ascents Psalm 123, and a one-letter change in Psalm 145, making 'A Prayer of David' into 'A Praise-Song of David'.[1] The third-century BC Septuagint has Psalm headings. Of its two principal texts, Codex Sinaiticus has all the Masoretic headings, while Codex Vaticanus lacks only the 'David'

---

[1] That is, *tefillah l'david* to *tehillah l'david*. Both changes are in the large Psalms scroll, 11QPs[a] (Flint 2006: 235).

headings for Psalms 122 and 124.[2] More, the Septuagint shows that the Psalms headings were already ancient in its time. For the Septuagint translators were clearly as puzzled by the meanings of some of the headings as we are now, which would not have been the case if they were dealing with headings which were relatively new in their time.

Going back further, to the mid-first millennium BC, the book of the prophet Habakkuk features a psalm complete with author ascription at the top and ascription to the temple Director of Music at the bottom.[3] The hymn of Hezekiah, from the end of the eighth century BC, likewise bears an author ascription at the top.[4] In fact, almost every psalm or song in the Bible has a heading naming its author, such as the Blessing of Jacob, the Song of the Sea, Moses' Song of the Ark, the Song of Moses, the Song of Deborah, and many others.[5]

But the practice of adding author names to the head of a song was not confined to Israel. It was standard throughout the ancient east. The forty-two Sumerian Temple Hymns, of the third-millennium BC, possess colophons naming their priestly authoress, En-hedu-ana, together with information about the tune, the instruments employed, and other details.[6] The practice continues throughout Mediterranean literature down to the Odes of Horace. Kitchen says:

> The use of titles, colophons, and terminology for various kinds of hymns and psalms is widely attested in the biblical world, from many centuries before David's time, and remained habitual down to his time *and* long afterward. So biblical titles and terms are a normal phenomenon. From the early second millennium in Mesopotamia, we have Sumerian hymns of various kinds labeled as *ershemma, balbale, shagidda,* etc., and used in the cults of the gods.[7]

Why then, if there is no evidence against them, have the headings of the Psalms been so frequently dismissed? There are several reasons. Here are some of them.

First, some said, as some still do today, that David was a legendary figure whose actual existence is to be doubted. However, there is evidence enough for his existence. In 1868, the Mesha Stele or Moabite Stone was discovered at the site of the ancient Moabite city of Dibon, east of the Dead Sea. The stele, which dates from the mid-ninth century BC, tells how King Mesha of Moab

---

[2] That is, LXX Pss. 121, 123. For the date of the LXX Psalter, see Mitchell 2006c: 546-47.

[3] Hab. 3.1, 19. Habakkuk lived in the period before the Babylonian destruction of Jerusalem in 587 BC (Hab. 1.6).

[4] Isa. 38.9.

[5] Gen. 49.1–2; Exod. 15.1, 20–21; Num. 10.35; Deut. 31.30; 33.1; Judg. 5.1; 1 Sam. 2.1; 2 Sam. 1.17; 22.1; 23.1; Jon. 2.2; Prov. 10.1; 25.1; 30.1; 31.1; Song 1.1.

[6] Wilson 1985 uses the headings and colophons of the Sumerian Temple Hymns and the catalogues of Mesopotamian Incipits to show the structural significance of the headings in the Book of Psalms.

[7] Kitchen 2003: 107.

recovered land from Israel. It gives the Moabite account of the events of 2 Kings 3.4-8, relating how Mesha conquered the territory of the 'House of David'.[8] The Tel Dan Stele, discovered in fragments in 1993, also dates from the ninth century BC. Erected by King Hazael of Aram, it relates his victorious incursion against Israel, as described in 2 Kings 10.32. It says: 'I killed Joram son of [Ahab] king of Israel, and I killed [Achaz]yahu son of [Joram kin]g of the House of David' (Lines 7–9).[9] A third inscription, the oldest of all, is by Pharaoh Shoshenq (Shishak), dating from the year after his attack on Israel in 925 BC. It refers to the southern highlands of Judah as *hadabiyat-dawit*, that is, 'the heights (or highland) of David'.[10] A recent publication says that, 'At the supposed time of David and Solomon's rule, the record of the surrounding peoples contain absolutely no references to them.'[11] This is simply untrue. Here are three inscriptions, from within a century of David's time. They constitute strong evidence for his existence.

Another view was that the Hebrew-Phoenician alphabet did not exist in David's time. Therefore, it was said, the Psalms were orally transmitted for many centuries before being written down, during which time they picked up imaginative titles. Yet, as long ago as 1905, Flinders Petrie discovered inscriptions in Proto-Sinaitic, the earliest Hebrew alphabet, dating from the middle of the second millennium BC. These were followed, in 1999, by the discovery of Proto-Sinaitic inscriptions in Egypt dating from the eighteenth or nineteenth centuries BC.[12]

From around 1,000 BC, we have an ostracon, an inscribed pottery shard, found at a fortress by the valley of Elah, where David met Goliath. Its inscription contains uniquely Hebrew words like '*asah* (did), '*avad* (worked) and *almanah* (widow).[13] It testifies to a kingdom in the land of Israel at that time, reading and writing early Hebrew. In fact, if Émile Puech is correct, it is a regional ruler's copy of an official message, testifying to the setting-up of an Israelite royal house which, in five key essentials, reflects the basis of the monarchy in 1 Samuel 8–9: (1) the need for judges to protect the foreigner, widow, and orphan; (2) the installation of a king; (3) a class of servants to serve the king;

Figure 9. Khirbet Qeiyafa ostracon

---

[8] Lemaire 1994: 30–37; Mykytiuk 2012: 41–43. The stele, broken by Bedouin soon after its discovery, now stands reconstructed in the Louvre.
[9] Biran & Naveh 1993: 81–98; 1995: 1–18; Shanks 1994: 26–39; Mykytiuk 2012: 41–43.
[10] Mykytiuk 2012: 43; Kitchen 2001: 44-46; Shanks 1999: 34–35.
[11] Gravett *et al.* 2008: 30.
[12] Goldwasser 2010: 40–53.
[13] Puech 2010: 162–84; Leval 2012: 41–43, 70; Garfinkel 2012: 58–59.

(4) an injunction not to oppress, but to serve God; and (5), most importantly, the designation of a new monarch.

Others feel David might have had little share in this literacy. But a wine jar found in Jerusalem, dating from about 960 BC, bears the words *yayin ḥalaq* (cheap or 'milk' wine) and other markings recording the date and source of the contents.[14] It shows that literacy was widespread in Jerusalem one generation after David, not only among trained scribes, but even among potters, who helped keep account of the large quantities of food and drink brought in to feed the labourers on Solomon's building projects. If literacy in Iron Age Israel extended to potters, it is not unlikely that a Bethlehem shepherd boy, whose father was a prominent landowner in his community, shared in it also.

Others think David is too good to be true. Warrior, king, poet, musician, theologian, prophet. Not the usual type of the Iron Age hardman. But other historical figures have shown similar gifts, if not on the same scale. Royal songsters include England's Henry V and Henry VIII, and military and literary talents were found in Samuel Ha-Nagid, Sir Walter Ralegh, Sir Philip Sydney, Cyrano de Bergerac, Alexandre Dumas, Napoleon, Churchill and many others. The one who united the tribes of Israel, defeated their enemies, and established the pattern of Hebrew worship for the next three thousand years, may surely have possessed the intelligence to express himself in song. David's gifts, though impressive, are not beyond belief.

Another objection is that certain psalms are not by the named author because they describe events after his time. This view usually assumes that psalms referring to Israel's defeat and invasion, like Psalms 77 or 89, must date from the Babylonian attack of 587 BC and so are at odds with their ascriptions to tenth-century patriarchs like Asaph or Ethan. But such views overlook earlier invasions of Jerusalem. Psalm 77 is actually better suited to Shishak's invasion of 925 BC. For it describes the desecration of the temple and the destruction of Jerusalem, as in Shishak's invasion, but not the destruction of the temple itself, as in the Babylonian conquest. Likewise, Psalm 89 tells how the king withstood the invader, something which never happened in the Babylonian invasion when Zedekiah and the army fled by night.[15]

Another view is that the headings do not mean what they were formerly thought to mean. For instance, *Of David* may not mean that a psalm was written *By* David, but rather that it was written *For* or *About* David. Now, from a linguistic point of view, Hebrew *l'david* can mean these things. But if we press this argument too far, then the initial *l–*, the *lamed* prefix, can mean all sorts of things. And, in that case, the ancient Hebrews would have continually misunderstood one another. It is clear from passages such as Isaiah 38.9 and Habakkuk 3.1, and from a comparison of the heading of Psalm 18 with 2

---

[14] M. Newman, *The Times of Israel*, December 31, 2013; cf. Millard 2014. The sherd was discovered by Professor Mazar and deciphered by Professor Galil.

[15] Ps. 89.40-43; cf. 2 Kgs 25.4–6; Jer. 52.6–9.

Samuel 22.1, that in these contexts the *lamed* prefix generally implies authorship. The same usage is found among Israel's neighbours. As Gesenius says, 'the introduction of the author, poet, *etc.*, by this *lāmed auctoris* [*lāmed of authorship*] is the customary idiom also in the other Semitic dialects, especially in Arabic.'[16] Anyone who wrote simply *l'david* to mean 'for' or 'about' David would have courted confusion. Hebrew has a perfectly good way of saying *about*, as in the heading of Psalm 7, which is *about ('al) Cush, a Benjamite*.

But, on occasion, a psalm can indeed have two *lameds*, one of the author, and one of the addressee. Such usage is attested in the Samaria Ostraca and the Lachish Letters, where the first *lamed* indicates the sender and the second the recipient.[17] But when this is so, it is unambiguous, as in the heading of Psalm 39: *Of [l] the director of music, of [l] Jeduthun. A psalm of [l] David.* Although both Jeduthun and David have the *lamed* denoting possession, the word order removes any ambiguity.[18] So Jeduthun and the director of music belong together: in this case, they were the same person. And the psalm and David belong together, he being the author.[19] In fact, many psalms make it perfectly clear that the *l'david* heading is meant to be authorial, for they say specifically for what event in David's life he composed the psalm. For instance, Psalm 3: *A psalm of David, at his fleeing from before Absalom his son;* or Psalm 34: *A psalm of David, when he feigned madness before Abimelekh, so that he drove him out and he went away;* and so elsewhere.[20]

This is not to say that the headings were 'original' (in Driver's phrase) from the moment of authorship. Indeed, numerological patterns concealed in the psalms tend to operate without the heading.[21] But the evidence in support of the headings, and the complete lack of evidence against them, makes it reasonable to assume that they are 'original enough' to reflect the actual origins of their respective psalms and actual details of how they were sung and played in antiquity. One imagines that they would have been affixed to their individual psalms by the time the various lyrics were first incorporated into collections.

---

[16] GKC §129c.

[17] Ross 2011: 1.43.

[18] The cantillation's *revia gadol* on Jeduthun further confirms it, forcing a semantic pause at his name. The dating of the Masoretic cantillation is addressed in chapter 11.

[19] *Midr. Teh.* says Ps. 72 was written *for* Solomon by David, and similar traditions (cited in chapter 13) surround the other Solomon psalm, Ps. 127. The themes of these psalms – Solomon's accession and his building of the temple – suit authorship by either king. But the fact that the rabbis see fit to clarify this point implies that elsewhere the default meaning of the *lamed* prefix is authorship.

[20] Pss. 18, 51, 52, 54, 56, 57, 59, or 60.

[21] See the chapters two and thirteen on Psalm 127, where the total of 28 words on each side of the central *yedid-ô* does not include the heading. Or again, Psalm 92, discounting the heading, has 52 words (twice the Tetragrammaton) on each side of v. 8, the shortest verse in the Psalter.

AUTHORSHIP OF PSALMS 122, 124, 131, AND 133

The four Songs of Ascents ascribed to David, Psalms 122, 124, 131, and 133, form a test case in this matter. For the tone, theme and language of the Songs of Ascents are so different from other David psalms that we might well doubt his authorship of these Ascents psalms that bear his name. After all, the Songs of Ascents are songs of peace and blessing, while David's other psalms are marked by conflict and urgent pleas for help.

But there may be good reasons why the Songs of Ascents ascribed to David should differ from his other psalms, written in different times and situations. The psalms of David's youth arose out of his persecution by Saul. This is clear from the headings of, say, Psalms 34, 52, 54, 56, 57, and 59. His songs of triumph and victory, such as Psalms 18, 60, or 68, came from his conquering years. Then there are pleas for deliverance and mercy dating from his later years, as in the headings of Psalms 3 and 51. But by the time we get to the Songs of Ascents, David is no longer persecuted outlaw, young lion, or beleaguered late-middle-ager. He is now the wise old king of a peaceful land and a submissive people. Every artist's speech changes with age. The best of them mellow. Compare the bellicose Shakespeare of *Henry VI* with the tranquil enchanter of *The Tempest*, or the rumbustious Beethoven of the Fifth Symphony with the ethereal minstrel of the late quartets. The events alluded to in the Songs of Ascents – Solomon's completion of the temple and the beginning of its rituals – were foreseen by David only in the last years of his life. There is every reason why the last psalms of David, who wrote so urgently and forcefully in his youth, should display the serene tone of the Songs of Ascents when looking ahead to the promised reign of the son who would build a house for the divine Lord (cf. 2 Sam. 7.12–13).

But there is also the matter of the Songs of Ascents' idiosyncratic language, inflected by Aramaisms. The idea that Aramaisms are easy to detect in Hebrew was knocked on the head long ago by R.D. Wilson.[22] More recently, archaeological finds suggest that the languages of Aram, Israel, Moab, Canaan, and Philistia – so many dialects of North-West Semitic – were not so distinct as was previously thought. Indeed, northern and southern Israelite dialects resembled each other less than they did the surrounding languages. To maintain that this or that linguistic feature of the Songs of Ascents is an irrefutable Aramaism is simply not possible.[23]

For instance, the relative particle *še–* ('which' or 'that'), found in the Songs of Ascents, is routinely given as evidence of Aramaized Judean Hebrew of the mid-first millennium BC, and therefore of a post-exilic date for the Songs of Ascents.[24] But this same particle appears (as *ša–*) in the Ephraimite Song of

---

[22] Wilson 1925: 234–66.
[23] Apart from those mentioned here, see Booij 2010: 250–51, who lists still others.
[24] *E.g.*, Goldingay 2008: III.463. It occurs in 122.4; 123.2; 124.1, 2, 6; 129.6, 7; 133.2, 3.

Deborah (Judg. 5.7), which is recognized on all hands as one of the most ancient lyrics in the Bible.[25] A recent study sums it up.

> From its distribution in the Bible, we may conclude that -שֶׁ *še*- was characteristic of IH [Israelite Hebrew] at first; later it penetrated to Judah and became more common in LBH [Later Biblical Hebrew]. In MH [Mishnaic Hebrew] it is the dominant form.[26]

The classical Judean Hebrew equivalent of *še*– was *ašer*. But this form was exclusive to the southern Jordan area, to Judah and Moab.[27] It was unknown among the Ephraimites. And even in pre-exilic Judah, *še*– was the preferred form in poetry.[28] So the presence of *še*– in the Songs of Ascents proves little. It could be later Judean Hebrew, but it could just as well be pre-exilic northern Hebrew or a pre-exilic Judean poetic form.

Again, the asseverative *ki* is sometimes said to be an Aramaism. In classical, pre-exilic Judean Hebrew, *ki* means 'that', 'when' or 'for'. But in Aramaic it has the extra asseverative sense of 'indeed'. So the issue is not simply that *ki* appears in the Songs of Ascents. For it does, frequently, as it does throughout biblical Hebrew.[29] The issue is where does *ki* have the asseverative sense 'indeed'. The answer is in two Songs of Ascents only, in Psalms 128.2, 4 and 130.4, 7. These may be Aramaisms.[30] But once again, they may be Aramaisms of the pre-exilic north rather than of the post-exilic south.

Another Aramaic-looking linguistic feature of the Songs of Ascents is *rabbat*, appearing as an exclamatory adverb at the beginning of a phrase in Psalms 120.6, 123.4, and 129.1, 2.

> Much [*rabbat*] have they troubled me from my youth! (Ps. 129.1)

However, like *ki*, it is not the word itself which is significant, for *rabbat* appears throughout Judean Hebrew meaning simply 'much' or 'many'.[31] It is this particular rhetorical adverb form which is unique to the Songs of Ascents, and may be an Aramaism.

Another such feature is the suffix *–lah*, usually meaning 'of it' or 'to it', but used reflexively in the Songs of Ascents, to mean 'itself'. This feature occurs together with *rabbat* in two of the songs of Ascents.

---

[25] Sáenz-Badillos 1993: 56–7.
[26] Khan 2013 II.724.
[27] Sáenz-Badillos 1993: 43.
[28] Sáenz-Badillos 1993: 57, 71.
[29] Pss. 120.7; 122.5; 123.3; 125.3; 128.2, 4; 130.4, 7; 132.14; 133.3.
[30] Although Sáenz-Badillos (1993: 59–60) notes that *ki* can be an 'emphatic' particle even in Judean Hebrew.
[31] It appears in 1 Sam. 2.5; Jer. 51.13; Ezek. 22.5; 24.12 as a construct form (many of, much of); and in 2 Chr. 30.17, 18 as an adjective (many). The only other adverbial use of it, as in the Songs of Ascents, is at Ps. 65.9 (you greatly enrich), but it lacks the rhetorical power that it has in the Songs of Ascents.

Much [*rabbat*] has dwelt itself [*shakhnah-lah*] my soul with the hater of peace (120.6)

Much [*rabbat*] has sated itself [*sav'ah-lah*] our soul [of] mockery of the proud (123.4).

Their use in this way is unique in the Bible and it is fair to say that those who wrote Psalms 120 and 123 did speak an Aramaized form of Hebrew. But since neither of these psalms bear the name of David, it does not prove that David did not write the four Songs that do bear his name.[32] All that we might conclude from this is that the Songs of Ascents are something of a multi-author work. But that was already known.

Nor, again, do such Aramaisms provide any evidence for the date of a text. As noted in chapter one, the Israelites knew Aramaic from patriarchal times. They confessed their father to be an Aramean, and the Arameans to be their close kin.[33] The Ephraimites had continual dealings with Aramean tribes east of the Jordan long before the ninth century BC, when Aramaic became the lingua franca of the east, and Ephraimite speech shared many Aramaic features.

So there is no reason why David could not have written the four Songs of Ascents which bear his name. But did he have a motive to write them? Let us recall the picture. He was told that he must not build the temple, but he might prepare for it. As we have seen, he made 'extensive preparations' and went to 'great pains' and worked 'with all his resources' to achieve this only goal, building up the Temple Mount, drawing up plans, gathering vast quantities of gold, silver, bronze, iron, stone, and cedar, planning the labour of the builders and the details of the ministry that would follow.[34] Can we imagine that, amidst all these preparations, the sweet singer of Israel did not write any liturgy or songs for the great day of the dedication? Would he not have taken 'great pains' over this as well? Since there is another psalm, Psalm 30, which claims to be written by David for just this event, should we be surprised if he wrote other songs for the day of the dedication? Certainly, the Talmud thinks he did. Noting the anachronism in Psalm 122 of David going to the house of the LORD which was not built in his time, R. Joshua ben Levi comments:

> What is that which is written: *A Song of Ascents of David. I was glad when they said to me: Let us go to the house of the Lord*? David said before the Holy

---

[32] The reflexive use of -*lah* also occurs in David Ps. 122.3. If this single reflexive usage (without *rabbat*) is also an Aramaism (which it may be), then David's psalm may have been redacted by the Aramaic-influenced Levites who wrote the other Songs of Ascents.

[33] Gen. 22.20–23; Deut. 26.5; Judith 5.6–9. The Passover Haggadah shuns the Aramean connection by vocalizing Deut. 26.5 as 'an Aramean destroyed my father' (*arami ibed avi;* Laban sought evil against Jacob) instead of the Masoretic 'a wandering Aramean [was] my father' (*arami oved avi*). Although endorsed by Rashi, it is rejected by Ibn Ezra and Rashbam (Rashi's grandson) as ungrammatical and incomprehensible in context.

[34] 1 Chr. 22.5, 14; 29.2; cf. 1 Chr. 21.22–26.32; 28.1–29.9; Ps. 132.1–5.

One, blessed be He: Master of the universe, I have heard people saying, 'When will this old man die, so that his son Shlomo will come and build the promised Sanctuary and we will go on pilgrimage?' And *I was glad.* (B. *Makkot* 10a)

Surely it is possible that, before his death, David did write these four Songs of Ascents for the great day that he would not see, when the temple would be dedicated in the reign of Solomon.

Finally, amidst the David psalms there is Psalm 127, which bears the heading *Of Solomon.* While the apparent interpretation is that the psalm was written by Solomon, we come up here against a prevalent Jewish tradition that says the psalm was written by David for Solomon. This is the view of Rashi, Kimḥi, and Ibn Ezra, who cites the 11th-century sage Moshe Ha-Kohen Gikatilla, saying,

> Rabbi Moshe said that David composed this song so that it would be recited with the [other] songs in the house of God when it would be built.

The psalm text alone gives no ground for choice between the two options, except that the *lamed*-prefix, without further indicators, would normally denote authorship. However, the united testimony of the *rishonim* is weighty. What can one conclude? I maintain a healthy respect for both views.

David, like all people of faith, worked for things he would never see. Abraham waited a lifetime for the child of promise, but never saw Isaac's children. Moses led his people from Egypt through the wilderness, gave them law and sacrifice, and forged them into a force to conquer Canaan, yet never saw them cross the Jordan. So with David. All his deeds – the capture of Jerusalem and the subjugation of Israel's enemies – were but a prelude to his greatest work, the establishment of the temple and its worship, which set the pattern for divine worship for all ages to come. Yet he never lived to see the temple built, nor heard the songs sung within it. It may not be given to us to complete the work, but we are not free to neglect it.

WHO WROTE THE OTHER SONGS OF ASCENTS?

If then David wrote four or five of the named Songs of Ascents, then who wrote the other ten with their Aramaic elements? There are three clues.

First, the person or persons who wrote the Songs of Ascents came from eastern Israel. For, in David and Solomon's time, Aramaic was spoken only in Aram, to the east of Israel, in the region of modern-day Syria. Later on, after the Assyrian empire, it was the *lingua franca* of the middle east; by New Testament times, it was the everyday language of Galilee. But, in the time of Israel's united monarchy, Aramaic proper was confined to the Arameans. Now, where languages meet, they mingle. In Alsace one finds Germanic French; in the Alto Adige one finds Germanic Italian. In the same way,

Aramaized Hebrew of this period would come from Transjordan on the Aramean border.

Second, whoever wrote these psalms was closely connected with Israel's temple worship. They are saturated with the language of the Priestly Blessing and the atmosphere of the temple courts. They are designed for temple worship and must have been written by temple ministers. Songs from any other source would not have been included in the Book of Psalms. Gunkel, in his day, imagined that the Psalms were written by 'conventicles of pious laymen'. But for such an idea there is no evidence at all. All the psalms-headings bear the names of Israelite rulers or temple singers. There are no psalms by Iron Age buskers or Zebulunite beach-bums. Radak understands this point well: 'The other Songs of Ascents, which do not bear the name of David, were added by the other temple singers.'[35] Whoever co-wrote with David and Solomon must have been a prominent Levite singer.

Third, since the dialect of the unnamed Songs of Ascents is unique in the Book of Psalms, we may conclude that whoever wrote these psalms did not write any other psalms. We can therefore exclude the Korahite and Asaphite temple singers. Their psalms have their own distinct linguistic features, but they are quite different from the Songs of Ascents.

Therefore these songs were written by someone from Transjordan, an Israelite leader of temple worship, who left behind no other psalms or Bible books. Who could this be? Perhaps the likeliest candidate is the Merarite Levite Jeduthun and his clan. The Merarites were the third clan of Levite temple musicians, together with the Korahites and Asaphites. At the settlement of the Promised Land, Joshua gave them eight towns in Transjordan, among the Reubenites and Gadites, and four towns to the west in the territory of Zebulun (Josh. 21.36–39).[36] They were not the only Levites in the east. The Gershonites had two towns in transjordanian Manasseh, though the bulk of their territory, another eleven towns, was west of the Jordan (1 Chr. 6.71–76). But the Merarites were the main Levite population east of the Jordan and many of their towns fell within the sphere of Aramaic influence. The most important of these towns was Ramoth-Gilead. It was the only Merarite town with the important legal status of a city of refuge, and it would have been their clan capital and the seat of their ruling families.[37] Lying on the very border, it was frequently attacked by Aram and often changed hands from one side to the other.[38] As we shall see in chapter thirteen, its precarious situation among hostile foreigners is exactly the situation represented in Psalm 120. Of all the

---

[35] Kimḥi on Ps. 122.1.

[36] Albright, Aharoni, Kallai, Mazar, and others have defended the historicity of the settlement narratives in Joshua as based on documents of the united monarchy period (Kallai 1986: 479–481; Galil 2000: 11–15; Levin 2010: 214–215).

[37] The cities of refuge were instituted by Moses (Exod. 21.13; Num. 35.6–34; Deut. 4.41-43; 19.1–13) and established by Joshua (Josh. 20.1–9). As centres of the Israelite legal system, they would have been the residence of clan leaders, who were responsible for matters of judgment.

[38] 1 Kgs 22.3-4; 2 Kgs 8.28–9.1; 2 Chr. 18.2–3.

Levites in Israel, the Merarites of Ramoth-Gilead would have been most likely to have spoken Aramaized Hebrew.

Jeduthun was one of the three chief leaders of temple music. He and his Merarite singers were entirely dedicated to the ministry of song and would certainly have written psalms. But only a few scattered lyrics bear Jeduthun's name – Psalms 39, 62, and 77 – and none was written by him, but they were written for him, as Director of Music, by David and Asaph. (Psalm 89 may have been written by Jeduthun under the cognomen of Ethan ha-Ezraḥi.[39]) But, if King David wrote psalms for him – something he never did, as far as we know, for Asaph or Heman – then Jeduthun was a leader of some stature. Would we not expect Jeduthun's own songs to be preserved somewhere among the Psalms? Indeed, the rabbinic dictum that 'Ten men wrote the Book of Psalms' includes the name of Jeduthun.[40] Where then are his psalms to be found? Would not the compiler of the Psalms, having preserved psalms by the Asaphites and Korahites, complete his collection with songs of Jeduthun and the Merarites? Would not the Merarite temple singers living at the time of the Psalter's compilation have insisted on it? Where would their songs come, as the youngest of the three clans, if not after the Korahites and Asaphites psalms in Books II and III?[41] Where then are they to be found if not in the Songs of Ascents?

SUMMARY

The four Songs of Ascents bearing the name of David appear to have been written by David in his later years as part of his preparations for the building of the temple. The song headed *Of Solomon* would appear to be by Solomon, although weighty rabbinic tradition makes it David's composition *For Solomon*. The other songs, with their Aramaic elements, look like the work of Jeduthun and the Merarite Levites.

As to how the collection was compiled, one may suppose that David and Jeduthun wrote their own songs for the great day, each with reference to the other. It was not the first time they had collaborated; they had worked together, as we shall see in chapter nine, since their youth. They may also have collaborated on the final recension of the fifteen psalms. But it is also possible that the final version was compiled by Jeduthun, who lived well into

---

[39] Mitchell 2006a: 245.
[40] *Song R.* IV.4.1, cf. IV.19; B. *B.B.* 14b/15a; cf. Y. *Pes.* 1c.
[41] The Merarites were the last born of the three Levite clans and bore the least holy temple artefacts, that is, the boards, bars, pillars, and sockets, of the sanctuary (Num. 3.17; 4.29–33). The Kohathites, of which the Korahites were a sept, bore the most holy things – the ark, the altar and other furnishings (Num. 4.1–20); from them came Moses, Aaron, and the Aaronite priesthood (Exod. 6.16–20). The Gershonites, of which the Asaphites were a sept, bore the sanctuary curtains, coverings and screen (Num. 4.21–28).

Solomon's reign and was present at the dedication itself (2 Chr. 5.12). In this final recension he may have collaborated with Solomon. One way or another, the collection reached its present form some time between the last years of David's reign and the dedication of the temple, that is, between 975 and 959 BC.

8

The Temple Orchestra: Origins and Instruments

Israelite music shared in all the folk music contexts of the ancient east: in family parties, weddings, festivals, mourning, and funerals; in shepherd songs, work songs, love songs, youthful improvisations; in military celebrations and royal coronations; in prophecies and exorcisms.[1] This old Hebrew music must have shared something of the musical language of the Levant, but also of the rich musical culture of the Israelites' Egyptian sojourn and of their ancestral heritage in Paddan Aram and Chaldean Ur.

Moses, wise in all the wisdom of Pharaoh's palace, would have been taught the arts of music, which the Egyptians prized highly. In the Sinai, he composed songs for Israel – a chant for the ark and a song of testimony – which would have been in the style of Egyptian music of the New Kingdom period; he also fashioned silver trumpets for gathering the people.[2] The people too knew all about dancing and singing, both for good and for ill.[3] Yet, in spite of all this, there is no sign of any regular cultic music during the years of Moses' tabernacle. The Levites, supported by the community's tithes and offerings, oversaw transportation of the holy things under the eye of Aaron and his sons.[4] But this was all they did. There is no hint that they, or anyone else, sang or played music at the tabernacle.

ORIGINS OF THE TEMPLE ORCHESTRA

However, when Israel settled the Promised Land, the ark and the tabernacle settled with them and were no longer borne from place to place. The Levites sought a new role in relation to the holy things. The one who found it for them

---

[1] Gen. 31.27; Jer. 33.11; Judg. 21.21; Isa. 5.12; Jer. 48.36; Job 30.31; Jer. 9.17; 1 Sam. 16.18; Isa. 16.10; 23.16; Lam. 5.14; 1 Kgs 1.40; Judg. 11.34; 1 Sam. 18.6; 1 Sam. 10.5–10; 19.20; 2 Kgs 3.15; 1 Sam. 16.16–23.

[2] Num. 10.35–36; Deut. 31.30–32.47; Num. 10.1–10.

[3] Exod. 15.1–21; 32.18–19.

[4] Num. 3.5–7; 8.14–19.

was himself a Levite, the prophet Samuel, from the Korahite town of Ramah.[5] Just outside his home town, on clan property, Samuel founded a community called Naioth or 'dwellings', named from the nature of the simple huts which they built there.[6] To Naioth in Ramah gathered Israelites wanting to devote themselves to the prophetic ministry under Samuel's leadership. These 'sons of the prophets' ministered in musical prophecy on the high place near Ramah, called Gibeah, the 'hill', of God.[7] Musical worship and prophecy formed the core of their communal life. One imagines that most of these 'sons of the prophets' would have been Levites, as Samuel was. Many, no doubt, came from Ramah town.

Yet some non-Levites knew the place and visited there. Saul the Benjamite, whom Samuel first anointed king, lived nearby, and was moved on several occasions by the powerful prophetic spirit that rested on Gibeah and its prophets.[8] Later, Samuel's second anointed king and *protégé*, the young David, fled from Saul to Naioth and lived for a time among the prophets there.[9] Being himself a skilled musician and a devotee of Israel's God, David must have been deeply impressed by the movement blossoming in Samuel's town. It was surely among the young prophets there that David met Heman the Korahite, the son of a weak father, but grandson of Samuel himself.[10] Heman is likely to have been among those Korahites who gathered around David after he fled from Naioth into the wilderness.[11] At Naioth, David would also have met other young Levite prophet-musicians, like Asaph ben Berekhiah the Gershonite and Ethan ben Kushaiah the Merarite, who took the cognomen Jeduthun or 'Praising'. These men later became leaders of cultic worship in David's kingdom.[12]

In time, David came to the throne. With characteristic *éclat*, he took as his capital ancient Shalem (Salem), the city of Melchizedek, where Abraham worshipped and offered up his promised son, the city straddling the border of the territories of Judah and Josephite Benjamin. David renamed it Jerusalem, Yeru-shalayim, 'Possession of Entire *Shalom.*' His next move was to bring the holy ark to his new city. In doing so, he implemented Samuel's musical initiative in a way that Saul had never done. The ark ascended to Zion, fêted by a band of Levite musicians, amidst singing and dancing.[13] There it was

---

[5] 1 Sam. 1.1, 19; 2.11; 7.17.

[6] 1 Sam. 19.19, 22. Cf. 2 Kgs 6.2, where Elisha's disciples make huts of logs.

[7] 1 Sam. 10.5.

[8] 1 Sam. 10.5–13; 26; 19.23–24.

[9] 1 Sam. 19.18–20.1.

[10] For Heman's genealogy see 1 Chr. 6.33–38. Heman's father, Joel, did not walk in Samuel's ways (1 Sam. 8.1–5).

[11] 1 Sam. 20.1–22.2; Korahites came to David in exile at Ziklag (1 Chr. 12.6), some of whom – Elkanah and Azarel (=Azariah) – are familiar to us from Heman's genealogy (1 Chr. 6.33–38). The young Heman is not mentioned by name, but his immediate elevation to leadership in David's kingdom suggests the king knew and trusted him before he came to the throne.

[12] 1 Chr. 6.33-47; 15.17.

[13] 2 Sam. 6.5, 12–15; 1 Chr. 13.8; 15.16–28.

installed in the city, inside its tent, where it was celebrated continually, morning and evening, with Levite psalms of praise.

David's institution of sacred song as an integral part of Israel's sacrificial worship was a major innovation. The law of Moses never envisaged any such thing. David apparently never had to justify it to his own generation. No doubt his royal will carried weight. But something of his reasoning is preserved by the Chronicler, who relates that the ministry of song was instituted by divine command through the prophets Nathan and Gad, and was implied in Moses' legislation on worship and ministry, particularly in the Levites' commission to minister before the ark, in the mandate to blow trumpets over the burnt offerings, and in the command to present sacrifices with rejoicing.[14]

This new cultic ministry was committed to the oversight of the Levites Heman, Ethan, and Asaph. Heman, apparently the chief of the three, ministered with Ethan and their respective families before Moses' tabernacle and altar in Gibeon, while Asaph, with Obed-Edom and their kinsmen, ministered before the ark on Mount Zion.[15] There is no solid evidence that the Zion ministry offered blood sacrifices of any kind.[16] It may have been only a ministry of praise. Yet the continual sacrifices were offered at the altar in Gibeon, and the Holy One was praised, both there and on Zion, morning and evening, with songs and musical instruments.

The instruments employed in temple worship – the *k'le shir* or 'vessels of song' – can be grouped in two categories. There were those which accompanied the Levites as they sang: the harp, lyre, pipe, flute, and, in much later times, a small positive organ. And there were those which played in between the singing of the Levites: trumpets and cymbals. Images of ancient Israelite instruments are few, due to the second commandment's pervasive prohibition of representational art. Yet the few images we do possess show them to be much like musical instruments throughout the ancient east. Egyptian, Assyrian, Babylonian, and Hurrian instruments therefore enable us to reconstruct the details of their Israelite counterparts.

---

[14] Kleinig 1992: 75–83. Cf. 2 Chr. 29.25; Deut. 10.8, 18.5 in 1 Chr. 15.2–16; Num. 10.10 in 1 Chr. 16.4–6; Deut. 12.6–18, 16.10–11, 26.11; 27.6–7 in 2 Chr. 23.18; 1 Chr. 15.16; 2 Chr. 29.30.
[15] 1 Chr. 16.37–42.
[16] Ps. 27.6 may point to such a scenario. But it is possible that it speaks of the Tabernacle in the high place at Gibeon.

NÉVEL AND KINNOR

Chief among the instruments which accompanied the song were the *minìm* or string instruments. These were of two kinds, the *kinnor* or lyre and the *névél*, often identified with the harp. The Hebrew *kinnor*, a child of the Akkadian *kinnarum*, was a small hand-held instrument, its strings made of the small intestines of a sheep.[17] It was usually played with a plectrum, although skilful players, like David, would play with the hand.[18] The oldest illustration of a *kinnor*-type instrument is from the tomb of the vizier Khnumhotep in Beni Hassan, Egypt, dating from the 20th century BC. The instrument is square; the plectrum is quite visible. The man carrying it is identifiable, by his kilt and pointed beard, as one of a procession of Hyksos, or western Asiatics, who have come to pay their respects to the dead vizier. In case anyone should miss the point, the leaders of this procession have the word 'Hyksos' written in hieroglyphs above their heads. The Hyksos, at some point, included the people who were to become the tribes of Israel.[19]

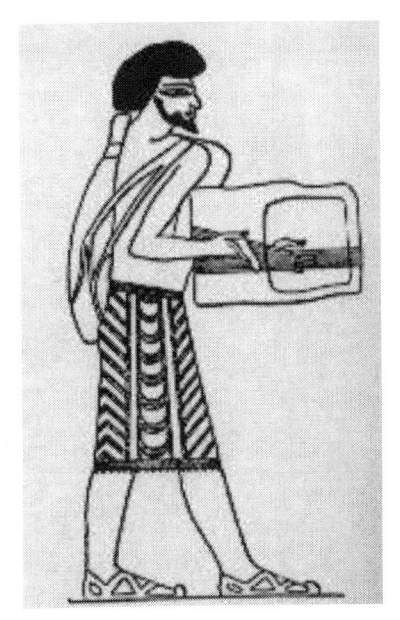

Figure 10. Lyre-playing Semite from the tomb of Khnumhotep

A rounder lyre is shown on the 13th century BC ivory plaque of the King of Megiddo.[20] Then, a millennium and a half later, a temple lyre, not unlike that of Megiddo, is depicted on the coins of Simon bar Kokhba's brief rule, during the Second Jewish Revolt of AD 132-135. All these lyres are similar in design, with a resonating cavity at the bottom, and two projecting arms, between which a bar carried the strings that stretched down to the sound box. The temple lyre had ten strings and was made of sweet-toned cedar wood.[21] Josephus relates that it was inlaid

Figure 11. Temple lyre on Bar Kokhba coin

---

[17] Mishnah, *Kinnim*, 3.6.
[18] 1 Sam. 16.16.
[19] Josephus, *Con. Ap.*, 1.86–90. Finkelstein agrees 'that the Biblical tradition likely contains vague memories of the expulsion of the (West Semitic) Hyksos.' (Warker 2012).
[20] Shown in Chapter 5.
[21] 2 Sam 6.5; 1 Kgs 10.12; Ps. 33.2; *Ant.* VII.xii.3. Cypress, or cedar, is used even today for the soundboards of top-quality classical guitars.

with incorruptible moon-yellow electrum, a naturally-occurring alloy of gold and silver much prized by the ancients.[22]

The *nével* was a larger instrument than the *kinnor*. It is commonly identified as the triangular harp, shown in Assyrian friezes as the instrument of the Assyrian military.[23] It stood half the height of a man, with a wooden frame on two sides, the top part forming the resonating chamber, with the strings stretched across the frame and forming the third side of the triangle. It was played with bare fingers and its ten or twelve strings, being made from a larger section of the sheep's intestine, were thicker than those of the *kinnor*.[24] These thicker, longer strings allowed the *nével* to produce lower notes than the *kinnor*.[25] It follows that the two instruments served different functions within the temple orchestra.

Figure 12. Assyrian harps played by eunuch and bearded man

PIPES AND FLUTES

The other instruments that played while the chorus sang were the *neḥilot* or 'woodwind' instruments.[26] These came in two kinds: the *ḥalil* and *ugav*. The *ḥalil*, though often translated 'flute', would be better called a 'pipe', for its sound was produced by the vibration of a double-reed, like an oboe or bassoon. Nor was its tone what we imagine of the gentle, soothing flute, but something more strident altogether. The *ḥalil*, like the ancient Egyptian *mat* or Greek *aulos*, or their modern descendants, the Egyptian *arghul* and Levantine *mijwiz*, was a double-pipe instrument. Such instruments can be of two kinds. The first kind are those, like the *arghul* or bagpipe, where one melody pipe is accompanied by one or more drones. Such pipes were in use in Egypt from 2,800 BC and the Israelites would certainly have known them. The other kind

---

[22] *Ant.* VIII.iii.8.

[23] So Sendrey 1969, *et al*. Dumbrill feels the case is not proven, and the *nével* may have been like the Sumerian *balağ*, a huge monumental lyre, taller than a man standing, and played by two players.

[24] *Ant.* VII.xii.3; M. *Kin.* 3.6. Josephus speaks of twelve strings, but Ps. 33.2 has *nebel asor* or 'ten-stringed *nével*', to which Ps. 92.3 (on *asor*, on *nével*) may allude as well.

[25] B. *Arak.* 13b.

[26] Found in the heading to Ps. 5; cf. Sendrey 1969: 318–20.

are those, like the *aulos* and *mijwiz*, where both pipes have finger holes, giving six notes on each pipe, and the player has one hand on each pipe. The Israelites would known this instrument too, for a bronze figurine from Megiddo, from late Canaanite or early Israelite times, shows a girl playing a double pipe, with one hand on each pipe. Later Israelite terracotta figurines show the same thing.

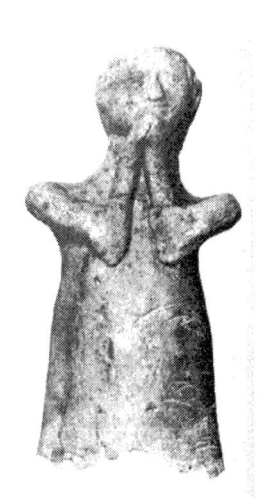

Figure 13. Playing *ḥalil* with one hand on each pipe. Bronze figurine of the 2nd millennium BC (*left*) and terracotta figure of Israelite monarchy times (*right*).

In the temple, the *ḥalil* was reserved for the high feasts.

> On twelve days in the *year* was the *ḥalil* played before the altar: at the killing of the first Passover sacrifice, at the killing of the second Passover sacrifice, on the first festival day of Passover, on the festival day of Pentecost, and on the eight days of the Feast [of Sukkot].[27]

And Isaiah speaks of people going up to the mountain of the LORD to the sound of a *ḥalil* on the night of a holy feast.[28]

Another wind instrument which, according to Psalm 150, was employed in temple worship was the *ugav*, often rendered 'pipe'. The few biblical references give little information about it.[29] But it appears to have been rather a 'flute', like the ancient Persian *ney*-flute. Its nearest modern relatives would be the penny whistle or the bamboo flute sold in charity shops. Like these flutes, the *ugav* had no reed, but produced its sound by splitting the airstream. Like them, it was blown from the end, not transversely like a modern orchestral

---

[27] M. *Arak.* 2.3; Y. *Suk.* 5.1 (55a).
[28] Isa. 30.29; the Feast of Sukkot was surely in view, as having the only night service in the temple; cf. chapter 3.
[29] Gen. 4.21; Job 21.12; 30.31; Ps. 150.4.

flute. The *ugav* was the pipe of shepherds in the field, the pipe of love and dalliance and courtship, sharing the verbal root *agav*, 'to love inordinately', with words such as *agavim* and *agavah*, ardent or illicit love.[30]

The Mishnah speaks also of a pipe called *abuv*, which was played in the temple and valued for its sweetness of tone.

> There was an *abuv* in the sanctuary, which was smooth [in sound], made of reed, and dated from the times of Moses. At the king's command it was overlaid with gold, but its sound was no longer sweet. They removed the overlay and its sound became sweet as it was before.[31]

Yet even the Talmud is unsure as to what this instrument was, discussing whether it is the same as a *halil* or not.[32] But since the same passage speaks of never less than two *halilim* being played before the altar, yet of only a single *abuv*, it would suggest they were different instruments.

> They played never...on less than two *halilim* or more than twelve....And they did not play on an *abuv* of bronze but on an *abuv* of reed, because its tune is sweeter. Nor was any but a single *abuv* used for closing a tune, because it makes a pleasant finale.

All in all, it seems, from the resemblance of their names and from its sweetness of tone, that *abuv* was simply an Aramaic name for the *ugav*. Together the *halil* and the *ugav-abuv*, the keen and the sweet, made up the woodwind section of the temple orchestra.

MAGREFAH

The Talmud remarks tantalizingly on the presence of an organ in the temple. The discussion revolves around whether or not the temple contained a *hydraulis*, that is, an organ powered by water pressure, an instrument invented by Ctesibius of Alexandria in the third century BC. Following a description of the water pressure from the Siloah spring, the discussion continues as follows:

> R. Simeon b. Gamaliel said: There was no *hirdolim* in the Sanctuary. What is a *hirdolim*? Abaye said: A musical instrument worked by pressure [of water]. [It was not used] because its sound was heavy and disturbed the music. Rabbah b. Shela, in the name of R. Mattenah, on the authority of Samuel, said: There was a *magrefah* in the Sanctuary; it had ten holes, each of which produced ten different kinds of sounds, with the result that the whole amounted to one hundred kinds of sounds.[33]

---

[30] Ezek. 33.31–32; 23.11.
[31] B. *Arak.* 10b; a shorter form is preserved in Y. *Suk.* 5.6 (55c).
[32] B. *Arak.* 10b; M. *Arak.* 2.3.
[33] B. *Arak.* 11a; cf. M. *Tam.* 3.8; 5.6; Rashi (on B. *Arak.* 10b–11a) thinks it was a rake.

The meaning of the passage is not, as some have said, that there was no organ in the temple. Rather, there was an organ, but it was a *magrefah* and not a *hirdolim* or *hydraulus*. In other words, there was no water-powered organ, whose noise would have disturbed the music, but they did have an organ blown by a wind-sack, an instrument which long-predated Ctesibius's automatic *hydraulis*. They called this instrument a *magrefah*, that is, a 'rake', perhaps because its vertically-projecting pipes looked like the prongs of a rake. In this, they demonstrated the same Israelite love of analogy which called the temple's great laver 'the Sea', or its thirteen horn-shaped money depositories *shofars*.[34] If Greek organs of the period are anything to go by, the *magrefah* would have been modest in size, more like a portative than a positive organ.[35] The Talmud passage says that it had ten holes, which may suggest that, like the temple *kinnor*, it played ten notes. And these ten holes could somehow produce a hundred sounds, though how this is done is unclear. (It is unlikely to be a reference to organ 'stops', which are otherwise unknown until the fifteenth century of our own era.) The *magrefah* was placed between the temple portico and the altar, and was played before the Levites sang, serving as a signal to them to gather.[36] One may surmise that, when the Levites sang, it served to accompany the voices, playing two or more notes at a time. Yet, while it appears that a *magrefah* was in use in Herod's temple, there is no evidence at all of such an instrument in the early second temple, much less in Solomon's temple.

TRUMPETS

While the *minim* and *nehilot*, the strings and woodwind, served to accompany the singing of the Levites, the trumpets and cymbals were played during breaks in the singing. This was not a musical interlude in the modern sense. Rather, the trumpets and cymbals were to rouse the attention of the deity and invoke his presence, as was the practice throughout the nations of the ancient east.[37]

The trumpets employed in the temple came in two kinds: the *hatsotserah* – plural, *hatsotserot* – and the *shofar*. The *hatsotserot* were played by *kohanim* to whom this role was allotted in the law of Moses.[38]

---

[34] Jer. 52.17–20; 2 Kgs 25.13–16; M. *Shek.* 2.1; 6.1, 5.

[35] A portative organ is small enough to be carried and played in procession; a larger positive organ can be moved, with some difficulty, but is only played when static.

[36] M. *Tam.* 5.6.

[37] In the third millennium BC, the conch shell was employed for the same purpose in Minoan Crete, and later spread into the Levant and Syria (Gorris and Verhulst 2005: 21–28).

[38] Num. 10.1–10; cf. 1 Chr. 16.6 and the descriptions of temple worship in the Mishnah and Talmud. However, we read in 1 Chronicles 16.42 that the Levites Heman and Jeduthun had *with* them *hatsotserot* for sounding.

The *kohanim*, the sons of Aaron, are to blow the *ḥatsotserot*. This is to be a lasting ordinance for you and the generations to come. When you go into battle in your own land against an enemy who is oppressing you, sound a *teruah* [fanfare] with the *ḥatsotserot*, and you shall be remembered before the LORD your God and you shall be saved from your enemies. Also on your festival days, and at your appointed feasts, and at the new moon, you shall blow the *ḥatsotserot* over your burnt offerings and over your peace offerings, and they will be a remembrance for you before the LORD your God (Num. 10.8-10).

An exact representation of temple *ḥatsotserot* has been preserved for nineteen and a half centuries in the Arch of Titus, near the Coliseum in Rome.[39]

Figure 14. Temple *ḥatsotserot* in the Arch of Titus

The Arch, celebrating Titus's conquest of Jerusalem in 70 CE, shows Roman soldiers in the victory procession carrying temple artefacts: the seven-branched *menorah* candelabrum, the table of shewbread, and a pair of *ḥatsotserot*. The frieze shows the *ḥatsotserot* to have been about half a metre in length. And, whether the Romans knew it or not, they were rightly depicted as a pair, for they were always played in pairs in the sacred service, as the law specified, the trumpets of each pair being made exactly the same size so as to produce notes of the same pitch.[40] While the minimum number of *ḥatsotserot* employed in the daily service was two, their number could be increased without limit, as at the dedication of the temple, when 120 *kohanim* played trumpets.[41]

The other trumpet, the *shofar*, was made of horn with a hole drilled in the end for blowing. In biblical times they were usually made of ram's horn. However, more exotic material could be used, as in this *shofar* of the Yemeni Jews, made of kudu horn from Africa across the Red Sea, and inscribed around with biblical texts.

---

[39] For another view of the Arch of Titus, see the 17th century engraving by Pietro Santi Bartoli (c. 1635-1700) in Appendix V.
[40] Num. 10.8–10; Y. *Yoma* 6.1 (43b).
[41] M. *Arak.* 2.5; 2 Chr. 5.12.

Figure 15. Kudu horn *shofar*.

Like the *ḥatsotserah*, the *shofar* was regarded as the preserve of the *kohanim*, but the regulations, being not prescribed in the law of Moses, were treated more leniently. During feasts it could be blown by non-priests – Levite cantors, boys, and even women, if necessary.[42]

Both *shofar* and *ḥatsotserah* had a place in temple worship, and both shared the common function of being blown to put the LORD in remembrance of his people, to 'wake up the Supreme Mercy', as the *Zohar* has it.[43] However, they also had particular functions. The *shofar* sounded the beginning and end of feasts and Sabbaths, both inside and outside the temple. The silver *ḥatsotserot* accompanied the army to war to rouse the divine power on Israel's behalf.[44] For the daily service, and on some festal days, only the *ḥatsotserot* were blown. But on Rosh Ha-Shanah – the autumn New Year's Day before the Feast of Sukkot – and on fast days, the *shofar* and *ḥatsotserot* were sounded together, the *shofar*-player standing between the two *ḥatsotserot*.[45]

Both types of trumpet had a core range of only two notes, the tonic and the fifth above, followed by a take-off note at the upper octave.[46] With these notes they had a repertoire of fanfares of long, short, ascending, and trilling blasts:

- *tekia*, a sustained blast, scooping up a fifth.
- *teruah*, or 'outburst', a jubilant fanfare of short notes; '*ta-ra!*' or '*tantara*'.
- *shebarim*, or '*broken*' notes, a series of short scoops, like a hunting horn.
- *meshekh*, a long drawn-out blast.

---

[42] T. *Suk.* 4.22; M. *RH* 4.8; B. *RH* 133a.
[43] *Zohar*, Emor 99b.
[44] Num. 10.9; 31.6; 1 Macc. 4.40-41; 5.31–33; 16.8; 1QM II.15; III.11; VII.9; IX.9. For the *zikhron* rite of 'remembrancing' YHVH in time of war, see Mitchell 1997: 93–99.
[45] M. *RH* 3.3-4.
[46] Sendrey 1969: 336, plausibly suggests that they must have known more than the second and third partials of the harmonic series, and may have employed higher notes on occasion.

Example 1. Trumpet fanfares

Tekia: Sounding

Teruah: Rejoicing-Tara

Shebarim: Brokens

Meshekh: Extended

Shebarim-Teruah

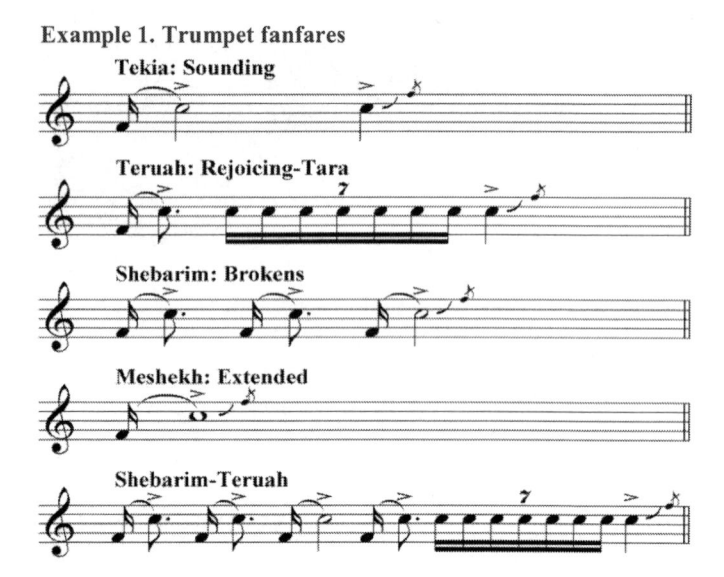

These fanfares were combined, on different liturgical occasions, in different sequences, such as *shebarim-teruah,* shown above, or *tekia-teruah-tekia* at the Passover sacrifices and on the first day of Sukkot, or, at other times, *tekia-shebarim-tekia* or *tekia-shebarim-teruah-tekia*.[47] The combinations and the number of times the trumpets could be blown on each occasion were strictly regulated.

> They never sounded less than twenty-one *tekia* in the temple, and never more than forty-eight. Every day they blew twenty-one *tekia* in the temple, three at the opening of the gates, nine at the daily morning sacrifice, and nine at the daily evening sacrifice. At the additional sacrifices they sounded an additional nine; and on the eve of the sabbath they added six, three as a sign to the people to cease from work and three to mark a distinction between the holy and the profane.[48]

PERCUSSION INSTRUMENTS

Temple worship also featured percussion instruments.[49] Chief among these were cymbals or *tsiltsayim.* Several kinds of ancient near eastern bronze

---

[47] M. *Pes.* 5.5; M. *Suk.* 4.5; 5.2.
[48] M. *Suk.* 5.5 (5.3 in some eds.).
[49] 'Percussion' is a widely-understood term for struck instruments in general, used by professional musicians as much as by the general populace. Yet the term is organologically imprecise. The Sachs–Hornbostel catalogue divides musical instruments into idiophones, membranophones, chordophones, and aerophones. Most instruments popularly called

cymbals have been found, varying in size and concavity, but divisible into two categories: large cymbals played with two hands and small cymbals played by the fingers of one hand, like metal castanets. Therefore, when Psalm 150 refers to two kinds of cymbals, *tsiltsle-shama* and *tsiltsle-teruah* – 'sounding' cymbals and 'fanfare' cymbals – it may well be contrasting these two kinds of cymbals. If so, the *tsiltsle-teruah* would be the larger ones, sounded with the *hatsotserot* fanfare, while the *tsiltsle-shama* would be small 'ringing' finger cymbals for use in joyful contexts, with dancing.

Figure 16. Small clapper cymbals and Assyrian hand-held cymbals.

Apart from Psalm 150, all the evidence for Israelite cymbals points only to the large pair of cymbals. These were held and sounded by the overseeing chief Levite. While it seems that in biblical times several pairs of cymbals might be sounded together, in later times, as the Mishnah reports, 'of cymbals, there was but one [pair]'.[50] These large cymbals made a loud and sonorous crash, as recorded both by the Chronicler and by Josephus, who calls them 'broad and large and made of bronze'.[51] They would have resembled the Assyrian cymbals shown above, slightly smaller than modern orchestral cymbals and more conical, like a pointed hat. Their tone, of indeterminate pitch, might have been as loud as modern cymbals, but their conical form would have produced a more gong-like sound.

'percussion' belong to the first two categories, although some, like cimbaloms and bull-roarers, are in groups three and four. Of the instruments detailed here, the cymbals, large and small, are concussion idiophones, the *tof* is a directly-struck membranophone, the sistrum is a shaken idiophone, and clapper bells are percussion vessel idiophones.

[50] Mishnah, *Arak.*, 2.5; 2 Chr. 5.12. While at 1 Chr. 15.19 Heman, Asaph, and Ethan sound bronze cymbals, it is not actually stated that they sounded them together (cf. 2 Chr. 5.12).

[51] 1 Chr. 15.19; *Ant.* VII.xii.3.

Also employed in temple worship was the *tof* or timbrel. The word is sometimes misleadingly translated 'tambourine', but it had no metal jingles and was larger than the modern tambourine. It was, in fact, a hand-held frame drum, about half a metre across, like the medieval tambour or Celtic *bodhran*, but beaten with the hand. What is interesting about the *tof* is that it was played mostly by women. When the Israelites came through the Sea, Miriam and the Israelite women took up *tuffim* and danced a victory dance; when Jephtah and David were victorious, the girls came out dancing with *tuffim*. Psalm 68 describes a victory procession up to the temple led by dancing girls with *tuffim*.[52] But in cultic celebrations, when the ark went up to Zion, or in the temple courts, where it accompanied trumpets, cymbals, and festal dancing, as on the first night of the Feast of Sukkot, it was played by Levite men.[53] This Israelite terracotta figure of a bearded man playing a *tof*, from early second temple times, would therefore represent a Levite, for the simple reason that, outside the temple, women had the monopoly on this instrument.

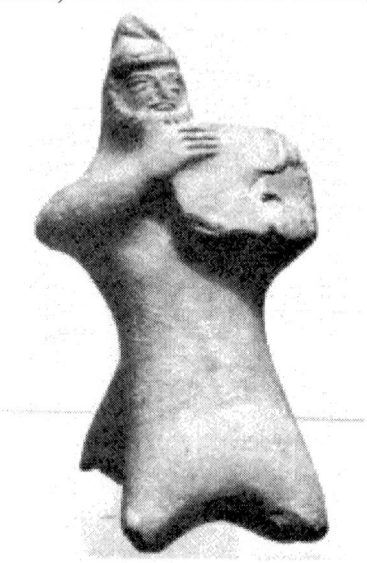

Figure 17. Bearded Levite with *tof*.

The Israelites had many other percussion instruments, some of which, like the sistrum, appeared in cultic processions.[54] But only one other 'instrument' is recorded as being used inside the temple, namely, the golden bells or *pa'amonim* which hung around the hem of the robe of the *kohen ha-gadol*, together with little, decorative pomegranates, symbolizing fruitfulness. The bells themselves were pomegranate-shaped, little round globes, like the bell on Noddy's hat. Josephus, an eye-witness of the temple service, says bells and pomegranates alternated on the hem of the robe.[55] But Kimḥi imagines the bells concealed within the pomegranates.[56] The bells were to be heard when the high priest *enters the Holy Place...so that he will not die* (Exod. 28.35). Just as household slaves in the ancient east had bells on their robes lest they surprise the master unawares and incur his wrath, so the *kohen ha-gadol* might not enter unannounced into the divine master's presence. The bells were not part of the musical worship, nor were they played by Levites, but, when the *kohen ha-gadol* appeared, their jingling on the hem of his robe would have added its own brightness to the soundscape of the Temple Mount.

---

[52] Exod. 15.20; Judg. 11.34; 1 Sam. 18.6; Ps. 68.25; cf. Jer. 31.4.
[53] 2 Sam. 6.5; 1 Chr. 13.8; Ps. 81.2; Ps. 149.3; Ps. 150.4.
[54] 2 Sam. 6.5.
[55] *Ant.* 3.7.4.
[56] On Exod. 28.35; bells of gold 'between' the pomegranates can equally mean 'inside' them.

MUSICAL STYLE OF TEMPLE WORSHIP

The nature of these instruments reveals much about the music sung and played in the temple. First, we know that the Hebrews knew the seven-note diatonic scale.[57] A series of cuneiform tablets, discovered last century, popularly known as the Babylonian Tuning Texts, show that the diatonic scale was already known in Mesopotamia in the early second millennium BC.[58] It was in use in Egypt around 1600 BC, when diatonic flutes replaced pentatonic ones. And it is found in Ugarit around 1400 BC. So the melodic lines of Hebrew chant were not based on primitive four or five note scales, but used seven-note scales, like our modern musical system.

Further, it is often imagined that temple music would have been single-line monodic chant, like an eastern version of Gregorian chant. But such an idea is refuted by the existence of the *ḥalil*. For a double-pipe, with finger holes on each pipe, shows that the players were employing two-note harmony, just like modern players of the *mijwiz*. The two pipes could not have been playing in octaves, for then the two pipes would have been different lengths, which they are not. Nor would the two hands have played in unison, for that would only have divided the air pressure of the pipe to no effect. They can only have been playing in two-part counterpoint.[59] This second melodic line may have been relatively simple: perhaps only an ison, a tonic drone, below the melody, varying by a few notes at cadence points, as is found today in the diaphony of Byzantine chant. Or it may have been more adventurous, as in Greece of the latter first millennium BC, where *aulos* players played an upper harmony – a descant – above the melody line.[60] Certainly, harmony had long been in the air. The Mesopotamians knew harmony of thirds, fourths, and sixths in the early second millennium BC.[61] Likewise, the multiple cheironomers – 'conductors' hand-signalling the notes to their musicians – of Egyptian friezes signal different notes to different harpists, who pluck different strings simultaneously.[62] So we may be confident that the Hebrews knew harmony too.[63] The mere possession of *ḥalil*, *névél*, and *kinnor* were a standing invitation to harmonic experimentation. How could one possess a lyre and not experiment with different strings sounding together? And if an ison could be

---

[57] I use the word 'diatonic' in the modern sense of denoting a heptatonic scale with a tonal centre, and not simply the major or minor scales, as the term was formerly used.

[58] For more on the 'Tuning Texts', see Chapter 12.

[59] Varro (116–27 BC), describing the two-note counterpoint of the Roman double-oboe, the *tibia*, calls the melody, played on the right pipe, the *incentiva*, and the accompaniment, played on the left pipe, the *succentiva* (*De agricultura*, I.ii.14–16). In the same way, he speaks of singers as *accanit* (he sings the lead part) and *succanit* (he sings the second part) (*De lingua latina*, VI.75).

[60] Landels 1999: 45.

[61] Kilmer & Civil 1986: 94–98; West 1994: 161–179. Sachs, 1929: 168–70, also suggest that harmony was employed in ancient Elam and Egypt.

[62] For more on cheironomy, including illustrations, see chapters 9, 11, and 12.

[63] Hickmann 1956: 97–100.

sustained below a melody, why not above? And if it could be transmuted into diaphony below the melody, then why not above? And once they had upper diaphony, it might be combined with a lower ison or double-ison on tonic and fifth. The result would be a simple but rich harmonic texture consisting of two or three parts.

The *nével* and *kinnor*, played by the singers as they sang, would double the vocal part of their respective players. Those playing the smaller *kinnor* would sing and play a higher part, those with the *nével*, a lower part. An account of their musical deployment is given by the Chronicler.

> Zechariah, Aziel, Shemiramoth, Jehiel, Unni, Eliab, Maaseiah, and Benaiah with *nevalim* [harps] on *alamot;* and Mattithiah, Eliphelehu, Mikneiah, Obed-Edom, Jeiel and Azaziah with *kinnorot* [lyres] on the *sheminit* to lead (1 Chr. 15.20–21).

Sheminit means 'eighth' and, since they knew the diatonic scale, we may surmise that this musical term means 'octave'.[64] Further, since it applies to the higher instrument, the *kinnor*, we may conclude that the upper octave is meant. The term *alamot* is trickier. It has two distinct meanings, either 'maidens' or 'hidden, eternal things'. The more popular understanding takes the 'maidens' line, making it equal to maidens' voices, that is, in the treble range. Yet this runs contrary to the passage, which gives the larger, lower-toned harps the *alamot* or 'maidens' part, while the smaller, higher lyres would then 'lead' at the *sheminit* or octave below. Sendrey concludes that the harps here were particularly small and played the upper part while larger lyres played the lower.[65] But that not only goes against the normal sense of *nével* and *kinnor*, but also leaves the orchestra without the standard large harp, which would have been desirable to fill out the lower sound spectrum. A likelier explanation is that the lyres 'led' by playing the melody in the upper octave or *sheminit*, while the harps played on *alamot*, in the range of hidden things, that is, in the mysterious realm of the bass diaphony, adding plagal cadences and lower harmony. If so, then, in the Chronicler's account, there was no upper harmony. Perhaps it was not yet known. Or perhaps the Levites were disinclined to flamboyance.

---

[64] The term occurs also in the heading to Pss. 6 and 12.
[65] Sendrey 1969: 280–83, 532.

9

The Temple Orchestra: The Levite Singers

Music, like all things human, is political. In a modern orchestra the chief authority is the musical director, who is nominally the orchestra's principal conductor, although he may conduct them for only a few weeks a year. He – it's usually a he – makes the key choices as to repertoire, assistant conductors, guest conductors, soloists, and section leaders. The routine work of rehearsal and day-to-day performance is done by assistant conductors, bright young things aiming for the lights. Then there is the lead violin or concertmaster, a remnant of eighteenth-century leadership from the string section, who has charge of orchestral discipline, tuning, and influences issues of interpretation for the strings. Solo players also have great influence. When Glenn Gould played the Brahms Piano Concerto with Leonard Bernstein, Gould insisted that the first movement be played at half the usual speed. The great Bernstein told the audience, 'I am not responsible for what you are about to hear.' Bring singers into the picture, and things get more complicated still. More conductors, more soloists, some with immense authority. Good luck to the conductor who clashes with a top tenor or soprano! Music has always been like this. In Renaissance times, in the Basilica of San Marco, the *maestri da capella*, giants like Willaert and Monteverdi, worked with first, second, and third organists, with *cori spezzati,* split choruses, each with its own head singer, each with their own view. And while each office was nominally more important than the one below, the relationships were always influenced by seniority, musical gifts, force of character, and popularity.

The music of the temple was much the same. There were musical directors, conductors, solo singers, chorus singers, split choruses, boy choristers, instrumentalists, and a support team. Together they formed a core institution of ancient Israelite society with its own strict codes and constitutions.

THE DIRECTOR OF MUSIC

The headings of fifty-five Psalms contain the Hebrew word, *la-mnatseaḥ*, which means, literally, 'for the prominent, shining one'. Clearly, this person was important. The underlying verb, *natsaḥ,* can indicate an overseer in general.[1] But the noun *mnatseaḥ* invariably indicates a musical overseer.[2] And therefore English Bibles, from the King James Version onward, rightly translate the heading *la-mnatseaḥ* as 'To the Chief Musician' or 'For the Director of Music.'

The first such musical leader we meet in the Bible is Kenaniah, 'prince' or 'commander of the Levites for the *massa*', who, when David brought the ark to Zion, directed 'the *massa* of the singers for he understood it'.[3] Although *massa* commonly means 'burden', the word may have as many as three senses here: namely, a weighty divine prophetic revelation, or the burden of the oracular song itself, or the literal burden of carrying the ark.[4] Once again, this is surely a deliberate play on words covering the multiple facets of Kenaniah's prominent role. What then was Kenaniah's *massa*? Probably his role was to oversee the ceremonial procession for the occasion, to be head of the procession and chief liturgist, responsible for both the physical and musical 'bearing' of the ark. His brief was to devise and execute ceremonies for the occasion, so that they would be ritually appropriate and properly coordinated, a role which would have included the singing of prophetic song.[5]

Kenaniah then is the first-known Levite director of music. Yet we hear little of him after the ark is installed on Zion. The likely explanation is that his authority was born of years of service as leader of the prophet-musicians of Samuel's time, and he was now nearing fifty, the age of retirement from full-time Levitical service. After the ark ascended to Zion, he was assigned an honourable position as judge over his Izharite clan, in the hill country of Ephraim and Manasseh, and passed his mantle to younger men, to the generation of Samuel's grandson, Heman.[6]

David then charged the Levite chiefs to appoint leaders over the music. They chose three younger men: Heman, the chief, with Asaph the Gershonite and Ethan-Jeduthun the Merarite, together with a number of lieutenants.[7] David appointed Asaph, with nine Levite assistants and two trumpeting *kohanim*, to supervise the ministry of song before the ark on Mount Zion.[8] Meanwhile, he appointed Heman and Jeduthun to supervise the ministry of song at Moses' Tabernacle and the altar of burnt offering in the priestly city of Gibeon, eight kilometres north-west of Jerusalem, under the ministry of Zadok the *kohen*.[9] This was not a second-class posting. Both David and Solomon

---

[1] 2 Chr. 2.2; Ezra 3.8–9.
[2] 1 Chr. 15.21; Hab. 3.19.
[3] 1 Chr. 15.22, 27.
[4] Each view finds biblical support: (1) Jer. 23.33–40; Mal. 1.1; (2|) LXX of 1 Chr. 15.22: *archōn tōn hōdōn* or 'chief of the hymnody'; (3) Num. 4.4–15.
[5] Kleinig 1993: 47–50.
[6] 1 Chr. 26.29; 1 Chr. 6.61; Josh. 21.20–26.
[7] 1 Chr. 15.16–17, where Heman is named first, as in 1 Chr. 6.33–39.
[8] 1 Chr. 16.4–38.
[9] Josh. 21.17; 1 Chr. 16.39–42.

recognized Gibeon's 'great high place' as the foremost shrine for cultic sacrifice until the inauguration of the temple.[10] The presence of Zadok and Heman there confirms its importance. The Gibeon shrine continued to function, with Moses' sacred artefacts, until it was closed just before the dedication of the temple. Then Moses' Tabernacle went up to the temple to be stored there, and Heman and Ethan went to share the Jerusalem ministry with Asaph, ministering together at the dedication of the temple.[11] Heman became chief of the three who, together with their twenty-one sons, led between them the twenty-four wards of Levite singers appointed by the king.

One passage illuminates the roles of these *mnatseḥim* or Directors of Music.

> These are the men whom David appointed over the hands of song of the house of the LORD after the resting of the ark there. They ministered before the tabernacle of the tent of meeting with song, until Solomon built the house of the LORD in Jerusalem; and they served according to the regulations for their ministry (1 Chr. 6.31–32).

Two roles are outlined here: the hands of song and the ministry of song. The 'hands of song' refer to the technique of conducting in the ancient world, known to us as cheironomy, a practice widely attested in pictures and friezes from Mesopotamia to Egypt. In a *bas relief* from an Old Kingdom mastaba, three cheironomers direct two flutes and two harps.

Figure 18. Egyptian cheironomers of the 3rd millennium BC

And below, in a detail from a steatite vase found in Tell Bismaya, near Ur, two harpists, a drummer, and a trumpeter are led by two cheironomers, one to the left, carrying a wand or rattle, and one above and between the two harps.

---

[10] 1 Chr. 21.29; 1 Kgs 3.4; 2 Chr. 1.3–6.
[11] 2 Chr. 5.12–13. Heman and Ethan also ministered at the Zion tent before the dedication of the temple, perhaps on the basis of rota or of lot (2 Chr. 6.31-48).

Figure 19. Sumerian cheironomers (c. 3200 BC).

Although ancient cheironomy is the ancestor of modern conducting, the two techniques differed in significant ways. Whereas modern conductors indicate a clear tempo to musicians following a musical score, the cheironomer was a 'living score' who indicated, by a two-handed vocabulary of gestured symbols, the musical pitches to be sung and played, together with other necessary details of the musical performance.[12] In Israel, these cheironomic traditions continued until the destruction of Herod's temple, after which they passed gradually into obscurity. A talmudic comment of Rabbi Akiva, from within two generations of the temple's destruction, refers to cheironomy in the Holy Land being practised with only hand.[13] Rashi's eleventh-century commentary on this Talmud passage shows that, in his time, some form of cheironomy was still preserved by Jewish communities in the east after it had long died out among western Jews. Indeed, to this day a form of two-handed cheironomy is preserved by the Jewish cantors of Cairo. Their gestures still preserve ancient symbols found on Pharaonic friezes, some apparently with the same meanings as in Pharaonic times.[14]

However, the Director of Music was not only a cheironomer. He was also a worship leader who, as precentor, led the singing of the whole chorus. Unlike modern church music, where everyone sings the whole song together, ancient eastern music was characterized by responsorial singing, one voice leading, the others answering. Thus the women sang to one another at David's triumph

---

[12] The nearest modern equivalent is the Curwen-Kodaly system, which indicates steps of the scale by hand signs. Zoltan Kodaly (1882–1967) inherited the system from John Curwen (1816–1880), who invented hand-signs to accompany the Sol-fa system of Sarah Glover's (1785–1867) *Manual of the Norwich Sol-fa System*. Glover's system followed the 11th-century theorist Guido d'Arezzo, whose own cheironomy, the Guidonian hand, had roots in the ancient traditions of the church.

[13] B. *Ber.* 62a.

[14] Gerson-Kiwi & Hiley 2001.

over Goliath; thus the *serafim* sang before the glorious throne.[15] As the Israeli musicologist Hanoch Avenary wrote, 'The various kinds of Jewish psalmody arose altogether from one formal principle: the confrontation of soloist and choir.'[16] In this way, Heman, Asaph, and Ethan, with their sons, were each solo singers who led the responsorial singing of their ward of singers.

From a combination of archaeological evidence and practice among modern eastern cantors, we can piece together a picture of how they would have sung. As is standard throughout the east, they would have sung with a tighter throat and a higher larynx than a modern classical singer, and the tone would have been correspondingly sharper and more penetrating. At the same time, they probably employed manipulated vocal trills, executed by pressing the thumb of the left hand against the larynx while singing, a practice preserved today among Jewish cantors in the east, and depicted in ancient Egyptian and Assyrian friezes.[17]

Something of these practices – the forceful, manipulated tone – is preserved in the Mishnah's account of the second temple *mnatseah*, Hygros the Levite.[18]

> When he tuned his voice to a trill, he would put his thumb into his mouth and place his finger between the two parts of the moustache, so that his brethren the *kohanim* staggered backwards suddenly (M. *Yoma* 3.11).

It is likely too that, while the left thumb manipulated the larynx, the left hand rested over the left ear, another practice found among Jewish cantors of the east to this day, signifying their status as chief singer and their receptivity to divine inspiration.

> There is one manual position that has remained alive through the millennia without a break or change of meaning: the hand covering the ear of a musician. In this case no technicality of intonation, interval or motif is intended, but rather the status of the musician as a professional singer. In addition, its purpose is to convey his prominence among the musicians as the most exalted personality, gifted with an inspired and ecstatic disposition. Today, as in Pharaonic times, great singers from Morocco to Persian and Kurdistan will enter a state of meditation by putting their left hand over their ear (often also pressing the thumb against the throat), thereby intimating a change of personality through change of their vocal resonance or timbre.[19]

---

[15] 1 Sam. 18.7; 21.11; 29.5; Isa. 6.3.
[16] Avenary 1963: 1–13.
[17] Sendrey 1969: 256; Gerson-Kiwi & Hiley 2001: V.556–57.
[18] See too B. *Yoma* 38a-b; Y. *Shek.* 5.2 (48d); T. *Yoma* 2.5.
[19] Gerson-Kiwi & Hiley 2001: V.556–57. The late Robin Gibb, born to a Jewish mother and a lover of Israel, was known for his hand-on-ear singing style.

Figure 20. Egyptian cheironomer (3rd from left) covering left ear.

For the *mnatseah* was a prophetic singer. Like Kenaniah, chief of the oracle, before them, Heman and Asaph were 'seers', Jeduthun 'prophesied with the lyre', and their sons, moved by the divine spirit, were set apart to 'prophesy' with lyres, harps, and cymbals.[20] Traditionally, their being prophets was thought to indicate their receptivity to divine messages while singing. And that is part of how their role was understood. But there is more to it. The more we learn about ancient views on music – views that originated a millennium before David's time – the more we understand that music and song were seen as prophetic in essence.

The Babylonians, who developed the seven-note scale, also had seven modes or patterns of scales, which they sang with the seven vowels of vocal music.[21] These compounded sevens were no accident. Seven was the number of magic, of the numinous, reflecting the sevens of calendar and astrology: the days of the week, the rainbow, the seven heavens, and the seven spheres, after whose deities the Babylonians named their harpstrings. For the Babylonians, their heptatonic incantations bathed everything within the soundscape in wave upon wave of magical sevens, the mode of the scale determining the particular astrological and magical effect. As for the instruments of music, they were not simply mundane objects; they were sacred artefacts for crossing the chasm separating gods and men. To these instruments they made sacrifice. With the sacred harp or lyre, one could receive and communicate divine instructions and channel the power of the stars to the wishes and needs of mankind.

The Babylonian wonder before the magical power of music was shared to some extent by all the ancients, not least the Hebrews. For them, music was the language of the heavenly beings, when the 'morning stars sang together and all the sons of God shouted for joy', before the foundation of the earth, before the existence of mankind.[22] The very act of singing and playing music was heavenly speech and prophecy, communicating with the world of the

---

[20] 2 Chr. 29.25; 1 Chr. 25.5; 2 Chr. 29.30; 1 Chr. 25.3, 1; 2 Chr. 20.14–17.
[21] For Mesopotamian musical theory, see chapter 12.
[22] Job 38.4–7.

heavens.[23] It had power to drive out evil spirits, to sanctify earthly objects, to open the way to the divine spirit and heavenly messages, to propitiate the deity, and to deliver from attack.[24]

This meant that where song was, a channel to the heavens was, through which heavenly messages might flow. And this in turn led to the prophetic status of the Levite singers. The *mnatseah* communicated with the heavens in temple worship, and from these communications came the divine oracles of the Psalms, in Ascents Psalm 132 and elsewhere.[25]

> The LORD has sworn truth to David, he will not turn from it:
> 'Of the fruit of your body will I set upon your throne' (Ps. 132.11).
>
> For the LORD has chosen Zion,
>   he has desired it for his royal seat:
> 'This is my resting place for ever and ever;
>   here I will dwell for I have desired it.' (Ps. 132.13-14).

Whether such oracles were first sung under the influence of the divine spirit and later transcribed, or whether they were pre-received and pre-composed is something we may ponder. No doubt many escaped the biblical record. But those which remain show how wide a range of subjects they covered: promises of divine favour and protection, promises of progeny and succession, exhortations, judgments on foreign armies, and even on Judah's kings.[26]

Linked to the role of the *mnatseah* as prophet was his role in sounding the cymbals along with the Aaronite *kohanim* who blew trumpets.[27] Throughout the ancient world, the concerted sounding of trumpets and cymbals was seen as a means of attracting the deity's attention to the worshippers. The Levites' cymbals therefore formed at the one time a call to the deity and a signal for the chorus to begin singing. At pauses during the singing, the trumpets would sound again, not as a musical intermezzo, but as an invocation to the deity, and all would bow down and the *mnatseah* would pray or prophesy. A Mishnah passage describes it in the time of the second temple.

---

[23] E.g., 1 Sam. 10.5–10; 2 Kgs 3.15; Ezek. 33.32; music and prophecy are also united in David (1 Sam. 16.23; 2 Sam. 23.1–2), and in Miriam and Deborah, prophetesses who led cultic song (Exod. 15.20–21; Judg. 4.4; 5.1). Among other ancient peoples, as Quasten says, "The expression for 'making music' and 'prophesying' was often identical in ancient tongues" (1983: 33).

[24] 1 Sam. 16.23; 1 Sam. 10.5–10; 1 Macc. 13.47–51; 2 Kgs 3.15; Ps. 69.30–31; Num. 10.9; 2 Chr. 20.22.

[25] Pss. 2.6; 12.5; 46.10; 50.5–23; 60.6–8; 68.22–23 75.2–5; 81.6–16; 82.2-4, 6–7; 89.19–37; 91.14–16; 110.1; 108.7–9; 110.1, 4; 132.11–18 ; cf. also 62.11; 87.6; 95.10.

[26] Ps. 132.11–18; 2 Chr. 15.1–7; 20.14–17; 24.27.

[27] 1 Chr. 15.19. The Levites' prerogative of sounding cymbals was by divine command through prophecy of David, Gad and Nathan (2 Chr. 29.25). On Zion, from David's time on, sounding the trumpets was the prerogative of the priests (1 Chr. 15.24; 16.6; 2 Chr. 5.12). However, in the high place at Gibeon, the trumpet-blowing was in the hands of the Heman and Ethan (1 Chr. 16.42)

Ben Arza clashed the cymbals and the Levites broke forth into singing. When they reached a break in the singing they blew upon the trumpets and all the people prostrated themselves; at every break there was a blowing of the trumpet and at every blowing of the trumpet a prostration. This was the rite of the Daily Whole-offering in the service to the house of our God.[28]

Finally, the Levite chiefs, Heman, Asaph, Ethan and their sons, being patriarchs of their own musical clans, had pastoral oversight of their own communities. Temple discipline was severe. In second temple times, the guard discovered asleep on duty was beaten and had his garments set on fire, while the Levite who trespassed into another's ministry might face death.[29] Nor can we imagine that David's Levites were any softer. Yet these were communities of kinship, and the patriarchs would be at pains to enforce discipline within their own clan, not only to ensure high standards, but to protect errant singers from the stricter discipline of other cultic officials – the gatekeepers, guards and *kohanim*.

Therefore the *mnatsehim*, the Levite Directors of Music, oversaw every aspect of temple music: cheironomy, solo singing and prophecy, striking of cymbals, musical direction, corporate discipline, inditing new songs. Did they exercise all these roles simultaneously? Clearly, the creative, pastoral, and leadership roles might take place in between public singing. But, in the live performance roles, the *mnatseah* certainly could and often would exercise them alone. He would strike the cymbals to rouse the Holy One. Then, handing them to an assistant, he would initiate the singing, either with his solo voice, or signalling a choral entry with a breath and a gesture. When he led as precentor, his left hand would cover his ear and, at times, press his larynx to produce the intense vibrato applied to the key words of the psalm. When he led the choral responses, his hands would gesture the cheironomic symbols which were regarded as essential to the music. When multiple wards of singers sang together at the feasts, he would take precedence over all to direct the antiphonal choruses of singing Levites. Rightly was he called 'the bright shining one' – *mnatseah* – the great general over the holy city's legions of praise.[30]

---

[28] M. *Tam.* 7.3; B. *Erub.* 54a.

[29] M. *Mid.* 1.2; cf. Rev. 16.15. B. *Arak.* 11b discusses what transgression of temple protocol leads to the death penalty. The young singer, Joshua b. Hananiah, wanting to 'help' with duties at the gates, is warned 'Turn back, my son, for you are of the singers not of the gate-keepers.'

[30] Sendrey, however, thinks the *mnatseah* is the virtuoso solo singer, the precentor, who was given opportunity to 'shine' and 'triumph' for the glory of God (1969: 118, 138). He suggests that at the ascent of the ark in David's day, the roles of cheironomer and solo singer were fulfilled by different people, by Kenaniah on the one hand and Asaph, Heman, and Jeduthun on the other (533).

THE LEVITE CHORUS

By the end of David's lifetime, there was a pool of 4,000 Levites to supply the temple ministry. From these, 288 were selected from among their fellows to serve as singers, being chosen, no doubt, on the basis of their fine voices, as was the case in later times.[31] These were organized into twenty-four wards of twelve men, each ward serving weekly shifts, drawn by lot.[32] In this way, a minimum of twelve men served at the daily sacrifices, a regulation that continued for a thousand years, while multiple wards of singers served together at New Moon days and feasts. In practice, this meant that each singer would serve for two 'low' weeks each year and perhaps one week at the feasts. In between, they tended their pasture-lands and rehearsed for their next period of public ministry. In this way they were freed from the repetitive weariness of constant ministry and the soul-deadening effect of over-familiarity with the holy. Instead, they prepared for each public appearance as footballers prepare for the World Cup, and would have sung with eager fervour, ward outdoing ward in their zeal to declare the divine glory.

From the inception of David's ministry of song, all the singers were male Levites.[33] Women might sing and dance in the royal palace or, when their youthful bloom faded, work as wailing women, but they were excluded from any part in temple worship.[34] This had not always been the case. In earlier times, women fulfilled some ministry at the entrance to Moses' Tent of Meeting and at the Tabernacle, but this ceased because of abuses arising from contact between the sexes.[35] In one diaspora form of Judaism, the Alexandrian Therapeutae, women continued to sing and worship beside men.[36] But, in

---

[31] B. *Meg.* 24b relates that a hoarse voice disqualified a Levite from the ministry of song.

[32] 1 Chr. 23.3–5; 25.1–31. The weekly changing of the Levite singers is recorded by Josephus (*Ant.* VII.xiv.7), who served in the temple priesthood, and by the Mishnah (*Suk.* 5.6; *Ta'an.* 4.2) and its remark that twelve men stood on the *dukhan* (*Arak.* 2.6). The weekly changing of the Levite guard in 2 Kgs 11.5–9; 1 Chr. 9.25, suggests that the same practice pertained in biblical times.

[33] 1 Chr. 6.16.

[34] 2 Sam. 19.33–35; Eccl. 2.8; Jer. 9.17.

[35] Exod. 38.8; 1 Sam. 2.22, which speaks both of the ministry and its abuses (cf. Deut. 23.17).

[36] Philo recounts both sexes singing in worship among the Therapeutae, a Jewish sect in Egypt in the early Christian era: 'And after the feast they celebrate the sacred festival during the whole night. And this nocturnal festival is celebrated in the following manner: They all stand up together, and in the middle of the entertainment two choruses are formed at first, one of men and the other of women. And for each chorus there is a leader and chief selected, who is the most honorable and most excellent of the band. Then they sing hymns which have been composed in honor of God in many meters and tunes, at one time all singing together, and at another moving their hands and dancing in corresponding harmony, and uttering in an inspired manner songs of thanksgiving, and at another time regular odes, and performing all necessary strophes and antistrophes. Then when each chorus of the men and each chorus of the women has feasted separately by itself, like persons in the bacchanalian revels, drinking the pure wine of the love of God, they join together and the two become one chorus, an imitation of that one which, in old time, was established by the Red Sea, on account of the wondrous works which were displayed there... When the Israelites saw and experienced this great miracle, which was

Herod's temple, women were confined to the lower Court of Women and, finally, in the temple's last years, the sexes were separated even within the Court of Women – the women sitting in an upper gallery – to preclude levity, it is said.[37]

On their weeks of ministry, the Levite singers stayed in the rooms surrounding the temple and were exempt from all other duties, being responsible for the music day and night.[38] They were admitted to the chorus at the age of thirty years, when the male voice attains full maturity, and were compulsorily retired at the age of fifty, when the voice might start to lose its strength. While they sang, they also played, some on the lyre, others on the larger harp. They had five official years of training, beginning at age twenty-five. However, their training really began in childhood. For, as boys, the sons of the singers, alone of all the children in Israel, were permitted to enter the Court of Israel, to sing at the high feasts. The Mishnah relates,

> There were never less than twelve Levites standing on the *dukhan* [platform] and their number could be increased without limit. No minor could enter the court of the sanctuary to take part in the service except when the Levites stood up to sing. Nor did they [the boys] join in the singing with harp and lyre, but with the mouth alone, to add sweetness to the music. R. Eliezer b. Jacob said: They did not help to make up the required number, nor did they stand on the *dukhan*. But they would stand on the ground, so that their heads were between the feet of the Levites. And they were called the 'troublers' of the Levites (M. *Arakhin* 2.6).

Their being dubbed the 'troublers' of the Levites was a pun on the similar-sounding words *tso'arei*, 'troublers' and *tse'irei*, 'youngsters', this being due, no doubt, to their youthful high jinks. But their unlevitical levity was borne for the sake of their training and for the sweetness of their voices. For, in the temple, as in cathedral choirs today, the air and sweetness of boys' voices was treasured as a complement to the strength of men's voices.[39] And, as in cathedrals, the training in boyhood was considered the best possible formation for the adult singer.

---

an event beyond all description, beyond all imagination, and beyond all hope, both men and women together, under the influence of divine inspiration, becoming all one chorus, sang hymns of thanksgiving to God the Savior, Moses the prophet leading the men, and Miriam the prophetess leading the women.' (*Vit. Con.* XI:83-90)

[37] M. *Mid* 2.5; *Suk.* 5.4; B. *Suk.* 51a. The gallery in the Court of Women was built in the last fifteen years before the Roman destruction (Mitchell 2005: 77–90).

[38] 1 Chr. 9.33.

[39] This effect of 'air' or 'brightness' in children's voices is due to a presence boost at 8 KHz, whereas the presence or 'formant' of a trained adult male singer is in the 3 KHz range.

DEPLOYMENT OF FORCES

The chorus responded to the lead of the precentor, line by line. The responsorial exchange between soloist and choir is reflected in the parallelism of the psalms, where each verse repeats or develops the same idea in different words. The precentor-chorus exchange is clearest in cases where the speaker abruptly switches from singular to plural. In the Songs of Ascents, for instance, we find:

Precentor	*I* was glad when they said to me, 'Let us go to the house of the LORD'
Chorus	*Our* feet are standing in your gates, Jerusalem (Ps. 122.1–2).

Or elsewhere:

Precentor	Blessed is *the man* whose strength is in you,
Chorus	The pilgrim ways in *their* heart (Ps. 84.5).[40]

Or again:

Precentor	*I* will give thanks, for you answered *me*; you have become *my* salvation.
Chorus	The stone the builders rejected has become the capstone; The LORD has done this; it is marvellous in *our* eyes (Ps. 118.21–23).

Or again:

Precentor	They will speak of the glorious splendour of your majesty;
Chorus	And I will meditate on your wonderful works (Ps. 145.5).

Abrupt changes in the sense also suggest a change of speaker. In Psalm 91.9, the first half addresses the Holy One, while the next half must address a human being.

> Because you, LORD, are my refuge;
> You have made Elyon your dwelling (Ps. 91.9).

Clearly, an individual – a precentor or perhaps a king – addressed the first line to the LORD, while the chorus sang the second line, addressing the first speaker.

The exchange between precentor and chorus was the foundation of temple psalmody. But there were other permutations. Sometimes the whole congregation of assembled Israelites joined in the responses. Where Psalm 106 closes, *Let all the people say: Amen! Halelu Yah!* we may surmise that the

---

[40] So the Hebrew. The translations become creative here, in attempting to smooth over the perceived problem of the change of speaker. Likewise in Ps. 91.9 below.

people did join in with just those words. And in Psalm 118 the precentor exhorts different groups in the congregation – Israelite men, Aaronite *kohanim*, and proselytes or 'God-fearers' – to respond in turn with one refrain.[41]

Let Israel say	His love endures for ever.
Let the house of Aaron say	His love endures for ever.
Let those who fear the LORD say	His love endures for ever.

Similarly, the congregation may have chanted the *Halelu-Yahs* of the Haleluyah psalms, the twenty-six-fold refrain of Psalm 136, and the blessings of the Songs of Ascents, such as *From now until forever* and *Peace on Israel*.

We read also of antiphonal singing, chorus against chorus. At the dedication of the walls of Jerusalem in Nehemiah's time, two large choirs processed in opposite directions around the city wall toward the temple, singing 'section against section' and 'answering one another' under the direction of a *mnatseah* called Yizrah-yah, who directed 'according to the hands of David'.[42] Since his cheironomy would have preserved both the melodies and the musical deployment of David's time, we may assume that such antiphonal singing was current also in David's day. This is borne out by Psalm 24, which gives every appearance of being David's liturgy for the entry of the ark into Zion citadel in 1004 BC.[43] It features distinct groups of singers, both inside the city and in the procession outside. As the ark ascends Zion hill to the citadel gates, the precentor, probably Kenaniah, issues a command to the city gates, which is taken up by the ark's entourage.[44]

Precentor	Lift up, you gates, your heads!
Chorus	And stand upright, everlasting doors!
All	And the King of Glory will come in.

A voice from the gate-house replies for the gates:

Who is this King of Glory?

An answer comes back from the procession:

| Precentor | The LORD, mighty and a hero. |
| Chorus | The LORD, hero of battle. |

Then another command – *Lift up, you gates, your heads!* – is followed by another challenge from the gates and another response from the procession

---

[41] Something similar may have been the case at Ps. 115.9–11. Though on occasion the same refrain was clearly chanted by the Levite chorus (2 Chr. 5.13; Ezra 3.11).

[42] Ezra 3.10–11; Neh. 12.24, 31, 40-42. Generally, 'responsorial' is where one voice leads and others respond, while 'antiphonal' denotes separate choirs singing in response to one another.

[43] As explained in chapter 8.

[44] 1 Chr. 15.22–27.

around the Ark: *The LORD of hosts, he is the King of Glory.* The psalm is constructed around different singers chanting in response to one another.

Undoubtedly, there were still other ways in which the musical forces were deployed in performance. In the Dead Sea Psalms Scroll (11QPs[a]), Psalm 145 has, after each verse, the doxology, *Blessed be the LORD and blessed be his name for ever and ever*, indicating that this congregational response was sung in response to every verse of the psalm. Avenary finds evidence in the Talmud for seven different types of responsorial performance:[45]

- Type 1 Repetition of the precentor's every phrase or verse by the chorus.
- Type 2 An intonation by the precentor, followed by a choral hymn.
- Type 3 A motto from the first verse recurs as a refrain.
- Type 4 *Haleluyah* as a responsorial call.
- Type 5 Alternate singing of psalm hemistichs.
- Type 6 Repetition of verses.
- Type 7 Additional responses added to a psalm text.

In similar ways, the Levite chorus of David's time would have sung responsorially and antiphonally to the lead of their cantors, who deployed their singers with as much musical imagination as any Renaissance *maestro di capella*.

SINGING IN PARTS

Since boys sang with the men, the temple singers were aware of singing in octaves. And, with trebles, counter-tenors, tenors, and basses, they would certainly have been able to sing in triple octaves if they chose. But how far did their harmonic sophistication extend? As we saw earlier, second-millennium BC figurines of people playing double-pipes with one hand on each pipe are incontrovertible evidence that the early Israelites knew some form of diaphony, where the melody line is accompanied by a lower counterpoint. Their Mesopotamian ancestors had harmony in thirds, fourths, fifths, and sixths by Abraham's time.[46] Their Egyptian neighbours caught up a couple of centuries later, when their pentatonic scale gave way to the diatonic in the early New Kingdom period (17th century BC).[47] The Hebrews could hardly have been ignorant of such practices. So we would expect, at least, a melody held by the tenors and doubled at the upper octave by boys, and a diaphonic bass line underneath. If there were also bass-baritones singing a lower counterpoint against the tenors, in thirds, fourths, fifths, and sixths, and if this counterpoint

---

[45] Avenary 1979: 108–10.
[46] Kilmer 1971; 1984; Crickmore 2009: 5–6.
[47] Hickmann & Hickmann 1996: 6–14; the Cairo Institute of Arabic Music at http://egyptsound.free.fr.

were perhaps doubled at the octave by the older boys, the harmonic texture of temple song might have been surprisingly rich.

REHEARSAL AND PUBLIC APPEARANCE

The temple musicians rehearsed, stored, and maintained their instruments in chambers under the Court of Israel, entered by doorways in the western wall of the Court of Women.

> And there were chambers beneath the Court of Israel which opened into the Court of Women, and there the Levites kept harps and lyres and cymbals and all instruments of music (M. *Middot* 2.6).

The sound emanating from these chambers was such a feature of temple life that the gate above the northern Levite chamber was called the Song Gate.[48]

> And opposite them on the north, counting from the west: the Gate of Jeconiah, the Gate of the Offering, the Gate of the Women, and the Gate of Song (M. *Middot* 2.6).

This layout, with the singers' chambers under the upper court of the temple, appears to have originated with Solomon's temple. For Ezekiel's visionary replacement for Solomon's temple has rooms for the Levites in the same area, opening in the wall running along the west side of the Lower Court.

> And from without to the inner gate, were the chambers of the singers in the inner court, which were at the side of the north gate facing south, and the other at the side of the east gate facing north (Ezek. 40.44).[49]

When the Levites emerged from their chambers to sing, they stood in one of two locations. On most occasions, they stood on the *dukhan* or platform between the long, narrow Court of Israel and the Court of the *Kohanim*. Here they stood directly east, facing the temple, and sang across the altar and the Court of the *Kohanim*, the *azarah*, toward the great portico of the temple. This was their position both in Solomon's and in Herod's temple. Only ministering Levite singers were permitted to ascend the *dukhan*.[50] The Levite boys, as we saw, sang with their heads at the level of their fathers' feet, as their fathers stood upon the *dukhan*.[51] They would therefore have stood on the last step before the Court of the *Kohanim*. (They would not have been permitted to stand in the court itself.) The *dukhan*, on which their fathers stood behind them,

---

[48] See Chapter 3 for a picture of the Gate, the fifteen steps, and the doors to the singers' chambers.
[49] LXX, more reasonably, has 'the other at the side of the south gate facing north'.
[50] 2 Chr. 5.12; B. *Suk.* 51a.
[51] M. *Arak.* 2.6.

was built over the middle between the Court of Israel and the Court of the *Kohanim*.

A difficult Mishnah passage allows for two views on the shape of the *dukhan*.

> The Court of Israel was 135 cubits long by eleven wide, and likewise the Court of the *Kohanim* was 135 cubits long by eleven wide, and the ends of beams separated the Court of Israel from the Court of the *Kohanim*. R. Eliezer b. Yaakov says: There was a step, and it was a cubit tall, and the *dukhan* was placed on it, and on it three steps of half a cubit each. Thus the Court of the *Kohanim* was higher than the Court of Israel by two cubits and a half. (*Mid.* 2.6)

One view is that the three steps of half a cubit were the *dukhan*, so that it was a stepped platform, rising away from the temple, where the Levites might sing toward the holy place in three tiers.[52] This is outlined in the model below.

Figure 21. The *dukhan* between the Court of Israel and the Court of the *Kohanim*

The other view is that the three steps of half a cubit were not part of the *dukhan*, but were built upon the step of one cubit, making an uneven four steps rising from one court to the other, and the *dukhan* was simply a flat platform astride the middle of these four steps.[53] I prefer the first hypothesis – the stepped *dukhan* – for it well explains how the young Levites could sing between their fathers' feet. But the second hypothesis – the flat *dukhan* – better explains the two and a half cubits from one court to the other.

---

[52] Sendrey, 1969: 425, 436.
[53] Ritmeyer, 358–59, 345, 369.

The other position from which the Levites sang was, as we have seen, the fifteen steps leading from the lower Court of Women up to the Court of Israel. With the *mnatseaḥ* standing in front, they ascended, singing as they faced the One indwelling the holy house above them, one song on each step.

PRIVILEGES AND STATUS

As pure-blooded Levites, the temple singers were among the upper ranks of Israelite society. In the kingdom period, they lived in their own cities dispersed throughout the land, where they had pasture-lands for their sheep and cattle.[54] They also received substantial provision of meat, oil, wine, and corn from the temple tithes. When they went up to minister in Jerusalem, they lived in rooms within the temple. By Nehemiah's time, though probably long before, they were distinguished as a guild apart from other Levites.[55] Also in Nehemiah's time, they received land and houses in or around Jerusalem, and a tax-exempt regular salary in addition to tithes.[56] In second temple times, they sang in synagogues, no doubt supplementing their income thereby.

> It was taught: R. Joshua b. Hananiah stated, When we used to rejoice at the place of the Water-Drawing, our eyes saw no sleep. How was this? The first hour [was occupied with] the daily morning sacrifice; from there [we proceeded] to prayers; from there [we proceeded] to the additional sacrifice, then the prayers to the additional sacrifice, then to the House of Study [the synagogue], then the eating and drinking, then the afternoon prayer, then the daily evening sacrifice, and after that the *Simḥat Bet Ha-Sho'evah* (Rejoicing at the House of the Water-Drawing) [all night] (B. *Suk.* 53a).

The singers were supported by a back-up fleet, for the construction and maintenance of their instruments, and for their wardrobe. This team included Levites of ministering age who were not selected as singers. It also included the temple servants or Nethinim, a group probably not of Israelite origin, but who enjoyed some of the privileges of temple employees, including houses around Jerusalem and freedom from taxes in Nehemiah's time.[57]

---

[54] The Asaphites, with the whole Gershonite clan, lived among eastern Manasseh, Issachar, Asher and Naphtali (Josh. 21.27–33; Josh. 21.6; 1 Chr. 6.62, 71–76 [56–61]). The Merarites had twelve towns in Reuben, Gad and Zebulun (Josh. 21.34-42; 1 Chr. 6.63, 77–80). The Korahites, with the other Kohathites, were appointed lands in Ephraim, Dan and western Manasseh (Josh. 21.20–26), but the Danites vacated their inheritance (Judg. 18.27–31) and the Chronicler records Kohathite settlement only among Ephraim and Manasseh (1 Chr. 6.61, 67–70 [46, 53–55]).

[55] Ezra 2.41, 70; 7.7, 24; 10.23–24; Neh. 7.44, 73; 10.28, 39.

[56] Neh. 11.3, 15–18; 12.27–29; Ezra 7.24; Neh. 11.23; 12.47.

[57] The name Nethinim, or 'given ones', appears only in post-exilic texts (1 Chron. 9.2; Ezra 2.43, 58, 70; 7.7, 24; 8.17, 20; Neh. 3.26; 7.46, 60, 73; 10.28; 11.3). That they were temple servants is clear from Josephus who calls them *hierodouloi* (*Ant.* XI.i.6). They were 'given' by David to the service of the temple (Ezra 8.20), and their origin is often traced to the Gibeonites

All in all, with their rigorous training, their professional pride, their closely-guarded secrets, their strict internal discipline, and their clan privileges jealously defended by watchful patriarchs, the Levite singers formed a distinct and influential guild within the temple hierarchy and Israelite society. This guild, called the Sons of Maḥol, was a formidable force in temple politics.[58] For the ministry of song was essential to the temple rite. The temple rule was that 'The omission of the song invalidates the sacrifice.'[59] Without the Levite singers, morning and evening sacrifice could not be offered, nor Sabbath, New Moon, and feast be sanctified. And it happened that, at times, tensions arose between the singers and the *kohanim*, disrupting the daily sacrifice. We know of two occasions when this occurred.

On the first occasion, the Levites' grievance was legitimate. In Nehemiah's time, the false *kohen*, Eliashiv, gave a large chamber in the temple to the arch-enemy of the Judean returnees, Tobiah the Ammonite. Since this chamber had been used for storing the tithes given to the Levites, the Levites' supply of tithes was disrupted. In response, they ceased the sacred service and went to their fields, returning to the temple only when Nehemiah returned from Babylon to right their wrong (Neh. 13–14). The second occasion was when the singers sought and received King Agrippa's permission to wear the priestly white linen ephod.[60] This, Josephus the *kohen* observed, was 'contrary to the laws of our country'. The *kohanim* objected strenuously to this Levite presumption, but were overruled not only by the royal will but by public lack of sympathy. For they had made themselves so contemptible in their robbery of tithes that no respect for them remained.[61] The shameful feud was finally stilled, as Josephus foresaw, by the sword of Vespasian and Titus.

Yet, by and large, the Zadokite *kohanim* and the Levites did manage to co-operate in the sacred service for the best part of a thousand years. The inevitable tensions were resolved partly through their common dependence on temple tithes, but also through their observance of temple law and their common devotion to the temple and its divinely-ordained rites which they honoured above factional rivalries.

---

of Joshua's day, who were 'given' by Joshua to be servants to the altar (Josh. 9.27). This agrees with the Mishnah's teaching that the Nethinim are forbidden to intermarry with Israelites in perpetuity (Yeb. 8.3). Yet they laboured together with the Judeans on the rebuilding of the wall (Neh. 3.26).

[58] *B'ne Maḥol* or 'sons of dance' (1 Kgs 4.31) is not a patronymic (cf. 1 Chr. 2.6; 6.33; 15.17), but rather the name of the singers' guild (Albright 1968: 217–18). Likewise Hengstenberg renders it *sacras choreas ducendi periti*, 'leaders of the sacred choral procession' (1845–48: II.491, n.1).

[59] B. *Arak*. 11a. Such was the consensus after debate. The view won the day because its rubric, *tannu rabbenan*, 'Our rabbis taught', announced its temple-period origin.

[60] *Ant*. XX.ix.6.

[61] *Ant*. XX.ix.6; viii.8; ix.2.

10

---※---

Moonlight on Moriah

The language of the Songs of Ascents is suffused with the atmosphere of a night-service in the temple at the Feast of Sukkot. The Bible says nothing of such a service or of how the Songs were sung in the temple. However, rabbinic literature preserves for us an exact picture of how the Songs of Ascents were sung at the Feast of Sukkot in the last decades of the temple's existence, before the Roman destruction of AD 70. They tell, in particular, of the festivities of the first night of the celebrations, known as *Simḥat Beth Ha-Sho'evah*, that is, the Joy of the Ceremony of the Water-Drawing.

SIMḤAT BETH HA-SHO'EVAH

As the sun set on the fourteenth day of Tishri and the rising full moon ushered in the fifteenth night, the blast of priestly trumpets on the Temple Mount announced the beginning of the Feast. The people assembled in the lower court, the Court of Women, which was illuminated by four immense candelabras, twenty-five-metre-high pylons each topped with four golden bowls, having wicks woven from the old girdles and breeches of the *kohanim*.[1] The nightlong demand for fuel of these flaming torches was met by strong lads of priestly descent who, bearing ten litre jars of oil, continually climbed ladders to feed them.[2] Such was the light these candelabras emitted that 'There was not a courtyard in Jerusalem that was not illumined by the light of the ceremony of the water-drawing,' while, in the city below, one could sift wheat by it.[3] Festivities began in the Court of the Women. While the women sat above in galleries, the leading men of the nation – 'men of deed and of name' – danced into the night with burning flambeaux, singing hymns of praise, shouting, clapping, jumping, and dancing. The 'men of piety and good deed'

---

[1] B. *Shab.* 21a; B. *Yoma* 23a.
[2] Mishnah *Suk.* 5.2; says they carried 120 log (c. 40 litres), while the Talmud (B. *Suk.* 52b) specifies that this was 30 log (10 litres) each.
[3] M. *Suk.* 5.3; B. *Suk.* 53a.

would sing: 'Happy our youth that has not disgraced our old age.' The 'penitents' would reply: 'Happy our old age which has atoned for our youth.' And both would sing together: 'Happy he who has not sinned, but let him who has sinned return and He will pardon him.'[4]

Rabbi Simeon b. Gamaliel, it is said, would take eight burning torches and juggle them in the air, none touching another; and when he prostrated himself, he would dig his two thumbs in the ground, bend down, kiss the ground, and push himself up again on his thumbs, a feat which no other man could achieve.[5] Even allowing for exaggeration, the festival was clearly a time of great joy and exuberance.[6] As it was said, 'He who has not seen the rejoicing at the ceremony of the water-drawing has never seen rejoicing in his life.'[7]

FIFTEEN STEPS TO THE HOLY HOUSE

After these festivities, well into the night, the Levite singers appeared from the door of their chambers that opened onto the Court of Women and assembled at the bottom of the fifteen steps that led up from the western end of that court to the Court of Israel above.[8]

At the top of the steps, overshadowing all by its massive bulk, was the great Nicanor Gate. Its great doors fashioned of Corinthian bronze, it was one of the glories of the temple, excelling the other gates in breadth, height and splendour. Josephus relates that it was fifty cubits high and forty wide, not including the postern gates on each side, and that twenty men were required to open and close each gate.[9] The bronze of these gates, he adds, was overlaid with silver and gold. The Mishnah, more mysteriously, remarks,

> All the gates that were there were overlaid with gold, save only the doors of the Nicanor Gate, for with them a miracle had happened; and some say, because their bronze shone like gold (M. *Middot* 2.3).

This magnificent gate, a fitting portal to the holy house above, was approached by the fifteen steps leading from the lower to the upper court. Yet not everyone could ascend these steps. This was not an egalitarian society. No Gentile could go anywhere near, not even in the lower court. The temple guards would see

---

[4] B. *Suk.* 53a; T. *Suk.* IV.2.

[5] M. *Suk.* 5.4; B. *Suk.* 53a.

[6] Rubenstein 1995: 141 remarks not only on the exaggeration but on the rabbinizing nature of the sources, where the founding fathers of rabbinism, Hillel and Shimon b. Gamaliel, 'put on the elaborate celebrations before the people while the priests passively stood at attention'.

[7] M. *Suk.* 5.1.

[8] M. *Mid.* 2.6. Each step was some five inches (12.5 cm) in height. They lie today beneath the eastern stairway leading to the Dome of the Rock (Ritmeyer 2006: 354–55, 361). See Figure 2 in chapter 3.

[9] Josephus, *War* V.v.3; M. *Mid.* 2.3; cf. M. *Mid.* 1.4; 2.6; *Sot.* 1.5; *Neg.* 14.8;

to that. No Israelite woman or child could ascend from the lower court. No Israelite ritually-unclean or of doubtful parentage could go up. Only men and youths of recognized Israelite lineage could ascend these steps and pass through the glorious gate. Arriving at the top, in the Court of Israel – long and narrow from north to south – they faced four more steps which only the *kohanim* might ascend. In the midst of these steps, directly opposite the temple portico, was the platform or *dukhan* where the ministering Levites stood to sing. Ahead and slightly to the left was the huge altar where the *kohanim*, robed in barefoot silence, walked among the fires on top. And straight ahead was the door of the temple itself, the entry to the throne room of heaven. These fifteen steps were important because of where they led.

The Mishnah tractate *Middot*, which preserves the measurements of the temple, describes the steps as follows:

> And fifteen steps ascended from within [the Court of Women] to the Court of Israel, corresponding to the fifteen Songs of Ascents in the Psalms, and upon them the Levites stood in song. They were not straight but rounded, like half a round threshing-floor (M. *Mid.* 2.5).

These steps then were not straight but curved outward into the lower court, a protruding semi-circular mound.

As the Levite singers emerged from their chambers, a hush fell upon the assembled crowds below. The Levites took their place at the bottom of the fifteen steps and began their ascent singing, as the Mishnah relates:

> Countless Levites [played] on harps, lyres, cymbals, and trumpets, and musical instruments on the fifteen steps which descend from the Court of Israel to the Court of Women, and which correspond to the fifteen Songs of Ascents in the Psalms. On these steps the Levites stood with musical instruments and played melodies (M. *Suk.* 5.4).

They sang, as we saw in chapter three, one Song of Ascents on each step as they ascended. As they stood on the steps in rows, looking upward toward the holy house, the *mnatseah* stood above them, leading their singing, while the semi-circular layout of the steps preserved the all-important sight-lines of the ensemble, enabling the singers to see and hear one another and the cheironomer.

When they arrived at the top of the steps, at the *dukhan*, the last Song was sung antiphonally between the Levites and another group, as the Tosefta says:

> What did they [the Levites] sing? A Song of Ascents. Come bless the LORD, all you servants of the LORD, who stand by nights in the house of the LORD (Ps. 134.1). Some of them sang: Lift up your hands to the holy place and bless the LORD (Ps. 134.2). And when they parted, what did they sing? The LORD bless you from Zion who made heaven and earth (Ps. 134.3) (T. *Suk.* 4.7–9).

This other group – who lift their hands in the holy place and bless the LORD – could only be the Aaronite *kohanim*, for they alone could enter the temple and bless the people from the portico in the sacred name.

After their ascent by the steps, the Levites took their place on the *dukhan* to sing for the rituals of the *nisukh ha-mayim*, the 'pouring of water' ceremony, to invoke the divine blessing of rain for the coming year.[10] Amidst a great crowd, a *kohen* brought water in a golden ewer of three logs' capacity from the Shiloah pool to the temple. It was borne in solemn procession to the Water Gate, where it was met with *shofar* fanfares – *tekia, teruah, tekia* – while the multitude sang: *With joy you will draw water from the wells of salvation* (Isa. 12.3).[11] The *kohen* took the ewer up the *kebesh* or ramp to the altar and turned to the left, where, on the rim of the altar, were two bowls, connected to two pipes running down into the Temple Mount below. Into one of these bowls he poured the water libation while, into the other, one of his fellows simultaneously poured the *nisukh ha-yayin*, the wine libation. Mingling together beneath the altar, the libations ran beneath the foundations of the temple into the Kidron brook.[12]

BACK DOWN THE STEPS

When the *Nisukh ha-mayim* was complete, the ceremony, as related by the Mishnah, continued as follows:

> Two *kohanim* stood at the upper gate [the Nicanor Gate] which leads down from the Court of Israel to the Court of Women, with two trumpets in their hands. When the cock crowed they sounded a *tekia*, a *teruah*, and again a *tekia*. When they reached the tenth step they sounded a *tekia*, a *teruah*, and again a *tekia*. When they reached the Court they sounded a *tekia*, a *teruah*, and again a *tekia*. And when they reached the ground they sounded a *tekia*, a *teruah*, and again a *tekia*. They proceeded, sounding their trumpets, until they reached the gate which leads out to the east (M. *Suk.* 5.4).

'Cock-crow' here does not refer to the crowing of a rooster. The breeding of chickens was prohibited in Jerusalem, lest they spread ritual uncleanness (in picking through dunghills).

> They may not rear fowls in Jerusalem because of the Holy Things, nor may priests rear them anywhere in the Land of Israel because of clean foods. (M. *BK* 7.7).

---

[10] B. *RH* 16a;

[11] For more on the question of whether the Isaiah quote arose from a procession festival of water-drawing at pre-exilic Sukkot celebration, see Rubenstein 1995: 148, n. 168.

[12] M. *Suk.* 4.1, 9–10; T. *Suk.* 4; B. *Yoma* 26b.

Despite this, other Mishnah passages speak of cock-crow marking temple rites.

> Sometimes he [the officer over the lots] came at cock-crow and sometimes a little sooner or later (M. *Tamid* 1.2).

> Every day they took up the ashes from the altar at cock crow or near it, either before it or after it; but on Yom Kippur at midnight, and on the Feast at the first watch. And never did the cock crow before the courtyard was filled with Israelites. (M. *Yoma* 1.8).

But the temple rites were not determined by the crowings of illicitly-concealed fowls. Measurement of time was vital in Israel. It was not regulated by chickens, which may crow at any time, nor even by witnesses, but by the astronomical and calendrical calculation of the Sanhedrin.[13]

In fact, the 'cock-crow' here was the trumpet signal – called the *gallinus* or 'cock-crow' – from the Roman Antonia Fortress, overlooking the temple. The Roman night-guard was divided into three-hour watches, ending at 9 p.m., midnight, 3 a.m., and 6 a.m. A trumpet call sounded the end of each watch. Therefore the 'cock-crow' in our passage was the Roman *gallinus* at the end of the night watch, at exactly 6 a.m., at sunrise, which marked the moment for the *kohanim* to begin their descent.

The trumpeting *kohanim* descended the fifteen steps, passed through the eastern gate of the temple amid the multitude of worshippers and, turning their backs to the rising sun in the east and facing west toward the Holy Place, they chanted, as the sun rose behind them:

> Our fathers in this place turned with their backs toward the temple of the LORD and their faces toward the east, and they worshipped toward the rising sun in the east; but as for us, our eyes are turned toward the LORD. R. Judah says: They used to repeat the words: 'We are the LORD's and our eyes are turned toward the LORD.'[14]

THE DOWNWARD PROCESSION MIRRORS THE UPWARD

This slow downward procession at dawn, following the night of festivities, sheds light on how the earlier upward procession was performed during the night. Just as the downward procession was slow, with deliberate pauses and actions on particular steps, the same was true of the upward procession, with psalms sung on every step. Likewise, the trumpet-playing on the descent of the steps had its parallel on the way up, as the Mishnah relates:

---

[13] When witnesses claimed to have seen the new moon, Rabban Gamliel, head of the Sanhedrin, delivered a funeral oration (forbidden on the New Moon), in honour of Ben Zaza's mother, to show that the Sanhedrin, not witnesses, decides time (RH 25a).

[14] M. *Suk.* 5.4 (B. *Suk.* 51b); cf. T. *Suk.* 4; Ezek. 8.15–16.

> Countless Levites [played] on harps, lyres, cymbals, and *trumpets*, and musical instruments on the fifteen steps which descend from the Court of Israel to the Court of Women, and which correspond to the fifteen Songs of Ascents in the Psalms (M. *Suk.* 5.4).

On the descent, trumpets were blown on the tenth step and at the arrival in the lower Court of Women.

> When they reached the tenth step they sounded a *tekia*, a *teruah*, and again a *tekia*. When they reached the Court [of Women] they sounded a *tekia*, a *teruah*, and again a *tekia* (M. *Suk.* 5.4).

And if we should ask the meaning of the particular steps for trumpet playing in the descent, no obvious answer occurs. But read the steps in reverse order, as an ascent, and the answer becomes plain. The fanfare on the tenth of the fifteen steps marks off ten and five, the numerical value of the letters *yodh* and *heh* which form the name of Yah. They also count off the festal days of the seventh month, based on the same ten-five division, with the Feast of Trumpets on the first day-step, the Day of Atonement on the tenth day-step, and the first day of Sukkot in the Upper Court. Therefore, since the pattern of fanfares makes sense on the way up rather than on the way down, it suggests that the downward procession was the mirror image of an upward step-by-step procession where trumpets were blown in the Lower Court, then on the tenth step, and in the Upper Court to mark off the name of Yah, which was itself spelled out in the feasts of the seventh month.

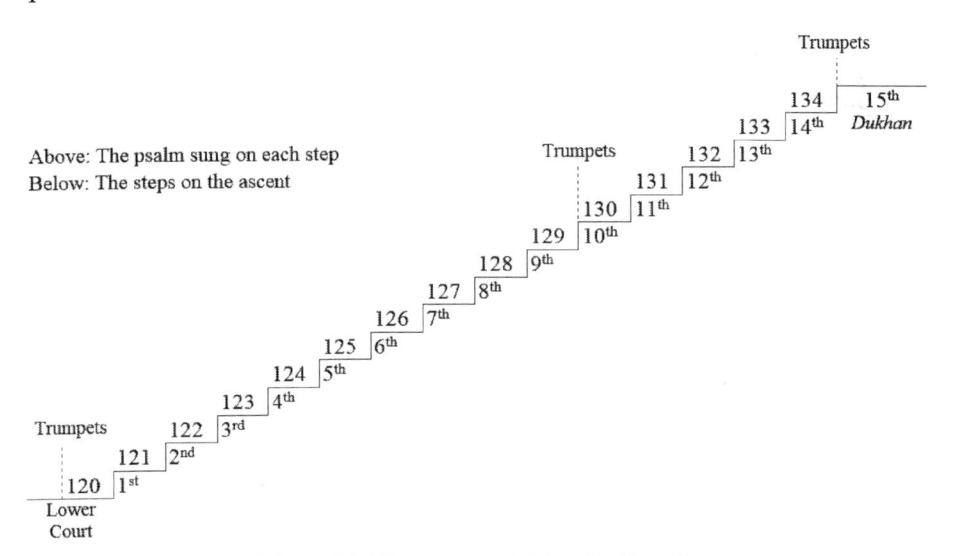

Figure 22. The Ascents in Herod's Temple

Such an upward progression agrees with internal evidence in the Songs of Ascents. The first Song, Psalm 120, represents the faraway land from which the pilgrim ascends to the holy house, before the outset of the journey. We would therefore expect it to be sung at the point of departure, the lower court, before they begin their ascent. As for Psalm 134, which the Tosefta says was sung antiphonally between Levites and *kohanim*, this could only have been sung within sight of the *kohanim* ministering in the temple *ulam* or portico, from where the *Birkat kohanim* was pronounced.

Other details fit too. Psalm 125, sung a third of the way up the steps, tells of the mountains surrounding Jerusalem. It would be at this point on the upward ascent that the Mount of Olives, under the moonlight, would be visible to the cantor looking over the orchestra to the temple's low eastern wall. Psalm 130's words about waiting for the LORD *more than watchmen for the morning* also suggest a view to the east, waiting for the first light over the Mount of Olives. Likewise, Psalm 130 was sung on the tenth step, after the sounding of the trumpets to signify the second letter of the name of Yah and the Day of Atonement. And we find that Psalm 130 pronounces the name of Yah and that its central theme is atonement.

FROM HEROD'S TEMPLE TO SOLOMON'S

If this is how the Songs of Ascents were sung during the Feast of Sukkot in the last decades of Herod's temple, how far does it reflect the rites of Solomon's temple, a thousand years before, with its more modest courts and walls? As we have seen, several architectural details of the first and second temples were the same. There was the same low eastern wall and the same Levite chambers opening onto the lower court.[15] But many other architectural details were carried from the first temple into the second.

First, Solomon's temple, like Herod's, had fifteen steps leading to the upper court. For Ezekiel's visionary new temple, based on Solomon's temple where Ezekiel had ministered, has fifteen steps on the east-west ascent to the court. But there is one important difference between Ezekiel's temple and Herod's: in Herod's temple the fifteen steps are continuous; in Ezekiel's temple they are arranged in two flights.[16] After ascending the first seven steps, the singers reached, with the eighth step, an intermediary gate with its own platform or semi-court. Ezekiel's arrangement is likely to have been the arrangement found in Solomon's temple. And such an arrangment agrees well with the prominence of Psalm 127 as the mid-point of the Songs of Ascents.

---

[15] See chapters 6 and 9.
[16] Ezek. 40.6, 22, 32–34.

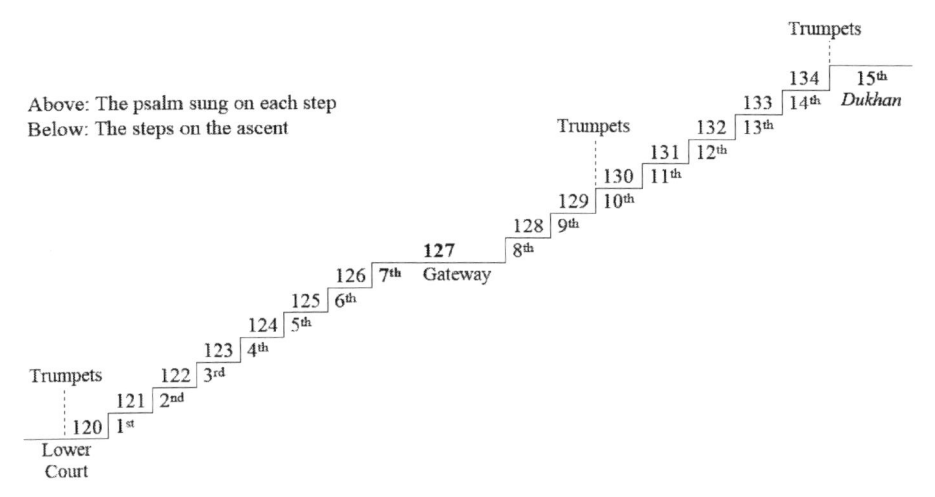

```
                                                    Trumpets
                                                       ⋮
                                              134 | 15th
Above: The psalm sung on each step       133 | 14th   Dukhan
Below: The steps on the ascent    Trumpets   132 | 13th
                                      ⋮   131 | 12th
                                   130 | 11th
                                129 | 10th
                             128 | 9th
                         127   8th
                     126 | 7th   Gateway
                 125 | 6th
              124 | 5th
           123 | 4th
Trumpets  122 | 3rd
    ⋮   121 | 2nd
    120 | 1st
Lower
Court
```

Figure 23. The Ascents in Solomon's Temple

Second, as we saw in chapter three, the 'Songs of Ascents' heading shows that these Songs were written for singing on steps. The heading was not an afterthought: it was part of the conception of the fifteen songs, as the step parallelism and pilgrimage imagery confirm. The link between the fifteen steps and the fifteen 'Songs of the Steps' – beginning far from the temple, journeying toward it, and culminating with a greeting to the *kohen* in the temple portico – was built into the liturgy from the first.

Finally, ancient Israel was conservative in its traditions of worship. The Levites in Herod's temple sang the same psalms their ancestors sang a thousand years before. The *kohanim* wore the same vestments and made the same sacrifices commanded by Moses. The liturgies, ablutions, and every other aspect of temple life, were prescribed in detail, and no changes were permitted.[17] The Mishnah was compiled specifically to preserve these traditions after the temple's destruction. The Mishnah and Talmud would inevitably have remarked on it if the ritual described in Mishnah *Sukkah* had been a recent innovation.

Therefore the rite which accompanied the Songs of Ascents in Herod's time was essentially the same as that in Solomon's time. At the dedication of the temple at dawn on the Feast of Sukkot 959 BC, the Levites ascended the fifteen steps singing the Songs of Ascents, just as they did in Herod's temple a thousand years later. The difference was what happened at the top of the steps. It was not simply the *nisukh ha-mayim* ritual – though that may well have taken place along with Solomon's prayer for rain – but rather Solomon's prayer of dedication and the entry of the ark into the new temple.

---

[17] As Alexander Jannaeus found, to his cost (Josephus, *Ant.* XIII.xiii.5; B. *Suk.* 48b).

11

Temple Song, Where Are You Now?

Once the psalms were songs for singing. But now their ancient melodies are gone. Instead, we read them as poems. Or we sing them to other tunes: plainsong, chant, metrical hymns, or ballads. But what happened to the ancient melodies? Where did they go? Have they really disappeared? Or what traces have they left so we can find them?

WHERE DID THE TEMPLE PSALMODY GO?

As we saw in chapter nine, the temple directors of music led their singers by two-handed cheironomy, indicating by different signs the notes that made up the song. Such cheironomy was standard musical practice throughout the ancient world, from Mesopotamia to Egypt, from 3,000 BC down to Roman times.

Figure 24. Egyptian cheironomers and musicians (2700 BC).
Bas-relief **from the tomb of Nencheftkai.**

It was inevitable that such cheironomers would wish to write down the music they sang, in order to teach it, transmit it, and preserve it from ever-threatening corruption. This they did by annotating the sung text with symbols derived from their cheironomical gestures. Such symbols became the earliest form of music notation.[1] Such symbols existed in Mesopotamia 4,000 years ago and are found in Levantine Ugarit half a millennium later.[2]

Now, in ancient times, all the Hebrew scriptures were sung. Therefore, when Moses was instructed to *write down this song*, or when the Talmud tells how Solomon included cantillation marks in his writings,[3] there is every possibility that they did indeed record musical symbols along with the text, just as Greek dramatists did in the mid-first millennium BC. Indeed, just as the ancient peoples of the Mediterranean shared certain melodies, so there is evidence that by Greek times they employed a common set of cheironomical symbols.[4] There are, for instance, resemblances between the cheironomical symbols found in second-century-BC Dead Sea Scrolls texts and the neumes of Byzantine *kontakia*.[5]

The temple directors of music, of all people, would have been well-versed in these forms of musical notation. It would have been due to some form of cheironomical notation that the Levites were able, five and a half centuries after David, and after the Babylonian destruction and exile, to direct and sing according to 'the hands of David' (Ezra 3.10). And it would have been around this time, when they gathered the scriptures and stored them in the rebuilt temple library, that scriptural texts were compiled, annotated with cheironomical symbols and signs indicating the vowels to accompany the consonants of the Hebrew text.[6] This was the view of the Talmudic sages.

> What is meant by the text, And they read in the book, in the law of God, with an interpretation and they gave the sense, and caused them to understand the reading? [Neh. 8.8] And they read in the book, in the law of God: this indicates the text; with an interpretation: this indicates the targum; and they gave the sense: this indicates the verse divisions; and caused them to understand the reading: this indicates [the singing of] the cantillational symbols. (B. Meg. 3a)

The same view is found in medieval times as well:

> Ezra put into written form everything relating to the vowels and cantillational accents, just as he did for the targum, the prayers, and the benedictions. Of course, we speak only of the forms and the names of the vowels and the accents;

---

[1] The origin of musical notation from cheironomy is widely recognized: Baer & Strack 1879: 17; Fleischer 1895: 29–34, 92; Sendrey 1969: 236, 434, 477, 569 n. 275; Flender 1992: 135; Haïk-Vantoura 1991: 81–91; Gerson-Kiwi & Hiley 2001: 556–57.
[2] Kilmer 1971: 131–49; Kilmer, Crocker, Brown 1976.
[3] Deut. 31.19–22; B. *Erub.* 21b.
[4] In the 5th century BC, Herodotus, *History* II.68–70, tells of a melody, *Linos*, sung in Egypt, Phoenicia, Cyprus, and Greece.
[5] Werner 1957: 21–37, on 1QIsa and 1QpHab.
[6] 2 Macc. 2.13; 4 Ezra 14.37-48; B. *Meg.* 4a.

the [actual] vocalization and accentuation were orally taught and were given to Moses on Sinai.[7]

In temple times, master copies of the biblical scrolls were kept in the temple and employed by the temple's official correctors to verify the accuracy of copies made for synagogue use.[8] In the same way, accented scrolls would also have been kept, showing the vowels and cantillational symbols. One imagines that the chief Levites would have had regular recourse to them, and might have kept copies in the Levite chambers beside the Song Gate. Such accented scrolls remained in the temple until the time of the Roman incursion, when they would have been hidden, some beneath the temple, others in the dry caves of the Judean desert. In this way, it was hoped that they would be preserved for future generations after the cataclysm had passed.

The Roman destruction touched different Israelite groups in different ways. The Nazarene community, forewarned by prophecy, left Jerusalem during the Roman withdrawal in the winter of AD 66–67, and sought refuge in Pella, where they escaped the siege and its aftermath.[9] With a commission to evangelize a world to whom Israel's temple rites meant nothing, the early church did not see the preservation of the temple song as its prime concern. Nevertheless, its first cantors would have been temple-trained Levites, leading congregations who sang in response. Temple-style responsary singing remained the Church's pattern throughout the first millennium. Chrysostom wrote, 'The cantor sings alone, and then all respond, the sound issuing as if from one mouth.'[10] Reminiscences of the temple melodies passed into the worship of the church, as far away as Rome, and ultimately into the church's plainsong, as it was systematized by Ambrose and Gregory the Great.[11] As Flender says, the Levites' song 'was continued more in the hymns of the oriental Christian churches than in the synagogue.'[12]

Other survivors of Jerusalem's fall were fewer. The *kohanim* who came to the temple for the fateful Passover of AD 67 perished in large number.[13] The Levites are likely to have fared similarly. Among the leaders of the Pharisees, only Yoḥanan ben Zakkai, who had long foreseen the city's destruction,

---

[7] From *Maḥberet ha-Tijan* (Derenbourg 1870: 467; my trans.), a rabbanite version of *Horayat ha-qore*, a Hebrew translation of the Arabic *Hidāyat al-qāri* (Guide to the Reader) by the 11th-century Karaite, Abu al-Faraj Harun of Jerusalem (Eldar, 1992: 67–73; 1994: 40-43).

[8] B. *Ket.* 106a; Y. *Shek.* 4.2; Y. *Sanh.* 2.6. The proof-readers were paid from temple funds lest financial dependence on those who brought copies for verification sway their judgment (Rashi on B. *Ket.* 106a).

[9] Eusebius, *Hist.* 3.5.3; cf. 3.5.4, citing Josephus (cf. *War* II.xx.1; cf. IV.vi.1; IV.vii.3). For the historicity of Eusebius' account, cf. Houwelingen 2003: 181–200.

[10] Chrysostom, *In I Corinthios*, Hom. XXXVI, 5–6 (*PG* LXI, 313–15).

[11] Werner 1959; see the following chapter.

[12] Flender 1992: 52; cf. Acts 4.36; 6.7.

[13] *War* VI.vi.1.

survived.[14] Smuggled through the siege in a coffin, he gathered a community in Yavneh in Galilee, which functioned as a continuation of the Sanhedrin. There Ben Zakkai and his disciples began to collect what they thought essential for the preservation of Israel's faith. First, they gathered and collated the Hebrew scriptures, preserving them from almost-certain destruction. Then they collected the traditions concerning the temple service and its regulations, which were codified, in the second century, in the Mishnah and Tosefta. To these were added later the collected teachings of the rabbis, from Hillel and Shammai on, which, in time, were codified around the Mishnah, to become the two Talmuds. And so Rabbinic Judaism was born.

One might have expected that the founders of Judaism would have tried to preserve the temple song. But, even before the destruction, some cantors were reluctant to pass on their art lest it should fall to the service of idolatry.

> Hygros ben Levi was an expert in song, but he did not want to teach it to anyone. They asked, Why? He answered, In my father's house they know that the temple will be destroyed and they do not want to teach lest their songs be sung to idols.[15]

And, after the destruction, there would have been few Levite musicians to pass on their art. Nevertheless, there are tantalizing remnants which suggest that the Jews of the early first millennium did try and preserve the temple song. The Talmud speaks of cheironomically-led chanting of the scriptures following written accents in the second century.[16] Bible manuscripts from the sixth to ninth centuries contain simple cantillational systems with a handful of symbols. There are two such systems, the Babylonian and Palestinian, but both are fragmentary, not only in survival, but in conception. Their cantillation symbols are rudimentary and no two texts are consistent in their use of them. It appears that, having lost the Levites' cheironomical notation, the rabbis were devising their own systems.

Yet, however crude the notation, the temple melodies were still orally transmitted in some form, and with some form of cheironomy, in the first millennium. The Babylonian Jews, the largest Jewish community in the world, particularly prided themselves on preserving the temple song. In the early tenth century, the historian Nathan ben Isaac ha-Kohen tells of responsorial psalm singing at the installation of the Exilarch, the king of the Jewish community in Babylon. On a Sabbath morning, the whole community gathered together.

---

[14] B. *Yoma* 39b: 'Forty years before the destruction of the temple...the doors of the *heikhal* (the temple) opened of their own accord, until Rabbi Yoḥanan ben Zakkai rebuked them. He said: 'O Heikhal, Heikhal, why do you foretell your destruction? I know full well that you are destined to be destroyed, for Zechariah ben Iddo has already prophesied concerning you, *Open your doors, O Lebanon, that the fire may devour your cedars* (Zech. 11.1).'

[15] T. *Yoma* 2.5. B. *Yoma* 38a also records Hygros' refusal to teach.

[16] B. *Ber.* 62a, where cantillation of the scroll (*ta'amey torah*) is shown with the right hand.

And when he said *A psalm for the Sabbath Day,* they replied, *It is good to give thanks to the LORD* [Ps. 92.1]. And all the people chanted the *pesûqey de-zimrah* [the introductory psalms of the morning service] until they had completed them. And [then] the cantor stood up and opened with *Nishmat kol ḥai*, and the young men responded after him.[17]

Likewise, Rashi speaks of cheironomy among cantors from the Holy Land in the eleventh century.[18] And yet, soon after this time, the temple melodies disappeared. And to discover why, we need to bring yet another Israelite sect into the picture.

The group that assembled in Yavneh under Ben Zakkai and his successors in the first century were not Jews in the modern sense: they had no Talmud. They would have diverged, in particular, on the Pharisaic doctrine of the 'oral law', which recognized the legal rulings of the Sanhedrin as equal to the law of Moses. This had been a divisive issue since the high priesthood of John Hyrcanus in the mid-second century BC. It was rejected flatly by the priestly Sadducees, the Essenes, and the Nazarenes.[19] After the fall of Jerusalem, oral-law and non-oral-law Jews lived in one community. But as the views of the oral-law party hardened into orthodoxy and were promulgated in the Talmud, the non-oral-law Jews became a separate community, eventually taking the name Kara'im, that is, 'Scripturalists'.

Figure 25. Medieval Jewish cheironomer and singers with Psalm 149 (Parma Psalter, 1280). Their music part in neumes, *Eyn kamokha ba-elim adonai* (Exod. 15.11; Ps. 86.8), precedes synagogue chanting of the psalms to this day.

THE MASORETES AND THEIR WORK

The Kara'im or Karaites rejected the Mishnah and Talmud and, as their name suggests, were devoted to the Scriptures. In the last centuries of the first

---

[17] Nathan ben Isaac ha-Bavli, *Aḥbar Baghdad* in Neubauer 1895: 83.
[18] Rashi on *Ber.* 62a.
[19] *Ant.* XIII.x.6.

millennium, there arose among them biblical scholars known as the Masoretes, from Hebrew *Ba'ale ha-Masorah* or 'Masters of the Transmission', who lived in Tiberias in Galilee.[20] Beginning with the Codex Orientales in the early ninth century, the Masoretes began to produce Bible texts unlike anything known at the time, texts in which the Hebrew letters were surrounded by an astonishingly sophisticated system of symbols.[21]

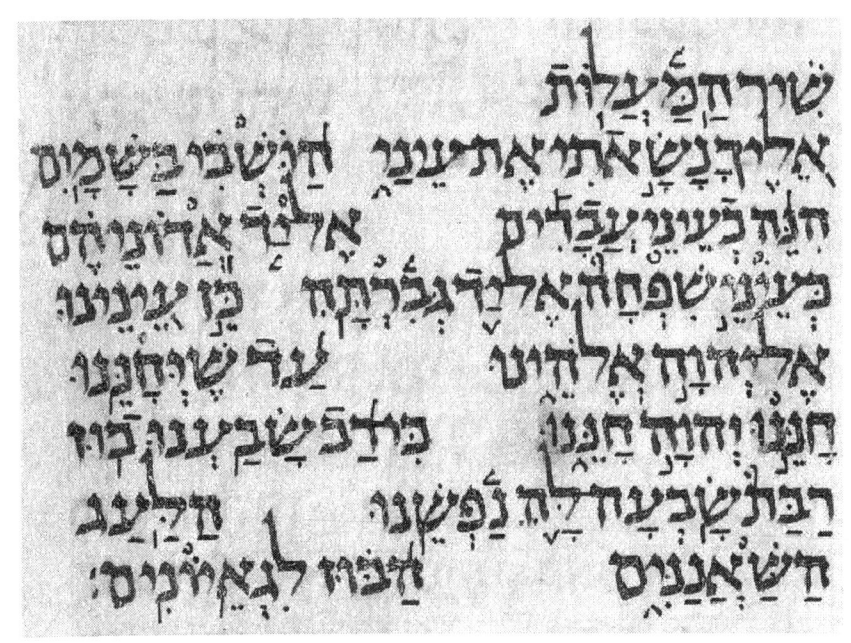

Figure 26. Aleppo Codex text of Psalm 123.

There were ten signs indicating vowels and inflections of the Hebrew consonants.[22] Here are these *nekudot* or vowel symbols for the *Shir ha-ma'alot* (Song of Ascents) heading.

שִׁיר הַמַּעֲלוֹת

---

[20] Graetz, 1853–70: III.206, first proposed that the Masoretes were Karaites, arguing that the lack of reference to the Talmud in their work is unthinkable in medieval Rabbanite literature. Kahle too regarded 'the Karaite affinities of the Ben Asher Masoretes' as 'decisive' (1959: 82). Yet Dotan (1957) always insisted that Ben Asher was a Rabbanite, and in some quarters the debate rumbles on. I am persuaded by the arguments of Graetz and Kahle, and by the facts that (1) the Aleppo Codex was delivered to the Jerusalem Karaites on Ben Asher's death, and that (2) the first person after Ben Asher to explain the *te'amim* was a Karaite, Abu al-Faraj Harun of Jerusalem.

[21] British Museum Codex Or. 4445; Ginsburg (1897: 469) dates it to c. 820–850 CE.

[22] Permitting the omission of vocalic *aleph*, *vav*, and *yodh*, the *nekudot* allowed an orthography more ancient than even the Dead Sea texts of 1,000 years before.

In addition, there were cantillational symbols or *te'amim* for singing the text. Here is the *Shir ha-ma'alot* heading with the *te'amim*.

שִׁיר הַמַּעֲלוֹת

And in these Masoretic codices both sets of signs unite to produce an accented text of a complexity and precision never seen before.

שִׁיר הַֽמַּעֲלוֹת

Moreover, unlike the probative attempts of the Babylonian and Palestinian accent systems, and unlike the 1,000 year evolution of western musical notation from neumes, the Masoretic system appeared fully-formed, without precursor, like a rabbit from a hat, and was employed with remarkable consistency throughout the Masoretic manuscripts.[23]

Now, the cantillation symbols or *te'amim* are commonly understood as nineteen in number.[24]

I ⌒ ↳ ⌐ ⌐ ⟨ ⌐ ⌐ ⌐ ⌐ ⌐ : I: ♦ ⌐ ⌐ ⌐ ⌐ ⌐

Figure 27. The Masoretic *te'amim*

Most are employed throughout the Bible, though a few are limited to the prosodic books, and a few others to the poetic books. Some are used in combination, making sign-pairs, while others are used both above and below the text. In this way, they make up a total of some twenty-six different significations.

Where did this system come from? The Masoretes, who were better placed to know than most, had an answer. The ninth-century master, Mosheh ben Asher, relates, in his 'Song of the Vine', kept with his Codex of the Prophets in the Ben Ezra Synagogue in Cairo, that they received the accents from a group called the Elders of Bathyra:

> The vine of God [was] the tribes of Jacob...The branches of the vine are the prophets...The perfect ones of the vine are the Elders of Bathyra, the heirs of the prophets, who possess knowledge of understanding. Deep waters that utter mysteries; their heart brings forth wisdom like a flowing brook. As delights they have established the *te'amim* of the Scripture [*hitqinu ta'ame miqra*], which give sense [to the Scripture] and interprets its word... Afflictions

---

[23] That is, the Codex Orientales (820–845), Codex Cairensis (895), Aleppo Codex (c. 920–30), Damascus Pentateuch (Codex Sassoon 507) (10th century), and Leningrad Codex (c. 1008).

[24] But see the discussion on *etnaḥ hafukh*, in chapter 12.

surrounded them from the kings of the Greeks, and they exiled them and dispersed them to No [Egypt] and its provinces.[25]

The elders or 'sons' of Bathyra were an Israelite priestly clan of temple times. They lived, both in Babylon and in the Holy Land, in their own clan towns called Bathyra.[26] Their origins are unknown, although their afflictions at the hands of the Greeks, referred to by Ben Asher, suggests they were a political force before Judah Maccabee (r. 166-160 BC). The Talmud relates that they led the Sanhedrin in the first century BC, but were ousted from leadership by Hillel, to whom they surrendered the presidency.[27] The tale is a strange one. The sons of Bathyra were apparently so ignorant that they did not know the regulations for a Passover falling on the Sabbath. One assumes that the Talmud, written by Hillel's disciples, is telling only part of the story. More likely, since the sons of Bathyra were Sadducees, the dispute hinged on their opposition to calendrical innovations appearing in the name of Pharisaic Hillel's oral law.[28] Thanks to Hillel, the Elders of Bathyra lost the presidency of the Sanhedrin, yet their family remained influential well into the Mishnaic period, especially in Babylon.[29]

Paul Kahle, who studied Ben Asher's 'Song of the Vine' in his Cairo Geniza research, sums up its import as follows:

> Moses b. Asher traced the chain of Karaite tradition to the Elders of Bathyra, the spiritual ancestors of Karaism who had inherited the prophetic traditions and transmitted them to the Karaites.[30]

Therefore, if Mosheh ben Asher's testimony about his own work is accepted, then Bible texts, annotated with the vocalic and cantillational symbols of the temple, were transmitted from the Elders of Bathyra to the Karaites. How this happened is not clear. It may have taken place by manual transmission over hundreds of years. Kahle also suggests that the cache of scrolls discovered near Jericho in AD 800, which, according to the Nestorian Patriarch Timotheus I, caused a great stir among Jerusalem's large Karaite community, were these Bathyrean texts complete with accents.[31] But, one way or another, accented texts came into the hands of the Masoretes, who recognized them as the work

---

[25] Kahle 1959: 84–5, where the Hebrew text will also be found.
[26] *Ant.* XVII, ii, 2; Mantel 1961: 19, 109–115.
[27] B. *Pes.* 66a; Y. *Pes.* 6.1 (33a).
[28] For the calendrical innovations, see Appendix III.
[29] B. *Pes.* 3b; B. *Sanh.* 32b; B. *RH* 29b; B. *Git.* 59a.
[30] Kahle 1959: 85–86.
[31] Kahle: 'The well-known letter of the Nestorian Patriarch Timotheus deals with a great find of Hebrew Manuscripts made shortly before A.D. 800 in a cave not far from Jericho. We hear that the Jews from Jerusalem who had been informed collected the manuscripts and studied them. The Jews chiefly interested in these manuscripts seem to have been Karaites, and we have to assume that the Karaites were considerably influenced by these manuscripts.' (1953: 82; 1959: 16.)

of their spiritual fathers. They combined the accents with the best scribal practices of their own day, and began to reproduce them in manuscript codices from the early ninth century on.[32]

The Rabbanite community did not welcome this initiative. The appearance of the Codex Orientales, sometime between 820 and 850, elicited a rebuke from the head of the Babylonian Rabbanites, Mar Natronai ben Ḥilai, Gaon of Sura academy from 853 to 861. He wrote:

> We are forbidden deliberately to add [to the text] anything at all for fear of transgressing the Law, *You shall not add anything to it* [Deut. 12.32]. This is why we do not vocalize the scrolls of Torah. Neither may we add the cantillation signs, even though these latter signs were revealed at Sinai.[33]

The following century, Sa'adya ben Yosef al-Fayumi became Gaon of Sura. Sa'adya had opposed Karaism from his youth in Egypt, and his appointment as Gaon in 927 coincided with the zenith of Karaite influence in the Holy Land. In the same decade, Aharon ben Mosheh ben Asher, the greatest of the Masoretes, completed his codex of the entire Bible, now known as the Aleppo Codex. Sa'adya, in a desperate bid to contain Karaite audacity, launched a three-pronged counter-attack. He castigated the Masorete in his *Book of Refutation against Ben Asher*, he unleashed persecution on the Karaites in Babylon, and, with the full weight of his authority as Gaon, he imposed a moratorium on chanting the Scriptures throughout the Rabbanite world.[34] It was not fitting, he pronounced, for the Psalms to be sung with instruments anywhere other than in the temple. Until the temple might be rebuilt, the Psalms were only for meditation, to be declaimed on a single tone without instrumental accompaniment.[35]

Sa'adya's ban was not received with joy. The preservation of some form of the temple melodies had always been a matter of pride to Jewish communities, especially in Babylon. And, in spite of Sa'adya's opposition, the practice seems to have continued for a time under the protection of the Exilarch.[36] The Bohemian rabbi, Petaḥiah of Regensburg, who visited Baghdad in the following century, observed psalm-singing similar to that described by Nathan a century before.

---

[32] Cf. Sanders 2014: 1–22, who concludes that the consonantal text underlying the Aleppo Codex was the fragmentary Ashkar-Gilson MS, a high-quality MS from the 7th or 8th century. Its consonantal text of the Song of the Sea is identical in orthography to the Aleppo text, as attested in Rambam's description. (The Aleppo text of the Song of the Sea was lost in 1947.)

[33] Cited by Weil 1963: 332.

[34] Sa'adya's *Book of Refutation [Kitab al Radd ala Ben Asher]* is known only by its title; the text is lost. While views on the severity of Sa'adya's persecution of the Karaites vary, the Karaites remember it as a time of bloodshed.

[35] Sa'adya, Commentary on Ps. 33.

[36] Avenary (1968: 154) explains this contradictory state of affairs with the remark that custom (*minhag*) has precedence over rabbinic law (*halakhah*), but one suspects it had more to do with the balance of power between the Exilarch and the Gaon.

Then a choir of boys assembled under the platform: boys who had been chosen from the elite of the community, well-trained boys with beautiful voices, experts in the melodies, proficient in all matters of the prayers. ...The ḥazzan began the prayers at *barukh she'amar*, and the boys responded antiphonally to each line.[37]

But the Gaon's ruling was *halakhah* and could not be ignored forever. Eventually, even the Babylonians capitulated. The Spanish rabbi, Benjamin of Tudela, who travelled in the Orient from 1160–73, tells in his diary of Eleazar ben Zemaḥ, master of one of the ten Hebrew colleges in Baghdad of that time:

> [He is] a man who knows the melodies that were sung in the temple of Jerusalem during the time of its existence. His lineage goes back to Samuel the prophet, the Korahite. He [Eleazar] and his brother know how to chant the melodies as did the singers at the time of the holy temple when the temple was standing.[38]

But the implication is that Eleazar and his brother were the last men in Babylon who possessed this knowledge. By the 12th century, it seems, the old melodies were no longer sung in the Babylonian synagogues, and were soon forgotten.

THE DISSEMINATION OF THE MASORETIC TEXT

After Aharon ben Asher's death, his Codex was endowed to the Karaite community in Jerusalem by a wealthy Karaite, Israel b. Simḥa b. Sa'adya b. Efraim of Basra.[39] In Jerusalem it was kept as a sacred treasure, a master copy to determine the Jewish world's enquiries regarding the sacred text, much as the scrolls of the temple library had done a millennium before. They appended to the back of the manuscript a dedication that read:

> This is the complete codex of the twenty-four books copied by the master and teacher Shlomo ben Buya'a, the ready scribe, may the spirit of God give him rest, and it was vocalized and given a full Masorah by the great scholar and wise sage, the master of scribes, father of sages, and chief of scholars, quick of deed, and understanding in action, unique in his generation, the master rabbi Aharon the son of the master Asher, may his soul be bound up in the bundle of life together with the prophets, saints, and pious men.

But soon after the Codex arrived in Jerusalem, the brief Karaite flowering in the Holy Land was cut short. In the tumult of the eleventh century, most of their community perished. The Codex was seized, either by the Seljuks in 1071 or by the Franks in 1099, and taken from Jerusalem to Egypt, where the Jews

---

[37] Grünhut 1905: 24–5.
[38] Adler 1907: 39 (ET), 39, §60 (Hebrew).
[39] Kahle 1947: 58–59.

of Fustat, to their eternal credit, purchased it at great cost. There, in the late twelfth century, it was consulted by Maimonides, who proclaimed it to be the most trusted of all Bible texts.[40] From Cairo, it made its way to Aleppo in the fourteenth century, by which time manuscript copies of portions of the Masoretic codices were circulating.[41] Finally, the Masoretic symbols were included in the first ever printed Hebrew Bible, published by the Soncino Press in 1488. Through the Soncino Bible and its successors, the Masoretic text, punctillated with vocalic and cantillational symbols, was gradually disseminated throughout the Jewish and Christian worlds.

Meanwhile, in far-flung Jewish communities, Yemen, Bukhara, Kurdistan, and even Egypt, where Sa'adya's writ did not run as large as in Babylon, cantors still sang their own ancient melodies which, after more than one and a half millennia of oral transmission in foreign lands, had become estranged from their ancient prototypes. When these communities received copies of the punctillated text, sixteen, seventeen or more centuries after the temple's fall, each cantor and community tried in its own way to reconcile the newly-received symbols with the tradition of cantillation they had preserved. They had learned to sing the Torah and Prophets to melodies which repeated for every verse. To these underlying melodies, the cantors now added vocal inflections for each of the *te'amim*. The cantillation of the prosodic books therefore became doubly divergent: different underlying melodies of different communities were inflected according to different understandings of the *te'amim*. As for the Psalms, the pioneering accentologist, William Wickes, could write in 1881, that 'the Jews themselves allow that the musical value of the accents of the three poetical books is altogether lost.'[42] In the twentieth century, Dotan agreed.

> ...the reading tradition for the books of Psalms, Proverbs and Job was not preserved by various Jewish communities, and the system of the signs – and even more so, the rules behind them – were not understood by the scribes and printers, and lacked all meaning for the reader.[43]

---

[40] *Mishneh Torah*, Hilkhot Sefer Torah 8.4. In 1973, Cassuto wrote that Maimonides did not work from Ben Asher's codex. But Ofer 2002a: 37–38, explains that Cassuto's view was based on an altered text of *Mishneh Torah*.

[41] See, for instance, the Parma Psalter of 1280 (MS Parm. 1870; *Cod. De Rossi* 510) in the Palatine Library, Parma, Italy; or the Rothschild Miscellany (Rothschild MS 24) of 1479 in the Israel Museum, Jerusalem. Pages are visible in Gillingham 2013b: pls 1 & 14, and at www.facsimile-editions.com.

[42] Wickes 1881: 2; so too Delitzsch 1887: 36.

[43] Dotan 1972: 1458; cf. likewise Herzog (1972: 1332): 'Although the psalms are furnished with accents in the masoretic texts, the question, whether they were ever, or still are, sung according to the accents is still moot.'

THE ALEPPO CODEX TODAY

Ben Asher's great Codex rested in Aleppo for some six hundred years. Then, in December 1947, at the UN partition of Palestine, the Aleppo synagogue was ransacked in anti-Jewish riots. The Codex was smuggled out of Syria to Israel, to President Itzhak Ben-Zvi. However, on its return to Jerusalem, after ten centuries of exile, some forty percent of the priceless manuscript, including most of the Pentateuch, was found to be missing.[44] The remainder of the Codex was carefully restored. A photographic facsimile was published in 1976. Then the entire Codex was made available online in 2004. Today that treasure, which was formerly most concealed, can now be seen, freed from its sequestration of centuries, by all eyes.

In perfection, the Codex stands head and shoulders above all other Masoretic texts. Professor Israel Yeivin stated,

> This manuscript is vocalized and accentuated in the most exact fashion, preserving intact the early tradition of accentuation, which was lost in later manuscripts. In sum, with regard to these features, it is the most exact of all the Tiberian Bible manuscripts.[45]

Rabbi Mordechai Breuer wrote:

> Anyone who examines the Aleppo Codex carefully, both along general lines and in detail, cannot help but be amazed by the almost superhuman ability of the Masorete who produced such perfect work.[46]

Professor Menachem Cohen of Bar Ilan University simply says it is 'flawless, like the work of an angel'. Breuer and Cohen, in their respective Jerusalem Crown (*Keter Yerushalayim*) and *Bar Ilan Keter* Bibles have largely restored the missing portions of the Codex with help from notes and descriptions from medieval times until the mid-twentieth century. The results are the most accurate Masoretic texts ever published, clarifying the many errors that crept into the punctillation of earlier printed Masoretic texts.[47]

---

[44] The Ben-Zvi Institute state that the Codex was sent to the State of Israel on the instructions of the Aleppo community leaders, and that the missing portions were lost during the looting of the Aleppo synagogue. But the Aleppo rabbis testified that they sent it to the Aleppo community in Jerusalem, and that the Codex was illegally seized by Ben-Zvi for the State of Israel. Current legal appeals maintain that the Codex was complete on its arrival in Israel, and the missing portions disappeared when it was in the custody of the Ben-Zvi Institute. See Friedman 2012, and www.tabletmag.com/jewish-arts-and-culture/books/176903/aleppo-codex (2014).

[45] Yeivin 1968, p. 10.

[46] Breuer 1996, p. 4; cited by Ofer 2002a, p. 11.

[47] Cohen's *Bar Ilan Keter* is the most faithful reproduction of the Aleppo text. Breuer, in the Jerusalem Crown, took the editorial decision to include what he regarded as 'missing' *te'amim* which he supplied from other Masoretic codices.

ANTIQUITY OF THE MASORETIC PUNCTILLATION

The Masoretes maintained that the punctillation of their codices derived from temple times. Their view was unquestioned until, six centuries later, the Hebrew humanist Elias Levita argued that they arose after the codification of the Talmud, in the second half of the first millennium of our era.

> Having now reached the place in which I, at the beginning of this Introduction, promised to state my own opinion about the *nekkudot v'ha-te'amim* [vocalic and cantillational signs], I shall first do battle against those who say that they were given on Sinai, and then state who invented them, and when they were originated and affixed to the letters. But if anyone should prove to me, by clear evidence, that my opinion is opposed to that of our rabbis of blessed memory, or is contrary to the genuine Kabbalah of the Zohar, I will readily give in to him, and declare my opinion as void. Up to this time, however, I have neither found, nor seen, nor heard, any evidence, nor anything approaching it, that is worthy to be relied upon, that the *nekkudot v'ha-te'amim* were given upon Sinai... Now this is my opinion upon this subject. The *nekkudot v'ha-te'amim* did not exist either before Ezra or in the time of Ezra, or after Ezra until the close of the Talmud.[48]

Levita's views generated much opposition, both Jewish and Christian.[49] But the idea that the Masoretes invented the accent system stuck. In the nineteenth century, Wickes assumed as much without discussion, as most have done since.[50] Indeed, most modern writers seem unaware that any other origin was ever proposed. The Masoretic system is now widely assumed to be the apogee of a long period of development which included the Palestinian and Babylonian accent systems. Yet there are substantial difficulties with this view. And, while it may seem sensational that the temple Levites' musical notation suddenly came to light in the ninth century after eight centuries of obscurity, it should not on that account be dismissed.[51] Therefore, since the value of the *te'amim* is inextricably linked to their origin, we must briefly review the evidence for their origins.

First, as stated above, Mosheh ben Asher testified in his 'Song of the Vine' that the Tiberian Masoretes received the accents from the temple-period priestly house of Bathyra. This is a remarkable testimony. Here is the first-known Masorete, the patriarch of their foremost family, testifying that they received the punctillation from a temple-period source, and his testimony is widely ignored. Yet it adequately explains the sudden appearance of the Masoretes' sophisticated system, which proponents of a late date for the accents are at a loss to explain. As Dotan remarks, 'The Tiberian system is a

---

[48] From the introduction to the third section of Levita 1538, tr. Ginsburg 1861: 121.
[49] Dei Rossi 1573–75, §59; Buxtorf 1620; Ledebuhr 1647; Buxtorf 1648; Florinus 1667.
[50] Wickes 1881: 1–2; cf. Tov 2009: 12.
[51] Cf. also Haïk-Vantoura 1991 and Weil 1996: 307–18.

highly perfected system, but no previous stages of its graphemic development are known to us.'[52]

Second, Mosheh ben Asher's testimony explains the Masoretes' inability to elucidate their own system. If it were their own work, they should have been able to explain it satisfactorily. But Aharon ben Mosheh's own commentary, *Diqduqe ha-te'amim* (Fine points of the *te'amim*) is, as Graetz says, 'for the most part incomprehensible'.[53] While it speaks of hand-signs for certain symbols, or of a rising and falling voice, it lacks any systematic clarification as to how the signs should be sung.[54] Its central concern is the notation and pronunciation of the *sh^{e}va* vowel.

Third, if the Masoretes had invented this entire new gamut of symbols and added it to the Bible text, they would have done so in direct defiance of their own epithet, 'Masters of the Transmission', and of their own guiding philosophy of 'hiding nothing and adding nothing to what was received'. For 'the goal of the Tiberian Masoretes was not to innovate, but to preserve the finest textual traditions that they knew.'[55]

Fourth, the Masoretes' Rabbanite contemporaries – Natronai b. Ḥilai and Saʿadya – objected to the Masoretes' work not because they thought the *te'amim* a novelty, but because they thought them ancient but sealed. They evidently held this view sincerely, for it would have been to their advantage to simply deny the antiquity of the punctillation and undermine the Masoretes' credibility.

Fifth, the rabbinic sages who preceded Natronai and Saʿadya agree with one voice that the *te'amim* originated with the writers of the Bible books and were systematized by Ezra.[56] They were aware, in their own day, that there were cheironomic gestures and cantillational symbols associated with the Torah.[57] They were aware that these things sprang from an ancient and authoritative source.[58] Yet, despite this, it appears they did not have direct access to these symbols. For they speak of the fifteen *puncta extraordinaria*,

---

[52] Dotan 1981: 87.

[53] Graetz 1853–70: III. 207. For the text of *Diqduqei*, see Baer & Strack 1879; Ginsburg 1897: 983–99; Dotan 1967.

[54] '*Zakef* is represented by a single upright finger; the *teres* (? *garshayim*) is shown by two fingers spread one against the other like a hook, joined without a separation; *tavra* (*tevir*) is shown by turning the hand over' (Dotan 1967: 154). *Mahberet Tijan* says 'Those who are skilled ascribe, apart from the vocal sound, also to each *ta'am* a hand signal. *Tsinori* (*zarka*) - a quick motion of one finger. *Segola* (*segol*) - waving three fingers in front. *Pazer* - a great waving of two fingers. *Karney-parah* – moving two fingers on high. *Talisha* – a shaking of fingers. *Zakef katon* - a finger in a downward motion.' (Derenbourg 1870: 416 [Heb.], 492 [Fr.]).

[55] Sanders 2014: 22.

[56] B. *Meg.* 3a; B. *Ned.* 37b; Y. *Meg.* 4.1; Gen. R. 36.8, ascribe the *te'amim* to Ezra, after Neh. 8.8. B. *Ned.* 37b; B. *Erub.* 21b ascribe to Moses and Solomon the cantillation of their own books.

[57] B. *Erub.* 21b; B. *Meg.* 3a.

[58] *Yesh em l'miqra* (B. *Sanh.* 4a): There is [an ancient and authoritative] source for the cantillation [of scripture].

which appeared in every synagogue scroll both then and now, as something seen, but they speak of the *te'amim* as something only known about.[59]

Sixth, the detail and consistency of the cantillation shows that those who developed it were experts in such musical notation. This could not have been the Masoretes themselves, for there is no evidence of high musical culture in their community. The obvious possessors of such skills would be the temple Levites, with their years of musical training and practice. Nowhere else in Israelite history is found such a pool of musical expertise from which such a rigorous system might emerge.

Seventh, since the cantillation, no less than the vocalization, influences the very meaning of the recited scripture, such an intervention to the text would have been tolerated only with adequate authority, an authority such as existed only in the days of the temple.

Finally, cantillation marks *per se* are of great antiquity. They appear in Mesopotamian texts of the 2nd millennium BC, in Greek poetic texts, and in the Dead Sea Scrolls. There can therefore be no objection to a temple-period origin for the *te'amim* on the basis of the history of musical notation. Indeed, one is struck by how the Masoretic *te'amim* resemble the symbols of 1,000 or more years before their own time.[60] One must ask why the Masoretes, if introducing their own cantillational notation, did not employ neumes, which were already current in the Levant of their own time. To employ the system of a millennium earlier was as anachronistic as for us to annotate a modern Bible in runes.

WHAT TRACES REMAIN?

If then the Masoretic cantillation originates from the temple itself, it follows that it is our best and purest source for reconstructing the temple song. With the musical notation of the Levites in our hand, the lost temple song is recoverable once we can decode the *te'amim*. Such a task, though challenging, should not be beyond us. To aid us in our research we now possess an online Aleppo Codex and, in the *Bar Ilan Keter*, a published Masoretic text of a purity unimaginable a generation ago. Our deciphering of the *te'amim* must draw upon synagogue cantoral tradition, church plainsong, the writings of the Masoretes, and insights gleaned from the music of other ancient cultures. The

---

[59] M. *Pes.* 9.2; B. *Men.* 87b. The *puncta extraordinaria* are the dots at Gen. 16.5; 18.9; 19.33; 33.4; 37.12; Num. 3.39; 9.10; 21.30; 29.15; Deut. 29.28; 2 Sam. 19.20; Isa. 44.9; Ezek. 41.20; 46.22; Ps. 27.13.

[60] The 3rd-century BC fragment of Euripides' *Iphigénie in Aulis* (Jourdan-Hemmerdinger 1973: 292–302) has symbols resembling Masoretic *munah* and *silluq*. Liebermann (1950: 38-46) and Talmon (1969 i-xxvii) note the similarity of Masoretic accents to Greek accents of the Alexandrian period.

evidence from these sources is substantial, complex, diverse, and sometimes contradictory. But, taken together, they hold promise of progress.

The music that will emerge will not be like modern music. It will be monodic chant: a single melodic line without the lower diaphony. To our ears, it may sound repetitive. For every verse in the Psalms ends on the same *silluq* cadence, on the tonic note of the scale; another eighty percent of verses have a halfway pause (semi-cadence) on the *etnaḥ* tone, on the fourth step of the scale; and there are only two more cadences, *oleh ve-yored* and *revia gadol* to add variety. The impression of strangeness is a characteristic one when approaching any unfamiliar musical language. We shall find this music both familiar and unfamiliar. But, clearly, it was characterized by monolithic simplicity, as we shall see in due course.

12

Restoring the Temple Song

The two great nineteenth-century scholars of biblical cantillation, William Wickes and Franz Delitzsch, noted that any tradition of interpreting the poetical accents had disappeared from the Sephardi and Ashkenazi Jews. Yet they held out hope that remnants of the temple psalmody might be preserved among the Jewish communities of the east.[1] Following their cue, the Latvian cantor, A.Z. Idelsohn (1882–1938), began his pioneering work in Jewish musicology among Yemeni Jews. He hoped to find among this conservative community some evidence for their claim that they retained the ancient psalmody. Following his work in the Yemen in the early twentieth century, he concluded that, while Yemeni psalmody differed widely even from village to village, it did share common phrase structures and recurrent melodic tropes. He hoped that future research might make it possible to wind back these divergent melodies to a common source.[2]

However, later research, both in the Yemen and, by Robert Lachmann (1892–1939), in Tunisian Djerba, did not yield the anticipated fruit. Flender's study of Idelsohn's work concluded that the cantillational symbols *silluq*, *etnaḥ*, and *oleh ve-yored* ('rising and falling') marked cadence points, the last being characterized by a rising and falling of the voice, as its name suggests. Yet this only confirmed what was already apparent. And while the Yemeni cantors retained as many as eighteen different recitation melodies for the Psalms, these were not individual melodies for particular psalms, but melodies for various seasons and feasts, where every psalm was sung to the same melody.[3] As for the Djerba melodies, Flender concluded, their style showed similarities with music of 11th-century Palestine, but their diversity made any reconstruction impossible.[4] Subsequent investigations into oral tradition have reached similar conclusions. A recent publication on the music of the

---

[1] Wickes 1881: 2; Delitzsch 1887: 36. Wickes refers in footnote to Jacob Saphir's *Eben Sappir* (1866) 55a, which records that the Yemeni Jews have separate melodies for Torah, Prophets, Ketuvim, and the poetic books.

[2] Idelsohn 1914.

[3] Flender 1992: 110–115.

[4] Flender 1992: 102, fn. 56.

Babylonian Jews, the other great hope for the lost Psalm melodies, concludes, 'The temple psalms perished with the destruction of the temple and the disappearance of its rites.'[5] Despite the beauty of the cantoral traditions, and despite the regard in which they are held, trying to reconstruct the temple psalmody from such sources is like reconstructing an unknown picture from the fragments of a mosaic.

GREGORIAN AND SYNAGOGUE PSALMODY

However, the comparative study of synagogue and church psalmody has been more fruitful. Musicologists like Eric Werner and Edith Gerson-Kiwi saw in the influx of Jews to Israel in the 1950s the opportunity to collect and record from immigrant cantors the cantillational traditions of the whole Jewish world. From their recordings they were able to compare the oral traditions of Jewish psalmody and show the similarity not only between Jewish traditions, but also between Jewish and Gregorian chant. Werner's great triumph was showing that the melody to Psalm 114, both in Ashkenazi and Sephardi tradition, is essentially the same as the Gregorian 'tone', or chant-melody, to the same text. In Gregorian tradition, this tune is called the *tonus peregrinus* or 'wandering tone'.

Example 2. Ashkenazi and Gregorian chants to Psalm 114

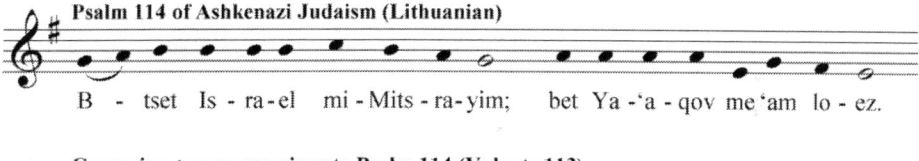

Psalm 114 of Ashkenazi Judaism (Lithuanian)

B - tset Is - ra - el mi - Mits - ra - yim; bet Ya -'a - qov me 'am lo - ez.

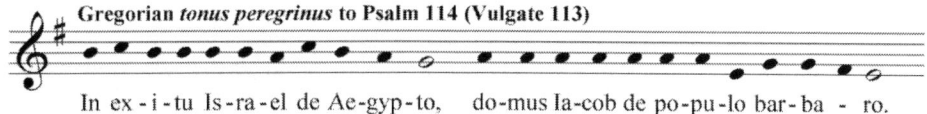

Gregorian *tonus peregrinus* to Psalm 114 (Vulgate 113)

In ex - i - tu Is - ra - el de Ae - gyp - to, do - mus Ia - cob de po - pu - lo bar - ba - ro.

Werner said, 'this mode occurs in almost all Jewish centres, and is used with the same text as the church (i.e. Ps. 114), during the very same liturgical season, Eastertide.'[6] He notes that the existence of the tone in Judaism cannot be explained by the influence of the Gregorian rite, for it is found not only in the west, but also in the east, beyond the influence of the Roman church. He concludes that the Jewish and Christian forms of the melody must date together from a single source predating both Church and Judaism, namely, the temple. The *tonus peregrinus* is therefore our best remaining fragment of temple

---

[5] Randhofer 2005: 262.
[6] Werner 1959: 419, 466.

psalmody. Werner also noted similarities between the other Gregorian tones and synagogue melodies. These were all advances. Yet one ancient chant and a number of fragments do not in themselves add up to restoring the temple psalmody. Something more was needed.

DECODING THE MASORETIC TE'AMIM

The only remaining way forward was an inductive approach to decoding the Masoretic cantillation, much as Champollion decoded Egyptian hieroglyphics. Some had attempted this before.[7] But the skills required were many – musician, Hebraist, specialist in Jewish and Christian liturgy – while the science of archaeomusicology, so vital to the task, was hardly born. Yet this was the approach taken by a French musicologist in the last quarter of the twentieth century.

Suzanne Vantoura was born to a Jewish immigrant family in Paris in 1912. While she was still a child, her father showed her the Hebrew text of the Psalms, surrounded by the mysterious marks which no-one understood. When she learned that they might be musical symbols, she longed to understand them. She went on to study at the Paris Conservatoire. But then came war and she fled the Nazi-occupied city. In the south of France, living in seclusion, she had the leisure to examine the Masoretic *te'amim* more closely. Armed with her school knowledge of Hebrew and a musician's instincts, she achieved a series of telling insights.

She noticed, first, that cantillation marks appear both above and below the line of Hebrew text. Observing that the sublinear signs appear everywhere, while the supralinear signs are sometimes absent for many verses at a time, she concluded that the sublinear signs were more important. Noting eight such signs in the prosodic books, she surmised that these represent the notes of a musical scale. Taking *silluq*, which appears under the final word of every Bible verse, to be the key-note or tonic, she proceeded to identify the other sublinear symbols with other notes of the scale, simply on the basis of the musicality of their mutual relations. The result was the first step of a musical system for the *te'amim*, a scale for the prosodic books rising six steps above the tonic and two steps below it. Taking E as the tonic, Haïk-Vantoura showed it as follows.[8]

---

[7] The first was probably Abraham ben David Portaleone in his *Shilte Hagiborim*, chapters 4 to 13 (Mantua 1612). He was followed by J.C. Speidel and C.G. Anton in the 18th century, by L. Haupt and L. Arends in the 19th and by H. Berl, O. Glaser and J. Yasser in the 20th. Anton, Haupt, and Arends published musical transcriptions of the purported music of the Psalms in the musical style of their own age ('Cantillation', *JE* III.538; Sendrey 1969: 205–207).

[8] The names of the *te'amim* symbols follow Ashkenazi use.

Example 3. The scale of the sublinear *te'amim* of the prosodic books

Darga	Tevir	Silluq	Merkha	Tifḥa	Etnaḥ	Munaḥ	Mehuppakh
Submediant	Subtonic	Tonic	Supertonic	Mediant	Subdominant	Dominant	Submediant

Then, building on her insight into the prosodic scale, she turned to the poetic books, Psalms, Proverbs, and Job.[9] She noted that they featured only seven sublinear signs. Six of these were identical to those of the prosodic books, but two of the prosodic signs were missing and in their place was another sign, *galgal*. She identified *galgal* with the sharpened subtonic ($D^\sharp$), and constructed *une échelle échappée* or 'gapped scale', a scale not forming a complete octave, rising six steps above and dropping one step below the tonic.[10]

Example 4. The scale of the sublinear *te'amim* of the poetic books

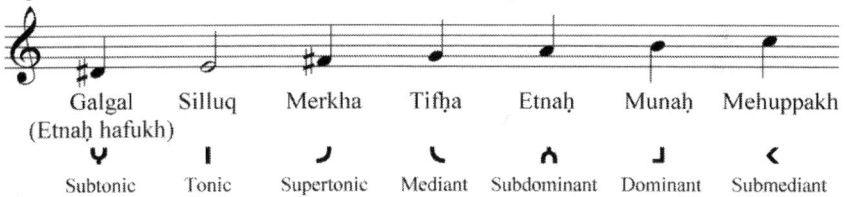

Galgal (Etnaḥ hafukh)	Silluq	Merkha	Tifḥa	Etnaḥ	Munaḥ	Mehuppakh
Subtonic	Tonic	Supertonic	Mediant	Subdominant	Dominant	Submediant

She assumed that each sublinear sign determines the tone of its own syllable and of all succcessive syllables until the next sublinear sign, a practice found in Byzantine and other ancient forms of psalmody. As for the supralinear signs, she surmised that they were to be interpreted in the fashion of the synagogue cantoral system, that is, as ornamental motifs which are applied to the notes of the sublinear signs, varying them in characteristic ways.

After the war, she returned to Paris, graduated with distinction in organ and composition from the Conservatoire, and married, becoming Haïk-Vantoura. Her busy life as a musician left little time to publish her findings. But she spent several decades thinking through its implications and studying Curt Sachs's foundational work in archaeomusicology. Finally, at the instigation of Marcel Dupré, she published the results of her work in 1976 in *La musique de la Bible révélée*.[11]

---

[9] Known as the *Sifrei Emet*, 'Books of Truth', because the initial letters of Job (א), Proverbs (מ) and Psalms (ת) form the mnemonic *emet* (אמת), 'truth'.

[10] Haïk-Vantoura calls the subtonic *galgal*. But Yeivin showed that the name *galgal* ('wheel') originally belonged to another sublinear symbol, a three-quarter-circle, absent from later Masoretic manuscripts (1968: 333). He renamed the v-shaped *galgal* symbol above *etnaḥ hafukh* (inverted *etnaḥ*). I am indebted to Professor Ofer for bringing this matter to my attention. It is discussed further below.

[11] Haïk-Vantoura 1976.

The book won the highest plaudits. Olivier Messiaen hailed Haïk-Vantoura as the Champollion of the Psalms. Other French musical luminaries, Duruflé, Dutilleux, Dupré, and Milhaud, pronounced her book a work of genius. The Chief Rabbi of France, Henri Schiller, spoke of her 'overwhelming discovery'. Israel Adler of the Hebrew University's Center for the Study of Jewish Music acknowledged the power of her system. The second edition of her book, in 1978, won the Prix Bernier, the highest award of l'Institut de France. The publication in 1985 of her two volumes of the Psalms was greeted as a breakthrough not only for biblical music, but for the whole infant science of archaeomusicology.

> Indisputably, Suzanne Haïk-Vantoura has rediscovered the methods of musical writing of antiquity... For it is difficult to imagine that a system founded on false suppositions could pertain so rigorously to such a large number of texts.[12]

WAS HAÏK-VANTOURA RIGHT?

Of course, Häik-Vantoura also had detractors, especially in the cantoral community, and continues to have to this day. Nevertheless, her system, even if imperfect, offers a fundamental breakthrough in deciphering the Masoretic cantillation. Here are the reasons why.

First, Haïk-Vantoura's identifying the sublinear *te'amim* as the notes of a musical scale is consistent with what we now know of the music of the ancient east. When Haïk-Vantoura formulated her theory, this idea went against all prevailing notions. There was no evidence that scales were known before the Pythagorean School, nor was it imagined that any form of music notation showing distinct notes existed in Bible times. Ancient musical notation, it was thought, was at best ekphonetic – mapping vague rises and falls of the voice – or built of quasi-melodic motifs, but quite unable to represent individual notes.

But a series of cuneiform tablets deciphered in the 1960s and 70s, popularly called the Babylonian Tuning Texts, shows that the Mesopotamians had a sophisticated music theory by the early second millennium BC.[13] In fact, another cuneiform text, the 'Self-Laudation of King Shulgi', relates that this system of musical theory was established in the 21st century BC.[14] It had seven

---

[12] Jourdan-Hemmerdinger 1986: 131. My translation.

[13] The key texts, first deciphered by Anne Kilmer in the 1960s, are CBS 10996 from Nippur, and UET VII 74 and UET VII 126 from Ur. The Nippur text was deciphered by Kilmer 1960: 273–308. The unfolding story of the deciphering between 1960 and 1984 is told by Duchesne-Guillemin 1984: 22, who cites R. P. Winnington-Ingram: 'It is really fascinating the way these documents have turned up in succession and provided a progressive illumination. And it is astonishing to find such a highly developed theory at this early date.'

[14] Duchesne-Guillemin 1984: 12.

different scales or 'modes'.[15] And each scale had seven notes from the first step to the eighth-note octave.[16]

Excursus. There is a lively debate in archaemusicology as to whether the earliest Babylonian scales were heptatonic, consisting of seven notes plus the octave, like our modern scales, or whether they were nine-note or 'enneatonic' scales, reflecting the nine strings of the early Mesopotamian lyre. The case for heptatonism was made by Kilmer and Duchesne-Guillemin when the Tuning Texts were first deciphered. The case for the nine-note scale is made by Dumbrill, who maintains that the word 'octave' is not found anywhere in ancient literature and that 'the concept of the octave was unknown during the Old Babylonian period'.[17] Of course, he is not saying that there was no actual octave in the Babylonian scales. There were indeed octaves between the first and eighth or second and ninth strings. But, he thinks that, despite this fact, the Babylonians were unaware of the octave as a special interval and had no word for it.

I tend cautiously toward the view that the heptatonic scale was foundational from the beginning, for three reasons.

(1) As Duchesne-Guillemin points out, 'The eighth string is always altered together with the first, or the ninth with the second, a proof that the division of the octave is heptatonic'.[18]

(2) While I cannot vouch for the Mesopotamian literature, there is certainly a word for octave in biblical Hebrew. It is *sheminit* or 'eighth' which the Septuagint translates as Greek *ogdoes* (octave).

> Zechariah, Aziel, Shemiramoth, Jehiel, Unni, Eliab, Maaseiah, and Benaiah with *nevalim* on *alamot;* and Mattithiah, Eliphelehu, Mikneiah, Obed-Edom, Jeiel and Azaziah with *kinnorot* on the *sheminit* to lead (1 Chr. 15.20–21).

> For the *mnatseah.* On *neginot.* On the *sheminit.* A psalm of David. (Ps. 6.1).

> For the *mnatseah.* On the *sheminit.* A psalm of David. (Ps. 12.1).

This *sheminit* is clearly a musical term. But it cannot refer to an eighth mode, for that would mean the singers of 1 Chronicles 15.20–21 were singing two different modes simultaneously, something unlikely even now and impermissible according to ancient musical theory. Nor is there any other suggestion of what it might represent if not a musical octave.

(3) Experience suggests the octave is a psycho-acoustic hard fact. A man and woman, or a man and child, or a mixed crowd of people, will sing together in octaves. This happens quite naturally, in every place where people sing, without any musical education or training. It is surely reasonable to assume that this natural phenomenon would have been recognized in the sophisticated musical theory of Mesopotamia.

Professor Dumbrill, however, cogently defends his views, and so the debate continues. Yet all agree that by the early first millennium, the time of Israel's temple

---

[15] A 'mode' is one of several different kinds or flavours of scale, as with our major and minor scales, which differ in their internal pattern of tone and semitone steps.
[16] Kilmer 1971; 1984; Crickmore 2009: 5–6.
[17] Dumbrill 2005: 119; cf. 116–22; he admits that many of his colleagues disagree (100).
[18] Duchesne-Guillemin 1984: 11.

cult, the seven-note scale that we use today was the established pattern. It would therefore have been the scale known to the Hebrews.

Here are the nine-note scales of the Mesopotamian lyres.[19] They are listed with notes – that is, lyre-strings – descending, following Mesopotamian practice. The tonic, or key-note, is the lowest note; the ninth is bracketed.

Example 5. The nine-note scales of Mesopotamian lyres

From the first scale, each subsequent mode was achieved by raising each harp-string one half-tone at a time. By raising the middle string a half-step, the first mode, *išartum*, became the second mode, *qablitum*. By raising the octave pair of the first and eighth strings, *qablitum* became *niš tuḥrim*. And so on until, by the raising of the last string, one regained the initial scale, *išartum*, a semitone higher. Note that the alterations occur in the same order as in our modern theory, the sequence of sharps being F C G D A E B.

---

[19] After Dumbrill 2010: 130, cf. 119.

Here are the same modes, transposed to 'white-note' ascending scales, with their equivalent Greek modes.[20]

Table 14. Babylonian and Greek modes compared

		Aristoxenos	Glareanus
išartum	B C D E F G A (B) [C]	Mixolydian	Locrian
qablitum	E F G A B C D (E) [F]	Dorian	Phrygian
niš tuḫrim	A B C D E F G (A) [B]	Aeolian	Aeolian (minor)
nid qablim	D E F G A B C (D) [E]	Phrygian	Dorian
pitum	G A B C D E F (G) [A]	Ionian	Mixolydian
embubum	C D E F G A B (C) [D]	Lydian	Ionian (major)
kitmum	F G A B C D E (F) [G]	Hypolydian	Lydian

With these scales, the Mesopotamians discovered harmony in thirds, fourths, fifths, and sixths, in the early second millennium BC. Each harp string had a name and symbol, enabling each note of the scale to be precisely notated. The different strings had different significations: the fourth was anciently named after Ea, the creator of mankind, the god of wisdom and music, and other strings existed in the 'god-number' ratios of Anu, Enlil, and Sin.[21] Therefore the diatonic scale, which the Greeks reckoned to be autochthonous, actually sprang from the sands of Mesopotamia. After it entered Greece, probably in the Orientalizing Period of the late 8th century BC, the only role that Pythagoras played was dressing it up in Greek garb.[22]

Around the same time as the Babylonian Tuning Texts were being deciphered, a German musicologist living in Egypt, Hans Hickmann, proposed that Egyptian friezes of performing musicians show a link between the cheironomers' gestures and the strings plucked by the harpists. He concluded that the Egyptians had the minor pentatonic scale, with distinct cheironomical gestures for each harp-string, in the third millennium BC.[23] More recent research on Egyptian flutes has confirmed the early use of the minor pentatonic

---

[20] The third-column nomenclature follows Aristoxenos 'the Musician' (4th century BC), the fourth column follows Glareanus, whose *Dodecachordon* of 1547 muddled the Greek terminology. While modern musicians follow Glareanus, musicologists follow Aristoxenos, often with a less-ambiguous description such as 'white-note scale from D to D' or 'D-mode'. From here on, I follow Aristoxenos.

[21] Dumbrill 2010: 115, 120.

[22] Dumbrill 2010: 122.

[23] Hickmann & Hickmann 1996: 6–14. Kuhn 2010: 11–18 notes that Egyptian depictions of music are not always detailed enough to be precise on fingering. Yet she regards Hickmann's work highly and accepts its general validity. She also accepts the central position played by cheironomy, but notes that it is less in evidence in Middle and New Kingdom murals, than in Old Kingdom and Coptic ones.

and has shown that it gave way to diatonic scales – the harmonic minor and Persian scales – by the 16th century BC.[24]

Meanwhile, the Ras Shamra tablets showed that the city of Ugarit, on the north Mediterranean littoral, had musical notation which represented each note – that is, each harp-string – with a particular numeric symbol in 1400 BC. A complete hymn, in the Hurrian language, to the goddess Nikkal was found, and was duly transcribed and recorded.[25]

Therefore, in Mesopotamia, Egypt, and the Levant, the lands of Israel's conception, gestation, and birth, the musical scale existed, with separate names and symbols for each note, before and during the period of Israel's residence there. It can hardly be doubted that the Hebrews shared in this musical lore and, like their neighbours, had diatonic scales with symbols for each step. That Haïk-Vantoura, knowing only the beginnings of Hickmann's work, should discover this and publish it as the Babylonian and Ugaritic texts were only emerging is a remarkable confirmation of her system.

Second, Haïk-Vantoura's system passes the litmus test for any attempt to decode the poetic *te'amim*: that is, it produces results consistent with the *tonus peregrinus* to Psalm 114, our best surviving fragment of temple psalmody. The Ashkenazi version of the *tonus*, cited earlier in this chapter, is closest to the Gregorian model. However, the Sephardi version of the *tonus*, preserved in the east beyond the influence of the Roman rite, is likely to be closer still to the temple original. Here it is.[26]

Example 6. Sephardi form of the *tonus peregrinus* to Psalm 114

Psalm 114 of Sephardi Judaism

B-tset Is - ra - el mi - Mits - ra - yim; bet Ya -'a - qov___ me 'am lo - ez.

The essential difference is that the mid-verse cadence or musical pause, on the last syllable of *Mitsrayim*, simply rests on the subdominant (A) and does not drop down to the mediant (G) as in the Gregorian and Ashkenazi versions.[27] And now here is Psalm 114.2–6 with its Masoretic *te'amim* decoded according

---

[24] The research, by a team from Cairo University, California State University, and the Cairo Institute of Arabic Music, is at http://egyptsound.free.fr. The harmonic minor is an altered Aeolian: E F♯ G A B C D♯. The Persian (or Byzantine or Arab) scale is E F G♯ A B C D♯.

[25] Kilmer, Crocker, Brown, 1976. Several versions of Hurrian Hymn VI have been proposed. The most recent is by Dumbrill, at www.youtube.com/watch?v=gynhfxQ1IO4.

[26] This version of the *tonus* is from Morocco. Idelsohn (1929.63) recorded it with Ps. 29 and Werner 1959: 419 has it for the same psalm. The *te'amim* of the first verse of Ps. 29 (without heading) are similar to Ps. 114 (as Werner 1959: 420 shows), and so the same tune serves the words of Ps. 114. But while the opening melodies of Pss. 29 and 114 were alike, the *tonus* does not fit Ps. 29 throughout. The bipartite verses of Ps. 114 fit the bipartite phrases of the *tonus* like a glove, but Ps. 29's tripartite and unipartite vv. 3 & 7 fit the *tonus* only under duress.

[27] Werner (1959: 436) confirms that the Sephardi *tonus* cadences on the subdominant, as does Herzog's (1972: 1330) version of Ps. 114 from the Djerba tradition. Cf. Herzog & Hajdu 1968.

to Haïk-Vantoura's system. (Verse 1 is omitted because its second stich takes a different melodic route from the rest of the psalm.)

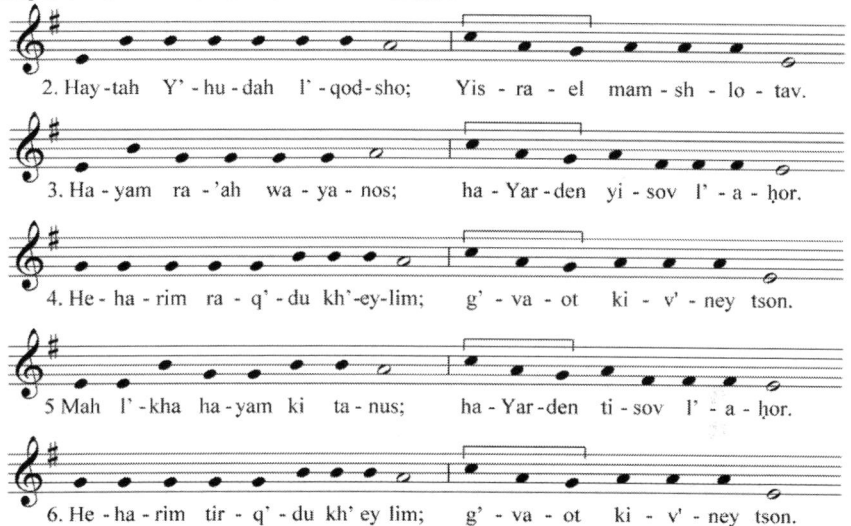

Example 7. Psalm 114.2–6 after Haïk-Vantoura

[musical notation]
2. Hay-tah Y'-hu-dah l'-qod-sho; Yis-ra-el mam-sh-lo-tav.
3. Ha-yam ra-'ah wa-ya-nos; ha-Yar-den yi-sov l'-a-ḥor.
4. He-ha-rim ra-q'-du kh'-ey-lim; g'-va-ot ki-v'-ney tson.
5 Mah l'-kha ha-yam ki ta-nus; ha-Yar-den ti-sov l'-a-ḥor.
6. He-ha-rim tir-q'-du kh'ey lim; g'-va-ot ki-v'-ney tson.

The resemblances are immediately noticeable. In the first hemistich of each verse, the tenor, or reciting note, revolves around the tonic triad (E G B) until the cadence on the subdominant (A). Then the tenor continues around the same note (A), decorated by the supralinear sign-pair *revia mugrash* – shown by the bracket – before passing, sometimes by way of the supertonic (F♯), to the inevitable close on the tonic (E).[28] Thus the *tonus* suggests that Haïk-Vantoura is right at least in identifying the mid-verse *etnaḥ* symbol with the fourth step of the scale (A) and in identifying the final *silluq* symbol with the tonic (E). Note too that the *tonus* opens with the dominant (B) and Haïk-Vantoura renders the opening *munaḥ* symbol of her transcription with the same note, suggesting that she is right in reading *munaḥ* as the dominant. This is confirmed by the fact that the highpoint of the psalm – the word *eloah* (high god) in verse 7 – would demand a strong high note (and nothing is stronger than the dominant); and on this word falls the only *munaḥ* occurring after the mid-verse pause.[29]

Example 8. Psalm 114.7 after Haïk-Vantoura

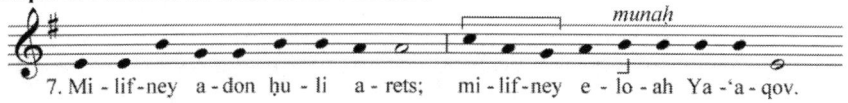

[musical notation]
                                                    munaḥ
7. Mi-lif-ney a-don ḥu-li a-rets; mi-lif-ney e-lo-ah Ya-'a-qov.

[28] The interpretation of the supralinear sign-pair *revia mugrash* is discussed in Appendix IV.
[29] Rightly is the bold and assertive fifth step, the strongest step of the scale, called the 'dominant'. See its declarative power at, e.g., Pss. 2.5; 91.13; 150.3.

The three sublinear signs *silluq*, *etnah*, and *munah* are therefore established as the three principle poles of the scale, the tonic (E), subdominant (A), and dominant (B). The two remaining signs found in Psalm 114, *merkha* and *tifha*, fall into place as the supertonic (F#) and mediant (G). For, if one reverses their values, singing F# for *tifha* and G for *merkha*, then the melos crumbles as the opening E-G-B sequences become harmonically-garbled E-F#-Bs, while the second hemistichs lose their 'answering' quality as the F#s become tonic triad Gs. So comparing the *tonus* compared with the cantillation of Psalm 114 confirms Haïk-Vantoura's interpretation that five sublinear symbols represent the first five steps of the scale: *silluq* (E), *merkha* (F#), *tifha* (G), *etnah* (A), and *munah* (B).[30]

What about the other sublinear signs of the poetic books that do not appear in this psalm? *Mehuppakh* is routinely connected with the idea of height or rising, and so it seems reasonable to connect it with the note above *munah*, that is, the submediant (C).[31] However, Haïk-Vantoura's other sign, the v-shaped sign usually called *galgal*, is less certain altogether. True, it is frequently connected with the idea of depth, and so she may have been right to connect it with the low subtonic (D#).[32] However, the Aleppo Codex poetic texts feature a three-quarter-circle, wheel-shaped sign, absent from later manuscripts. Yeivin identified this 'wheel' sign as the true *galgal* ('wheel'), and he renamed the v-shaped sign *etnah hafukh*, 'inverted *etnah*'. Haïk-Vantoura was not even aware of the wheel-shaped *galgal* sign, for in her texts both signs were represented by the v-shaped sign.[33]

Third, despite the widespread confession that the cantillation of the poetic books is lost, some old traditions for the Psalms *te'amim* have come to light which corroborate Haïk-Vantoura's system. One tradition comes from the Jewish community of Syria.[34] This shows notable parallels with Haïk-Vantoura's interpretation of the sublinear *te'amim*: *silluq* is (a step to) the tonic; *merkha* is (a step to) the supertonic; *tifha* (*dehi*) is (a step to) the mediant; *etnah* (*atnah*) rises to the subdominant (then falls to the supertonic); *revia* is a falling and rising melisma; *oleh ve-yored* is a rising and falling; and *tsinnor* is a turn.[35]

---

[30] For further discussion of the cantillation of Ps. 114, see Mitchell 2012: 374–76.
[31] See, e.g., 7.6 [7]; 88.10 [11]: 'Arise'; 24.7, 9: 'Lift up!'; 44.23 [24]: 'Awake!'; 92.8: 'sprout'; 93.3: 'lifted up'; 148.14: 'raise up'.
[32] See, *e.g.,* Pss. 1.3: 'planted'; 23.4: 'valley'; 35.14; 57.6: 'bow down'; 124.7: 'snare'.
[33] Yeivin 1968: 333.
[34] This was kindly sent to me by Professor Joshua Jacobson. It appears in Jacobson 2014: 16. All that he can ascertain about its origins is that it was adapted by Rabbi Joseph Silverman from Syrian traditions. My transcription is transposed from tonic D to E, but otherwise unchanged.
[35] For a fuller discussion of *revia mugrash* and *oleh ve-yored*, see Appendix IV. An old Sephardi mnemonic on the *te'amim* says: 'after *tarha*, *etnah*', that is, after 'dragging' or 'effort' (*tarha*) comes rest (*etnah*). Of course, *etnah* follows *tarha* (*tifha*) in the *zarqa* table, the mnemonic device for the *te'amim*. But, in Haïk-Vantoura's system, *etnah* also follows *tarha* in the musical scale.

Example 9. Syrian cantillational system compared with Haïk-Vantoura

[Musical notation: Syrian tradition (left column) compared with Haïk-Vantoura's system (right column), showing: Silluq, Merkha, Dehi (Tifha), Atnah, Mugrash revia (Revia), Tsinor]

So too Werner records a Sephardi tradition, not for the Psalms, but the prophets, where *etnah* cadences on the subdominant (A) and *silluq* on the tonic (E).[36]

Example 10. Sephardi tradition for the prophets

[Musical notation showing Atnah and Sof pasuq (silluq)]

A similar pattern, with the semi-cadence on the subdominant and the final on the tonic, is found in the chants of the Maronite Church of Antioch, which the Maronites trace to the liturgy of Saint Ephrem of Nisibe (306–373). Here is one of the chants of Holy Week, *Dahṭō lō nehṭē*.[37] It uses the quarter-sharp supertonic (F) of the zalzalian scale.[38]

---

[36] Werner 1959: 436; transposed from tonic D to E.

[37] With thanks to Professor Abou Mrad. The chant appears in the forthcoming volume by Abou Mrad, Maatouk, Chédid.

[38] The Zalzalian (or Mansouri) scale is named after the 8th-century Persian musician, Mansour Zalzal, who divided the minor third into two equal three-quarter tone steps, making the supertonic equidistant between the tonic and mediant.

Example 11. Maronite liturgy for Holy Week

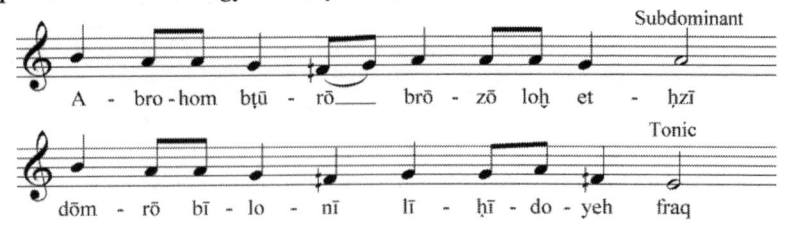

A - bro - hom bṭū - rō___ brō - zō loḥ et - ḥzī

dōm - rō bī - lo - nī lī - ḥī - do - yeh fraq

Maronite chants have, of course, no direct link to the Masoretic symbols. But, since the earliest Christian chants grew out of those of ancient Israel, it testifies to the same cadence structure as found in the *tonus peregrinus* and so corroborates Haïk-Vantoura's interpretation of *etnaḥ* and *silluq*.

Yet another old tradition for the cantillation of the Psalms is from the early seventeenth century *Sefer ha-niggunim* of Jacob Levi Finzi, which preserves an Ashkenazic tradition known to Abraham Segre, Finzi's predecessor as cantor in Casale Monferrato.[39] This system is fragmentary and lacks the most important signs. However, it may elucidate the meaning of the upper sign-pair *oleh ve-yored*.[40]

Fourth, Haïk-Vantoura's system produces melodies which are singable and which illustrate the words as one would expect in music written for particular texts. This is what composers call 'word-painting', where the melodic movement illustrates the meaning of the text. In Psalm 114, as we saw, the voice rises to the high dominant (B) for *eloah*, 'high god'. Likewise, in the initial verse of Psalm 121, the voice rises from tonic (E) to dominant (B) for *I lift*, then drops, as to a valley, for *my eyes to the* (G), and then rises again to the *etnaḥ* pause on *hills* (A). Or, in Psalm 23, the voice sinks to the depths for the *valley of the shadow of death*. Other examples shall be seen in the following chapter.[41]

On the basis of the above evidence, I am inclined to think that Haïk-Vantoura is right in identifying the sublinear symbols with the steps of a scale, and mostly right in identifying each symbol with the step of the scale that she does: *silluq* (E), *merkha* (F♯), *tifḥa* (G), *etnaḥ* (A), *munaḥ* (B), and *mehuppakh* as (C). However, I am less confident about her identification of the v-shaped *galgal* (Yeivin's *etnaḥ hafukh*) as the subtonic (D♯).

Haïk-Vantoura is not the only one to have tried to decipher the *te'amim* inductively. Others, following her example, have proposed systems at variance with hers.[42] But since these systems, when applied to the cantillation of Psalm

---

[39] Finzi's book survives only in *Ta'amei tehillim* (1669/1670) by Abraham Joseph Solomon Graziano. The transcription is in Adler 1989: 25.

[40] See Appendix IV.

[41] See also Mitchell 2012: 367–71; 2013: 122; See too Appendix IV, where the melodic shape of *revia mugrash* fits language about prostration and bowing-down.

[42] Weil 1995; McCorkle: www.musicofthebible.com. Weil admits to Haïk-Vantoura having inspired his search, but abandons her hypothesis for his own motivic 'chain-system' which he

114, do not produce anything like the *tonus peregrinus*, they fall at the first hurdle. And, since synagogue psalmody is so diffuse as to offer no hope of recovery from cantoral traditions alone, Haïk-Vantoura's system is the only one left standing to point the way toward the recovery of temple song.

WAS HAÏK-VANTOURA TOTALLY RIGHT?

Haïk-Vantoura's system is the best one going, but it is not infallible. For a start, she worked from an inferior text. The Aleppo Codex was not available to her. Her choices were the Letteris text, the Ginsburg text, and the Leningrad Codex as it appeared in *Biblia Hebraica*. She chose, apparently on the advice of Gérard Weil, to work principally from the Letteris text, not knowing that it was the most muddled of the three. All these printed editions omit the sublinear three-quarter-circle symbol found in the Aleppo Codex, which Yeivin identified as the true *galgal*.[43] Clearly, the addition of an extra sublinear symbol makes a difference to Haïk-Vantoura's system. One might suspect that it means the poetic books have eight sublinear symbols, like the prosodic books. And if it has another musical meaning, where is it to be found? Sometimes this circular *galgal* symbol would seem to suit a high note, as in Psalm 122.4, where it sings the ascent of the tribes, and sometimes a low note, as at the bowing-down in Psalm 138.2. And, strangely, in these instances the printed editions replace the sign with *mehuppakh* and the inverted *etnaḥ hafukh*, high and low notes respectively in Haïk-Vantoura's system. But why they did so is a mystery. I have not hazarded any guesses as to what the distinction between *etnaḥ hafukh* and *galgal* may be, but have simply followed the older printed editions, who render the three-quarter circle *galgal* sometimes as *mehuppakh* (C) and sometimes as *etnaḥ hafukh* (D♯).

Next, although I feel Haïk-Vantoura was largely right in regard to the musical values of the sublinear *te'amim*, I am less sure of her interpretation of the supralinear signs. Yes, the idea that they are tropes, or decorations on the lower signs, seems plausible. But we lack external proof for her interpretation of them, such as the *tonus peregrinus* provides for the lower signs. And some of them seem highly conjectural. She proposes that the sublinear arrowhead sign, *mehuppakh*, the sixth above the tonic, when placed above the text (as *oleh ve-yored*), signifies a leap of a fourth from the underlying tone. But why a fourth, and not a sixth again? She proposes that sublinear *munaḥ*, which represents the fifth above the tonic, when placed above the text (*illuy*),

---

hopes is not his own 'intellectual artefact' (p. 291). McCorkle follows Haïk-Vantoura in seeing the sublinear signs as notes of a scale. He agrees on *silluq* as tonic and *merkha* as supertonic, but posits different tonal values for the other signs.

[43] Yeivin 1968: 333; the symbol appears in other early Masoretic codices, from before the 11th century, but was later forgotten. It appears in the Songs of Ascents at Pss. 122.4; 123.2; 125.3; 126.2; 127.2.

becomes, as one might expect, a momentary jump of a fifth; but since this fifth is often too high to sing, she reckons it as a jump down to the same note in the lower octave. But the reasoning seems strained, and the effect is frequently unmusical. Then what can one say of *shalshelet*, which she defines as a semitone triplet run-up to the note from below? Yes, Mesopotamians, Egyptians, and Greeks all knew the twelve-note semitone scale, but the effect, again, seems unmusical, and no external evidence is given for this strange solution. Meanwhile, there is evidence from cantoral sources that suggest a modification of her approach to the *revia-mugrash* sign pair.[44]

Third, as regards the rhythm of psalmody, Haïk-Vantoura had her own unique view, saying, 'Equality and homogeneity of the succeeding time values are the bases of the meter of the Psalms.'[45] And so her transcriptions are written in successive eighth-notes without bar lines and her recordings sound like fluid ametrical Hebrew plainsong. One wonders if, in this matter, she was influenced by her great admiration for Gregorian chant. Perhaps too she was swayed by her own syllable-timed French tongue or influenced by views such as Sendrey's:

> Oriental vocal music does not know any conscious beats, or "counts," in the Western sense, consequently it has no metric units bound by bar-lines. Oriental rhythm has a different basis.[46]

But, although oriental song is fluid in its rhythm, it is still rhythmic.[47] Its *tempo* may be *rubato*, speeding up and slowing down, but there is a discernable pulse. It may break into florid cantoral cadenzas, but it will return to that pulse. Israel's temple rites involved processions, marches, and dances, accompanied by drums and sistrums, none of which can take place to ametrical chant. Josephus, who heard the songs in the temple with his own ears, testified to Greeks and Latins that the psalms were trimeter and pentameter, which implies a regular pulse.[48] And while the cantillational symbols do not contain detailed rhythmic notation, there are several things which indicate the rhythmic pulse of the song: namely, the stress of the poetic foot, the position of cantillation marks, the use of the *maqqef* hyphen, and the practice called *nasog aḥor*.

The poetic foot arises from the regular recurrence of stressed syllables. In classical poetry, the number of syllables in each foot – that is between each stress – is strictly defined in iambs, trochees, spondees, dactyls, and anapests. So too is the number of feet in each line. Hebrew poetics are less rigid. Yes, there are regular metres. The Hebrew metre of 3+2 stresses, often called *qinah* metre, resembles classical pentameter, both in structure and in its application

---

[44] See Appendix IV.
[45] Haïk-Vantoura 1991: 368.
[46] Sendrey 1969: 240; cf. also 377.
[47] Stocks 2012: 23–30. Dobbs-Allsopp (2014: 85) agrees, and points out this was recognized long ago in George Wither's *A Preparation of the Psalter* (1619).
[48] *Ant.* VII.xii.3.

to noble or solemn themes. But generally Hebrew metre is more subtle. There is no insistence on regular numbers of syllables within each foot; anything between one and four syllables is possible.[49]

> l'-|ma-'an a-|ḥai v-re-|'ai | a-da-b'rah-|na sha-|lom |bakh
> Ps. 122.8

Nor is there any insistence on successive lines having the same metre. A six-foot line can be followed by a five-foot line.

> ez-|ri me-|im yeho-|vah | o-|seh sha-|ma-yim va-|a-rets |
> al yi-|ten la-|mot rag-|lekha | al-ya-|num shom-|re-kha |
> Ps. 121.2–3

Further, the poetic line has pauses or caesuras, matching the musical cadences of the melody, and marked by the major cadence-points, *silluq* and *etnaḥ*, and the lesser cadences, *oleh ve-yored* and *revia*. Nor are all pauses of the same length. The usual pause is equal to a complete missing stress, as in the examples above. But a short pause, equivalent to one syllable, is found too.[50]

> Ash-|rey ha-|ish   a-|sher lo ha-|lakh   ba'a-|tsat rᵉsha-|im
> Ps. 1.1

Now it is essential to stress-timed languages, like Hebrew, that they be sung or declaimed with the stresses in the right place. To write poetry with the wrong stresses, or to mismatch the poetic and melodic stresses, is the work of a bungler; it is not what we would expect from kings and Levite chiefs. Therefore the first key to finding the musical pulse of biblical psalmody is to identify the stresses which mark out the poetic feet.

The second key is noting where the cantillation marks have been placed. Generally, these fall on the stressed syllables, confirming that the melos moves with the basic poetic pulse. But, occasionally, the cantillation mark is placed on what should be an unstressed syllable. This can signal one of two things. It can mean that, contrary to normal usage, the stress falls on a normally-unstressed syllable. Or it can mean a change of reciting tone within the poetic foot. The decision as to which of these principles to follow depends on the *maqqef* hyphen and *nasog aḥor*.

The *maqqef* hyphen joins words together so that, instead of each word having its own stress, the hyphenated word-group shares a single stress. Often this is a simple matter of showing that a one-syllable word is unstressed. However, sometimes the *maqqef* brings into play a principle called *nasog*

---

[49] Alter 1985.
[50] Stocks 2012: 26, 255, proposes that the pause is 'equivalent to an anapaestic foot for a major caesura and equivalent to a single stressed syllable for a minor caesura' (26), the major caesura occuring in the bicolon and long tricolon, the minor caesura in the short 'para-tricolon' of 2–2–2 syllables.

aḥor, or 'pulled back', which displaces the usual stress of a word. Usually the stress is 'pulled back' to the end of the group, although sometimes the stress can be pulled forward as well.[51] The main thing is that the hyphenated group has one single stress. Usually, *nasog aḥor* is used to shift the stress for the sake of the metre. But sometimes it is used to hurry syllables into a single poetic foot so they become a form of 'word-painting' to depict, for instance, wind blowing chaff away:

| ki 'im–ka-|**mots** a-sher–tid-|**fe**-nu |**ru**-aḥ

Ps. 1.4

Or a city closely compacted together:

Yerusha-|**la**-yim |**ha**-b'nu-|**yah** k'-|**ir** she-hu-brah-|**lah** yaḥ-|**dav**

Ps. 122.3

These various stress indicators, taken together, give a good idea of how the rhythmic and melodic elements of the song combine. We can see how they interact in, for example, the repeated words *yanum*, 'slumber' in Psalm 121. In v. 3b, the two words *al-yanum*, 'he does not slumber', are joined by the *maqqef* hyphen, showing that they have a single stress. And since the little supralinear diamond-sign *revia* falls on the second syllable of *yanùm*, it shows that the stress falls on that syllable, as normal. In v. 4a, the words *lo-yanum*, 'he does not slumber', are also joined with the *maqqef* hyphen. But, in that case, the sublinear *tifḥa* on the first syllable of *yanum* shows that *nasog aḥor* is applied and so the word stress is 'pulled back' to the first syllable, *yànum*.

³ al yi-|**ten** la-|**mot** rag-|**lekha** | al-ya-|**nùm** shom-|**rekha** |
⁴ hi-|**neh** lo-|**yànum**   v-|**lo** yi-|**shan**   sho-|**mer** yisra-|**el**

The effect introduces variety and colour to the metre as well as adding emphasis to the second *yanum*.

DECIPHERING THE PSALMS

All in all then, we approach Haïk-Vantoura's system with trust and caution. We must lean on it, for it is our best key to the lost temple song. But we must be aware of its failings. The transcriptions of the musical tones of the Songs of Ascents in the following chapter therefore depend on her deciphering system, with the following provisos.

---

[51] Waldman (1989: 148) speaks of *qofets qadimah*, 'jumping ahead', in addition to *nasog aḥor*.

Text. I have followed the online Aleppo Codex text, whose cantillation shows a pristine simplicity lacking in later texts.[52] I have departed from it only in reading the wheel-shaped *galgal* symbol as *etnah hafukh* (D♯) or *mehuppakh* (C), following the Leningrad Codex. The interpretation of *galgal* and *etnah hafukh* is the most important unknown in our current understanding of the cantillation.

Rhythmic notation. Instead of Haïk-Vantoura's unmeasured equal eighth-notes, I have used a musical bar marked off in 'tick' bar lines to coincide with the poetic foot, whose stressed syllables are given in bold. Within this bar I have employed a quarter-note beat divided into the likeliest sub-divisions, based on the interaction of word-stresses, cantillation symbols, *maqqef*, and *nasog ahor*. These notated rhythmic values are not meant to be declaimed woodenly, but are a guide to metrical singing. Every song is notated in duple time, although it is possible that some of them were sung in triple time.

At times, one might be tempted to see syncopation in lines such as Psalm 122.5.

Example 12. Syncopation in Psalm 122?

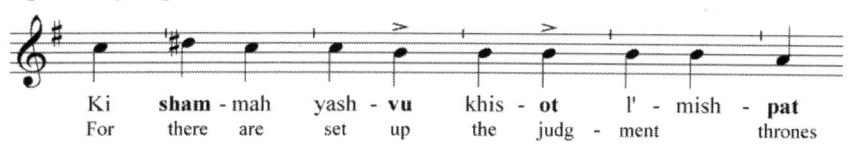

Ki **sham** - mah yash - **vu** khis - **ot** l' - mish - **pat**
For **there** are set **up** the **judg** - ment thrones

Yet I have not dared to open such a Pandora's box, but have kept the rhythmic values unsyncopated.

Supralinear signs. Following my misgivings about Haïk-Vantoura's interpretation of some supralinear signs, I have transcribed *revia* as a vocal trill, indicated by slashes above the note, *revia mugrash* as a vocal trill approached by the *geresh* ornament, and *illuy* as a momentary jump to the dominant.[53] Happily, *shalshelet* occurs in the Ascents collection only once, at Psalm 31.1, where I have left it untranscribed.

Choice of mode. Haïk-Vantoura suggests several scales were used in biblical cantillation, including the Dorian, Phrygian, Lydian (major), and altered Aeolian (harmonic minor), and the scale known in the synagogue as Ahavah Rabbah.[54] Many of these scales are recognized as being employed in Hebrew music in ancient times.[55] As for the Songs of Ascents, she transcribes them in an impressive array of modes:

---

[52] I use the *Bar Ilan Keter* and *Jerusalem Crown* to discern difficult readings of *silluq* and *merkha*.
[53] See Appendix IV for this interpretation of *revia* and *revia mugrash*.
[54] Ahavah Rabbah is the scale E F G♯ A B C D.
[55] As noted, the Egyptians had the harmonic minor in the 16th century BC. Idelsohn notes the ancient use of Dorian, Phrygian, Lydian, and Ahavah Rabbah in Israelite music (1948: 25–26). Sachs too, citing Clement of Alexandria, notes Jewish use of the Dorian, Phrygian, and Lydian (1943: 81–95).

Psalms 120, 121, 127 are in E harmonic minor, with an altered G♯ appearing in the lowest note of the *revia mugrash* ornament.
Psalm 122 is in E major throughout.
Psalms 123, 130, 131 are in unaltered E harmonic minor throughout.
Psalms 125, 128, 133, 134 are in the 'major-minor' scale (major lower tetrachord with a minor sixth): E F♯ G♯ A B C D♯.
Psalms 124 and 129 feature a mode with a raised fourth: E F♯ G A♯ B C D♯. This resembles the Jewish *Mi sheberakh* mode, allowing for the altered sixth and seventh which is a feature of this mode.

In fact, four of Haïk-Vantoura's psalms even change mode halfway through:

Psalms 124 and 129 begin in the Mi sheberakh mode, then, in the closing verses, revert to the altered harmonic minor of Psalm 120.
Psalm 126 is in the major-minor scale for the first three verses, then reverts to the G natural of the altered harmonic minor of Psalm 120.
Psalm 132 begins in the altered harmonic minor of Psalm 120 but, at v. 6, changes to the permanent G♯ of the major-minor scale.

Her decision to change mode in the middle of a psalm is surprising. For in ancient times different modes denoted different moods. The writer of Job refers to 'turning' or 'tuning' one's harp to a mode for mourning, and there would have been modes for weddings, victories, and for different times and seasons, just as there were among the Greeks some centuries later.[56] Haïk-Vantoura herself notes that in Greek music each song could be in only one mode.[57] One must therefore ask whether it is likely that the Levites re-tuned their harps as they ascended from step to step, or even in the middle of a single short psalm.[58] One suspects the answer is no, and that all fifteen songs should be in the same mode.

Which mode should this be? It should reflect the underlying hope and brightness of the Ascents collection, and be suitable for joyful psalms such as Psalm 122, while also lending an element of piquancy to the more wistful psalms. Again, if *revia* is a vocal trill, the fact that the Ascents have *revia* on the supertonic step of the scale may suggest that this step is a half tone, to facilitate the trill. And again, it should be a scale known to have existed in Israel's monarchy period. The best contender for these criteria is the Persian scale.

---

[56] Job 30.21. Clement of Alexandria notes that the modes of ancient Jewish melodies were determined by the character of the songs. Epic melodies (narrations of the Pentateuch) were Dorian, lyric chants and lamentations were Phrygian, and songs of praise were Lydian (Sachs 1943: 81–95). Plato, *Republic* III: 398-400, speaks of the different qualities of the Ionian, Lydian, Dorian, Phrygian, and Mixolydian modes, asserting that the Dorian is the noblest of modes and that the Mixolydian has undesirable effects upon young men.
[57] Haïk-Vantoura 1991: 229, 232.
[58] Haïk-Vantoura 1991: 361; 1985: Ps. 126.

E F G♯ A B C D♯

The bright major third gives it the necessary strength and joy, the minor sixth and augmented seconds give the necessary piquancy; the semitone step from tonic to supertonic would facilitate vocal trills between these two notes. Moreover, since archaeology has uncovered Egyptian flutes tuned to this scale, dating from the early New Kingdom period, it is a scale which the Hebrews would certainly have known.

Cantor-chorus exchange. We saw in chapter nine how the passing of the sung psalm between cantor and chorus was an essential part of temple psalmody. So any attempt to reconstruct the psalms as they were sung of old must make some guess where these exchanges happened. I assume the following principles.

First, the likeliest place for the cantor-chorus exchange is straight after the *etnah* cadence. This cadence is the commonest point for the break in the sense of the poetic parallelism, and hence for the exchange in voices.

> He will not let your foot be moved (*etnah*),
> he will not slumber your keeper (Ps. 121.3).

We also find that florid melodies with many supralinear signs, which look like cantoral solos, appear before the *etnah* cadence, while passages which must have been choral – refrains and response formulae – routinely occur after the *etnah* cadence.[59] The response formulae of Psalm 136, for instance, all appear after the *etnah* cadence. In addition, there are indications of a fresh breath after the *etnah* cadence, suggesting a change of forces.[60] The other, subordinate exchange points within the verse are the *revia gadol* and *oleh ve-yored* cadences.[61]

Second, although the semantic break, the pause in poetic thought, usually occurs within the verse, sometimes it falls between two successive verses, as in Psalm 122.8–9.

> [8] For the sake of my brothers and friends, I will say 'Peace within you!'
> [9] For the sake of the house of the LORD our God, I will seek your good.

Here, a cantor-chorus exchange at verse 8's *etnah* (the comma at 'friends') would not agree with any semantic break in the verse; it would simply interrupt the flow of thought. Instead, the semantic division is at the end of verse 8,

---

[59] Refrains: Pss. 115.9–11; 118.1-4, 8–12, 15–16, 29; 135.19–20; 136.1–26. Response formulae: *Maker of heaven and earth* (115.15; 121.2; 124.8; 134.3); *from now until forever* (115.18; 121.8; 125.2; 131.3); *Let Israel now say* (118.2-4; 124.1; 129.1); *Peace on Israel* (125.5; 128.6).

[60] In Ps. 90.5, after the *etnah* cadence, *ba-boqer* begins with daghesh forte, although the previous word ended with an open vowel. This indicates at least a fresh breath and, probably, a new speaker.

[61] Werner 1959: 418 regarded *revia gadol* as a cantor-chorus exchange point.

while verse 9 repeats the structure of verse 8, but develops the thought. The two verses form a pair, bound by their Hebrew rhyming ends, and should be treated as a pair. So, in this case, it looks like the cantor-chorus exchange point was at the end of verse 8 rather than at the *etnah* cadence.

Third, another marker of the cantor-chorus exchange is the change of speaker from singular to plural, or a change of address from second to third person, or an abrupt change of the person addressed. Frequently, these also occur at the *etnah* cadence, as in the following examples.

> Blessed is the man whose strength is in you;
> pathways in their hearts (Ps. 84.5).

> Because you Yehovah are my refuge;
> you have made Elyon your dwelling (Ps. 91.9).

Fourth, step parallelism (anadiplosis) between verses is another likely marker of the exchange point. When a word at the end of one line is repeated at the beginning of the next, one should assume that, for variety, that word was sung by different vocal forces.

Fifth, internal repetition of words and phrases within a verse, as in Psalm 131, also indicate likely points for the cantor-chorus exchange, the chorus repeating and confirming the words of the cantor.

| Cantor | Like a child upon its mother, |
| Chorus | like that child upon me is my soul. |

By a combination of these principles, we are able to reconstruct the metres, modes, and deployment of voices in the psalms. So equipped, we now proceed to decrypting and transcribing the cantillation of the Songs of Ascents.

13

The Songs of Zion

We now turn to look at the Songs of Ascents one by one, with reconstructions of their original music. The musical notes largely follow Haïk-Vantoura's system. The cantillational symbols have been notated as follows. (The sign-pairs – *revia mugrash* and *oleh ve-yored* – read from left to right, as in the musical transcriptions, not from right to left, as in the Hebrew text.)

Sublinear signs		*Supralinear signs*	
Etnaḥ hafukh	V	Revia mugrash	/ ♦
Silluq	|	Revia	♦
Merkha	/	Geresh	/
Tifḥa	\	Tsinnor	2
Etnaḥ	∧	Pazer	⊢
Munaḥ	⌐	Illuy	⌐
Mehuppakh	<	Azla (Qadma)	\
Circular *Galgal*	∪	Shalshelet	⟨
Supra- & sublinear		*Interlinear*	
Oleh ve-yored	< /	Makkef	–

In the transcriptions, the sharp signs on G♯ and D♯ last while the note repeats.

I do not suggest that the following reconstructions are one hundred percent correct. Science proceeds by hypotheses, not certainties. But, as Max Stern says, 'To say that there is no evidence as to how they [the Psalms] sounded strikes me as insufficient academic posturing, the security of not being proven wrong.'[1] Our reconstructions, if not perfect, will still give a real flavour of the temple song, and may make a way to introduce the cantillation of the Hebrew scriptures, and of the Psalms, to Biblical Studies.

---

[1] Stern 2010: 170.

Psalm 120
The Lower Court

1. Shir ha-ma-'a-lot / Song of the Ascents.
2. El-y'ho-vah ba-tsa-ra-tah li / qa-ra-ti va-ya-'a-ne-ni
   To Y'ho-vah in my distress I cried and he answered me
3. Ye-ho-vah ha-tsi-lah naf-shi mi-sfat-she-qer, / mi-la-shon r' mi-yah
   Ye-ho-vah, rescue my soul from lying lip, from tongue of deceit.
4. Mah-yi-ten l'-kha u-mah-yo-sif lakh, / la-shon r'-mi-yah
   What will he give to you and what bequeath you O tongue of deceit?
5. Hi-tse gi-bor sh'-nu-nim 'im ga-ha-le r'-ta-mim
   A warrior's arrows sharp with burning coals of broom.
6. O-yah-li ki-gar-ti me-shekh / sha-khan-ti im-o-ho-le qe-dar
   Woe is me that I stay in Meshekh, that I dwell with tents of Qedar!
7. Rab-bat shakh-nah-lah naf-shi / im so-ne sha-lom
   Too long has dwelt my soul with the hater of peace.
8. A-ni-sha-lom v' khi a-dab-ber, / hem-mah la-mil-ha-mah
   I am for peace but whenever I speak, they are all for war.

Under the moonlight of the first night of Sukkot, the night preceding the fifteenth day, the Levite singers gather in the Court of Women below the fifteen steps leading up to the sanctuary. In their midst stand the ark-keepers, the Levites of the family of Shemaiah ben Elizaphan, bearing the holy ark upon their shoulders.[1] The singers raise their song, singing in the persona of an Israelite persecuted by cruel foreigners.

Verses 1 and 2 divide between cantor and chorus at the *etnaḥ* cadence. The cantor sings of how in his distress he *cried* to Yehovah and was *answered*. The past (*I cried...he answered*) rather than the present tense (*I cry...he answers*) is certainly the natural reading of this verbal form, and it is endorsed by the

---

[1] Num. 3.27–31; 1 Chr. 15.8.

aorist *ekèkraxa* of the Septuagint.² The psalmist is recalling his own words of urgent prayer in the past. In distress he prayed with his face to Jerusalem and the LORD in mercy heard him, the very picture Solomon will repeat in his prayer of dedication at daybreak (1 Kgs 8.46–51).

In verse 2, he cites his former petition. He had prayed to be saved from lying lips and deceitful tongues. The word, *remiyah*, 'deceit' or 'shooting' or even 'making fall' suggests that they shoot lies treacherously and without warning, like archers. The idea of being under attack from arrows of treachery recalls Joseph whose betrayal by his brothers is likened by his father to an attack by archers (Gen. 49.23). Indeed, arrows of treachery are a key motif of the Josephites, like Benjamite Jeremiah, whose neighbours' *tongue is a deadly arrow*.³ Such imagery confirms what we saw in chapter seven, that the psalmist dwelt among the tribes of Joseph.

Verse 3 forms one long question. It repeats the chorus's *lashon remiyah* but has no *etnah* cadence, which suggests that it was sung entirely by the cantor. It recalls Semitic oaths of the kind, 'The god do so to me and add so to me, if I lie in this matter.' (2 Sam. 3.9; 1 Kgs 2.23). His enemies, it seems, swore a self-maledictory oath and then broke it. He wishes the consequences of their broken oath to fall upon them.

In verse 4, the chorus answer the cantor's question with bold affirmative dominants (B) to close the first quatrain. Yes, the Holy One will pay back deceitful, shooting tongues as they deserve, with arrows which are barbed, or 'toothed'. More, they will be fiery arrows – a fearsome weapon of ancient warfare – furnished with burning coals of white broom, said in the east to provide the hottest, longest-burning coals.⁴ The arrows of the Holy One will burn up his enemies.

At the slight risk of splitting a semantic unit in verse 6, I have divided verses 5 to 7 between cantor and chorus at the *etnah* cadence.⁵ This allows *shakhanti* and *shakhnah* in verses 5 and 6 to be assigned to different voices. Note how verses 5a and 7a trace the same rising melodic contour, while verse 6, sandwiched between, takes a contrasting falling and rising route.

The cantor laments his hostile environment. His 'Woe' comes from sojourning by the people of Meshekh and dwelling 'with', that is, beside or

---

² LXX Ps. 119.1. Thus the opening lines of Ps. 120 resemble Ps. 130.1. In both cases, the psalmist is citing his own past speech.

³ Jer. 9.8, where the tongue is an arrow that speaks deceit (*mirmah*). Cf. the parallels with Ps. 120.2 in Jer. 9.3 (*they prepare their tongue like a bow to shoot lies*); and with Ps. 120.7 in Jer. 9.8 (*each one speaks peace to his neighbour, but in his heart sets a trap for him*). Cf. Prov. 26.18–19.

⁴ Rashi, *ad loc.*, says they continue to burn inside when extinguished outside. Kirkpatrick says that from broom 'the Arabs still manufacture charcoal of the finest quality, which makes the hottest fire and retains heat for the longest time' (1902: 735). The eastern name (Heb. *retamim*) is preserved in the Latin-Linnaean *Retama raetam*.

⁵ The other option, to preserve v. 6 whole, would be to assign v. 5 entirely to cantor and v. 6 to chorus.

near, the tents of Kedar. Some suggest that, since he could not simultaneously dwell in Meshekh in the Caucasus and Kedar in Arabia, the two terms are a *merismus* representing total foreign hostility to the nation of Israel.[6] Others think the psalmist is describing hostile Israelite neighbours as virtual pagans. Another solution is that one verb should be read as past and the other as present tense – *I sojourned in Meshekh, I [now] dwell beside the tents of Kedar.* Both verbs are in the Hebrew perfect tense, which can sometimes be read as present tense in English. But they cannot be taken as two different tenses in one line. And, since his woe is not in the past, but ongoing, the natural reading is the present tense: *I sojourn in Meshekh, I dwell beside the tents of Kedar.*

How is this possible? Kedar was in the north-west Arabian desert, south of Damascus, east of transjordanian Israel. It was populated by Ishmaelites, that is, Arabs, known to all as *archers, the mighty men of the children of Kedar,* a reputation traceable to their earliest ancestry and their bellicose spirit.[7]

As for Meshekh, even the name has an archery ring to it, sounding like the Hebrew for 'drawing [a bow]'.[8] Its location, however, is trickier altogether. Most commentators opt for Meshekh in the Caucasus between the Black and Caspian Seas, an obvious candidate since most biblical references to Meshekh indicate this place.[9] There, in the 8th century BC, arose the Scythians, archers and merciless scalp-hunters.[10] But there is another, less familiar, option: a Semitic tribe called Meshekh. Outside this psalm, they appear only once by this name in the Bible, in 1 Chr. 1.17. But a comparison with Gen. 10.22–23, where they are called 'Mash', shows that they were Arameans. They would therefore have lived among the Aramean confederacy, with transjordanian Israel to the west and Kedar to the south. Their war-god would have resembled Asshur, the 'feather-robed archer' of the Aramean Assyrians.

Can we choose between these two Meshekhs? The first has the advantage of being better known. But in Solomon's time, the Scythians were a small nation of no consequence to Israel, and it would be impossible for the psalmist to live near Scythia and Kedar simultaneously. Aramean Meshekh, on the other hand, has more to commend it. Since it bordered both Israel and Kedar, an Israelite living in Transjordan would indeed dwell beside Meshekh and Kedar at the same time. Second, although we know the Caucasus Meshekh better than the Aramean one, the familiarity would have been otherwise in Solomon's Israel. For, unlike the early Scythians, the Arameans were Israel's powerful near neighbours, controlling the Fertile Crescent from Damascus to Babylon. They sprang from Abraham's brother, Nahor; the Israelites knew the various Aramean tribes and leaders by name; David even intermarried with

---

[6] *Merismus* is a literary device where two extremes embrace all between, like 'wet from head to toe.'
[7] Gen. 25.13; 1 Chr. 1.29; Isa. 21.17; Gen. 21.20; Gen. 21.9; 16.4.
[8] The root is *mashakh* (1 Kgs 22.34; 2 Chr. 18.33; Isa. 66.19).
[9] Gen. 10.2; 1 Chr. 1.5; Ezek. 27.13; 32.26; 38.2-4; 39.1–3; cf. Herodotus, *Hist.*, III.94; VII.78.
[10] 2 Macc. 4.47; 3 Macc. 7.5; 4 Macc. 10.7.

The Songs of Zion

them.[11] And although ancient treaties recognized the heights of Gilead as a border from early times, the Arameans eyed the territory hungrily after Israel annihilated Og and Sihon.[12] During David's time they made a bid for it, but were crushed, subjected, and controlled by David's garrisons in Damascus.[13] But during Solomon's reign, they flexed their muscles, overthrew David's garrisons, and on Solomon's death they broke loose.[14] Gilead fell bit by bit into their hands, and Israel's best efforts to retake it failed, resulting in Ahab's death at Ramoth-Gilead.[15] So all told, it is more likely that it is this Aramean Meshekh which the psalmist means. He recalls their deeds, and the deeds of the desert Kedarites to the south, the continual threat, hostility, and deception. Among these haters of peace, says he, his soul has dwelt too long (vv. 6–7).

Now we see our psalmist a little better. He is a Levite chief – only kings and Levite chiefs wrote psalms – living among the Josephite tribe of Manasseh in southern Transjordan, in the only Levite city of the area, the Merarite city of Ramoth-Gilead, hard against the desert, with Arameans to the north-east and Kedarites to the south-east (Deut. 3.12 13). The reference in verse 3 to a broken self-imprecatory oath suggests that their neighbours treacherously broke territorial and peace treaties with his community. Indeed, reading the last letter of every verse reveals an encoded message: יה המרמה, *Yah, ha-mirmah!* 'O Yah, the treachery!' The Israelites tried to speak *shalom* to them, to reason with and pacify them. But the response was treachery and violence which, borrowing the imagery of Joseph, was like attack by archers.

Yet they prayed and at last their prayer was answered. There arose a strong dynasty over a united Israel, defending the Gilead population against the foe and preserving their territorial boundaries intact. Now, with David's garrisons subduing the Arameans and peace in Israelite Transjordan, this Levite chief rejoices to leave his hostile neighbours and ascend to Zion to worship and give thanks at the dedication of the temple there. The tread of pilgrim feet is heard in his soul. We hear it in the step parallelism of verses 5 to 7, in the repetition of *dwell* (vv. 5–6), and *shalom* (6–7). The psalm is, as it were, uttered on the point of his departure, as he packs his bags, loads his beast, and walks through the city gate westward to Zion, the city of his heart. There he will be no longer a despised foreigner, but a valued citizen. The man of peace sets his face for the city whose name is peace, *Yerushalayim*, plurality of peace, peace above and peace below.[16]

---

[11] Gen. 22.20–21; 2 Sam. 10.6–8; 1 Chr. 19.6–19; Ps. 60.1 [heading]; 1 Kgs 11.23–25; 2 Sam. 3.3 (cf. 15.8).

[12] Gen. 31.45–54; Num. 21.21–35; Deut. 1.4; 2.24–3.11; Josh. 9.10; 12.1–6; Judg. 11.19–22; Ps. 136.19–20.

[13] 2 Sam. 8.6.

[14] 1 Kgs 11.23–25.

[15] 1 Kgs 22.3; 2 Kgs 5.2; 1 Kgs 22.1-40; 2 Kgs 8.28–10.32–33.

[16] *Shalayim*, plural of *shalom*, is a plural of majesty (like *elohim* or *adonai*), meaning 'totality of peace'. The holy city will extend peace into all dimensions, making peace below and peace above.

The psalm speaks of divine justice. The psalmist cries to God to avenge him on his enemies: barbed arrows for barbed lying tongues. Goldingay finds it contradictory that the psalmist, who proclaims himself a man of peace, should pray for judgment on his enemies; the psalm, he says, ultimately 'deconstructs'.[17] I disagree. This cry to God for justice is fundamental to the Psalms. I like the comment of C.S. Lewis on the cursings of the Psalms:

> I saw also the natural result of injuring a human being. The word *natural* is here important. This result can be obliterated by grace, suppressed by prudence or social convention, and (which is dangerous) wholly disguised by self-deception. But just as the natural result of throwing a lighted match into a pile of shavings is to produce a fire...so the natural result of cheating a man, or "keeping him down" or neglecting him, is to arouse resentment.[18]

Resentment arouses retribution. Yet the distinctive thing is that the psalmists do not seek retribution with their own hands. Instead, they cry for divine retribution on their behalf. Of course, both the Old and New Testaments speak of the place of contrition, reconciliation and forgiveness. But what if the offender is impenitent, making reconciliation and real forgiveness impossible? How is the offended party to deal with the sense of injustice and abuse, if not by appeal to the justice of God? In such cases, divine nemesis can and does weigh in on behalf of those mistreated.

The psalm also teaches us anagogically (to use the ancient term of fourfold exegesis) about our life's daily pilgrimage. For, like the Levite cantor, all our blessing begins with seeking the city of God. And seeking begins with the faith that his city exists and has a place for us. By this faith, the righteous of ancient Israel were blessed. By this same faith, we rise from mundane pursuits to seek the Jerusalem which is to be revealed from on high.[19] Like a pilgrim, we leave the City of Destruction for the Jerusalem which is to come, seeking the hope of eternal life.

---

[17] Goldingay 2008: 453.
[18] Lewis 1961: 26.
[19] Rev. 21.2; *Ta'an* 5a.

Psalm 121
The First Step

1. **Shir** la-ma-'a-**lot**
   Song for the A - scents;

2. E - **sa** ey - nai el-he-ha-**rim** / me - a - yin ya - **vo** ez - **ri**
   I lift my eyes to the hills! / From where shall come my help?

3. Ez - ri me - **im** ye-ho-**vah** / o - **seh** sha - ma-yim va - **a** - rets
   My help is from Ye-ho-vah / who made the heavens and earth.

4. Al - yi - **ten** lam - mot rag - **le** - kha / al - ya - **num** sho-m - **re** - kha
   He won't give to slip your foot, / He won't slumber your kee-per.

5. Hin - **neh** lo - ya - num v' - **lo** yi - shan sho - **mer** yis - ra - **el**
   Be - hold! he nei - ther slumbers nor sleeps, the keeper of Is - ra - el.

6. Ye - ho - **vah** sho-m - **re** - kha / ye-ho-**vah** tsil - **kha** al - **yad** y'-mi - **ne** - kha
   Ye-ho-vah is your kee-per; / Ye-ho-vah your shade at your right hand.

7. Yo - **mam** ha - she-mesh lo - ya - **ke** - ka / v' - ya - re - ah ba - **lay** - lah
   By day the sun shall not smite you; / nor the moon by night.

8. Ye - ho - **vah** yish-mor - **kha** mi - kol - **ra** / yi - sh - **mor** et - naf - **she** - kha
   Ye - ho - vah will keep you from all harm; / he will keep your soul.

9. Ye - ho - **vah** yish-mor - tset - **kha** u - vo - **e** - kha / me at - **tah** v' - ad - o - **lam**
   Ye - ho - vah will keep your com - ing and go - ing, / from now till e - ver - more.

The Levite singers around the ark ascend to the first step, where they raise the second Song of Ascents. It paints the psalmist, the man of *shalom* who has sojourned in Meshekh and by Kedar, on his pilgrim ascent to Zion. It is called 'A Song *for* the Ascents' – not '*of* the Ascents' like its neighbours – because it is *for* the journey, whereas the other songs deal with the pilgrim's origin and destination.

Travel was a risky business in the tenth century BC. No Thalys whisked you there in half an hour. No smooth highways rolled ahead. Instead, a long and arduous trudge by foot – with a donkey, if you were lucky – on dry tracks, blazing sun by day, cold by night. There was no health insurance, no Nivaquine or Imodium. Yet the waters had bacteria, the swamps malaria, the sands snakes and scorpions, the hills lions and bears. Even under the *pax Salomoni* the badlands of Israel's borders may have felt little obligation to wayfaring strangers. No friendly policemen pointed the way, but bandits and hard men lived by pillage and robbery. Fall foul of them and only vultures and dogs cared for your corpse. Travellers needed protection. Of course, they would travel in armed groups. But they sought higher protection than arms could give. And so this song was written as a song of blessing, an amulet for the road, confessing how the LORD will defend his faithful ones. Six times in this little song he is called their *shomer*, that is, their 'keeper' or 'protector'. He is their ever-wakeful helper, their shield from the very elements, the omnipotent Maker of all.

Verse 1, being all one question, suggests it was sung entirely by the precentor, the Levite chief from Ramoth-Gilead. The hills to which he looks in his mind's eye can only be the hills of Judah, with Jerusalem nestling in their midst. On every approach to the city, the central mountainous ridge which runs up through the Holy Land dominates the horizon. The pilgrim, on his journey, looks up to the hills ahead and asks from whence his help shall come if not from Zion. The melos traces the sight-line of the psalmist, with a rise upward on *lift*, then drops, as if looking westward over the Jordan Valley, and rises again to the *etnah* cadence on the *hills* of Jerusalem.

Appropriately to its upward-journeying theme, this song has more 'step-parallelism' than any other psalm. Verses 1 and 2 form a step with 'help'; verses 3 to 5 are stepped with 'slumber' and 'keeper'; and the last couplet, verses 7 and 8, forms a step with 'keep'. The whole song becomes a rhythm of ascending footsteps, one upward climb, as the Levites, on their slow ascent of the temple steps, sing of the pilgrim ascending toward Jerusalem.

In verse 2, the chorus answers the cantor's question. His *help* will come from these hills, that is, from the One who dwells amidst them, where the Levites sing and the newly-built temple glistens in the moon and torch light. In the second part of the verse, the words *Maker of heaven and earth* are sung to the same melos as accompanies the phrase throughout the Songs of Ascents and elsewhere in the Psalms.[1] This suggests that the phrase was a congregational refrain, where cantor, chorus, and others joined together.

At verse 3, the first person speech changes to second person 'your' and 'you', suggesting that the chorus now address the cantor. They pronounce a blessing on him, assuring him of the divine protection he seeks. The bold declaration on the dominant (B) reflects the surety of divine protection on

---

[1] Pss. 124.8; 134.4; 115.15. The exception is Ps. 146.6 which, being the first stich of the verse, was sung by the cantor and ornamented accordingly.

rough roads where a broken ankle might mean permanent disability or worse. But the ever-wakeful Lord, who keeps Israel, will keep his pilgrim (vv. 3-4). He will be on his right hand, like the faithful comrade in battle, who protects the fighting warrior's unshielded right flank. He will protect from the elements. The sun will not strike with feverish sunstroke, nor the moon with baleful lunacy (vv. 5-6).

The psalm closes, in verses 7 and 8, with a blessing of protection, each phrase being set to very much the same melody, binding the little couplet together. The God who dwells on Zion hill is fully able to protect. A series of merisms portray his total power. *Heaven and earth, now and forever,* express his sovereignty over space and time. *Day and night, sun and moon, going and coming,* depict his control over the things that impinge on human experience. He can protect his pilgrim worshippers everywhere and always.

As part of the Ascents collection, sung in the temple courts, one may ask what was this psalm's relation with actual pilgrims coming to the feast. Did it first exist as a song for the road before it was taken into the Ascents collection? Or was it first written for the Ascents collection and the temple, and was later sung by pilgrims on the road. Perhaps, like many songs, it was a bit of both. Perhaps the Levite composer borrowed parts of songs that were already sung by pilgrims, and formed them into a new song, which the pilgrims would learn and, in turn, sing as they travelled up to the festivals in Zion.

The psalm teaches us, anagogically, that God will keep us in our ways. We may certainly ask the blessing of heaven on our coming and going. When we sit behind the wheel, when the tram or metro pulls out, or the plane takes off, we can affirm the promise of verse 8 and expect protection on our ways. But those who have set their hearts on pilgrimage have a bigger journey ahead, a lifetime's trek through an uncertain and often hostile world to the city of God. Yet he who called us to his feast will keep our coming and going now, will keep us always, until we enter the gates of his city with joy.

Psalm 122
The Second Step

CANTOR
1. Shir ha-ma-'a-lot l'-da-vid.
   Song of As-cents. Of Da-vid.

CANTOR
Sa-maḥ-ti b'om-rim li bet ye-ho-vah ne-lekh
I was glad when they said to me, 'Let's go to the house of the Lord.'

CHORUS
2. Om-dot ha-yu rag-le-nu bi-sh'a-ra-yikh ye-ru-sha-la-yim
   Now stan-ding are our feet in your gates, Je-ru-sa-lem.

CANTOR   **CHORUS**
3. Ye-ru-sha-la-yim ha-b'nu-yah k'-ir she-ḥub-rah-lah yaḥ-dav
   Je-ru-sa-lem which is built like a ci-ty close-ly set as one.

CANTOR   **CHORUS**   **CANTOR**   **CHORUS**
4. She-sham a-lu sh-va-tim, shiv-tey-yah e-dut l'-yis-ra-el l'ho-dot l'-shem ye-ho-vah
   For there go up the tribes, tribes of Yah, a law for Is-ra-el, to thank the name of the Lord.

CANTOR   **CHORUS**
5. Ki sham-mah yash-vu khis-ot l' mish-pat kis-ot l'-vet da-vid
   For there are set up the judg-ment thrones, the thrones of Da-vid's house.

CANTOR   **CHORUS**
6. Sha-'a-lu sh'-lom ye-ru-sha-la-yim yi-sh-la-yu o-ha-va-yikh
   Pray for the peace of Je-rusa-lem, May they pros-per, those who love you.

CANTOR   **CHORUS**
7. Y'-hi-sha-lom b'-ḥe-lekh shal-vah b'-ar-m-no-ta-yikh
   And there be peace in your walls, sal-va-tion in your pala-ces.

CANTOR
8. L'-ma-'an a-ḥai v'-re-'ai a-da-brah-na sha-lom bakh
   For sake of my bro-thers and friends, I will say 'Peace u-pon you!'

CHORUS
9. L'-ma-'an bet-y'ho-vah e-lo-he-nu a-vaq-shah tov lakh
   For the house of Y'ho-vah our God, I will seek your good.

The ark and its Levites ascend to the second step, where the singers take up the third Song of Ascents, which is the first one written by David.[1] Here they sing of themselves as pilgrim travellers arriving in Jerusalem. The precentor lifts his voice to sing the first verse, with its singular 'I' and 'me', and the Levite chorus respond with the plural 'our' in verse 2. We see him, singing toward his singer kinsmen and friends on the fifteen steps, as to those who encouraged him to come on the arduous journey, and declaring: *I was glad when they said to me, Let us go to the house of the* LORD. And his brothers, standing beneath the great overshadowing gate, respond, *Our feet are standing in your gates, Jerusalem.*

The repetition of *Yerushalayim* at the beginning of verse 3, suggests it was sung by another voice, by the precentor again. He speaks as one seeing Jerusalem, as if for the first time, in all its beauty. He praises the city's strong, solid construction which seems to him the outward reflection of its inner nature. The *maqqef* compresses together the words *she-ḥubrah lah yaḥdav*, 'well compacted together', as a sound-picture of the compact city. The houses are compact together, as they are within Jerusalem's walls today, for the inhabitants of the city were not strangers who feared one another, but brothers who lived together.

The melismatic opening of verse 4 suggests it was sung by the cantor. How to interpret the circular *galgal* under *alu* is a puzzle. But I have followed Ginsburg, whose sources take it as *mehuppakh*, a rising sixth.[2] Certainly this fits well, as the cantor's voice soars with excitement as he describes the ascent of the tribes, now standing assembled in the courtyard below him. The repeated words which follow – *tribes...tribes, thrones...thrones* (vv. 4–5) – may have been sung in short responsory bursts.

v. 4	Cantor	There the tribes go up...
	Chorus	The tribes of Yah!
	Cantor	A statute of Israel...
	Chorus	To give thanks to the name of Yehovah!
v. 5	Cantor	There are set thrones of justice...
	Chorus	Thrones of the house of David!

Here then is the secret of the city's well-built strength and *shalom*: the heart of the city is the temple of the Holy One, where the people give thanks to his name. His presence brings strength and calm to all its soul; its citizens live under the righteous rule of divine law, administered by the house of David. *Yashvu* (v. 5) means 'sat', a verb where the melodic line of the Psalms sometimes drops or sits.[3] But in this case, it rises, for the sense of the verb is not sitting down but the setting up of high thrones. The thrones are plural since

---

[1] The 'David' heading is found in the Masoretic texts, the Qumran Psalms Scroll (11QPs^a), and LXX Codex Sinaiticus. It is absent from LXX Codex Vaticanus and the Targum.
[2] BHS, on the other hand, reads it as *etnaḥ hafukh* (D♯), the step below the tonic.
[3] See, e.g., Ps. 1.1.

they represent not only the king's throne, but the thrones of the judiciary who administer justice in the name of David's house.

Verses 6 to 9 stand out among the psalms as a perfect example of a rhyming song.

⁶ Sha'alú shalóm yerushaláyim	yishláyu óhaváyikh
⁷ Yehi-shalóm b'helékh	shalváh b'ármnotáyikh
⁸ L'má'an aḥái v-re'ái	adabrah-ná shalóm bákh
⁹ L'má'an bet-Y'hováh elohéynu	avaqsháh tóv lákh

There are rhyming couplets: *ohavayikh* and *armnotayikh*, *bakh* and *lakh*. There is first word repetition, or anaphora, in the repeated *l'ma'an*. There is a predominance of accents on *a*-vowels, with liquid *l* and *sh* consonants, soothing consonants that speak of peace: *sha-la-la, sha-la-la*. And it has a real melody. The first halves of verses six and seven have a different contour, for variety's sake, yet the second halves of each verse close with the same melody, pointing up the rhyme and unity of the couplet.[4] And verses 8 and 9 are identical in their melodic contour. Note how the single accented syllables at the end of these verses, especially verse 9, force longer time values on the notes, a favourite closural device in music.

The cantor-chorus exchange point, as noted in the last chapter, would be at the end of the semantic unit, at the end of v. 8. For there is no internal parallelism, or repetition, or halfway break in the sense, within either verse 8 or 9. Instead, the two verses share the same sense structure and are bound by their rhyming ends so as to form a parallelistic couplet together.

⁸ For the sake of my brothers and friends, I will say peace within you
⁹ For the sake of the house of Yehovah our God, I will seek your good.

So the natural place for the cantor-chorus exchange is where the semantic pause occurs, at the end of v. 8. Then, in v. 9, the chorus respond to the cantor and complete the song.

The person who composed this song loved Jerusalem and wrote this singable, memorable blessing for the city to turn the people's hearts toward it and urge them to pray for its *shalom*. Would it surprise us if David would conceive such a song for his royal capital that he wrested from the Jebusites and their Egyptian patrons? A prominent Scottish politician and lawyer of former years, Andrew Fletcher, said, 'Let me write the songs of a nation, and I care not who writes its laws.'[5] David too realized the culture-shaping power of song. With such a song as this in their mouths, the Israelites in their towns

---

[4] In western classical music it is more common for paired musical phrases to be identical in their *initium* and to vary in their closing cadence. But the opposite formula, is, globally-speaking, more widespread, occurring, for instance, in the traditional music of Africa and Asia and in much western popular music.

[5] Thanks to Gordon Wenham (2013: 13). Fletcher published these words in 1704.

and villages would sing blessings on the holy city all year round and seek its good.

This song had, for modern-day Israel, a fulfilment on 7 June 1967, when a crackly radio voice announced that the Israeli Defence Force had taken the Temple Mount, and then read the psalm: *Our feet are standing in your gates, Jerusalem.* Prayers for the fallen were led by Rabbi Shlomo Goren, and the Jewish populace erupted in celebration, singing Naomi Shemer's *Yerushalayim shel zahav.* The psalm became the liturgy of the moment in answer to 1900 years of Jewish prayers and the opening of a new chapter in world history.

But Jerusalem was no less precious to David and his Levites. For them too, it was the global epicentre of glory. There was the throne of the Maker of heaven and earth, with the *Mashiah* seated at his right hand, administering the just and heavenly law. They thought themselves supremely favoured to walk in this city, to belong there, to seek its good, to offer their lives in its service, to stand in the gates of its wonderful house and declare the praises of its God. To belong to such a city was life.

As for us, the goal of our pilgrimage is also to enter the gates of God's city with joy. I like the story of Cecil Rhodes, bivouacking in the bush late one night, waking his comrade, Leander Starr Jameson.

'Jameson, Jameson!' he insisted, 'Wake up! Wake up!'

Jameson awoke, seizing his Hauser against marauding Hottentots. 'What is it, Rhodes?'

Rhodes replied, 'Jameson, have you ever thought how fortunate you are to be British? Britain, the flower of history, the jewel of civilization!'

'Go to sleep, Rhodes.'

Few these days would subscribe to Rhodes's imperialist zeal. But to be proud of one's motherland is not all bad. And we wait for the revealing of a better royal city, whose glory shall not fade, and of whose citizenship we may gladly sing.

Psalm 123
The Third Step

1. Shir ha-ma-'a-lot
   Song of the As-cents.

   E-le-kha na-sa-ti et-'ei-nai ha-yosh-vi ba-sha-ma-yim
   To you I lift up my eyes, O En-throned in the hea-vens.

2. Hin-neh kh'-'e-ne 'a-va-dim el-yad a-do-ne-hem
   Be-hold! as the eyes of slaves to hand of their lord,

   k'-'e-ne shif-ḥah el-yad g'-vir-tah
   as the eyes of a maid to hand of mis-tress,

   Ken e-ne-nu el-y'ho-vah e-lo-he-nu ad she-y'han-ne-nu
   So our eyes are to Y'ho-vah our God, till he has mer-cy.

3. Ḥa-ne-nu y'ho-vah ḥa-ne-nu ki-rav sa-va-nu vuz
   Have mer-cy, Y'ho-vah, have mer-cy, for much are we sated with scorn.

4. Rab-bat sav'ah-lah na-f-she-nu ha-la-'ag ha-sha-a-na-nim
   For much sated is our soul of mock-e-ry of the proud,

   Ha-buz li-g'-e-yo-nim
   of the scorn of those at ease.

The singers ascend to the third step and raise their song, the first of the first 'dark' trio of the Songs of Ascents. At this point the narrative and physical actions of the Songs converge. The precentor-pilgrim, who has so far spoken like one arriving in the holy city, now speaks of himself as he actually is, looking to the temple, the heavenly throne, above him.

He lifts his eyes, not *to the hills* as in Psalm 121, but *to you* (v. 1), to the One who indwells the temple. The *qal* verb (*nasati*, I lifted) shows that this is not a single prayer of the moment, but, in a sense, the prayer he has always been praying. It is his habitual prayer, beginning in the past, continuing into the present, his prayer for the vindication of Israel. With his lifted eyes, his voice also rises on the melodic line of *I lift*, and the chorus bring the melody back down to depict the sitting of the heavenly One. The Hebrew definite article *ha-* in *ha-yoshvi* is a courtly vocative, while the verb (*yashav*) means dwell, sit, or sit enthroned. The form of address is therefore *O Enthroned One in the heavens*. But why does he say this? That God sits in heaven is a truism. But, gazing on the temple, one would expect him to say, 'O Dweller in the temple'. Instead he says 'O Enthroned One in the heavens'. There are two reasons why he speaks this way. First, as we saw in chapter five, there was indeed a throne in the temple, beneath the wings of the *keruvim* chariot, and there the invisible God sat enthroned. But, second, in Israelite thought, the temple was part of heaven itself.

This idea of a point at which heaven and earth conjoin, an *axis mundi*, has been held by many nations. As the Japanese had Mount Fuji, the Greeks Olympus, the Indians Kailash, so the Hebrews had the Temple Mount. Just as Ceuta is part of Spain on the African mainland, so the temple was part of heaven on earth. It was *the navel of the earth* (Ezek. 38.12), where earth, like a foetus, drew life from the land of the stars. At this centre-point, earth's needs and petitions were heard in heaven; there heaven's life and power flowed to earth. This idea is vital to understanding the ancient Israel's world-view. When David wrote *The LORD is in his holy temple; the LORD – in heaven his throne* (Ps. 11.4), he was not speaking of two dwellings but of one throne at the junction of heaven and earth. Those of us who live in the age of the Holy Spirit believe we are heard wherever we pray. But in ancient Israel, heaven and earth met in the temple and it was to the temple alone that prayer might be made.

In verse 2, at each mention of lifted *eyes*, the voice soars up, and then once more for *Yehovah*. The verse is particularly long. It must be read as a tetracolon, since the *etnaḥ* cadence at the end of *elohenu* means that the following words – *ad she-y'ḥanenu* – form a colon in their own right. The complex cantillation of the first three cola suggest that they were sung by the precentor as a cadenza, in fairly free rhythm, before the chorus responded with the last colon. He declares that, like a slave or maid-servant before master or mistress, he has nothing to bargain with. His only hope is in the master's compassion. The chorus plead that they will wait until he has mercy upon them.

In v. 3, the cantor takes up the chorus's word, *ḥanenu*, 'have mercy on us' with a strong declaration on the dominant. The chorus respond, asking mercy in recompense for the *contempt* they have endured through a millennium of hardships, from the slavery in Egypt on.

Throughout the psalm, the dominant image is not directly stated. But it is that thing which the master's hand might bestow upon his servants. It has been suggested that this refers to the cessation of punishment or a gesture indicating favour, but the likelier explanation is that it refers to provision of food. It is when the Holy One opens his hand that his creatures are filled (Ps. 104.27–28). The provision they hope for is contrasted with what they have already received. For instead of being filled with blessings, they have been *sated* with contempt. They ask that they might be filled with good things instead of bitter fare. As David first rolled back their reproach, so may Solomon continue to do. Yet, the prayer contains no request for immediate deliverance from danger or for action against the contemptuous oppressors. The oppression, though formerly sore, has evidently ceased. The day of blessing has dawned.

Citizens of the holy city may offer up prayers from a humble heart before the divine throne and be heard. *Lord, have mercy on us!* is a good prayer for any time. Weary from the wilderness, worn out from failure, wandering, and opposition, how can we shine like a city set on a hill? But those who appeal to the merciful Lord, enthroned in heaven, will be filled and refreshed and guided, and raised from contempt to vessels of glory.

Psalm 124
The Fourth Step

1. Shir ha-ma-'a-lot l'-da-vid
   Song of Ascents. Of David.

2. Lu-le y'-ho-vah she-ha-yah la-nu yo-mar-na yis-ra-el
   Had not Y'-ho-vah been on our side... O say now, Is-ra-el.

3. Lu-le y'-ho-vah she-ha-yah la-nu b'-qum 'a-le-nu a-dam
   Had not Y'-ho-vah been on our side when rose a-gainst us men.

4. A-zai hay-yim b'-la-'u-nu ba-ha-rot a-pam ba-nu
   Then had they swal-lowed us live when burned their wrath on us.

5. A-zai ha-may-im sh'ta-fu-nu nah-lah a-var 'al-naf-she-nu
   And then the waters o-ver-whel-ming, the flood went o-ver our soul.

6. A-zai a-var al-naf-she-nu ha-may-im ha-ze-do-nim
   And then went o-ver our soul the wa-ters proud.

7. Ba-rukh y'-ho-vah she-lo n'-ta-na-nu te-ref l'-shi-ne-hem
   Blest be y'-ho-vah who did not give us as prey to their teeth.

8. Naf-she-nu k'-tsip-por nim-l'-tah mi-pah yo-q'-shim
   Our soul like a bird has e-scaped from snare of fow-lers.

9. Ha-pah nish-bar va-a-nah nu nim-lat-nu
   The snare is bro-ken and we have e-scaped.

10. Ez-re-nu b'-shem y'-ho-vah o-seh sha-ma-yim va-a-rets
    Our help in the name Ye-ho-vah who made the hea-vens and earth.

Rising to the fourth step, the Levites around the ark take up the fifth song. Having recalled the oppressions of the past in the previous psalm, they now raise their voices in a hymn of thanksgiving for the many deliverances which the Holy One has granted them. In verse 1, the words *yomar-na yisrael* have the same melody as the identical phrase in verse 1 of Psalm 129, which suggests the phrase is a group response, either from the Levite chorus addressing the men of Israel, or else by the assembled congregation of Israelites gathered around.[1]

This is the second of the Songs of Ascents authored by David.[2] Seeing in his mind's eye the realization of his great and glorious dream, the temple, he confesses that it was only because the Holy One was with them, only because of his covenant bias towards them, that Israel even survived, either before his reign or during it. For *men rose against* them in hot anger, like beasts to swallow them alive, like gluttonous death (Prov. 1.12; Hab. 2.5), and like overwhelming waters to wash them away (vv. 2–5). To paint the hostile nations as voracious beasts and unruly waters is familiar imagery, in the Psalms (Pss. 65.7; 68.30) and elsewhere (Isa. 5.29–30; 17.12-13; 51.9-10; Dan. 7.2–3). It recalls Canaanite belief, where Yam, the sea-dragon, rises to overthrow Lord Baal and the created order. Likewise, for the Israelites, the Flood rose to overthrow the LORD's rule of creation, but was defeated (Pss. 29.10; 93.3–4). And, certainly, the flood of nations did their best to overthrow the new creation Israel.[3] And not only the nations, but Israel's tribal conflicts and the harsh rule of Saul added to their woes. Finally, a thousand years after the promise to Abraham, David arose to cut off Israel's enemies on every side and to rule the twelve tribes. He handed to his son Solomon a nation with peace on every border, a nation respected on all sides, so that Solomon might build the holy temple.

Reviewing the past, David can only bless the One who saved them from the fangs of the beasts (v. 6). *Barukh Yehovah*, 'Blessed be the LORD' is a characteristic exclamation of the praising king, which he always sang to the same hopeful, rising melody (Pss. 28.6; 31.21). Israel has escaped alive from nigh-extinction. As only darkness shows the beauty of light, only the nearness of death teaches the sweetness of salvation.

In verse 7, the bird in a snare was a common picture of captivity in the ancient east: Sennacherib boasted that he shut up Hezekiah in Jerusalem like a bird in a cage.[4] And note how the vagrant, wind-blown melodic line lacks the strong mid-verse cadence – *etnaḥ*, the 'rest' – so as to depict Israel having no rest, but fleeing like a bird, painted by the fluttering *tsinnor* turn. Their harried lives of the past had been wandering and distraught.

---

[1] In vv 1–5, Haïk-Vantoura raises the fourth steps of the scale (the *etnaḥ* pause) by a semitone (to A♯), making the *Mi sheberakh* mode. The effect is attractive and exotic. However, the A♯ does not work throughout the song, as Haïk-Vantoura recognizes, for she does not include it in the psalm's heading nor in verses 6 to 8, where it would sound odd. The A♯ should therefore be omitted throughout, unless we can imagine the Levites retuning their harps between verses 5 and 6.

[2] The 'David' heading is found in the Masoretic texts, LXX Codex Sinaiticus, and the Targum. Its presence or absence in the Qumran Psalms Scroll (11QPs^a) cannot be determined due to the condition of the scroll. It is absent from LXX Codex Vaticanus.

[3] Aletti & Trublet 1983: 248–9.

[4] *ANET*, 287–88. Goldingay 2008: 481.

Verse 8 opens with a bold confession of faith to an altogether more familiar melodic pattern: mediant and dominant coming to pause, at long last, on *etnaḥ*. Their divine helper has brought them rest. The whole congregation responds with the refrain, *Oseh shamayim va-arets*, 'Maker of heaven and earth', to the same melos as its other appearances in 121.2 and 134.3.

Note again that there is no request for salvation from any current threat, for their deliverance is complete. The Holy One has set them free. With the architectural plans of the glorious temple in his hand, David already saw the day of its completion in his mind's eye as he wrote his song. There was undoubtedly reason to give thanks.

The metrical version of this psalm was sung in the churches and schools of Scotland in the dark days of the Second World War until victory was won. In time, divine mercy leads us out of overwhelming troubles into spacious places. Until then, we should wait, for he will surely come to save those who trust him. And when we are free, we should remember from what we have come, and bless him for his goodness. Deliverance begins with wisdom. For, although David gives glory to God, it was David's wisdom and courage that lifted his people from a thousand years of adversity. Leadership can do that. Yet few leaders see the full fruit of their labour. Moses died leaving his people in the desert. Yet, playing the part given him, he laid the foundation on which David built. David died not seeing the temple worship that was his life's goal. But he prepared the way for those who would follow. Happy are those who fulfil their mandate from on high.

Psalm 125
The Fifth Step

1. **Shir ha-ma-'a-lot** / Song of the Ascents.
   ha-bot'-ḥim bi-y'ho-**vah** k'har-tsi-**yon** lo-yi-mot l-'o-lam ye-shev
   Those who trust Ye-ho-vah are like Mount Zion, never shaken; it for ever abides.

2. Ye-ru-sha-**layim**, ha-rim sa-**viv** lah vi-y'ho-vah sa-viv l-'a-mo
   Jerusalem, the mountains surround it! And Y'ho-vah surrounds his people
   me-at-**tah** v'-ad-o-**lam**
   from now till evermore.

3. Ki lo ya-nu-aḥ she-vet ha-re-sha al go-**ral** ha-tsa-di-**kim**
   For shall not rest sceptre of wickedness on the portion of the righteous
   l'-ma-'an lo-yish-l-**khu** ha-tsa-di-**kim** b'-av-la-**tah** y'-de-**hem**
   so that they put not forth, the righteous, to evil their hands.

4. He-**ti**-vah y'-ho-vah la-to-**vim** v'li-sha-**rim** b'-li-bo-**tam**
   Do good, Ye-ho-vah, to the good, to the upright in heart.

5. V'-ha-ma-**tim** 'a-kal-k'lo-**tam** yo-li-khem y'-ho-vah et-po-'a-le ha-a-ven
   But those who stray in crooked ways, he will lead them, Ye-ho-vah, away with doers of evil.

   sha-**lom** 'al-yis-ra-**el**
   Shalom on Israel.

The Levites ascend one more step and look over the temple's low eastern wall to the Mount of Olives beneath the full moon of the fifteenth night.[1] They lift their harps and sing: *Jerusalem – mountains surround it; and the* LORD *surrounds his people from now until forever.*

After the cantor sings the heading and the words *Those who trust in the* LORD, the chorus respond with the greater part of the verse, their *revia* shake

---

[1] See Chapter 6.

on 'shaken' well depicting what will not happen to the faithful or to Mount Zion. The unshakeability of Jerusalem is a fairly frequent theme of the Psalms.[2] Isaiah too could sing, *We have a strong city; he sets up salvation as walls and bulwarks* (26.1). This is, of course, picturesque language for the city's enduring life and importance. But it also reflects a geographical fact, namely, that in a region prone to earthquakes, Jerusalem, on its rocky foundation, always escapes damage.[3] In addition to the eternal rock below, the city is defended by mountains. The city's natural defenses are only a picture of its supernatural defenses. For, more than all, the Holy One upholds and surrounds both the city and its people for ever. For, in comparison to other encomiums of Zion, and in comparison to the earlier Songs of Ascents, this psalm takes a more individual tone. It is not simply Mount Zion which will endure. That is undisputed. But *those who trust in the* LORD will also, like Zion, endure forever. Here there is more than a hint of eternal life for the faithful.

The complex cantillation of the first part of verse 2 suggests that it is a cantoral solo. Note that *Yerushalayim*, the sure-founded, is sung on the foundational tonic or key-note (E), while the surrounding mountains are sung on the notes on each side (D$^\sharp$, F). The simpler second colon would have been sung by the chorus, or a semi-chorus, while the third colon, the response, *From now until forever*, was declared by all present, its cantillated melody being the same as in Psalms 121.8 and 131.3.

Lengthy verse 3, without *etnaḥ* pause, clustered with supralinear signs, and difficult to scan (with eleven feet to the verse), looks like a cantoral solo throughout. The cantor sings of what he has observed in his own lifetime: the *sceptre of the wicked*, heathen domination, shall not continue forever over the heritage of righteous Israel. In the days of faithless Saul, much of the land was under Canaanite and Philistine kings, while the Jebusites held Jerusalem as Egyptian puppets. Such rulers had their day, but ceded their place to righteous rule, to the rule of David's house, who brought the promised inheritance, bit by bit, under Israel's control. Such rule is a gift from above to the righteous, so that evil rulers will not compel them to lift their hands to idolatry.

Verse 4, after the preceding cantoral solo, is assigned to the chorus. They ask the Holy One to continue and increase good to those who merit it, to bless the upright, who trust him, with peace, prosperity and righteous rule. Verse 5 is taken up by the cantor again, his *revia* shake now illustrating the unsteady ways of those who stray. The chorus sing the assurance that these unsteady ones, erring Israelites, will be removed together with foreign occupation (v. 5), such as the Philistine occupation of Gezer, which was ended, by the incursion of Solomon's Egyptian father-in-law, shortly before the construction of the temple.[4] Then the whole congregation close with the blessing formula, *Shalom on Israel*, sung to the same melody as in Psalm 128.

---

[2] Pss. 46; 48; 76.
[3] Arieh 1972: 340-42.
[4] Kitchen 2001: 41-43; 1 Kgs 9.16; *Ant.* VIII.vi.1; cf. Josh. 16.10; Judg. 1.29; 2 Sam. 5.25.

The psalm continues the thanksgiving mood of Psalm 124, but allows that unfaithful Israelites will be removed from the community while divine protection will rest on the faithful. The saying that 'people get the governments they deserve' is a modern one, reflecting the idea that democracy empowers those who model the values of the electorate. But the frequent match between rulers and ruled is not simply a human matter. It is an outworking of divine justice in human affairs (Matt. 7.2), appointing rulers as a blessing or scourge as each people merits. And so, while it is good to cast our vote in the polling station, it is the moral vote which we all cast with our lives which most determines the peace, or lack of it, in the nations where we live.

Psalm 126
The Sixth Step

1. **Shir** ha-ma-'a-lot / Song of the Ascents.
   b'-**shuv** ye-ho-**vah** et-shi-**vat** tsi-**on** ha-**yi**-nu k'-**hol**-**mim** / When turned Yehovah the fortunes of Zion, we were like those who dream.

2. **Az** yi-ma-**le** s'-**ḥok** pi-**nu** u-l'-sho-ne-nu ri-**na** / Then was filled with laughter our mouth, and our tongue with happiness;
   az yom-**ru** va-go-**yim** hig-**dil** ye-ho-**vah** la-'a-sot im-**e**-leh / then said they in the nations, 'Great things Yehovah has done for them.'

3. Hig-**dil** ye-ho-**vah** la-'a-sot i-**ma**-nu ha-**yi**-nu s'me-**ḥim** / Great things Yehovah has done for us and so we are glad.

4. **Shu**-**va** ye-ho-**vah** et-sh'vi-**te**-nu k'a-a-fi-**kim** ba-**ne**-gev / Restore, Yehovah, our fortunes like the streams in the Negev.

5. Ha-zor-**'im** b'-dim-**'ah** b'-ri-**na** yik-tso-ru / Those who sow in tears, with joy shall reap.

6. Ha-**lokh** ye-**lekh** u-va-**kho** no-**se** me-shekh ha-**za**-ra / He who goes out, weeping, bearing seed for sowing,
   bo-**ya**-**vo** b'-ri-**na** no-**se** a-lu-mo-**tav** / will return in joy, and carrying his sheaves.

The Levites ascend to the sixth step. Below, the streets and homes of the midnight-feasting city were full of the bread and new wine of the harvest. The Levites sing this psalm, its pictures of reaping and harvest and autumn rain so apt to the Sukkot Feast. Duhm calls it, 'One of the most beautiful psalms, perhaps the most beautiful in the whole Psalter, both in content and form.

Nowhere else is the eschatological hope expressed with such heartfelt, touching simplicity.'[1]

Verse 1 features the unusual word *shivat,* attested in the 8th century BC Seifire inscription as meaning 'fortunes'.[2] There is no need, then, to read it as *shevut* (captivity), as some do. However, the marginal reading in verse 4 shows that the choice between *fortunes* or *captivity* was an ancient one. The language borrows from the Song of Moses, who speaks of the LORD turning back Israel's fortunes when they repent, even in a foreign land (Deut. 30.3). And therefore, although the other reading, *captivity*, dates from a later period, from the end of the Judean captivity in Babylon following Cyrus decree to restore Jerusalem in 538 BC, it is perfectly in keeping with the spirit of the original psalm.

The cantor takes up the opening clause, and after the *etnah* cadence, the chorus respond, *We were like dreamers* (v. 1). The Israelites said to one another in the time of the Judges, *But if the LORD is with us, why has all this happened to us?* (Judg. 6.13). They imagined oppression would never cease, that any better future was a dream. But David's generation found their dreams come true; prophecy was fulfilled and prayers answered; the obedience of the nations belonged to the sceptre of Judah (Gen. 49.10). No longer did foreigners ravage family and field, nor internecine blood-feuds multiply bitterness, nor famine stalk the land.

The first part of verse 2 is clustered with complex cantillation, including the circular *galgal*. (I have again followed Ginsburg in reading it as *etnah hafukh* and therefore treating it as the subtonic.). Such cantillation signifies a cantoral solo. The cantor sings of how their *mouth was filled with laughter*, that is, they laughed and sang joyful songs, and of what the nations said about their good fortune. The chorus respond, after the *etnah* cadence, in the persona of the nations, declaring, *Great things the LORD has done for them*.

Verse 3 has no *etnah* cadence and one may imagine that it was sung by the cantor throughout. This would suit the *diminuendo* toward the end of the verse, where all the rejoicing and *Great things* are followed by a little conclusion: *We are glad.* Cohen thinks that this implies disappointment. But it is rather deliberate restraint for emphasis. The Greeks called it *litotes*. Some music critics call it 'under-exaggeration' (in the works, for instance, of Johannes Brahms). It is the gentle word which breaks a bone, the humble and reflective summary of a great triumph, the stepping back from the brink of bluster. As if a government were to say, 'We have grown the economy, expanded health services, provided education for all, reduced taxation, paid off the national debt, and established global peace. We have done not badly.'

Verse 4, by contrast, is a strong plea on the dominant. I have assigned the entire verse to the chorus alone, not only because of its urgency, but also to contrast with the solo cantor in verses 3 and 5. They ask that the Holy One

[1] Duhm 1899: 275.
[2] Allen 1983: 170.

might continue to turn their fortunes, just as he has already begun to do. Just as he blesses the dry Negev wadis with harvest rain in season, may he bless Israel and make them fruitful.

Verse 5 is extremely short, with only four feet, a range of two notes, and no *etnah* rest, as if painting a weary trudging to work. The lack of *etnah* cadence may suggest it was a cantoral solo. The psalmist ties their former sufferings to their current happiness. Just as, at the harvest feast, Israel celebrated the fruits of their hard work throughout the year, so now, in their time of prosperity, they celebrate the fruits of what they sowed in their former sufferings. This means, of course, that they continued faithful to their calling in times of adversity. But, more, there is the idea that suffering and adversity are in themselves a form of sowing, a deposit in the secret heart of God, which bear the sweet fruit of prosperity in due season.

The cantillation of verse 6 is, like verse 2, complex. But the verse can be divided into four cola: the first cadence at the *tsinnor* turn of 'weeping', the second at the *oleh ve-yored* of 'sowing', the third at the *etnah* pause of 'joy', the fourth at the close of the verse. One can imagine several possibilities for how it might have been sung. But the likeliest is that the complex first two cola were cantoral solo, as was the simpler third colon, whose rising tones ushered in the full chorus after the *etnah* cadence.

After a millennium of suffering, Israel's light came under David and Solomon. For a moment, their kingdom shone brightly. Then, on Solomon's death, their turnings turned again to struggle and adversity. Therefore the rabbis, particularly Kimḥi, routinely interpret the psalm as pointing to Israel in their long exile, whose faithful observance of Torah will eventually lead to a harvest of redemption. In this, they agree with Duhm, who saw the psalm pointing well beyond its own time to the bright future of the age to come.

Walt Disney famously said, 'If you can dream it, you can do it.' And, certainly, great achievements begin with a dream. But dreams do not come true of their own accord, but through labour and perseverance. *Omnia perseverando vinces* goes the Roman proverb: Perseverance conquers all things. Or as Plutarch said, 'Perseverance is more prevailing than violence, and many things which cannot be overcome when they are together, yield themselves up when taken little by little.' Harvest fields are ploughed in winter frost. Resolute sowing in adversity yields the sweet fruit of dreams come true. For perseverance is itself a sowing in the heart of God, and so we should never be weary in well-doing. For however glorious or otherwise the society we inhabit, the earth will soon host a kingdom outshining Solomon's, as the sun outshines the stars. Those who cherish this hope are marked not by despair but by virtue and fortitude, as they look to the day when ages of sowing in tears will be reaped in songs of everlasting joy.

Psalm 127
The Seventh Step

CANTOR
1. Shir ha-ma-'a-lot li-shlo-mo.
   Song of the Ascents. Of Shlo-mo.

im-ye-ho-vah lo-yiv-neh va-yit shav 'am-lu vo-nav bo
If Ye-ho-vah build not the house, vainly labour builders in it;

CHORUS
im-ye-ho-vah lo-yish-mar-'ir shav sha-qad sho-mer
If Ye-ho-vah guard not the city vain-ly watch the guard.

CANTOR
2. Shav la-khem mash-ki-me qum m'aḥ-re-she-vet
   Vain for you, ri-sing ear-ly and late to rest,

o-kh'ley le-ḥem ha-'a-tsa-vim ken yi-ten li-di-do she-na
eating bread of an-xious toil, for he gives his be-lo-ved rest.

CANTOR
3. Hin-neh na-ḥa-lat ye-ho-vah ba-nim sa-khar p'-ri ha-ba-ten
   Behold! a be-quest of Ye-ho-vah are sons, a re-ward is the fruit of the womb.

CHORUS
4. K'-ḥi-tsim b'-yad-gi-bor ken b'-ne ha-n-'u-rim
   Like arrows in the hand of a hero so are the chil-dren of youth.

CANTOR
5. Ash-re ha-ge-ver a-sher mil-le et-ash-pa-to me-hem
   Most hap-py the man of whom is full his quiver of them.

CHORUS
lo-ye-vo-shu ki-y'-dab-ru et o-y'-vim ba-sha-'ar
they won't be a-shamed when they con-tend with foes in the gate.

Rising to the seventh step, the Levites of Solomon's time were now standing midway on the two flights of stairs in Solomon's temple, in the semi-court beneath the gate over the eastern stairway. They take up the eighth Song of Ascents, the centre and capstone of the entire collection, the densest in metaphorical language. It follows on from the sowing of Psalm 126, but now its theme is sowing the seed of men, that is, human fertility. This simple, profound psalm has its roots in 2 Samuel 7 where David longs to build a house for the LORD, but is told that the LORD will build a house, that is, a dynasty, for David, and David's son will build a house for the LORD. The chapter hinges on the Hebrew word-play of 'build' (*banah*), 'sons' or 'children' (*banim*), and the dual meaning of 'house' (*bet*) as dwelling and dynasty. The word-play passed into later Hebrew as a proverb in its own right: "Do not read 'your sons' (*banayikh*) but 'your builders' (*bonayikh*)."[1] For those who truly build one's house are not the builders, but the sons who establish a family in one's name.

The psalm is in two stanzas. The first speaks of human endeavour within the overarching providence of God; the second of how the building-blocks of a family are children, who can defend the dynasty and continue its strength and prosperity. The interplay of these themes produces a palette of images with many colours.

Verse 1 unrolls itself in Solomonic magnificence as the longest verse in the Psalms. Its fifteen metrical feet are too many to form a tricolon. (How could one colon have five or six metrical feet?) No, it must be divided into five sections, each with its own cadence, making it a pentacolon, five cola of three metrical feet each.

A song of Ascents. Of Solomon.		(3)
If the LORD build not the house	vainly labour its builders in it;	(3+3)
If the LORD guard not the city	vainly watches the guard.	(3+3)

The heading ascribes the psalm to Solomon. The simple understanding would be that Solomon is the author (and the psalm's rich, allusive imagery might well have arisen from that subtle, proverb-forming mind). Yet Rashi, Ibn Ezra, and Radak all regard it as David's psalm *for* Solomon.[2] And certainly the themes it deals with are ones that must have been much in David's mind, as he foresaw in his crown prince the promised builder of the holy house.

The cantor opens, singing the heading and the first *If...vainly* statement; the chorus answer with the second. The cantor establishes the tone of this ardent psalm by leading off with high *mehuppakh* notes from the beginning, and the chorus respond with a similarly high tessitura. The phrase *build the house* can refer to a spectrum of human endeavours. It can mean building the royal palace, or the city of Jerusalem, or the nation of Israel. It can mean building up a family – particularly the house of David – by procreation. But its first meaning in the temple context is the construction of the glorious new temple itself. Without the co-working of the Holy One, the builders would have laboured in vain.

In AD 363, Julianus Caesar, called the Apostate, tried to rebuild the temple on the Mount. His friend the historian Ammianus Marcellinus recorded:

---

[1] אל תקרי בניך אלא בוניך Babylonian Talmud, *Ber.* 64a; cf. *b. Tam.* 32b; *b. Ker.* 28b; *b. Yeb.* 122b.

[2] See Rashi, Ibn Ezra, Kimḥi, *ad loc.* Ibn Ezra's fragmentary commentary is in Simon: 1982. Cf. also B. *Mak.* 10a cited in the fuller comments on the subject in chapter 7.

Julian thought to rebuild at extravagant expense the proud temple once at Jerusalem...when fearful balls of fire, breaking out near the foundations, continued their attacks, till the workmen, after repeated scorchings, could approach no more.[3]

Two generations later, the historian Sozomen related the events in detail.

[Julian] gave them [the Jews] public money, commanded them to rebuild the temple, and to practice the cult similar to that of their ancestors, by sacrificing after the ancient way. The Jews entered upon the undertaking, without reflecting that, according to the prediction of the holy prophets, it could not be accomplished. The emperor, the other pagans, and all the Jews, regarded every other undertaking as secondary in importance to this. Although the pagans were not well-disposed towards the Jews, yet they assisted them in this enterprise, because they reckoned upon its ultimate success, and hoped by this means to falsify the prophecies of Christ. Besides this motive, the Jews themselves were impelled by the consideration that the time had arrived for rebuilding their temple. When they had removed the ruins of the former building, they dug up the ground and cleared away its foundation; it is said that on the following day when they were about to lay the first foundation, a great earthquake occurred, and by the violent agitation of the earth, stones were thrown up from the depths, by which those of the Jews who were engaged in the work were wounded, as likewise those who were merely looking on. The houses and public porticos, near the site of the temple, in which they had diverted themselves, were suddenly thrown down; many were caught thereby, some perished immediately, others were found half dead and mutilated of hands or legs, others were injured in other parts of the body. When God caused the earthquake to cease, the workmen who survived again returned to their task, partly because such was the edict of the emperor, and partly because they were themselves interested in the undertaking. They had scarcely returned to the undertaking, when fire burst suddenly from the foundations of the temple, and consumed several of the workmen. This fact is fearlessly stated, and believed by all; the only discrepancy in the narrative is that some maintain that flame burst from the interior of the temple, as the workmen were striving to force an entrance, while others say that the fire proceeded directly from the earth. In whichever way the phenomenon might have occurred, it is equally wonderful. A more tangible and still more extraordinary prodigy ensued; suddenly the sign of the cross appeared spontaneously on the garments of the persons engaged in the undertaking. These crosses were disposed like stars, and appeared the work of art. Many were hence led to confess that Christ is God, and that the rebuilding of the temple was not pleasing to Him; others presented themselves in the church, were initiated, and besought Christ, with hymns and supplications, to pardon their transgression. If any one does not feel disposed to believe my narrative, let him go and be convinced by those who heard the facts I have related from the eyewitnesses of them, for they are still alive. Let him inquire,

---

[3] Ammianus Marcellinus, *Res Gestae*, 23.1.2–3.

also, of the Jews and pagans who left the work in an incomplete state, or who, to speak more accurately, were unable to commence it.[4]

The work stopped. The small beginnings were shaken to the ground by a devastating earthquake.[5] Within months, Julian was dead at the age of thirty-two, leaving the Mount desolate until the time of Abd al-Malik. No plan can succeed against the Lord, as Solomon also taught (Prov. 21.30).

Nor is any building, however so strong, protected by mere watchmen. It is not human guardians who protect city, temple, house, or family. It is on the collaboration of the Holy One that the building and security, the construction and protection, the inception and completion of all our works depend.

The next verse proceeds to the question of how to sustain one's 'house'. It is not by unceasing labour and anxious toil. No, the favour of the LORD provides for and gives rest to *his beloved* (*yedido*). We saw, in chapter two, how this word, *yedido*, is the centre of the psalm. Its value by *gematria* is twenty-eight and, omitting the title, there are twenty-eight words before it and twenty-eight after it. It is therefore the central word of the central Song of Ascents. It refers to Yedid-Yah (Solomon), the 'Beloved of Yah'. But it refers indirectly to all the people of Israel, whom the LORD has loved by sending just kings (1 Kgs 10.9) and giving them rest.

The second stanza of the psalm, at verse 3, moves to the issue of building a family. The collaboration of heaven is as necessary for building a dynastic house as for a house of stones. For *sons*, or more generally, *children* (for the masculine plural, *banim*, indicates both male and female offspring) are given to humankind as a portion or inheritance from the Holy One. They are his stones to build families, tribes, communities, cities, and nations. They are his protection for old age. They are one's glory and honour when one is gone. They are his gift through us to the world of the future. They are called *the fruit of the womb*, an appropriate metaphor for a song sung at harvest time, for they will ripen into blessings. They are his *reward*, his 'wages' for a righteous life, just as Abraham, of great reward, filled the earth with his seed.

The language of v. 4 sees children as a man's *arrows*, that is, as defence against attack. In ancient times, one's police, security guards, and private army were one's brothers, one's strong sons and nephews. And although modern societies provide police, which, at their best, work for our protection, a strong and supportive family is still a great blessing. Our children are *arrows* also in the sense that we send them beyond us into the future. This was the picture in the mind of the Maronite poet Khalil Gibran, who wrote:

> You are the bows from which your children
>   as living arrows are sent forth.
> The Archer sees the mark upon the path of the infinite,

---

[4] Sozomen, *Historia Ecclesiastica* V.22; see too Theodoret, *Historia Ecclesiastica* XV.
[5] A recent archaeological survey by the University of Haifa reports that the destruction wrought by this great earthquake took twenty years to restore (*Jerusalem Post*, 29 Sep. 2014).

and He bends you with His might
   that His arrows may go swift and far.
Let your bending in the Archer's hand be for gladness;
   For even as He loves the arrow that flies,
   so He loves also the bow that is stable.

In verse 5, *man* is the Hebrew *gever*, a free-born Israelite of high standing, as opposed to the more general *ish*, which is simply a male person. The implication is that honour and status will come to the one who has a quiverful of such strong young arrows. The psalm, so rich in double meanings, closes with one last flourish: They shall uphold the family honour when they contend with enemies in the gate. The verb *y'dabru* can mean both 'speak', or 'contend'. The gate was the place where the city was defended against invaders, but it was also the city law court, where the family was defended in legal dispute. Dynasties built by the LORD will defend themselves honourably against foes near and far. Solomon, a good son, will defend his father's house against all attacks.

Yet Solomon, for all his filial faithfulness, became unfaithful to *torah*. When his former wisdom turned to aged folly, he betrayed the blessing of children which the psalm speaks of. He made his multitude of sons princes over Israel (Ps. 45.16), but dealt otherwise with the children of others, whom he sacrificed to Moloch in the Tophet outside Jerusalem (1 Kgs 11.7). The cruelty of this Canaanite worship appalled even the Romans, who saw it in Tyre and Carthage centuries later. Human infants were placed alive in the scalding arms of a large bronze idol, heated by fire from within. There they shrivelled and burned, their screams covered by the banging of drums, until their charred remains fell into the fire-pit below.[6] For this quintessence of idolatry, Solomon's temple, kingdom, and people were purged by Shishak's overwhelming flood.

Dietrich Bonhoeffer spoke of 'the blessing and burden' of children. Sometimes, in these hard-pressed days, we forget the blessing when a little one interrupts or a youngster misbehaves from lack of parental care. Indeed, some have found children to be such a burden that they have been killed in large numbers. On Boxing Day 2006, a *tsunami* in East Asia killed some 300,000 people and the world was stirred to compassion. But in many countries now, there is a *tsunami* of the unborn every year, for whom few weep here below. It was for slaying children made in the divine image that the Canaanites fell before the sword of Joshua. It was for this that the Aztecs perished by the sword of Cortès. Societies enfeebled by infanticide reap the whirlwind.

Yet this little psalm of Solomon's wiser days, the capstone of the Songs of Ascents, expresses a capstone truth: it is the favour of the heaven which, like a capstone, keeps our house from crumbling. In all our getting, let us get this.

---

[6] Rashi on Jer. 7.31; Diodorus Siculus, *Bibliotheca historica* XX.14; Plutarch, *De Superstitiones*, 171. For modern corroboration, cf. Smith 2014: 54–56, 68.

Psalm 128
The Eighth Step

1. **Shir** ha - ma - ʻa - **lot**
   Song of the As - cents.

   a - shre kol y' - re ye - ho - vah; ha - ho - lekh bi - d'ra - khav
   How happy all who fear Ye - ho - vah; he who walks in his ways.

2. Ye - **gi** - a ka - pe - kha **ki** to - **khel** ash - re - kha v' - **tov** **lakh**
   The fruit of your hands you'll sure - ly eat; happy you, and pros - perity to you.

3. Esh - t' - **kha** k' - ge - fen po - ri - **ya** b' - yar - k' - te ve - te - kha
   Your wife like a vine fruit - ful in the thighs of your house;

   ba - **ne** - kha ki - shti - le ze - **tim** sa - viv l' - shul - ḥa - **ne** - kha
   your sons like shoots of o - live trees a - round your table.

4. Hin - **neh** khi - **khen** y' - vo - rakh ga - ver y' - re ye - ho - vah
   Be - hold, so is blest the man who fears Ye - ho - vah.

5. Y' - va - re - kh' - kha ye - ho - vah mi - tsi - **on** u - r' - eh b' - **tuv** ye - ru - sha - **la** - yim
   May he bless you, Ye - ho - vah, from Zi - on and see the good of Je - ru - sa - lem

   kol y' - **me** ha - **ye** - kha
   all the days of your life!

6. U - r' - eh va - **nim** l' - va - **ne** - kha sha - **lom** al - yis - ra - **el**
   And see the sons of your sons. Sha - lom on Is - ra - el.

The Levites ascend to the eighth step. Below them in the lower court stand the assembled Israelites, men, women, and children. Above them, King Solomon sits enthroned in the upper court. They take up their song.

This psalm is like the preceding one in its theme of nation-building through family and children.[1] Both mention progeny and fruitful labour. They share vocabulary: *sons (banim)*, *house (bet)*, *fruit of the womb (pri ha-baten)*,

---

[1] As many note: Cohen 1945: 430; Keet 1969: 64; Mannati 1979: 96; Miller 1986: 136.

blessed (*ashre*), *man* (*gever*). Both begin with a general statement in the third person singular and move to specifics in the second person singular. Both have two strophes, the second beginning with *Behold* (*hinneh*). The last two lines of each combine city and household. But their similarity invites comparison of their differences. While Psalm 127 asserts that civic welfare is unattainable without heaven's blessing, Psalm 128 shows that the way to obtaining this blessing is by individuals fearing the LORD and walking in his ways, by avoiding what he forbids and doing what he commands. It is this which leads to peaceable and fruitful domestic life, which lead in turn to civic and national security (vv. 5–6).

In verse 1 the cantor sings of the happiness of *all who fear the LORD*, and the chorus respond to his plural in the singular, speaking of *the one-walking in his ways*. In verse 2 the cantor tells this righteous one, perhaps Solomon himself, how *your* labour will be fruitful and provide sufficiently. The chorus confirm: *you* shall be happy and prosperity shall come to *you*, the words *tov lakh* falling on consecutive accented long syllables, as at the end of Psalm 122.

The complex cantillation of the first part of verse 3 suggests a cantoral solo until the *oleh ve-yored* cadence at the end of the second colon. Note how the parallel thought of the two parts of the verse is in tension with the cantillation. The parallelism suggests that the pause in the poetic sense comes after *house*. Yet the main musical pause falls later, at the *etnaḥ* cadence, three-quarters of the way through the verse, at *olive trees*. I have followed the principle that likeliest point for the choral entry is at the *etnaḥ* cadence, though it is certainly possible that the chorus came in at *banekha* (*your sons*), after the semantic pause, where the complex melodic line returns to simplicity.

The imagery gets fertile when it comes to the picture of the righteous man's wife. Translations do not convey it, but *b'yarkhete* means 'in the thighs' of the house. Elsewhere, the word is used figuratively. Psalm 48 speaks of Mount Zion *in the thighs of the north*, meaning the untouchable recesses of the mountains. The shared idea is that the inner thigh is a private place, not accessible to public viewing and touching. So the *thighs of your house* are the private recesses of the house, the *zenana* or women's quarters which every large oriental house possessed, entered only by the master of the house. That was where virtuous women of the ancient east stayed. But the phrase refers back to the wife and to the intimacy of the reproductive process, much as the biblical expression of *going in to* a woman refers both to entering the inner room and to the sexual act.

Rashi summarizes this verse by saying, 'It is customary to have conjugal relations in private.' Yet, obvious as this may seem, it was not so to Solomon's brother (2 Sam. 16.22), nor is it to all even now. But the result of procreation in the fear of God, the chorus testifies, is vigorous young striplings around the table, compared to olive saplings for their fresh suppleness and the anticipated blessing of their fruitfulness and oil of joy.

In verse 4, *man* is again *gever* (or more precisely *gaver*, since the vowel changes at the cadence), the free-born Israelite of high status. The Holy One will confer dignity on the one who fears him (cf. Ps. 91.15). The semantic unity of the verse, its brevity, and the absence of an *etnah* cadence, suggest that it was sung as a unit. I have assigned it to the chorus as befitting their declarative and closural role.

The psalm closes with a blessing (v. 5). The fertile family man will be blessed by the One who dwells in Zion, whom he has come to worship. He will see the prosperity of Jerusalem, the city of God, in whose prosperity he and his nation shall prosper. As in the previous psalm, the prosperous father is many-childed Solomon himself, upon whom these blessings are directed together with all his subjects. The good of Jerusalem is dependent upon Solomon and the men and women of Israel populating the nation and building its strength. It is a strong and populous Israel which will find peace, as the congregation affirm at the end. And so, while Psalm 127 begins with building the nation and makes it dependent on building the family, Psalm 128 begins with building the family and sees it leading to a prosperous nation.

My gentler readers may baulk at the testosterone-scented whiff of this reproductive talk. A quiverful of sons around the table may be fine for males, but less fine for those who endure multiple consecutive pregnancies or the downside of polygyny. Yet none born of woman can think that child-bearing is altogether a bad thing. Great nations have always put a high value on it. And although ancient Israel was patriarchal, women there had greater freedom and status than their counterparts in ancient Greece or Rome. The Israelite male, for instance, did not have the arbitrary power of life and death over his family exercised by the Roman *vir*. On the contrary, power in Israel ran along dynastic lines, women could inherit, and matriarchs had great influence. In Solomon's time, as in Jeremiah's, the power and influence of the Queen Mother – the *g'vurah* or 'great lady' – was second only to the king (1 Kgs 2.19–25; Jer. 13.18). In many ways, Israelite law protected women and advanced their rights.

Psalm 129
The Ninth Step

1. **Shir ha-ma-'a-lot**
   Song of the Ascents.
   Rab-bat ts'-ra-ru-ni mi-n'-'u-rai yo-mar-na yis-ra-el
   Much have they troubled me from my youth — O say now, Israel.

2. **Rab-bat ts'-ra-ru-ni mi-n'-'u-rai gam lo-yakh-lu li**
   Much have they troubled me from my youth — but they have not prevailed.

3. **Al-ga-bi hor-shu hor-shim he-e-ri-khu l'-ma-'a-no-tam**
   On my back the plough-men ploughed, they extended their furrows.

4. **Ye-ho-vah tsa-diq qi-tsets 'a-vot r'-sha-'im**
   Ye-ho-vah is just! He has cut the cords of the wicked.

5. **Ye-vo-shu v'-yi-so-gu a-hor kol so-n'-e Tsiy-yon**
   They will be shamed and turned back, all haters of Zion.

6. **Yi-h'-yu ka-ha-tsir ga-got she-qad-mat sha-laf ya-vesh**
   They will be like the grass of the roofs, which as soon as plucked will wither.

7. **She-lo mil-le kha-po qo-tser v'-hits-no m-'a-mer**
   Which does not fill the hand of reaper or bosom of binder.

8. **V'-lo om-ru ha-'ov-rim bir-kat-Y'ho-vah a-le-khem**
   And they do not say, the passers-by, 'The blessing of Y'ho-vah be on you,
   bê-rakh-nu e-t'-khem b'-shem Ye-ho-vah
   We bless you in the name of Y'ho-vah.

The Levites rise to the ninth step. Looking over the low eastern walls to the city roofs, tufted with grass, to the fields strewn with the last scattered stalks of the harvest, they take up their tenth song. The melodic line, in this psalm of painful recollection, is restrained and simple, without cantoral *bravura*.

In verse 1, the cantor sings the heading and the opening declaration; the chorus and congregation respond with the refrain, *Let Israel now say*, sung to the same melody as in Psalm 124. And, like Psalm 124, the repeated idea in verse 2a shares the melody of verse 1a. The similarities between the two psalms are intentional. Both reflect on foreign attacks endured in the past. The difference is distance of viewpoint. Psalm 124, the middle and darkest song of the first dark trio, is an alarming close-up. It emphasises the scale of the threat and Israel's nigh destruction. It reverberates with memories of recent cataclysm. Psalm 129, on the other hand, the first of the second dark trio, takes a longer view. It says less of the recent threat, but contemplates Israel's sorrows from youth, and the Holy One's continual mercies. Yes, many enemies attacked them, but they were not able to destroy them (v. 2).

In harvest imagery *noir*, the enemies were like *ploughmen* who ploughed long furrows *al-gabi*, a pun which can mean *on my back* or *on my mound*. The language recalls Israel in Egyptian slavery, their backs gashed with slavedrivers' lashes. But the effect of the pun is to minimize the affliction, giving again the impression of distance. For the pain is past. *The LORD is just* (v. 4). The words are sung in that distinctive opening phrase of *silluq* (E), *merkha* (F) and *etnah* (A) which here, as often elsewhere, speaks of something new and hopeful entering in. He has cut the cords of bondage, the ropes of the ploughmen.

Verses 5–8 are the closest the Songs of Ascents get to a malediction. For the haters of Zion hate not only Zion, but the One who dwells there. They will be ashamed by the failure of their schemes and turned backward. Zion's enemies will be – in harvest pictures again – like unwanted grass on the roof, withering as soon as it sprouts, ungathered by reaper or binder, useless and fruitless, unblessed by the harvest blessing which falls on the fruitful field and its harvesters (v. 8).

The last two verses rise to the higher notes of emphasis. The last words for the haters of Zion, in verse 8, are not a curse, but simply a blessing withheld. Freed from affliction, Israel can now regard their former slavers with equanimity. Yet the haters of Zion are justly unblessed. Who will bless them in the name of a God they hate? They are left to the destiny they have chosen outside his blessing. The cantor rises high for the blessing which Zion's friends will receive and her enemies forfeit. He pauses on a quavering *revia* cadence, introducing, as often it does, a passage of direct speech. He then speaks the blessing in the sacred name with the rising, hopeful *silluq* (E), *merkha* (F) and *etnah* (A) pattern. The chorus confirm the blessing upon those who love Zion. It washes over the temple courts and all assembled there. It covers the earth to this day, affirmed wherever the psalm is read, falling on all who love in truth the One who set his throne on Zion.

Psalm 130
The Tenth Step

1. **Shir** ha-ma-'a-**lot**
   Song of the As-cents.
   mi-ma'a-ma-**qim** q'-ra'-**ti**-kha ye-ho-**vah**
   Out of the depths I cried to you Ye-ho-vah

2. A-do-**nai**, shim-**'ah** v'-qo-**li**
   'My Lord, hear my voice;
   ti-h'-**ye**-nah oz-ne-kha qa-shu-**vot** l'-qol tah'-nu-**nai**
   in-cline your ear to at-tend to the voice of my pleas.'

3. Im-'a-vo-**not** tish-mar-**yah**, a-do-**nai** mi ya'a-**mod**
   If sins you marked, Yah!... My Lord, who could stand?

4. Ki-'im-m'-**kha** ha-s'li-**ha** l'-ma'an ti-va-**re**
   But surely with you is pardon so that you are feared.

5. Qi-vi-ti ye-ho-**vah** qiv-**ta** naf-**shi** v'-li-d'va-ro ho-**hal**-ti
   I wait for Ye-ho-vah, my soul waits, and in his word I hope.

6. Naf-**shi** l'a-do-**nai** mi-shom-**rim** la-bo-**ker** shom-**rim** la-bo-**ker**
   My soul for my Lord, more than watch-men for mor-ning, than watch-men for mor-ning.

7. Ya-**hel** yis-ra-**el** el-ye-ho-**vah** ki-im-y'ho-**vah** ha-**he**-sed
   O hope, Is-ra-el, in Ye-ho-vah, for with Y'ho-vah is loyal love
   v'-har-**beh** im-**mo** f-**dut**
   and plenti-ful with him re-demption.

8. V'-hu yif-**deh** et-yis-ra-**el** mi kol 'a-vo-not-**av**
   It is he re-deems Is-ra-el from all his sins.

The Levites ascend to the tenth step, the step which marks the beginning of the second letter of the name YaH. Trumpets are blown to mark the division, just as they will be later on the downward procession at dawn. It is now late night, around the tenth hour, about four in the morning. Below, the eastern temple courts are dark as the full harvest moon descends behind the massive edifice of the temple. On the temple walls, the guards of the fourth watch, who took their posts an hour ago, are looking over the low eastern wall to the Mount of Olives, where the imminent rising of the Morning Star will herald the first lightening of the sky and the rising of the warm fruitful sun. The Levites, looking up to the torch-illuminated temple above, take up their song.

The melody of the heading is quite different from the other fourteen Ascents songs. There is no *revia* shake, nor does it cadence with *oleh ve-yored* on the supertonic (F). Instead the first cadence is on *etnaḥ*. This makes it the only Song of Ascents with a bipartite first verse. It also suggests that the words following the heading are not sung by the cantor, as elsewhere, but by the chorus.

After the heading, the line drops one step for *the depths*.[1] The opening words are frequently translated *Out of the depths I cry to you*, like a plea for mercy. However, the translation above gives *qarati* its proper weight as a perfect tense verb: *I cried*. Verse 2 then follows as a citation of the psalmist's earlier words spoken when in distress. There are several reasons why this translation is preferable. First, the Septuagint renders *qarati* as a past tense with the aorist form *ekèkraxa*. Second, citation of past speech is a feature elsewhere in the Ascents, making it likely here also.[2] Third, the cry was from *ma'amaqim*, 'depths', which is precisely the opposite place to the present location, *ha-ma'alot*, 'the ascents' or 'heights' of the temple steps. Therefore the cry cannot originate from the present situation, but must be from an earlier one. This past tense 'cried' makes the psalm not a plea for help, but a thanksgiving for deliverance consistent with the mood of the rest of the Ascents collection. Just as Psalm 124 is followed by 125, so 129 is followed by 130, both pairs recalling attack by hostile nations and giving thanks for the deliverance wrought.

Verse 2 opens with the cantor, as the complex cantillation confirms. The change from the preceding chorus to the lighter solo voice reinforces the impression of one recalling the past. The citation of past speech probably finishes at the end of verse 2; though, alternatively, it may continue to the end of verse 4.

Verses 3 and 4 are a confession of Israel's error in sinning against their God. It is the only Song of Ascents in which such a confession occurs. Elsewhere, they tell how they have been badly treated by the nations. But now they confess that their troubles sprang from their unfaithfulness and idolatry. Because of their guilt, they do not deserve even to *stand* before the Holy One; they deserve only to be swept away. However, with him is the pardon which

---

[1] In this instance, Ginsburg's cantillation is more dramatic, dropping down to *silluq* (E) for the words *Out of the*, and then rising upward. However, I have followed Ben Asher.

[2] See 122.2; 126.2; 132.2-4, 11–12. The aorist *ekèkraxa* of Ps. 120.1 (LXX Ps. 119) suggests it should be read like Ps. 130.1, making Ps. 120.1–2 another example of significant past speech in the Ascents.

they sought and found, on the Day of Atonement, five days before. And therefore he is feared. For if he did not pardon, they would resign any hope of pleasing him and sink into despair. But his pardon encourages them to walk contritely with him in the fear of covenant obedience.

In verse 5, the upward fifth expresses the ardent longing of the soul, before the second colon settles down to two notes, expressing patient waiting for his word. Indeed, the tessitura of the psalm is low throughout, as befits its theme. There is no high D♯ or E, as found in the other Songs.

In verse 6, the cantor's hopeful rising sequence to the *etnaḥ* cadence ushers in the vivid picture of watchmen waiting for the dawn. The repetition, by the chorus, not only expresses the intensity of longing, but introduces a pause in the sense, forcing the singers and listeners themselves to wait, like the watchmen, a little longer. Upon the temple walls, the Korahite and Merarite watchmen hear the Levite song. Soon the sun will appear and follow the singers up these very steps and enter the temple by the main door from the east, as the forgiving Lord comes to his people in reconciliation.

In verse 7, the cantor exhorts the people: *Hope, Israel, in the* LORD. In the Aleppo Codex, the sacred name has the arrow-head sign of *oleh ve-yored* over the first letter, the *yodh*, while the Leningrad Codex has it on the second letter, the *heh*. I have followed the Aleppo Codex and begun the ornament on the *yodh*, but I have carried the latter part of the ornament onto the second syllable with its open *o*-vowel. This makes more musical sense than having the entire ornament on the half-vowel *sh^{e}va* of the *yodh*.

As the singers ascend from the lower courtyard to the temple courts above, they mirror the subject of their song: Israel's ascent from adversity to blessing, when, in the morning of redemption, they will shine in the world. Some may rage at God's hand. But he replies, *Hear now, house of Israel, is my way unjust? Is it not your ways that are unjust?* (Ezek. 18.25). The door to blessing and peace is repentance and patient hope.

Psalm 131
The Eleventh Step

1. Shir ha-ma-'a-lot l'-da-vid.
   Song of Ascents. Of David.
   ye-ho-vah lo-ga-vah' li-bi v'-lo-ra-mu 'ey-nai
   Yehovah, not lofty is my heart and not upraised my eyes

   CHORUS
   v'-lo-hil-lakh-ti big-do-lot u'v-nif-la-ot mi-men-ni.
   and I don't go about in great things or in wonders beyond me.

2. Im-lo shi-vi-ti v'-do-mam-ti naf-shi
   Have I not be-calmed and stilled my soul

   CHORUS
   k'-ga-mul a-le i-mo ka-ga-mul 'a-lai naf-shi.
   Like a child up-on his mother like that child on me is my soul.

3. Ya-ḥel Yis-ra-el el-y'ho-vah me-'at-tah v'-ad-o-lam
   O hope, Israel, in Y'hovah from now till evermore.

The Levites ascend to the eleventh step. Casting down their eyes before the glorious temple above them, they take up their twelfth song. This short lyric is a mere thirty-three words in length. Yet its almost Japanese brevity comprises what Cohen calls, 'a literary gem of exquisite beauty and surpassing spirituality'.[1]

David's meditation begins with four negatives: not lifted up, not raised high, not walking to and fro in great matters, nor in wonders beyond him. The melody follows the words, dropping one step from *Yehovah* to *not lofty*, rising again to *upraised*, then dropping for *I do not walk* and rising up for *great things or in wonders*.[2] This fourfold disavowal of pride has a continual outward movement. For pride begins in the heart, finds expression in the eyes, busies itself in great things, and reaches forth to the unattainable and forbidden. At the same time there is a descent from *lofty* to *high* to *walking* to *the little child*. This outward and downward movement is something that characterizes the closing Songs of Ascents, just as an inward and upward movement characterizes the opening Songs.

---

[1] Cohen 1945: 435.
[2] The Songs of Ascents only use of the supralinear sign *shalshelet* occurs on the emphasized syllable of *hilakhti* (v. 1). It is marked with a wavy line, but is untranscribed, as explained in chapter 12.

The opening words of verse 2, *If I have not* are an oath formula. The melody is correspondingly ardent; the syllables squeezed into each stress would be sung expansively, with *rubato*. Unpacked, the words mean, 'If I do not speak the truth' or 'If I do not do what I have said, then may heaven do this and this to me'. Such a phrase could vary in intensity from a vehement oath, illustrated with violent gestures toward one's body, to a more formal but emotional avowal, as here. For it was not only armies that David's will commanded. True mastery begins within. To 'level' one's soul to silence, as David did, requires a force which turbulent people do not possess.

He likens his soul to a little *child*; the chorus repeat his words in confirmation. The meaning of the word *gamul* (child) has been disputed since the medieval rabbis.[3] It means, literally, 'a weaned child'. But insistence on the weaning misses the point. It is simply a little child of two or three years old cuddled against his mother's breast. David was perhaps remembering the young Solomon with Bathsheba. Just as the child and the mother repeat comforting words to one another – for they speak love not instructions – so David repeats himself. The effect of the repetition is again one of pause, but not the pause of waiting, as in Psalm 130, but of resting. The repetition moves from *a child* to specifically *the* child, as if to say 'like that same child I just spoke of', underlining his words and making the picture yet more fixed and striking. And what a picture. The busy little bee, who has ranged and stomped around his small world all day, now lies quiet on his mother's lap, the active little limbs too tired for any further outbursts of autonomy. Like such a one is the soul brought to rest on the lap of the will, of the inmost 'I'. Such was the soul of David, looking back over his life as Israel's king and commander. We find this in the Jerusalem Talmud.

> It is written: A Song of Ascents of David. *O Lord, my heart was not haughty –* when Samuel anointed me [as king]. *Nor were my eyes lofty –* when I killed Goliath. *And I did not go to and fro in great things –* when I brought the ark up. *Or in things too wonderful for me –* when I was returned to my kingdom. Rather, *Surely I composed and stilled my soul, like a child upon its mother, like a child is my soul upon me* (Y. Sanhedrin 2.4; 20b).

David, reflecting on his life, says that in his greatest hours his soul was not haughty. For self-seeking was not his core characteristic. He did not seek the kingship, but Samuel the anointer sought him. When he killed Goliath, he confessed himself unworthy to marry Saul's daughter. When he had the opportunity to slay Saul, his persecutor, he stayed his hand. When he brought up the ark, he dressed not in royal attire, but in a linen robe. And when Absalom's rebellion was quelled, he did not seize the kingship, but waited for the people's bidding. In each situation, his soul tended to humility.

---

[3] Rashi (1040–1105) understood it to mean a child on the breast, feeding and content. But Radak (1160–1235) and Meiri (1249–c.1310) insisted that the *gamul* is one who has been fully weaned from the breast. VanGemeren 1982: 51–57 suggests only a young child is meant.

But now, in the Ascents collection, the psalm becomes the voice not only of David, but of Israel. That is why David added the words *Trust, Israel, in Yehovah* (v. 3), which occur, to a different melody, also in Psalm 130. For the humble trust resulting from the forgiveness in Psalm 130 continues into this psalm. After the busy fray of the millennial day from Abraham to Solomon, Israel's soul lies serene in the everlasting arms. Implicit in the picture is a promise of great hope. Israel may be only a little child, just entering the world, but, with such parentage, his future is glorious. That was surely how it appeared in Solomon's day. And if the days since Solomon were again restless and troubled, trust must continue *from now until forever.* There will yet be serenity and glorious maturity for all who are quiet before heaven. For inner quietness is the wellspring of character. It is the rendezvous of the human spirit, seeking the quiet place, and the Holy Spirit, who seeks the seeker. The resulting quietness is the entry to the house of prayer. And so we take the final steps into the silence of the temple courts, to hear the great prayer and the divine promise which will follow.

Psalm 132

The Twelfth Step

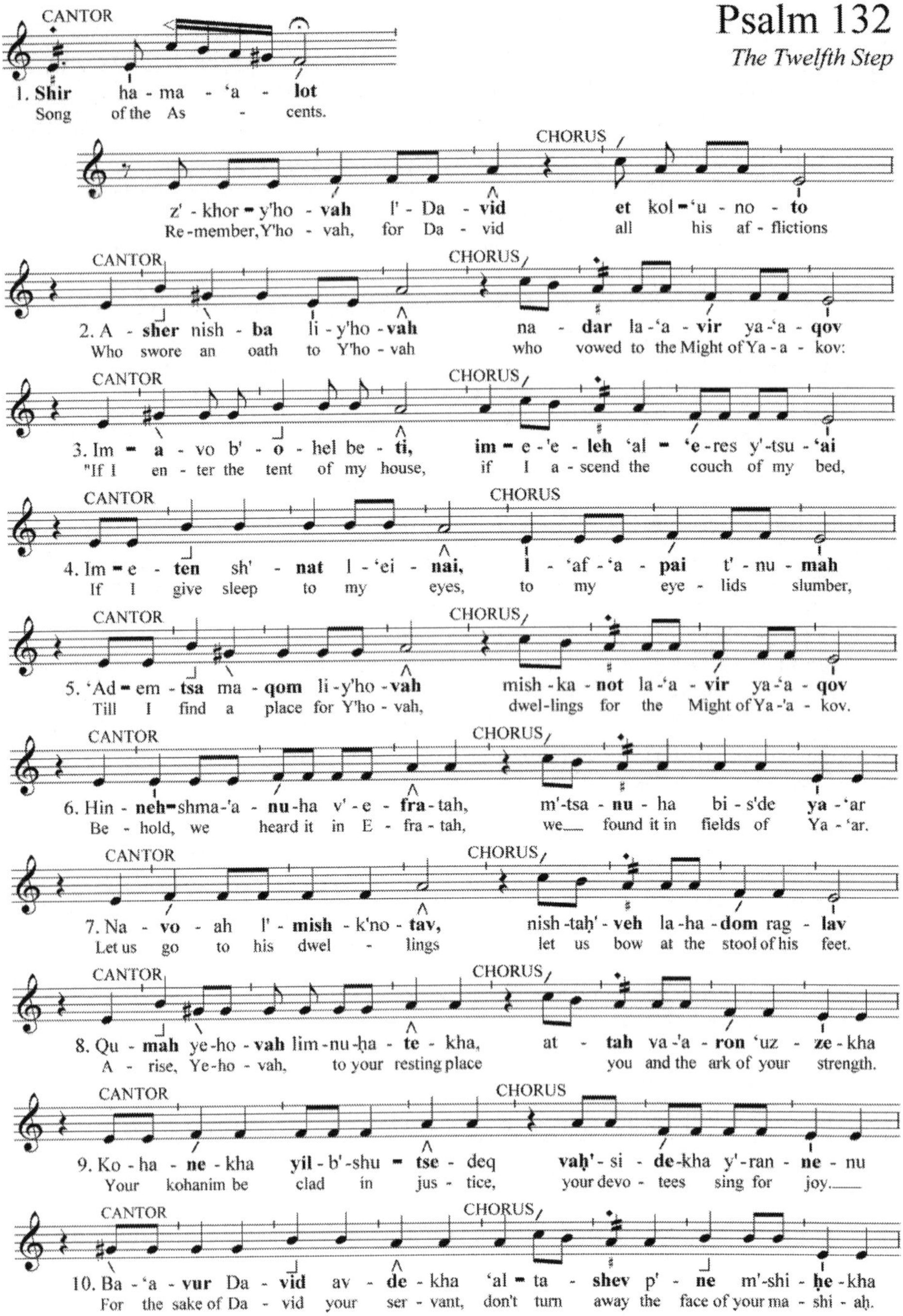

11. Nish-ba-ye ho-vah l'-da-vid e-met lo-ya-shuv mi-men-nah,
He swore, Ye-ho-vah, to Da-vid truth, he will not turn from it:

mi-p'-ri vit-n'-kha a-shit l' khi-se-lakh.
'Of the fruit of your body will I set u-pon your throne.

12. Im-yish-m'-ru va-ne-kha b'-ri-ti v'-e-do-ti zo a-la-m-dem
If they keep, your sons, my co-ve-nant and this my sta-tute I teach them,

gam-b'ne-hem a-de-ad yesh-vu l' khi-se-lakh
then their sons for ever will sit u-pon your throne.

13. Ki-va-ḥar ye-ho-vah mi-tsi-on i-va l'-mo-shav lo
For Yeho-vah has cho-sen Zion; he has desired it for his throne.

14. Zot m'nu-ḥa-ti 'a-de-'ad po-e-shev ki i-vi-ti ha
This is my resting place for ever; here will I sit for I have de-sired it.

15. Tse-da ba-rekh a-va-rekh ev-yo-ne-ha as-bi-a la-ḥem
Her pro-vi-sion blessing I will bless, her needy sa-tis-fy with bread.

16. V'-ko-ha-ne-ha al-bish ye-sha vaḥ'-si-de-ha ra-nen ye-ra-ne-nu
And her kohanim will I clothe in sal-vation, her devo-tees for joy will sing.

17. Sham ats-mi-aḥ qe-ren l'-da-vid 'a-rakh-ti ner lim'-shi-ḥi
There will I make grow a horn for Da-vid; I've set up a lamp for my ma-shiaḥ.

18. Oy-vav al-bish bo-shet v'-a-lav ya-tsits niz-ro
His foes will I clothe in shame, but on him will shine his crown.'

The Levites and the ark-bearing *kohanim* ascend to the twelfth step. Above them sits King Solomon on his royal throne, waiting to conduct the holy ark into its new home. They take up the thirteenth Song of the Ascents.

It is commonly said that this psalm consists of two ten-line strophes. This may be true of the words, but not of the music. The verse numbers give it away. The first ten lines are numbered one to ten, while the next ten are numbered eleven to eighteen. The twist is in the cantillation. Most of its verses are in two parts, with a mid-verse cadence on *etnah* and a final close on *silluq*. However, verses 11 and 12 each have four stichs. Verse 11 cadences on *pazer, oleh ve-yored, etnah,* and *silluq*. Verse 12 cadences on *tsinnor*, followed again by *oleh ve-yored, etnah, and silluq*. So verses 11 and 12 are longer because each contains two poetic lines in one long musical line. Apart from these two expansive verses, the song is simple and declamatory. Verses 2, 3, 5, 7, 8, 13, 16, and 18, all end with the same melodic curve; verses 9, 15, 17 come very close; and the other verses end in similar predictable ways.

The two strophes respond to one another. The first asks the Holy One to remember the hardships which David endured to find a resting-place for the ark; the second announces the Holy One's irrevocable promise of a royal dynasty to David and his descendants, again recalling 2 Samuel 7, where David's wish to build a house for the LORD is answered by the promise of a house for David.

In verses 1 to 5, the psalmist begs the Holy One to remember the hardships borne by David. For David swore an oath not to rest till the ark had a shrine in his new capital, Jerusalem. The threefold, *If,* in verses 3 and 4, is the same oath formula that we met in Psalm 131, but here it is altogether more forceful than before. David solemnly vowed to forego all comforts until he had found a resting-place for the ark.

Verses 6 and 7 date, one imagines, from the festivities when David and his men brought the ark to Zion. Ephratah or Ephrat is the ancient name for David's home town of Bethlehem (Gen. 35.19; 48.7). Here it is surely David who is relating how, in his youth, he and his friends heard about the mighty ark lying forsaken, neglected by Saul (1 Chr. 13.3), in Qiryat Ye'arim, while Moses' Tabernacle lay bereft of its holy treasure (1 Sam. 6.21–7.2). So, as soon as David established his capital, he gathered the Israelites and went to Qiryat Ye'arim, that is, 'Forest-town', where they retrieved the ark from Abinadab's house in the country around Qiryat Ye'arim (1 Chr. 13.6), which David in this psalm calls *s'de ya'ar*, that is, 'forest-fields' (v. 6). We may imagine that these words were sung as they brought the ark to Zion with joy and placed it in the tent which David set up there.

At verse 8, the cantor's summons to the deity soars to the *munah* dominant (B). Verses 8 to 10 appear to date from Solomon's time, rather than David's. The resting place spoken of in verse 8 sounds permanent rather than temporary. Verse 9 suggests regular priestly ministry before the ark, something of which there is no solid evidence in David's time. And verse 10 asks blessing on a *mashiaḥ* for David's sake, which implies that the *mashiaḥ* in question is not David himself, but Solomon, in whose day the ark, shoulder-borne and encompassed by singing Levites, ascended the temple steps and entered its rest (2 Chr. 6.41–42).[1]

But this great triumph is all to David's credit. He it was who brought the ark with honour to Jerusalem. He it was who conceived a house for it, who bought the land for it, who drew up the plans, who provided the materials, who begot the son to build it. Therefore it is *for the sake of David your servant* that the Holy One is now implored in the day of the temple not to reject his new *mashiaḥ*, David's son (2 Chr. 6.42).

In verses 11–12, as noted, each musical line contains two poetic lines. The melismatic cantillation in the first half of each verse suggests cantoral solos, while the shared melodic contours of the second half of each verse suggest choral responses. Such an innovation in the middle of the psalm makes for variety. It also casts lustre upon the start of the second strophe, where heaven answers the pleas of earth. We may imagine that the first strophe's simplicity derives from its being based on a popular song of David's day, while the cantoral cadenzas of verses 11 and 12 mark them out as new material composed for the great orchestra of the day of dedication, painting in song the bright new world which Israel is entering: Now they can truly sing! From the chorus part of verse 11 through to the end of verse 18 the singers sing the words of the Holy One himself, received in the spirit of prophecy, one imagines, by Jeduthun and set in song in this way.

The Holy One is not grudging in his response either to David's devotion or the psalmist's petition, but replies with a correspondingly great promise, derived from 2 Samuel 7. If David's sons keep the covenant and the divine law then they shall rule for ever on his throne. For as David has built the LORD a house, so the LORD will build David a house that will never pass away.

In verse 14, the LORD enters his temple. He speaks like a man who has just received the keys to his dream-house: *This is my resting-place for ever and ever. Here I will stay for this is just what I wanted* (v. 14). And because he now inhabits the city, the God of all blessing will make it overflow with blessings for people, *kohanim* and king. For the poor there shall be abundant food (v. 15). In verse 16, the 'and' of *and her kohanim* is emphatic.[2] It makes the link with the prayer back in verse 9, as if to say, 'And, yes, just as you asked, I shall clothe the *kohanim*, not only with righteousness, but with salvation.' And as for the devoted ones, they shall overflow with loud songs of joy. At verse 17, the cantor rises to the only sustained high *mehuppakh* of the entire song, as if to express the great exclamation of divine contentment: *po eshev*, 'Here I will sit' or 'rest' or 'dwell'. In this place, says the Holy One, *I will*

---

[1] Dahood, 1965–70 III.241-42, notes that 'the language of the psalm is extremely archaic' and it was 'composed in the tenth century as part of the liturgy for the feast when the ark was carried in procession to Jerusalem'.

[2] The emphatic use of *vav* is noted by Sáenz-Badillos 1993: 59–60.

cause a horn – that is, kingship – *to spring up for David. I will set up a lamp for my* mashiaḥ; that is, for David's sake, he will ensure the continuity of his dynasty. His enemies will be put to shame, to fulfil the promise made long ago in Psalm 2. But upon his brow his golden crown will both shine and flourish (*yatsits* can mean both), bestowing glory upon him and upon all who behold, and flourishing in his royal posterity, in whom David reigns for ever.

Hebrew literature is often multi-layered. Like the stones of the Holy Land, its words are remade by successive generations into new things. This psalm is a good example. The earliest layer is David's vow about the ark (vv. 3–5). The next layer is the song sung when they sought it out (vv. 6–7). The next layer is the addition of other words to complete the opening plea (vv. 8–10). Then come the divine oracles spoken by the Levite prophets (vv. 11–18). Then all is gathered in this Psalm for the installation of the ark in Solomon's temple. Finally, this psalm was joined with the other fourteen Songs of Ascents – parts of which may have had independent histories of their own – for the day of the dedication of the temple. The next 'layer' was when the Ascents collection became the annual Sukkot liturgy for the next millennium. Another layer was when the entire Ascents collection was included in the Book of Psalms. In this new larger context, they took on a new meaning altogether, pointing to things yet to come, as we shall see in the next chapter.

At the dedication of the temple on 15 Tishri 959 BC, two promises were fulfilled. David's promise of a house for the LORD and the LORD's promise of a house for David. Side by side they sat on the holy mountains, looking eastward to command the rising sun, the king of heaven and, at his right hand, the king of earth, his son the *mashiaḥ*, each in his own house built for him by the other.

Psalm 133
The Thirteenth Step

CANTOR
1. Shir ha-ma-'a-lot l'-da-vid.
   Song of Ascents. Of David.

   Hin-neh ma-tov u-ma-na-im shevet a-him gam ya-had
   Behold, how good and how pleasant, the dwelling of brothers as one!

CHORUS
   Hin-neh ma-tov u-ma-na-im shevet a-him gam ya-had
   Behold, how good and how pleasant, the dwelling of brothers as one!

CANTOR
2. Ka-she-men ha-tov al-ha-rosh yo-red 'al-ha-za-qan z'qan-a-ha-ron
   Like oil of the best on the head, descending on the beard, the beard of Aharon,

CHORUS
   she-yo-red 'al-pi mi-do-tav
   which descends on the mouth of his robes.

CANTOR
   Hin-neh ma-tov u-ma-na-im shevet a-him gam ya-had
   Behold, how good and how pleasant, the dwelling of brothers as one!

CHORUS
   Hin-neh ma-tov u-ma-na-im shevet a-him gam ya-had
   Behold, how good and how pleasant, the dwelling of brothers as one!

CANTOR
3. K'-tal-her-mon she-yo-red 'al-ha-r're tsi-on ki
   Like dew of Hermon descending on the hills of Zion; for

   sham tsi-vah ye-ho-vah et-ha-b'ra-khah ha-yim 'ad-ha-'o-lam
   there commands Yehovah the blessing, even life for evermore.

CANTOR
   Hin-neh ma-tov u-ma-na-im shevet a-him gam ya-had
   Behold, how good and how pleasant, the dwelling of brothers as one!

CHORUS
   Hin-neh ma-tov u-ma-na-im shevet a-him gam ya-had
   Behold, how good and how pleasant, the dwelling of brothers as one!

The Levites ascend to the penultimate step. In the Court of Israel, one step above them, they see the congregated Israelites. In the Court of the Kohanim, four steps higher, stands the *kohen ha-gadol* of the house of Aaron. They lift up their song.

There is an ancient synagogue tradition of repeating the first verse of this psalm as a refrain after every verse. Since, as we saw in chapter nine, such practices were current in temple times, and since the first line of this psalm lends itself so readily to this procedure, I have transcribed it in this way.

In verse 1, the *maqqef*-hyphen joining *uma-naim* forces the syllables into one metrical foot with a single stress on the final syllable, *-im*. The effect of moving the emphasis onto this last syllable is to bring the cadence forward by one foot (or bar), so that it falls on the third bar, leaving a pause on the fourth.

The brothers dwelling as one are the twelve tribes of Israel. As Kimḥi says: 'It speaks of Israel, for they are all brothers.'[1] This is clear from the picture of the dew of northern Mount Hermon, above Galilee, coming down upon Zion in the southern mountains of Judah. These two peaks symbolize the political power axes of Joseph and Judah. And now, like the freshness of dew, the children of Joseph are coming to worship at the Zion footstool. Centuries of conflict behind, centuries of undisclosed fratricide ahead, they now live in peace under the rule of Solomon, the man of peace. Yet, while the hand holding them together in peace is of David's Judean line, at the heart of their unity is quite another genealogy to which all the tribes confess allegiance: it is the legitimate *kehunah* or priesthood of the sons of Aaron. Therefore it is Aaron (and his beard!) – *z'qan aharon* – which are the middle words at the heart of this psalm. Aaron is portrayed complete with beard to dignify him, resplendent in his ornate robes, fragrant with the sacred oil which marks his anointing with the divine spirit as a *kohen* acceptable to God and man. Israel's *kohanim*, the sons of Aaron, are both glorious and fitting.

In verses 2 and 3, the movement is all down, down, down, with the thrice-repeated verb *yarad* or 'descend'. We might even dub this a Song of Descents. The good oil, that is, the fragrant oil of the priestly anointing, descends from Aaron's head to his beard, and thence to the collar of his robes, in the same way that the dew of Hermon (and its fresh young people) descends to anoint and sanctify ancient-gated Zion on its eternal hills. *Oil* and *dew* together make a fitting pair. *Dew* is the freshness of heaven, *oil* the freshness of earth, which Israel gained at Esau's cost (Gen. 27.28, 39). As a word-pair, they are a picture of blessing from above and below. The coming of the Ephraimites to worship in Judah is *dew* from heaven; the anointing *oil* of Aaron and his sons is blessing below.

The one who blesses the people is the *kohen ha-gadol* of Aaron's line. Blessing the people was his most important function. In the *Birkat kohanim*, he was given the exact words to chant over them, and the Ascents Songs are

---

[1] So too Berlin (1987: 141) who suggests the national image is borrowed from rural life, where brothers might dwell together on an undivided patrimonial land holding.

redolent with this blessing (Num. 6.24–26). Yet, in spite of his blessing, there were times when the blessing of heaven was withheld, in the days of idolatry and bitter tribal warfare, when a curse consumed the land (Isa. 24.6). Was this because the blessing was no longer spoken? Was it not because only heaven may endorse each blessing spoken in the sacred name? An undeserved blessing, like an undeserved curse, will not come to rest. For the LORD commands the blessing where his people dwell as one (v. 3). But here, in Solomon's days, with the tribes of Israel living in peace, each one who comes to worship in Zion will truly be blessed by Aaron's blessing.

The Levites finish their song and cast their eyes eastward to the brightening sky behind Olivet, where the blessing flows out from the temple to the entire land. Soon, when the Israelites depart from the feast, they will take with them the blessings of Zion to the nation dwelling as one. The blessings, like the sacred oil and the dew from heaven, will drip down, down, down upon the whole land from Zion the global epicentre of blessing. As a power station sends out warmth, light, and life to all the homes connected, so the heavenly courts of the temple send out blessing and life to all Israel.

Yet the psalm's picture of anointed Aaron does not represent only the *kohanim*. As often in the Psalms, an individual represents the whole nation of Israel. For, in the divine plan, all Israel was an anointed *kohen*, an Aaron in the midst of the nations (Exod. 19.6). From our perspective, 3,000 years on, Israel has blessed the world. The sweet wind of the law of Moses has blown through the lands. A king, heir to David's throne, has spoken peace to the nations. The blessings spoken on Zion have circled the world and all humankind has, to some degree, entered into them.

Psalm 134
The Fourteenth Step

CANTOR
1. **Shir** ha - ma - 'a - **lot** / Song of the Ascents.
hin - **neh** **bar** - **khu** et ye - ho - **vah** kol av - **de** ye - ho - **vah** / Behold! Bless Yehovah, all servants of Yehovah,
ha - om - **dim** b' - vet y' - ho - **vah** ba - le - **lot** / Who stand in the house of Y'hovah by nights.

CHORUS
2. S'u - y' - de - **khem** qo - **desh** u - var - **khu** et ye - ho - **vah** / Lift up your hands to the sanctuary and bless Yehovah.

KOHEN GADOL / ALL
3. Y-va-re-kh' - **kha** ye-ho - **vah** mi-tsi - **on** 'o - seh sha - ma-yim va - a - **rets** / Yehovah bless you from Zion, who made the heav'ns and the earth.

The Levites proceed from the steps to the *dukhan*. Looking across the upper temple precincts, the *azarah*, they see the *kohanim* preparing the altar for the morning sacrifice. Some twenty-five metres away, they see the *kohen ha-gadol*, standing in the *ulam* or portico to pronounce the blessing on the Israelites. They raise their final song.

The first fourteen songs were about the blessings which the LORD bestows on Israel. But now, in this final song, Israel bestows blessings on the LORD, who responds with one final blessing from his holy house, spoken by the mouth of the *kohen ha-gadol*.

In verse 1, the title is sung to the usual pattern, cadencing with *oleh ve-yored*. Since verse 1 is one unit of thought without any break or repetitions, it is given undivided to the cantor. He addresses the *servants of the LORD who stand in the house of the LORD* (vv. 1–2). Contrary to the Targum, the night-ministers in the temple are not Levite guards but Aaronite *kohanim*. For they are *in* the house of the LORD, where they *stand*, a verb customarily denoting Aaronite ministry.[1] And from there, in verse 3, they speak the Aaronite blessing, which was lawful only for the *kohanim* to speak. The cantor, on a rising tone, exhorts the *kohanim* to bless the LORD. His opening *Behold!* shows that this is not a general encouragement to them to praise at general times. Rather it is an immediate exhortation awaiting an immediate response there and then in the temple courts. The little psalm exhales its unmistakeable cultic and liturgical atmosphere. Since the *kohanim* whom he addresses *stand* in the temple *by nights*, we are reminded again that the context of the psalm can only

---

[1] Deut. 10.8; 18.1–7; 1 Kgs 8.11; 1 Chr. 23.28–30; 2 Chr. 5.14; 29.4–11.

be the Feast of Sukkot, the only time in Israel's cultic year when a night service was held in the temple.[2]

The chorus join with the exhortation of verse 2. With a slow rising melody, they exhort the *kohanim* to raise their hands and bless the LORD. The accented last syllable of *y'dekhem*, 'hands', is long to allow metrical space before the equally accented first syllable of *qodesh*. The *kohanim* are to lift up their hands *b'qodesh*. That is, either *toward the holy place* (*b* as an accusative of direction) or *in holiness* (*b* as an accusative of definition), that is, with ritually clean hands. The former, which most translations follow, is endorsed by the Septuagint, while the second is supported by R. Joshua b. Levi of the third century AD.[3] So both are linguistically possible, but the first and more ancient understanding, from the days when the temple still stood, is preferable.

In verse 3, the one whom all Israel have been blessing now blesses them through the *birkat kohanim*, the blessing which he gave the sons of Aaron. It is spoken by the mouth of the *kohen ha-gadol*, standing in the portico, who lifts his hands in blessing to the level of the golden plate on his brow, the plate inscribed 'Holiness to YHVH', and says, *y^{e}varekh^{e}kha Yehovah*, 'Yehovah bless you'.[4] To the ancient words have been added the suffix *from Zion* – now that the divine presence has settled in Jerusalem. Who is first to receive the blessing but those who have blessed and praised his name all up the fifteen steps. They and all the congregation respond, declaring the universal authority and power of Israel's deity: *Maker of heaven and earth*. Over the Levites flows the blessing, over the Israelite men and women in the courts below, and out to all Israel. The holy name is set upon the children of Israel and so he blesses them (Num. 6.27). And the blessing flows on, in our own day, to all who bless him, to the ends of the earth.

We have read in the Ascents of many blessings – of blessings of protection on the way and in the city, of the blessings of harvest, of the blessings of fruitfulness, children and family, of the blessings of just rule and true religion. We have also learned something of how to obtain the blessing: by seeking it, by living in unity. But the biggest blessing is to bless the LORD. To bless him is happiness and joy; it is the purpose of our being, the key and door to all blessings. As Hengstenberg says on this psalm, 'The sure way to obtain the blessing of the LORD is to bless him.'

I remember a discussion once as to whether unwilling children should be made to come to church. One lady said that they must come at all costs. Others asked why. After all, the unwilling might learn little. But she insisted, 'They will get the blessing.' Good parents do not excuse unwilling children from school. They haul them from bed, if need be, and get them there by hook or by crook. They figure that, once they are there, they may acquire some smattering of the good oil of learning. How much more should we compel them into

---

[2] Isa. 30.29; M. *Suk.* 5.4.
[3] B. *Sot.* 39a.
[4] M. *Tam.* 7.2; T. *Sot.* 7.7.

blessing? If they listen to nothing, yet the blessing will rest on them and the shield will surround them. In all our getting we must get blessing. We should not let our young people miss it because in the wisdom of youth they misprize it. On the contrary, we must 'compel them to come in' (Luke 14.23).

This last Song of the Ascents collection resembles Psalm 150, whose great chorus of praise provides the last reverberant close to the book of Psalms. They have this in common that they make no petition of any kind for individual or nation, but focus only on praising the Holy One for his own sake. How else should a collection of psalms close? We rightly ask the Lord for his help and his blessings, for he promises and loves to give them. But, as we honour the giver more than the gift, so we should celebrate the Lord not for his blessings but for himself. For blessing him is our destiny. And that is why Psalms 134 and 150 have the last word in their lesser and greater anthologies: they point the way to an as-yet-unspoken eternity of praise.

14

In the Latter Days

David and Solomon are gone, blown away by the winds of three millennia. The temple, built with such labour, stood in glory for only thirty-six years before its treasures were plundered by Shishak. Gone now is roof and walls, gone the kingdom, gone the *kohanim* and their sacrifice, gone the Levites and their song. And one must finally ask why these fifteen songs have been preserved to this day. Why were they carefully copied and transmitted during thirty centuries? Why should anyone should read them now? Or, for that matter, why should anyone write books on them?

THE PROPHETIC BOOK OF PSALMS

These questions are not new. Someone must have asked them in the fifth century BC. Why, after the Babylonian conquest of 587 BC, after the humiliation of Judah's king, after the destruction of Jerusalem and the profanation of the temple, why gather these old songs about the glory of the king, the inviolability of the city, and the sanctity of the temple and collect them into a Book of Psalms? Yet someone did exactly that.[1] And the reason why they did it can only be that it was a statement of faith. These songs, and the other psalms, were preserved in hope that there would again be a time when Israel would have national independence, when they would again have a king, the LORD's *mashiah*, when they would again have a strong city and a holy house in whose courts these songs would again be sung.[2]

A closer look makes it clear that this was indeed the compiler's purpose. The preservation of the royal psalms – such as Psalms 2, 21, 45, 72, 110, 132, and others – after the extinction of the monarchy can be explained only on the basis of hope in a coming king greater than David or Solomon. Indeed, the prominence of the royal psalms within the Psalter shows that this messianic hope is its central theme. As John Forbes said:

---

[1] The redaction of the Psalms is traditionally ascribed to Nehemiah and Ezra; see chapter 1.
[2] For the full case for the Psalms as eschatological prophecy, see Mitchell 1997.

But whatever may be thought of the original purport of these [royal] Psalms, when we look at the place which has been assigned them in the Psalter as now constituted (arranged certainly in its present form a considerable time before the Septuagint version), and to the order and connection in which they stand, it becomes impossible with any fairness to deny that they were intended to excite in the Jewish worshippers an expectation of the Messiah.[3]

This messianic bias in the Psalms was instinctively understood in the past. The Dead Sea texts, the New Testament, Patristic and Rabbinic literature all routinely interpret the Psalms as speaking of the Messiah.[4] The Book of Psalms was never meant to be a museum piece of ancient Israel's songs. Instead, it paints a picture of the longed-for Messiah and his coming kingdom. As John Barton says, 'The thrust of the whole collection is strongly eschatological.'[5] In short, the Psalms form a book of prophecy, like Isaiah or Zechariah.[6]

Some of the hopes enshrined in the Psalms were partially fulfilled at the time when they were compiled, in Ezra and Nehemiah's time. The temple was rebuilt; Zerubbabel was a king of sorts. A few centuries later, the Maccabees were kings for a while. After the Maccabees, Herod made the temple most splendid. Yet Herod was a non-Israelite and a Roman puppet, and Israel never recaptured the national sovereignty or unity of the days of David and Solomon, much less the glorious vision presented in the Psalms and prophets. And, after the Roman destruction of AD 70, their hopes were more shattered than ever. Yet the Book of Psalms was preserved through all this because hope in the Messiah had become a central pillar of faith. And so the Synagogue treasured the Psalms as prophecy of the coming Messiah, the Church treasured them as testimony to the Messiah already come, and as prophecy this collection of ancient songs is still preserved twenty centuries later.

THE TIMETABLE OF THE BOOK OF PSALMS

The prophetic hope which lies at the heart of the Book of Psalms gives direction to the whole book, as its 'story' progresses from persecution, trouble, and distress to triumph. Augustine of Hippo discerned something of it long ago, saying, 'the sequence of the Psalms, which seems to me to contain the secret of a mighty mystery, has not yet been revealed to me.'[7] Yet the crux of

---

[3] Forbes 1883: 3.
[4] Mitchell 1997: 16-40, 64–65.
[5] Barton 1986: 22.
[6] The 'story' or 'meta-narrative' that underlies the Psalms has been a matter of debate since Wilson 1985. Some, like myself, have argued that it is eschatological and messianic (Mitchell 1997; 2006c; Cole 2013; McCann 2014: 350–362). But Wilson argued, until his death in 2006, that it is a non-eschatological, non-messianic history of David's dynasty (2005: 229–246). His view is still upheld by de Claissé-Walford (2014: 363–376).
[7] *Enarrationes* on Ps. 150 §1.

the story is found in Psalms 86 to 89. In Psalm 86, the psalmist, who is David the *mashiaḥ*, is surrounded by deadly enemies who seek his life. In Psalm 87 appears a brief vision of the future blessedness of the holy city. But in Psalm 88, someone is crying out from Sheol, the underworld, among the slain in the deepest pit of darkness. Then comes Psalm 89 with its urgent demand as to why, despite all the heavenly promises to David, the *mashiaḥ* has been so shamefully *cut short*, his *crown pierced in the dust* (89.45, 39). Yet after Psalm 89, the tone of hope begins to rise until the collection closes with the triumphant celebration of Israel's restored kingdom amidst praises and halleluyahs (Pss. 147-150). Each psalm and each group of psalms sits where it does in the collection as part of this ongoing narrative. However, as we meditate on it, parts of the narrative do become clear. It contains a host of details, an entire programme or timetable of future events, leading from the establishment of David's kingdom, through the death and resurgence of the *mashiaḥ*, to his final triumph.

THE ASCENTS OF ZECHARIAH

If then, the Psalter encodes a programme of future events, why have the Songs of Ascents been placed just where they are within the Psalms collection? The answer is in the book of Zechariah. It tells, in chapters nine and ten of the coming of the Messiah and the restoration of Israel, then, in chapters eleven to thirteen of a stricken and pierced shepherd for whom Israel's leaders mourn. Finally, in the last chapter, it tells how all the nations will go up to worship the LORD of hosts at the Feast of Sukkot in Jerusalem. The mention of Sukkot immediately alerts us to the Songs of Ascents: they were the liturgy that initiated the Sukkot festivities. But there is more. Five times in four verses, Zechariah uses the verb *alah*, 'ascend' or 'go up', to describe the nations going up to worship in Zion (or not going up and being smitten with drought). Nowhere else in the Bible does this verb get such emphasis. And this is the same verb that appears in the *ma'alot* heading of every one of the Songs of Ascents. In Zechariah's great vision of the Messiah's triumph, Israel and all the nations will make the 'Ascents' to worship at the Feast of Sukkot in the last days. Of course, this idea was not Zechariah's own invention. He inherited it from his prophetic forebears. Micah and Isaiah both sang of a time when the nations would ascend to Zion to worship Israel's God and learn his ways (Mic. 4.2; Isa. 2.3).

It was to represent this event – the ascent of Israel and the nations to the Feast of Sukkot in the messianic time – that the compiler of the Book of Psalms placed the Songs of Ascents near the end of his collection. Therefore, reading the Psalter as a prophetic text, we today can take the Songs of Ascents as foretelling the Feast of Sukkot in the coming days of the Messiah. Song by song, they tell once again the story of gathering to worship in Jerusalem, but now the story is in the future, not the past.

Psalm 120. As in the past, the Israelites went up from troublesome neighbours to the city of peace, so in the latter days, when the King Messiah sits on David's throne, Israel, with people from far away, shall turn their steps to Zion, to go up and worship there. The picture of being wounded by arrow-like tongues (vv. 2–5) suggests that some of them may be from the seed of Joseph (Gen. 49.23). They are the people of Ephraim returning home, as they first did in Ezra and Nehemiah's time, as they have done in our own time, and will do yet in the time to come.

Psalm 121. Those who go to celebrate at the Feast will be kept on their journey, as of old, by divine protection.

Psalm 122. Arriving in Jerusalem restored, they will praise the beauty of the well-built city, ruled again by the rightful heir of David's throne, who has made both throne and nation secure for ever. Thrones of justice will again be set up to judge the twelve tribes of Israel, even as promised (Matt. 19.28).

Psalm 123. They will look to the holy temple, now rebuilt, and ask the Holy One to bless them for the millennia of contempt they have endured.

Psalm 124. They will remember how the attacks of foreign nations almost overwhelmed them and bless the Holy One who has brought them escape and deliverance.

Psalm 125. They will rejoice in the security of the city of which they can now truly say that *the LORD surrounds his people from now until forever.*

Psalm 126. They will remember how the turning of their fortunes in these last days was a dream come true, how their sowing in adversity eventually led to a happy harvest, how all the nations now confess the great deeds of Israel's God.

Psalm 127. Instead of speaking of Solomon, the psalm now speaks of the Messiah, as Radak says:

> *Thus he gives his beloved rest.* 'His beloved' is the King Messiah and God gives him Jerusalem without struggle; and those who struggled over her will not remain and will not dwell in her.

They will sing of the blessing of a city rebuilt with the favour of heaven.

Psalm 128. They will confess the blessings on their families and, in particular, the blessing of the son of the royal house, the King Messiah who has brought peace and prosperity to the land.

Psalm 129. They will remember their past afflictions and confess the divine justice which cut the cords that bound them. They will confess that all who hate Zion will be unblessed for now Zion is the mother-city of the world.

Psalm 130. They will remember how, when the nations attacked them, they cried out of the depths for deliverance and their prayer was answered by the coming of the Messiah. They look ahead to the fullness of the kingdom which has just begun, when the Holy One will remove all the guilt and punishment of sin from Israel.

Psalm 131. In the knowledge of this pardon, they wait quietly on the will of heaven to be fulfilled in them.

Psalm 132. Once again the LORD comes to the holy house and enters his resting place. Once again prayers are offered for the King whose reign fulfils the promise to David. For Solomon and his sons were faithless, and their rule was cut off. But the one who will inherit David's throne will reign for ever.

Psalm 133. They celebrate their unity restored, under the true and faithful *kohen ha-gadol* who ministers before them, and look to their faithful worship being met by divine blessing and eternal life.

Psalm 134. They exhort the ministers of the holy city to bless the Holy One, and depart from the feast in blessing.

THE SONGS OF ASCENTS IN THE PSALTER

Therefore, reading the Book of Psalms as prophecy, as its compiler intended, the Songs of Ascents represent the Feast of Sukkot in the time of the Messiah. But how do the other psalms complete the prophetic timetable?

The Psalms tell of the Messiah. Because he loves Torah and meditates in it day and night (Ps. 1), the Holy One promises to overthrow every opposition to his rule and to establish his throne on Zion (Ps. 2). He comes as the divine Bridegroom-Messiah to rescue Daughter Zion and raise her to honour (Ps. 45). He issues a command to gather Israel (Ps. 50) and sets up a kingdom like Solomon's which will extend from sea to sea, and from the river to the ends of the earth (Ps. 72). However, his kingdom will be attacked by hostile nations (Pss. 73–83); he will surrounded by enemies and fall into the underworld (Ps. 86, 88). His people bereft of his presence, lament his death, and arraign the Holy One for the failure of his promise (Ps. 89). Israel will be exiled and perish in the wilderness, as they were in Moses' day, as Zechariah foretold, (Ps. 90; Zech. 13.7). But the king will be delivered from every evil (Ps. 91) to re-emerge from the underworld like a triumphant wild ox (Ps. 92).[8] Thereafter YHVH is praised and begins to rule among the nations (Pss. 93–99). Eventually, Israel regather to the land (Ps. 107), when the Messiah will announce his victory (Ps. 108), anathematize his enemy (Ps. 109), and descend from the right hand of Power to wage victorious battle (Ps. 110). This deliverance is celebrated in the Hallel Psalms (Pss. 113-117) which recall the joyful triumph of the Exodus. Then he ascends to Jerusalem amidst crowds and joyful celebrations (Ps. 118), while the scattered tribes of Israel, who have strayed like lost sheep, are gathered in (Ps. 119.176). Then the Songs of Ascents represent Israel and the nations ascending to keep the Feast of Sukkot

---

[8] For the wild ox as the resurrected Messiah of the House of Joseph, see Mitchell 2006b.

in Jerusalem when, in fulfilment of the promise of Psalm 2, the Messiah is installed on his throne (Ps. 132). Psalms 135 to 137 are a *codetta* to the Ascents collection. Psalms 140 to 144 feature a final attack upon the messianic throne. Evildoers threaten the new David with force, stratagems, and pursuits, but the threat is now easily dismissed.[9] Psalm 145 is a hymn of praise for the victory, and Psalms 146 to 150 are the grand *coda* of praise to the entire collection.

Along such lines runs the prophetic programme which underlies the Book of Psalms. From Israel's ancient collections of songs, the compiler, in the fifth century BC, put together a work of eschatological prophecy looking to the coming and triumph of the Messiah. He learned of these things from the prophets before him, whose sayings, if opaque to us, were sufficiently clear to him as to be harmonized into a single story running through his book of praises. We, who know a later version of the story, are amazed at what his ancient collection foresaw.

---

[9] The Psalms appear to see three attacks on the Messiah: Pss. 86–89, where the Messiah dies; Pss. 108–110 where the Messiah conquers; and Psalms 140–144, where he conquers completely. This idea is known from other Israelite texts. *Midr. Pss* 118.12 and 119.2 see Gog and Magog going up against Jerusalem three times. Sa'adya, *Kitab al-amanat*, VIII.6, speaks of three attacks: in the first, Messiah ben Joseph dies; in the second, Messiah ben David conquers; in the third, Ben David conquers overwhelmingly. And much earlier, the author of Revelation, whose Messiah was killed by foreign invaders just before his own time, foresaw two more attacks on Jerusalem which the Messiah would conquer overwhelmingly (Rev. 19.19; 20.7–9). See Mitchell 2006c: 526-48.

15

I Will Proclaim Your Name to My Brethren

I was glad when they said unto me, *Let us go to the house of the LORD.* Our feet are standing in your gates, Jerusalem, at the top of the fifteen steps. I thank you for coming with me on this journey to the well-springs of worship. In the light from the Holy Place, we can reflect on the way we have come.

Folowing the old pattern of fourfold exegesis, we have read the Songs of Ascents literally, tropologically, allegorically, and anagogically; we have sought the *peshat* (plain sense), the *remez* (the implied sense), the *derash* (allegorical sense), and the *sod* (the concealed mystery). This has enabled us to read the Songs of Ascents in different ways, in new ways. Taking their heading as a sign that they belong together, we discovered a narrative sequence running through them which tells of pilgrimage to and from the autumn Feast of Sukkot. We discovered that the occurences of the Ineffable Name encode numerological mesages that show the name of Yedid-Yah or Solomon watermarked throughout the collection. Other details of the Songs led us to conclude that they attained their present form in Solomon's reign. Further investigation showed that they were written as the liturgy for the celebrations of the first night of the fifteenth of Sukkot 959 BC and for the ark of the covenant's entry to the temple at dawn of that day. We saw that, in later years, they continued as part of the worship of the Feast throughout Israel's history. We discovered that the Levite singers sang the fifteen songs as they ascended the fifteen temple steps. We learned how the Levite orchestra sang and played. We reconstructed the melodies to which the songs we sung, and saw how each song fits within the ascending thought of the progress to the holy courts. And we saw how, after the return from the Babylonian exile, the Songs of Ascents became part of a collection speaking about the coming of the Messiah, and how, within that collection, they represent the ascent of all the nations to worship in Jerusalem, as foretold by Isaiah and Zechariah.

All these things we learned on our journey. But, like the Levites before us, the reason I came, and, I suppose, the reason you came too, was to offer up a worthy song before the holy throne. Let us speak a bit more of worthy songs.

THE POWER OF MUSIC

The Babylonians saw in music the language of the stars. The seven modes of seven notes brought the magical power of the stars to earth. The Hebrews shared the same philosophy. For them, the morning stars sang at the founding of the earth, before the creation of mankind.[1] And so they saw music as heavenly speech and prophecy, communicating with the world of the heavens. It had power to receive and communicate divine instructions, to channel the power of heaven, to heal, exorcise, and sanctify, to propitiate and invoke, to protect, bless, and deliver from evil.[2] The Greeks agreed. For Pythagoras, the sun, moon, and spheres emit their own music.[3] For Plato, music enters our being, imparting grace, wisdom, and discernment to the inmost soul.

> Musical training is a more potent instrument than any other, because rhythm and harmony find their way into the inward places of the soul, on which they mightily fasten, imparting grace, and making the soul of him who is rightly educated graceful, or of him who is ill-educated ungraceful: and also because he who has received this true education of the inner being will most shrewdly perceive omissions or faults in art and nature, and with a true taste, while he praises and rejoices over and receives into his soul the good, and becomes noble and good, he will justify, blame and hate the bad, now in the days of his youth, even before he will recognize and salute the friend with whom his education has made him long familiar.[4]

The Church too, drawing on the Bible, always recognized the power of music. For Boethius, music was a mirror of the divine order: *music mundana* was the music of the macrocosm, of the heavenly bodies in their spheres; *music humana* was the music of the microcosm, of mankind and of human society. That musical theologian, Martin Luther, wrote that 'Music is a gift of God…Next to the Word of God, the noble art of music is the greatest treasure in the world.'[5]

Music is the language of heaven, the *nomos* of the multiverse made audible, the daughter of Elysium to earth come down. The lustre of her descent sprinkled the songbirds, who melodize without rhythm. It brushed the higher vertebrates, elephants and chimpanzees, who beat rhythm without melody or ensemble. Yet only among mankind do her gifts converge in communal melody and rhythm in song and dance. Among our species music is primeval: early bone flutes, from the Geißenklösterle cave, have been dated to some

---

[1] Job 38.4–7.

[2] 1 Sam. 16.23; 1 Sam. 10.5–10; 1 Macc. 13.47–51; 2 Kgs 3.15; Ps. 69.30–31; Num. 10.9; 2 Chr. 20.22.

[3] Pythagoras, from Pliny, *Natural History*, II.xviii.20. Pythagoras designates the distance between the Earth and the Moon as a whole tone, between the Moon and Mercury as a semitone, and so on, until the seven tones produce the diapason or universal harmony.

[4] Plato, *Republic*, III.401d-402a.

[5] Luther, Foreword to Georg Rhau's collection of chorale motets, *Symphoniae* (1538).

50,000 years ago.[6] It is also universal: there is no species of mankind which does not sing.

Music has two poles. The heavenly component of melody, ruled by magical stellar sevens, and the earthly component of rhythm, ruled by twos and fours, like the bipedal and quadrupedal world of seasons and compass points.

Melody, the heavenly part, fills our minds and souls. It is melody, not rhythm, which we sing. Melody is the mirror of our spirits. Our sad melodies reflect the physiognomy of the depressed: low, soft, and of dropping contour. But when we are happy, our melodies bound up in Mannheim rockets. Melodies are what we remember, bringing back to us in a wash of pathos our memories of times past, the soundtrack of our days. Melody connects us with our ancestors, when we sing their ancient songs. Melody connects us with the ancient church, when we hymn their hymns. Melody touches our spirits.

But if music's stellar essence woos mind and spirit, its earthly component – rhythm – grabs us in the viscera. In rhythm we were all conceived. The first flicker on the screen of our dawning consciousness was our mother's heartbeat in the womb, its slow gradations of tempo and rhythm forming our total world. Heartbeat underscores all our doings to the end of our mortal days. But it is soon joined by other rhythms: the duple beat of breathing, chewing, walking, and all the body's circadian periodicity of eating and digesting, of sleeping and waking, of peristalses and hormonal cycles. Rhythm, the physical part of music, imperiously demands our heart. Children seek out fast music to match the racing pulse of youth. They turn the dance grooves on the Clavinova to 180 per minute and career around the *salle de danse*, frolicking in the beat of their intra-uterine memories. Older people find this disquieting. They do not want their quiet heart limbering up for the hundred metre sprint. But their poor heart, all reluctant, leaps to the call, as after some hypnotic demagogue. As for the truly aged, with trudging pulse, they seek music of increasingly sedate measure until the slow *Totentanz* ends in silence. Rhythm is life: its absence is death.

Joining sevenfold melody and twofold rhythm unites heaven and earth. And, if melody sways the spirit and rhythm the body, then harmony moves the heart. Harmony – the difference tones between notes – fills the space between melody and rhythm, adding shimmer to the melody, thickening it, teasing the mind and ear. At the same time, it augments the rhythmic undertow, as harmonic changes coincide with rhythmic patterns and cadences. Harmony's close friend is the bass line, supporting the harmonic movement from the bottom up, reinforcing the rhythm. And added to all this is *timbre* – the tone quality of instruments and voices – trumpets and bagpipes and spinto sopranos all adding their flash of colour to the inner eye.

---

[6] For more, see Mithen 2005. Dumbrill (2009–10: 108) cautions that these earliest bone-flutes may have been to lure birds within bow-shot. Yet that implies human recognition of the tonal nature of bird-song and the ability to reproduce it. In the same place, Dumbrill shows the Jiahu bone-pipe from China, a fully-functional, multi-holed, musical pipe, dating from 6,000 BC.

Music retains its primeval power. It recalls lost emotions. It calms stress. It makes cows give more milk and plants grow more luxuriantly. It reduces blood-pressure, triggers the release of mood-altering brain chemicals, and regulates the extremes of epilepsy. Participating in music is better still. Singing strengthens lungs and torso, promotes coordination, manual dexterity, beauty, posture, and poise. It is a great cardiovascular workout. It releases endorphins and Immunoglobulin A, it increases production of oxytocin and testosterone, promoting health and healing, relieving pain and anxiety, lowering blood pressure, making people healthier, happier and longer lived.[7]

Music benefits the mind. In one British study in the 1990's, children of equal abilities were divided into two groups. One group was given forty-five minutes of extra music every day; the other was given extra Mathematics and English. At the end of a year the music group were better in all subjects, including Maths and English,[8] and more attentive in all classes. Reports abound of children exposed to classical music excelling in IQ tests in comparison to others.[9] Music effects changes in the very structure of the brain. In professional musicians, the corpus callosum, that connects the two hemispheres of the brain, is enlarged and there are increased volumes of gray matter in motor, auditory, and visuospatial areas of the cortex, and in the cerebellum. To a pathologist, a musician's brain is easily identifiable.[10]

From this deep-penetrating efficacy springs music's mnemonic power. The processing of words and speech is localized in Broca's region in the brain's left frontal lobe. A brain-scan of speech shows activity in that area alone. But when music is heard, the whole brain flashes like a Vegas sidewalk, and the song is stored all across the brain. Therefore learning is easier with music. The rabbis knew this. As they said: If one reads Torah without a melody or recites without a tune, of him Scripture says, *Wherefore I have given them also statutes that are not good.*[11] And so we set scripture to song to make it memorable. From music's mnemonic power comes yet another of its healing properties. In patients with aphasia following stroke-related brain injury, songs lodged elsewhere in the brain, words wrapped in all-pervading music, can be recalled and speech may be brought back to use again.[12]

Yet music's power does not derive from the words joined to it. Music is numinous speech in its own right. A former Archbishop of Canterbury wrote: 'To listen seriously to music and to perform it are among our most potent ways of learning what it is to live with and before God.'[13] While the Hamburg *Kapellmeister*, Johann Mattheson, Handel's erstwhile enemy and reconciled

---

[7] From the review of Britain's *Silver Song* programme for the elderly in J. Murray, 'All Together Now', *The Guardian*, Tuesday 15 April 2008.
[8] Jenkins 2001: 170-72.
[9] See the *The Mozart Effect* series by Campbell 1997–2001.
[10] Sacks 2007: 94.
[11] *Meg.* 52, citing Ezek. 20:25.
[12] Sacks 2007: 232–242.
[13] Williams 1994: 249.

friend, wrote: 'Saving faith comes not from the sermon alone but equally from listening to a beautiful piece of sacred music, which may then be called a main sermon.'[14]

Yet, when music and words are aptly joined, the whole is greater than the sum of the parts. For the Babylonians, the addition of the seven vowels to the seven notes of the seven modes raised the magical power to the highest level. For us, a tune is one thing, a poem is another, but a song is more than both together. A fitting melody to beautiful words penetrates soul and spirit deeper than mere words ever can. What will a child learn sooner than a song? What brings memory flooding back, if not a song? Or to paraphrase Andrew Fletcher, what is more transforming than law, if not song?[15]

MUSIC AND THE WORD OF GOD

Yet if, as Luther says, music is second only to the word of God, what can we say when music and the word of God are joined in song? J.S. Bach owned the three-volume Calov Bible Commentary.[16] At 2 Chronicles 5.13, where the glory of the LORD fills the temple at the Levites' praises, Bach wrote in the margin, 'In devotional music God is always present with his grace.' The apostle Paul said the same thing. His recommended means for being filled with divine grace is sacred song: *Be filled with the Spirit, as you sing psalms, and hymns and spiritual songs among yourselves; sing and make music in your hearts to the Lord* (Eph. 5.18-19).

Bach also wrote, at 1 Chronicles 25.1, where the temple musicians are to proclaim God's word in the composition of psalms and singing with musical instruments, that this chapter is the true foundation for all God-pleasing church music. Then, at 1 Chronicles 28.21, where Calov remarked that David had not arranged the temple and its services on his own initiative but at divine command, Bach notes that, through David, God's Spirit instituted not only the divine service of the temple, but the music of the church.

The Holy One set music at the heart of worship, to mediate his presence and proclaim his word. In the temple service there was no sacrifice without a song: 'The omission of the song invalidates the sacrifice.'[17] Yet the merit of the song over animal sacrifice was long recognized (Ps. 69.31). In time, the sacrifice was completed, but the song remained. It flowed from the temple into the synagogues and churches of the Holy Land, and then into all the lands. And so the holy house in Jerusalem filled the world with music.

---

[14] Mattheson 1721: 132-33.
[15] See Chapter 13.
[16] Calov, *Commentary on the Bible* (Wittenberg, 1681–82); noted by Kleinig 1993: 13. Facsimiles of Bach's marginal comments are in Leaver 1976: 16–22.
[17] B. *Arak.* 11a.

A church without music is therefore inconceivable. For the Lord inhabits the praises of his people and the wings of the Holy Spirit are upborne on currents of melody. Start a church without music and be confounded, for the flock gather at the spring of sacred song. It is the first-listed activity of the gathered saints: *When you come together, everyone has a hymn* (1 Cor. 14.26). Sacred song holds up half the ecclesial sky.

Biblical worship is vocal worship. The human voice is its foundation. 'The Rabbis are of the opinion that the essential feature of the [temple] music is the singing.'[18] Some say that since most people have no experience of singing 'outside of football matches', singing in church, especially choral singing, is alien and should be replaced by a DJ.[19] But in a packaged world, the Holy One still requires and inspires the sound of his people's voices. To offer anything less is a dishonour.

Biblical worship is choral. In Jerusalem, never less than twelve men ministered in song before the altar. The cathedrals of Christendom, throughout medieval and renaissance times, maintained similar bodies of professional singers to offer up praises. Yet, in the last few centuries, there has been a global explosion of choral singing. The London Handel Centenary of 1784, and the invention of lithographic music printing, combined to produce a new phenomenon – the amateur choral society whose members gather for love of singing. This movement has now surpassed all bounds. From Tokyo to Los Angeles, from Oslo to Wellington, any major town or city has multiple choral ensembles. One website, noting that its list is partial, lists 25,000 choirs in the United Kingdom alone. Most of these choral groups feature sacred music as a central part of their repertoire. Wherever the gospel river laps, songs spring up, and choirs, orchestras, and musical directors sing them. The seed planted at David's tabernacle 3,000 years ago has become a tree in which the birds of the air may roost. They have filled air with singing.

Biblical worship has solo singers. The best temple singers were chosen as cantors, and the exchange of solo and chorus voices was essential to Hebrew music. The exchange of soli and chorus is equally essential to the great music of western tradition from medieval times to the present. Many forms of contemporary worship music also have a prominent place for the soloist. Solo singing should not be dismissed on the ground that soloists are prone to vanity. Such temptations afflict the best of us.

Biblical worship is congregational. The singing of the temple cantors was answered by congregational Halleluyahs, Amens and other responses. The church, being altogether a holy priesthood, rightly involves the congregation more than the temple ever did. So congregations should be encouraged to sing. They will not sing like a well-trained choir, but strophic hymns and songs are ideally suited to their use and the church's vast repertory of hymnody was

---

[18] B. *Suk.* 50b.
[19] Leach 2011.

composed for just this purpose.[20] Yet the congregation may worship also in hearing the singing of others, solo or choir. Meanwhile, the church, unlike the temple, welcomes the participation of women, as co-heirs of the gift of life.

Biblical worship has instruments. The temple orchestra of Psalm 150 contains the seed of the symphony orchestra: strings, woodwind, trumpets, and percussion. Yet instrumental worship elicits strong views. For the best part of the first millennium of church history instruments were little used, not from the lack of them, but from their association with Greco-Roman orgiastic cults. Eusebius wrote:

> Of old, when those of the circumcision were worshipping with symbols and types, it was not inappropriate to send up hymns to God with the psalterion and cithara and to do this on Sabbath days... But we render our hymn with a living psalterion and a living cithara with spiritual songs. The unison voices of Christians are more acceptable to God than any musical instrument.[21]

John Chrysostom was more direct: cymbals and pipes were 'rubbish of the devil'.[22] But in time, instruments were gradually permitted. The organ was introduced to worship by Pope Vitalian in AD 658.[23] Yet church music still remained largely vocal for another 1,000 years. As late as the Reformation, Calvin branded instruments a thing of Popery and Judaism.

> Musical instruments in celebrating the praise of God would be no more suitable than the burning of incense, the lighting of lamps, or the restoration of the other shadows of the law. The Papists therefore, have foolishly borrowed this, as well as many other things, from the Jews.[24]

But Calvin's criminations were unfounded. The Jews (as opposed to biblical Israel) had banned instruments since Sa'adia's time. As for the Papists, while basilicas and cathedrals employed organs, the sound of unaccompanied vocal polyphony was still the ideal. The Sistine Chapel, completed in Calvin's day, has no organ.

---

[20] The church has sung congregationally from the beginning. Pliny wrote to Trajan, in AD 111, of Christians gathering before sunrise to sing a hymn antiphonally to Christ as to a god (Pliny, *Letters*, 10.96). This may have been an early version of *Phos hilaron* (reliably attested from the 3rd century). The fourth century saw *Hymnum dicat turba fratrum* by Hilary of Poitiers and *Te Deum laudamus*, perhaps by Nicetas. The succeeding centuries saw, to give only a few examples, *Corde natus* by Prudentius (4th–5th), *Vox clara ecce intonat* (5th) and, westward, *Rop tú mo baile* (Be thou my vision) by Dallán Forgaill (6th century) and Caedmon's Hymn (7th century). Medieval times produced, for instance, *Dies irae* by Thomas of Celano (13th century), *In dulci jubilo* by Henrich Suso (13th–14th century), and *O filii et filiae* by Jean Tisserand (15th century).

[21] Eusebius, Commentary on LXX Ps. 91:2-3 [MT Ps. 92].

[22] *In I Corinthios*, Hom. XII,5; *PG* LXI,103; cited in McKinnon 1987: 86.

[23] Faulkner 1996: 216-224, outlines the elaborate process by which the organ eventually became the Christian instrument *par excellence*.

[24] Calvin, Commentary on Ps. 33.

It was the Reformation movement, particularly in England and Germany, which gave the greatest impetus to the use of instruments in church. Since the seventeenth and eighteenth centuries, they have become widespread. Some still resist instrumental worship on the basis of church history and the New Testament's silence on instrumental worship. Now, of course, there is no compulsion to employ instruments. 'The essential feature of the music is the singing.' But to forbid them, as some still do, is an error. *Praise him on the trumpet*, says the psalmist.[25] Therefore on the trumpet we shall praise him. What the Old Testament commands and the New does not prohibit is certainly permitted. And instruments shall bestow all the blessings of music, not least the presence of the divine Spirit. And they shall serve to enhance the voices, as the crown sets off the diamond. Then instruments, like voices, shall be for the divine glory and for our blessing.

Bible worship is festal. Celebrations lighten our hard lot. Holy feasts of happy song punctuate time's turbulent stream with islands of joy; they make stepping-stones over the Slough of Despond; they print the deeds of God in the calendar, bring down the Spirit's power, and exalt the one who said, 'When I am lifted up from the earth, I will draw all people to me.' We rightly celebrate Easter, Christmas and Pentecost. But we should not forget the harvest Feast of Sukkot. As the only Israelite feast not fulfilled in the New Testament, the imperative for keeping it may not be obvious. But it awaits its fulfilment, as many ancient liturgies and lectionaries, and the best harvest hymns, make clear.

> Even so, Lord, quickly come;
> Bring the final harvest home.
> Gather all your people in,
> Free from sorrow, free from sin.

Celebration of the Feast of Sukkot fulfils Zechariah's prophecy of the time when all nations will celebrate the Feast with Israel. We applaud those who already go up to Jerusalem to celebrate Sukkot year by year. But all those who celebrate Harvest in the Sukkot season may share in this testimony to the world.

Singing is the audible witness of the Church's divine unity. Mankind mirrors God's image of unity in diversity. Just as the notes of the scale only make music in their concordant and discordant relations to one another, so we only reflect the divine image in the complexity of our relations. 'Human beings are *imago trinitatis* and only correspond to the triune God when they are united with one another.'[26] Much discord has marred the divine image. But when we sing together, many voices become one, simultaneously following one melody, each contributing without losing its individuality. None runs ahead,

---

[25] Ratzinger 1981: 114: 'In contrast to theology, the psalms manifested an utterly unpuritanical delight in music.'
[26] Moltmann 1985: 216.

none lags behind; all walk in step. This power of song unites humankind, in football crowds, children's games, folk clubs. But it is seen most clearly in the diversity of the Church, when old and young, rich and poor, from all corners of the globe, join in the communal song that heralds the new humanity.

This is seen particularly in the singing of the Psalms. For while other songs and hymns differ from community to community, the Psalms are shared by the church in all the world. This is what Ambrose wrote:

> [A psalm is] a pledge of peace and harmony, which produces one song from various and sundry voices in the manner of a cithara.... A psalm joins those with differences, unites those at odds and reconciles those who have been offended, for who will not concede to him with whom one sings to God in one voice? It is after all a great bond of unity for the full number of people to join in one chorus. The strings of the cithara differ, but create one harmony.[27]

When we join with others in singing the Psalms, we join not only with our own congregation, but with the faithful in all ages. We sing with Moses and Israel coming through the sea; with David dancing before the ark and the Levites in the temple; with children running down Olivet waving eager palm branches, with the disciples in the upper room; with the apostles before the Sanhedrin and in Pisidian Antioch; with the churches of Corinth and Ephesus; with the Fathers and the Schoolmen, the Reformers and Counter-Reformers; with Catholic, Orthodox, Protestant, and Pentecostal; with the 144,000 and the innumerable multitude who sing before the throne the psalms of the age to come.

> In the vigils in the churches,
> David is first, middle, and last.
> In the singing of hymns at dawn,
> David is first, middle, and last.
> In the monasteries, in the hosts of holy warriors,
> David is first, middle, and last.
> In the convents of virgins, the imitators of Mary,
> David is first, middle, and last.
> In the deserts where men crucified to the world hold
>   converse with God,
> David is first, middle, and last.[28]

And not only in the church. For in the Psalms, Christian meets Jew: Rabbi and Karaite, Exilarch and Gaon. All meet together in these songs, our differences shelved as we pray with one voice for the meek to inherit the earth, for the kingdom of God to come, for his praise to fill the earth.

The Psalms teach us to pray. They are, as Calvin said, 'the design of the Holy Spirit...to deliver to the church a common form of prayer.'[29] Praying the

---

[27] Quoted in Stapert 2007: 26.
[28] Pseudo-Chrysostom, *De poenitentia*; PG LXIV, 12–13.
[29] Calvin 1563 [1949]: I.334.

psalms frees us from our own private litanies. In their praises of God in creation, we meditate on the mystery of his works. In their praises of God's deeds, we learn of his saving power. In their praises of God in his sanctuary, we meditate on the wonder of his being. In their curses against enemies, we feel the bedrock of evil and judgement, we sense the sufferings of the Messiah and our share in them. In their praises of Israel's king we proclaim the one who will yet rule the world. And so we are renewed.

> What is more pleasing than a psalm? David expresses it well: Praise the Lord, for a song of praise is good; let there be praise of our God with gladness and grace. Yes, a psalm is a blessing on the lips of the people, a hymn in praise of God, the assembly's homage, a general acclamation, a word that speaks for all, the voice of the Church, a confession of faith in song. It is the voice of complete assent, the joy of freedom, a cry of happiness, the echo of gladness. It soothes the temper, distracts from care, lightens the burden of sorrow. It is a source of security at night, a lesson in wisdom by day. It is a shield when we are afraid, a celebration of holiness, a vision of serenity, a promise of peace and harmony. It is like a lyre, evoking harmony from a blend of notes. Day begins to the music of a psalm, day closes to the echo of a psalm.[30]

WILL THE REAL DIRECTOR OF MUSIC PLEASE STAND UP?

Fifty-five psalms bear the heading *la-mnatseah*, 'For the pre-eminent one', in reference to the Levite Chief Musician. Our modern translations are therefore justified in rendering the term, 'For the Director of Music.' Yet the ancient translations emphasize the pre-eminence rather than the musicianship. The Septuagint renders it, *Eis to telos*, 'For the pre-eminent one.' Aquila gives *tō nikopoiō*, 'For the conqueror.' Jerome has *victori*, 'For the conqueror.'[31] Given the widespread messianic interpretation of the Psalms in their day, it seems that these translators saw the Levite *mnatseah* as a prophetic type of the Messiah.

But can the Messiah be a cantor? Certainly, the Holy One of Israel rejoices over his people with singing, and sounds the *shofar* for their victory.[32] Yet, while Judaism sees a *shofar*-sounding Messiah, it is the Church that sees the Messiah as a singer.[33]

The gospels record that Jesus, on the night of his Passion, sang a hymn with his disciples. The hymn was surely part of the Hallel – Psalms 114 to 118 – and Jesus, as the teacher of his little band, would have taken the cantor's part,

---

[30] Ambrose 1966: CSEL 64.7, on Psalm 1 (with thanks to John Barton 2013: 259).
[31] In his later and better 'Hebrew' Psalter. In his earlier Gallican (Vulgate) Psalter, he renders it 'In finem', a Latin translation of one sense of the Greek *Eis to telos*. Cf. Mitchell 1997: 37.
[32] Zeph. 3.17; Zech. 9.14.
[33] See O'Connor 2011, to whom I am indebted for many of the sources in these paragraphs.

with his disciples responding.[34] The next day, on the cross, in mortal suffering, he hymned to himself the prayer of Psalm 22 to a tune he would have learned in the synagogue or the temple.[35]

But Psalm 22 is the song not only of the Messiah's sufferings, but also of his triumph. This is the theme of the writer to the Hebrews. After being delivered from his sufferings, the Messiah will again lead the call-and-response praises among the congregation: *I will proclaim your name to my brothers; in the presence of the congregation I will sing [hymnesō] your praises*.[36] John Wesley remarks,

> Christ declares the name of God, gracious and merciful, plenteous in goodness and truth, to all who believe, that they may also praise him. "In the midst of the church will I sing praise unto thee" – as the precentor of the choir. This he did literally in the midst of his apostles, on the night before his passion. And as it means, in a more general sense, setting forth the praise of God, he has done it in the church by his word and his Spirit; he still does and will do it throughout all generations.[37]

Yet, while Jesus has led the church's singing in all ages, the real sense of the letter to the Hebrews points to the time when he will return in glory to judge the world and lead his brothers to the heavenly banquet with a song.

> The writer to the Hebrews locates here a reference to the exalted Lord who finds in the gathering of the people of God at the parousia an occasion for the proclamation of God's name and who as the singing priest leads the redeemed community [*en mesō ekklēsias*] in hymns of praise.[38]

The Messiah sang among his people during his earthly sojourn, he sings amidst them to this day, calling from heaven to their earthly response, and he will sing over them when he appears in triumph. But did his singing begin only at the incarnation? Not for the bishops of the Second Vatican Council. They saw the incarnated Messiah bringing to earth heaven's song of praise.

> Christ Jesus, high priest of the new and eternal covenant, taking human nature, introduced into this earthly exile that hymn which is sung throughout all ages in the halls of heaven. He joins the entire community of humanity to himself, associating it with his own singing of this canticle of divine praise. For he continues his priestly work through the agency of his Church, which is

---

[34] Matt. 26.30; Mark 14.26. In the Passover Seder, the first two Hallel Psalms (113–114) precede the Passover meal, the last four (115–118) follow it.
[35] Matt. 27.46; Mark 15.34.
[36] Heb. 2.12 citing Ps. 22.22; Greek *hymnesō* renders Hebrew *ahal^{e}lekha*.
[37] John Wesley, *Explanatory Notes on the New Testament*, vol. 2 (Grand Rapids: Baker Books, 1986); 'Reprinted from an undated edition published by the Wesleyan-Methodist Book-Room London'), no page numbers.
[38] Lane 1991: 59.

ceaselessly engaged in praising the Lord and interceding for the salvation of the whole world.[39]

Likewise, Johann Mattheson remarked, on Hebrews 2.5, that when the morning stars sang together at the foundation of the world, their precentor, their *mnatseaḥ* or 'shining one', could only have been the Bright Morning Star, the chorus-leader [*choragos*] of the heavenly princes, the *Oberkapellmeister* of the heavenly hosts; and he who sang praises before the earth's foundation, and during his sojourn in this *Jammertal,* will certainly sing among us at his appearing and in the world to come.[40]

The Bright Morning Star is the root and offspring of David. His song is David's song, the song of the holy temple. 'The very words uttered by David were at the same time being uttered in him by the Messiah who was to come... Christ himself offered them in the person of his ancestor David.'[41]

For a long time now we have sung new versions of the old songs, or new songs altogether. Perhaps this was by design. Otherwise we might never have had Allegri's *Miserere*, Rachmaninov's *Night-Vigil*, or Stravinsky's *Symphony of Psalms*. But the lost treasure gleams in the sand, and we go out to gather it, in preparation for the *mnatseaḥ* whom we await. For he will descend from heaven with a shout, with the voice of the archangel and the *shofar* of God, and with the song of David – *Let us go to the house of the Lord!* – and we shall answer with singing as he leads us up the ascents to the feast in his Father's house.

---

[39] Second Vatican Council, Constitution on the Sacred Liturgy (Sacrosanctum concilium) §83.
[40] Mattheson 1747: 99–100, 67, 121–22; cf. Rev. 22.16.
[41] Bonhoeffer 1961: 5.

Appendix I

Singing the Sacred Name

The sacred personal name of God, occurring 6,828 times in the Hebrew scriptures, is written with the Hebrew letters *yodh-heh-vav-heh* – equivalent to the English letters YHVH.

יהוה

In Hebrew this is called the *shem meforash* or 'explicit name'. In English it is sometimes called the 'ineffable name' or, more often, the 'Tetragrammaton', a Greek word meaning 'four letters'.

The antiquity of the Name is beyond question. It appears in three Egyptian lists, from Soleb (late 15th century BC), Amarah-West (13th century BC), and Medinet Habu (12th century BC). The Soleb list, of which the later two seem to be copies, was written by the scribes of Pharaoh Amenhotep III. The list speaks of six different groups of Shasu – Asiatic semi-nomads – known to the Egyptians as living in the Levant. One of these groups is the 'Shasu of Yhw'.

The phrase has given rise to various opinions. Some think it refers to the early Israelites as the 'Shasu of Yhw'. Others think it shows that the Edomites were the first to worship Israel's deity.[1] Still others think 'Yhw' is a place name, named after the deity.[2] Yet, despite all these different views, the consensus is that the name is an early mention of the sacred Name, to be pronounced Y^eho or Yahu or Y^ehowa or Y^ehova.

In pre-exilic Israel, the Name was spoken freely by all the Israelites, as both the Bible and archaeological sources testify. The

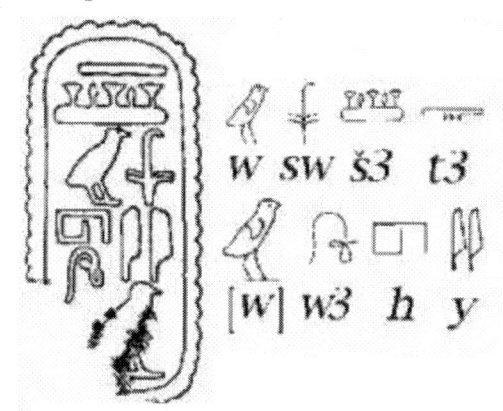

Figure 28. Shasu of Yhw
The text from Soleb (right to left)

[1] Redford 1993: 272–73.
[2] Astour 1979: 20–29.

Lachish ostraca, for instance, written during the Assyrian attack on the city in 701 BC, show a junior officer, Hoshayahu, continually using the Name when writing to his captain Ya'ush.[3] After the Exile, the speaking of the Name was increasingly circumscribed, in order to protect it from profanation. After the death of the *kohen ha-gadol* Simeon the Just, in the early third century BC, it was spoken only by the *kohen ha-gadol* on Yom Kippur.[4] Finally, following the Bar Kokhba Revolt of AD 132-135, the Romans banned the Name on pain of death, a ban which led to the martyrdom of R. Hanina ben Teradion.[5] Thereafter, the rabbis discouraged entirely the speaking of the Name, to protect the community. Not that this was done in any official way. The only Mishnaic authority in the matter is an addendum in the name of a minor second-century teacher, Abba Saul.[6]

> All Israel will have a portion in the World to Come, as it is said, *And all your people will be righteous; forever they will inherit the earth* (Isa. 60.21). But these have no portion in the World to Come: One who says there is no resurrection of the dead; [one who says] there is no Torah from heaven; and an Epicurean. R. Akiva says: One who reads heterodox scrolls, and one who murmurs over a wound and says, *All these diseases which I set upon the Egyptians, I will not set upon you* (Exod. 15.26). And Abba Saul says: Whoever pronounces the Name literally.

Yet, in time, the ban became binding and the spoken vowels that originally accompanied the four consonants gradually became obfuscated.

However, when the Masoretic codices appeared, from the ninth century on, it appeared that the Masoretes were in no doubt about the vowels of the Name. At its first occurrence in the Aleppo Codex Psalms, at Psalm 1.2, we find the Name written with vowel points, as follows:

$$יְהֹוָה$$

Reading from right to left, the first consonant, *yodh*, has two dots below it, representing the *sh^{e}va* half-vowel. The second consonant, *heh*, has a dot to the upper left, representing the *o*-vowel *ḥolam*. The third consonant, *vav*, pronounced as bilabial *v*, has the sublinear sign for the back *a*-vowel, *qamats*.[7] The closural fourth consonant, *heh*, although silent in later Hebrew, would

---

[3] Ahituv 1992: 36-41.
[4] B. Yoma 30b; 39b; cf. M. Sot. 7.6; Tam. 7.2; B. Sot. 38a; T. Sot 13.
[5] See the martyrdom of R. Hanina ben Teradion at B. *AZ* 17b–18a; B. Kal. 5.
[6] M. *Sanh.* 10.1.
[7] Some maintain that Hebrew *vav* or *waw* (ו) was anciently pronounced as *w*, like Arabic *waw*. However, every known form of Hebrew since medieval times pronounced it as bilabial *v*. So too in the Bible, from 10th century BC Ephraim to the 6th century BC Judean exile, the Hebrew word for 'back' is written גו (gav) or גב (gab) interchangeably, showing that *vav* was equal to the bilabial *v* or soft *bet* (1 Kgs 14.9; Ezek. 23.35; cf. 10.12). The *v* sound is therefore to be preferred, the more so because the *w* is comical to speakers of modern Hebrew.

have been pronounced in early biblical times as a short aspiration after the *a*-vowel.[8] Finally, since the Masoretic cantillation mark generally falls on the third consonant, it suggests that the last syllable was the accented one.

Taken together, these vowels make Y*ᵉ*-ho-**vàh**, which came into Latin as Iehova or Iehovah and so passed into the tongues of Europe as Jehovah. These vowel points appear on the Name throughout the Masoretic codices, although sometimes the middle vowel, the *ḥolam* dot, is omitted.

יְהֹוָה

The first seed of doubt for the 'Yehovah-Jehovah' pronunciation was Elias Levita's *Masoret ha-Masoret* (1538), which argued that the Masoretic punctillation was invented by the Masoretes themselves. This, as we saw in chapter nine, generated much opposition precisely because it threw into doubt the pronunciation of the sacred name. Yet Levita's cue was followed by Génébrard, whose *Chronologia* (1567) proposed the pronunciation 'Iahve' on the strength of the testimony of the fifth-century Syrian Father, Theodoret.[9] Nevertheless, Jehovah was largely accepted for another two-and-a-half centuries until Wilhelm Gesenius's influential *Lexicon* (1833), again on the testimony of Theodoret, proposed Yahᵉveh and Yahᵃveh.

יַהֲוֶה and יַהֱוֶה

Following Gesenius, Ewald (1803–1875) adopted 'Jahweh', omitting the middle half-vowel. Through Ewald's writings, the name came into widespread use. English writers, maintaining the German *w*, took it up as Yahweh. To our own day, numerous other conjectures have followed, including Yahaweh, Yahawah, Yahuwah.

DIFFICULTIES IN THE 'YAHWEH' CONSTRUCT

There are several difficulties with the 'Yahweh' or 'Yahveh' form of the Name. First, it is based on questionable testimony, that of the fifth-century Church Father, Theodoret, Bishop of Cyrus in Syria (c. 393–457). Theodoret wrote, 'The Samaritans call it IABE while the Jews AIA.'[10] From this Greek form, IABE, Génébrard and Gesenius derived Yahᵃveh. But Theodoret was no expert witness. He lived seven hundred years after the Name had ceased from

---

[8] This is evident from the way it modifies the opening *bgdkft* consonants of following words, as, for instance, at Ps. 127.3, where the *daghesh* on *banim* shows that the preceding sound is a consonantal *heh* and not simply an open *a*-vowel.

[9] Génébrard 1567: 79; cited by Parke-Taylor 1975: 79.

[10] Theodoret of Cyrus, *Question* 15 in Exodus 7.

common speech among the Jews. He did not know Hebrew, for his scriptural exegesis relies entirely on the Greek and Syriac translations. Further, whichever name Theodoret intended, he had the unenviable task of transcribing a Semitic name into the Greek alphabet, without any consonants corresponding to Hebrew *heh* or *vav*. It may even be that he was trying to write Yafeh, the Beautiful One, a Samaritan form of address for God.

Second, Gesenius suggested that the vowels supplied by the Masoretes were not the true vowels of the Name at all. Instead, he said, the Masoretes substituted the vowels of *Adonai*, 'my Lord', beneath the four consonants, to show that *Adonai* should be read instead of pronouncing the true name. This, he said, was in line with the scribal practice called *ketiv-kere* – meaning 'written-read' – which occurs throughout the Masoretic codices. In *ketiv-kere*, the letters of a word written in the text are given the vowels of another word, whose consonants are written in the margin, to show that the marginal word should be read. In this case, Gesenius said, the *sh^{e}va*, *ḥolam*, and *qamats* vowels of the Tetragrammaton were not its real vowels at all, but borrowings from *Adonai*.

This might be convincing if the Masoretic vowels for the Tetragrammaton were indeed those of *Adonai*. But since they patently are not, the argument collapses. For while the Masoretic vowels for the Tetragrammaton are *sh^{e}va*, *ḥolam*, and *qamats*, the vowels of *Adonai* are *ḥataf pataḥ*, *ḥolam*, and *qamats*. If the Masoretes intended that *Adonai* should be read, why did they write *sh^{e}va* instead of *ḥataf pataḥ*? You may say that this is because the *yodh* cannot take *ḥataf pataḥ*. And that's true. But if the Masoretes wished to indicate the true pronunciation, why did they not make it that much clearer by keeping the vowels of the word they wished to signify. That, after all, is exactly what they do in every other *ketiv-kere*. They insert the *kere*-vowels unchanged, even when the result is an impossible fit to the *ketiv*-consonants.[11]

Third, Gesenius's assumption that the Masoretes would change the vowels at all is doubtful. In Gesenius's time it was thought that the Masoretes were rabbinic Jews, who might well have attempted to conceal the Name. But it is now widely thought that the Masoretes were not Rabbanites at all, but Karaites, who rejected rabbinic tradition.[12] Unlike the Rabbanites, who did not speak the Name at all, the Karaite position was much more diverse. According to their 10th century historian, Jacob Kirkisani, some thought the Name should be greatly restricted; others thought it might be used in prayer, reading, and liturgy; yet others spoke it deliberately and often, rebuking those who replaced it with *Adonai*.[13] Yet all the Karaites were dedicated to preserving the Name. As for the Masoretes, it appears, as we shall see, that their position was to

---

[11] See, both in Leningrad and Aleppo, 1 Sam. 5.9; 6.4, where the *sh^{e}va* of *t^{e}ḥorim*, inserted in the consonants עפלים, produces the impossible *ayin* with vocal *sh^{e}va*; or Jer. 42.6 where the vowels of *anaḥnu* are added to אנו, giving the impossible combination of *shuruk* and *sh^{e}va* on a single *vav*.

[12] As discussed in Chapter 11.

[13] Gordon 2012: 103.

discourage the speaking of the Name in public Scripture reading. Yet they would have resisted any attempt to obscure its true pronunciation. Their great work of scholarship was designed to preserve the true knowledge of the Scriptures for their own community. They had every reason not to conceal the true pronunciation of the Name.

Fourth, the true pronunciation of the Name must possess three syllables. The second letter, *heh*, cannot be silent for, in pre-exilic Hebrew, there was no silent *heh* in the middle of words. It always carried a vowel or a half-vowel. In fact, the Leningrad Codex not infrequently places cantillation marks over the second *heh*, which may show that the second consonant was sung.[14] Since one cannot sing a silent letter or a half-vowel, the Name must have had had three vowels, of which the last two, which bear cantillation marks, were full and unreduced *holam* and *qamats* – that is, *o* and *a*.

Fifth, Gesenius himself was not nearly as convinced of the Yah^aweh-Yah^eweh form as is supposed. In his *Lexicon*, after noting Reland's view, he makes a surprising *volta-face*:

> Also those who consider that יְהֹוָה [Y^ehovah] was the actual pronunciation are not altogether without ground on which to defend their opinion. In this way can the abbreviated syllables יְהֹו [Y^eho] and יֹו [Yo], with which many proper names begin, be more satisfactorily explained.[15]

THE PLAUSIBILITY OF THE MASORETIC VOCALIZATION

Therefore, since even Gesenius thought his own proposals were not sufficient to dismiss the Masoretic vocalization, let us return to that vocalization – Y^ehovàh – and examine its plausibility.

Apart from the vocalized Tetragrammatons in the Masoretic text, hundreds of personal names in the Bible carry part of the sacred name. The Masoretes give these theophoric names a range of vowels – *yo, y^eho, yah, yahu* – some of which seem to refute the Masoretes' own vocalization of the Tetragrammaton as Y^ehovàh. This is surely testimony to the integrity of the Masoretic vocalization. For if they were trying to promote an alternative pronunciation, they would not have left the field so littered with contradictions. And if these variants can be reconciled on the basis of the 'Y^ehovàh' vocalization, it will confirm the correctness of that vocalization.

According to the Masoretic vocalization, there were two forms of the Name since ancient times: a form beginning Y^eho and a form beginning Yah.

---

[14] I say 'may' because, in each case, the Aleppo Codex positions the cantillation mark further right, nearer the yodh: *e.g.*, Exod. 3.15, 16 (*gershayim*); Pss. 80.19 [20] (*tsinnor*); 84:[8] 9 (*tsinnor*); 96.10 (*tsinnor*); 99.5, 9 (*tsinnor*); 104.1 (*oleh ve-yored*); 106.47 (*tsinnor*); 109.21 (*tsinnor*); 130.7 (*oleh ve-yored*); 142.6 (*oleh ve-yored*).

[15] Gesenius, *Lexicon* (tr. Tregelles), p. 337.

Reading through the biblical timeline, the first form we meet is Y^{e}ho: in Genesis 2.4 the name of the Creator is vocalized as Yehovah. Two chapters later we meet the Y^{e}ho vocalization again: the antediluvians, we are told, *began to call upon the name of Yehovah* (Gen. 4.26). Indeed, the Y^{e}ho form – in Y^{e}hovah – is the only form of the name throughout Genesis. Likewise, in Exodus, the Name is consistently vocalized as Yehovah until, after crossing the Sea, we meet the first appearance of the Yah-form, which appears in the Song of the Sea: 'Yah is my strength and song' (Exod. 15.2). Throughout the other books of the Pentateuch, the only vocalization of the Name is Yehovah. Therefore, if the first five books of the Bible are purporting to report a historical narrative, as they surely are, then they are saying that Yehovah is the most ancient form of the sacred name, whereas Yah is not heard until the Exodus and, even then, is rare.

The first person to bear the sacred Name in their own name is Moses' mother, Yo-kheved, 'Glory of Yo' (Exod. 6.20), where Yo is surely a contraction of Y^{e}ho, as it frequently is in the historical books (see below). The second person to bear the sacred name is Moses' lieutenant, Hoshea ben Nun, who was surnamed Y^{e}ho-shua (Joshua) (Exod. 17.9; Num. 13.16; Josh. 1.1). Thereafter, no one else bears the Y^{e}ho form for many centuries until, in the Judges period, we find Y^{e}ho as a suffix in Mikha-y^{e}ho (Judg. 17.1) although, unlike Y^{e}ho-shua, this is not a declaration of the deity's power, but a question, 'Who is like Y^{e}ho?' Not long after, we meet another Y^{e}ho-shua in the priestly town of Bet Shemesh (1 Sam. 6.14), after which names like Y^{e}ho-yada (2 Sam. 20.23) and Y^{e}honadav (2 Sam. 13.3–5) become quite common. From the Judges period on, the Yo prefix also appears: Yoash (Judg. 6.11); Yotam (Judg. 9.5, 7); Yonatan (Judg. 18.30; 1 Sam. 13.16); Yoav (2 Sam. 2.13); Yonadab (2 Sam. 13.3). Then, last of all, from the time of Saul, the Yah suffix appears in Israelite names: Ahi-Yah (1 Sam. 14.3); Ts^{e}ru-Yah (2 Sam. 2.13); B^{e}na-Yah (2 Sam. 20.23); Uri-Yah (2 Sam. 11.3); Adoni-Yah (1 Kgs 1.5).

Therefore, following the Masoretic vocalization, the Y^{e}ho and Yah forms of the Name are both old, but Y^{e}ho is the more ancient by far. It was known, according to the Masoretes, in antediluvian times; its contracted form, Yo, appeared during the Egyptian captivity, while the first person to bear the full Y^{e}ho prefix was great Y^{e}ho-shua in the Sinai wanderings. The Yah form is first encountered at the Exodus, but is not found in Israelite names until the early monarchy period, in the late 11th century BC; it is invariably a suffix, never a prefix, and is first borne by people of no repute, such as Ahi-Yah, son of the wicked *kohen* Pinhas ben Eli (1 Sam. 14.3). Therefore, the order of appearance of these variants suggests that the older vocalization of the Name begins Y^{e}ho and that Yah is a later, derivative form.

For the third syllable of the Tetragrammaton, the Masoretes give two options: *-vah* and the much rarer *-vih*, which we shall discuss below. The *-vah* form appears the more authentic, not only by its frequency, but also by the large number of instances where poetic texts place the accented last syllable of the Tetragrammaton to rhyme with another *a*-syllable. Here are a few examples:[16]

Arise, Yᵉhovàh	*Qumàh, Yᵉhovàh*
Return, Yᵉhovàh	*Shuvàh, Yᵉhovàh*
How long, Yᵉhovàh	*Ad-anàh, Yᵉhovàh*
The law of Yᵉhovàh is perfect	*Torat Yᵉhovàh temimàh*
The statute of Yᵉhovàh is pleasant	*Edut Yᵉhovàh ne'emanàh*
The command of Yᵉhovàh is pure	*Mitsvat Yᵉhovàh baràh*
The fear of Yᵉhovàh is clean	*Yir'at Yᵉhovàh t'horàh*
Your goodness, Yᵉhovàh	*Tuvkhà, Yᵉhovàh*
Your name, Yᵉhovàh	*Shimkhà, Yᵉhovàh*
Yᵉhovàh, save us now	*Anàh, Yᵉhovàh, hoshia-nà*
Yᵉhovàh, deliver us now	*Anàh, Yᵉhovàh, hatsliḥah-nà*

Finally, apart from the Masoretic text, there is ancient evidence for the pronunciation Yᵉhovàh. A Hebraic Greek magical text from the 2ⁿᵈ or 3ʳᵈ century states ελητε Ιεωα ρουβα, 'My God Ieoa is mightier.'[17] Ιεωα, being about as close as the Greek alphabet can get to writing Yᵉhovàh, supports the Masoretic pronunciation. Ten centuries later, the Name appears in Latin as 'Iehova' in Raimundo Martini's *Pugio fidei* (1270). Whether Martini learned this pronunciation from his mentor, the Jewish Christian Pablo Cristiani, or whether, as some have suggested, Martini was himself of Jewish origin, is not clear. But he knew 'Iehova' at a time when it existed, so far as we know, only in a few Masoretic manuscripts far away from Barcelona. So it seems that the Yᵉhovah pronunciation may have been known among the great community of Spanish Jews.

All in all then, there is evidence to confirm that the Masoretic vocalization, Yᵉhovàh (hereafter Yehovah), is a likely ancient pronunciation of the Tetragrammaton. But can it provide an explanation for all the anomalies of the case? Where did the name Yah come from? And what about Yahu and Yᵉhovih?

DOES 'YEHOVAH' EXPLAIN THE ANOMALIES?

Yah. After its first appearance in the Song of the Sea (Exod. 15.2), Yah appears in later poetic texts, especially the Psalms, with their ancient acclamation, 'Halelu-Yah!'[18] In every such case, the second letter of the Name, *heh*, contains the dot *mappiq*, showing that the final *h*-consonant is to be pronounced as an

---

[16] Num. 10.35; Ps. 3; Ps. 132.8; Num. 10.36; Ps. 13.1; Ps. 19.8–10; Ps. 25: 7, 11; Ps. 118.25.

[17] British Museum Greek papyrus CXXI 1.528–540 (3rd cent.); cf. Alfrink 1948: 43–62.

[18] Exod. 15.2. Yah occurs forty times in the Psalms: once in Book II (68.5), twice in Book III, seven times in Book IV, and thirty times in Book V, including the Halelu-Yah acclamations.

audible breath or aspiration just after the vowel, as with the last letter of Yehovah.

$$יָהּ$$

But proper names, from the time of Saul on, display Yah as a suffix without the *mappiq*-dot breath. There is no reason to doubt that this is the same name. However, it is not clear whether the dot reflects a later pronunciation or simply a later orthography of the final *heh*.[19]

The likeliest explanation for the origin of Yah is that it is a contraction of Yehovah, preserving the first consonant and last accented vowel and aspirated *heh*, and omitting everything in between: Y-(ᵉhov)-ah. Such contractions were always current among the Israelites: Baʻal Meon became Beon (Num. 32.3, 38), Yᵉhoshua (Num. 13.16) became Yeshua (Neh. 8.17), Yᵉhoash is Yoash (2 Kgs. 12.1; 11.2); Ananias is Annas, and Epaphroditus is Epaphras. The same is true nowadays: Alexander is Alasdair, Augustine is Austin, Magdalena is Malena, Philippa is Pippa, Willem is Wim.

Yo. Yo is a contraction of Yᵉho. Evidence appears in the early monarchic period in names given both in the Yᵉho and Yo form: Yᵉhonadav is Yonadav (2 Sam. 13.3–5); Yᵉho-ram is Yo-ram (2 Kgs 8.16; 9.15); Yᵉho-ash is Yo-ash (12.1, 19 [20]).

Yahu. From the ninth century BC, proper names appear with the suffix Yahu: Eli-Yahu (1 Kgs 17.1); Ḥizki-Yahu (Hezekiah), Yᵉsha-Yahu (Isaiah), Yirmᵉ-Yahu (Jeremiah), Tsidqi-Yahu (Zedekiah).

$$יָהוּ$$

The likely origin of Yahu is that it was naturally formed by expanding the final *mappiq*-dot breath of Yah to a carrier *u*-vowel, a paragogic *vav*. Although, in the Bible, Yahu is confined to theophoric suffixes on personal names, there is evidence that it was a spoken form of the Name among Judeans in late biblical times. In 407 BC, the Jewish *kohanim* in Egypt wrote the Name with the letters YHV, indicating Yahu or Yaho.[20] A Mishnah passage relates that a deliberate approximation to this name – Vahu – was spoken in the Hoshana Rabba festivities in late temple times (M. *Suk.* 4.5; B. *Suk.* 45a).

---

[19] The *mappiq*-dot may indicate that the orthography of Yah is later than that of YHVH. For, in early Hebrew, when the final *heh* was routinely vocalized, then a *mappiq*-dot on YHVH was unnecessary. But when, in kingdom times, the final *heh* became silent, the *mappiq*-dot was introduced to preserve the aspiration on the final consonant. Its presence in Yah therefore suggests a later written form. Such consistent use and non-use of *mappiq* not only supports a temple-period origin for the punctillation but testifies to the exacting nature of the Masoretes' work.

[20] The 'Petition to Bagoas', *Pap. I* of the Elephantine Papyri.

Appendix I. Singing the Sacred Name

Around the beginning of the Babylonian-Exile period, proper names ending with the *–yahu* suffix begin to feature instead a *–yah* suffix, without any *mappiq*-dot. The Books of Chronicles feature both *–yahu* and *–yah* forms for the same name, Zechariah (2 Chr. 20.14; 24.20). Jeremiah uses both forms for the same man, Zephaniah the *kohen*, who is first Ts^{e}fan-Yahu and then Ts^{e}fan-Yah (Jer. 21.1; 25.5). In post-exilic times, the *–yah* suffix replaces the *–yahu* form.

Yaho. In the Greek magical papyri is found Ιαω, which would represent Hebrew 'Yaho'. In Hebrew *o* and *u* are the same in consonantal spelling and often differ little in pronunciation. Yaho is therefore Yahu.

Y^{e}hovih. In the Masoretic codices, when the Tetragrammaton follows *Adonai*, the first vowel is changed from *sheva* to the short 'e', *hataf seghol*, and the last vowel is vocalized with the *i*-vowel *hireq*: Y^{e}hovìh.[21]

יְהֹוִה

In such cases, the Masoretes appear to have replaced the first and last vowels of the Name with those of *elohim* in order to show that the reader should read *Adonai Elohim* rather than an awkward *Adonai Adonai*.

From this we can discern the true practice and intent of the Masoretes. Their practice in reading was to substitute *Adonai* for the Tetragrammaton. When the infrequent *Adonai* YHVH combination appeared, they showed, by substituting two vowels of *elohim*, what form should be spoken. Wherever else the Tetragrammaton appeared, they either preserved the original vowels complete, assuming that the reader would know to substitute *Adonai*, or else they gave only two vowels, *sh^{e}va* and *qamats*, omitting the *holam* dot.[22]

יְהוָה

The frequent omission of *holam* is unlikely to have been an error. Aharon ben Asher was not so careless as to err so often, nor to leave so many errors uncorrected. More likely is that the omission of the *holam o*-vowel was another signal that the Name should not be pronounced. But otherwise, the Name was unchanged. The purpose was to signal, not conceal.

---

[21] See, *e.g.*, Aleppo Codex Judg. 16.28; 1 Kgs 2.26; Pss. 69.6 [7]; 71.5, 16; Isa. 22.5; Jer. 4.10; Ezek. 24.3, 6, 9, 14, 21, 24; *et passim*. The Leningrad Codex features this form also in the Pentateuch (absent from Aleppo), *e.g.*, Gen 15.22; Ezek. 24.3, 21, 24.

[22] See, for instance, throughout the first extant page of the Aleppo Codex (Deut. 28), and, in the Leningrad Codex, all occurences of the name up to Gen. 3.14.

THE MEANING OF THE NAME

The Bible tends to explain significant names. Many, like Noah, Abraham, Isaac, Moab, Ammon, Jacob, Judah, Benjamin, Moses, or Solomon, are explained where they occur; some, like Joseph, have two meanings; others, like Edom, require some deduction.[23] But the clarification is usually somewhere to be found. The Tetragrammaton receives its explanation at Exodus 3.14, where the Holy One calls himself *eh^{e}yeh asher eh^{e}yeh*, 'I am what I am.' Or as the Septuagint renders it, *Εγο ειμι ο ων*, 'I am the Existing One.' From this we deduce that the Tetragrammaton, which follows in the next verse, is what it appears to be, a form of the verb *hayah*, 'to be'.

Some think 'Yahveh' or 'Yahweh' is a *hifil* or causative form of *hayah*, meaning 'He who causes to be', this despite the fact that a *hifil* of *hayah* is unknown in the Bible.[24] However, unknown *hifil*-forms aside, *eh^{e}yeh asher eh^{e}yeh* refers to immutable self-existence rather than creative power and explains perfectly the form Yehovah. The first consonants suggest the future (imperfect) form of the verb, *yih*; the middle syllable suggests the present participle *hoveh*; and the last syllable suggests the perfect tense, *hayah*. Taken together, it would mean 'Who is and was and is to come' or, as the synagogue sings each Shabbat, 'And he was, and he is, and he will be in glory.'[25]

THE SACRED NAME IN THIS BOOK

One would not want to pretend that every question about the vocalization of the Tetragrammaton is now answered. Yet, on the basis of the evidence above, I suggest that Yehovah is more likely than Yahweh-Yahveh. It is certainly the vocalization indicated by the Masoretes. And so, for these reasons, I have employed 'Yehovah' in transcribing the Masoretic cantillation of the psalms in this book.

Their remains one last puzzle. How was the Tetragrammaton pronounced after prefixes?

In normal practice, the prefixes *w-* (ו), *l-* (ל), *b-* (ב), and *k-* (כ) receive the vowel *sh^{e}va*.

l^e-david   to David

When a prefix precedes a definite article or when the noun begins with an *a*-vowel, the prefix takes an *a*-vowel.

---

[23] Gen. 5.29; 17.5; 18.12–14; cf. 21.3; 19.37–38; 25.26; 29.35; 35.18; Exod. 2.10; 1 Chr. 22.9; Gen. 30.23–24; 25.25.

[24] Albright 1924: 374; Freedman 1960: 152; Cross 1962): 251–53; Dahood 1965–70: I.64, 177; Parke-Taylor 1975: 59–63.

[25] Rev. 1.4; 'Adon Olam', attrib. to Yehudah ha-Levi: *V-hu hayah, v-hu hoveh, v-hu yihyeh b'tifarah*.

Appendix I. Singing the Sacred Name

l^e-ha-melekh	→	la-melekh	to the king
l^e-^{a}donai	→	ladonai	to my Lord

But when a noun begins with *yodh* and *sh^{e}va*, the two *sh^{e}vas* and *yodh* coalesce to the *i*-vowel *hireq*.

l^e-y^{e}rushalayim	→	lirushalayim	to Jerusalem

What we would expect with prefixes before the name Yehovah, would be two *sh^{e}vas* becoming *hireq*.

l^e-Y^{e}hovah	→	lihovàh	to Yehovah

However, what is found everywhere is that the prefix receives the *a*-vowel, while the first letter of the Name has no vowel indicated at all.

la-yhovàh   to Yehovah

There are two possible explanations for this anomaly. The first is that the prefix + *a*-vowel signal the reader to read *Adonai* instead of the Tetragrammaton. For, as we saw, a prefix before *Adonai* simply joins the vowel:

l^e-^{a}donai	→	ladonai	to my Lord

The second possibility is that the *la*-prefix is a unique form of reverence for the Name. Saènz-Badillos notes such a usage, which resembles familiar vocative forms taking the definite article, like *ha-melekh*, 'O King' (Est. 7.3) or *ha-elohim*, 'O God' (Judg. 16.28).[26] In that case, the pronunciation would be either *lahovàh* – with no vowel on the *yodh*, as in the codices – or *la-y'hovah*, taking the missing *sh^{e}va* in the codices as defectively written.

While the second option sometimes appeals on poetic grounds – for instance, *la-Y'hovàh ha-y'shu'àh*, 'salvation belongs to Yehovah' (Ps. 3.8) – it is probably better for now to avoid unknown forms and stay with known procedures of vowel-modification. I therefore read *a*-vowel prefixes before the Tetragrammaton as a Masoretic sign that it should be pronounced *Adonai*, and that the true pronunciation of the Name with prefixes follows the rules of two coalescing *shevas*, that is, *lihovàh*, *vihovàh*, *bihovah*, or *kihovah*.

---

[26] "We have good evidence for לִי (la-Y.) 'truly, Y. is...' (Ps 89:19) or as a vocative (Ps 68:34)" (Sáenz-Badillos 1993: 60).

Appendix II

Temple Where and When

The testimony of the Bible, Rabbinic literature, and the ancient historians, Philo and Josephus, is that the first Israelite temple in Jerusalem was built by Solomon. This view has been challenged over the last twenty years by biblical historians who maintain that Solomon's temple either never existed, or never existed in any such way as described in the Bible.[1]

Their views are supported by the 'low chronology' of Israeli archaeologist, Israel Finkelstein, who has dated pottery types previously thought to be from the tenth century BC to the ninth century. The effect of this down-dating is that archaeological structures previously identified as belonging to David and Solomon are now said to have been built by Ahab and Omri, while David and Solomon were at best small-time clan chieftains who built nothing that remains. A new theory of pottery shards, though still widely disputed, has reduced biblical history to disdain.

It is strange that these historians do not give ancient Israelite texts the credence they give to the texts of Mesopotamia or Egypt or Rome. Instead, they seem to take obvious delight in subverting them. Liverani proclaims that his history shines among the all-too-similar dreary mass of biblical histories precisely because it presents a 'history' quite different from the others. He says,

> Biblical criticism has progressively dismantled the historicity of creation and flood, then of the patriarchs, then (in chronological order) of the exodus and of the conquest, of Moses and Joshua, then the period of Judges and the 'twelve tribe league', stopping at the era of the 'United Monarchy' of David and Solomon, which was still considered substantially historical.[2]

Then, of course, Liverani announces that he will complete the dismantling of David and Solomon in our generation. Others prefer mockery, laughing off those who do not share their scepticism, likening them to Balaam's talking ass.[3]

---

[1] Coogan 2013; Finkelstein and Silbermann 2007; Römer 2007; Liverani 2003; Thompson 1999; Davies 1992; 2004; Whitelam 1996.

[2] Liverani 2003: xvi.

[3] Whitelam in Burns and Rogerson 2012: 492.

But this book does not venture to speak of talking asses. Our concern is only whether an Israelite King Solomon really did build a temple in Jerusalem. In this matter, one must admit that the repeated plunderings of Jerusalem through the ages – by Shishak, Asa, Jehoash of Judah, Jehoash of Israel, Ahaz, Hezekiah, Nebuchadnezzar, and others – have stripped much evidence from the site.[4] So too the status of the Temple Mount has always made exploration there difficult. Yet, despite all this, there remains important evidence, both circumstantial and material, for the existence of Solomon's temple.

EXISTENCE OF SOLOMON'S TEMPLE

Circumstantial evidence. Galil shows that the biblical account of the architectural plan of Solomon's temple resembles the plan of Syrian temples of the early first millennium BC, particularly the Ain Dara temple in north Syria (c. 1300–740 BC), which resembles the biblical description of Solomon's temple in length, in its succession of rooms leading to a raised holy place, in its portico supported by two colossal pillars, in its side chambers, in its ornamental blocked windows, and in many other details.[5] There is therefore good reason to accept the Bible account of Solomon's temple at face value as describing an actual eastern Mediterranean temple of that period. Galil notes further that no ancient near eastern king ever caused his scribes to compose a building chronicle to honour another king. Nor, much less, did any such king ever build a temple or palace and credit the work to his predecessors. That being so, it follows that the temple was built by Solomon, as recorded, and the core material of the building chronicle, 1 Kgs 5.15–9.9, was composed by Solomon's scribes.

The Jehoash Inscription. In 2001, a sandstone plaque came to light. Some 30 by 60 centimetres (12' by 24') in size, and containing fifteen lines of Hebrew text, it appeared to be a royal inscription from the ninth century BC, recording King Jehoash's repairs to the temple, as detailed in 2 Kgs 12.4–16 and 2 Chr. 24.8–14. It reads:

> [I Yeho'ash ben A]hazyahu, k[ing of Ju]dah, and I made the re[pai]rs, when men's hearts were filled with generosity in the land and in the desert and in all the cities of Judah, to give money for the holy offerings (הקדשם) abundantly, to purchase quarry stone and juniper wood and copper of Adam to perform the work faithfully. I renovated the breach of the house and the surrounding walls, and the storied structure, and the meshwork, and the winding stairs, and the

---

[4] 1 Kgs 14.25–28; 2 Chr. 12.1–12; 1 Kgs 15.9–24; 2 Chr. 16.2; 2 Kgs 12.17–18; 2 Chr. 24.23; 2 Kgs 14.14; 2 Chr. 25.24; 2 Kgs 16.8–18; 2 Chr. 28.21; 2 Kgs 18.15–16; 2 Kgs 24.13–25.17; 2 Chr. 36.6–19; Isa. 39.5–6; 64.11. For an appraisal of the wealth of gold in Solomon's temple, see Millard 1989. Kitchen (2001: 46-47) notes that, less than five years after Shishak's invasion, his son Osorkon gave 400 tons of silver and gold to the temples of Thebes and Memphis.

[5] Galil 2012: 137–146.

recesses, and the doors. May this [stone] become this day a witness that the work has succeeded. May YHVH command his people a blessing.

The owner of this new discovery was an Israeli antiquities collector called Oded Golan. But, when Golan revealed the Saint James Ossuary in 2002, he incurred the suspicion of the Israeli Antiquities Authority. And so, in July 2003, he was arrested and charged with forty-four counts of forgery relating to the ossuary, the Jehoash inscription, and other items.

The IAA prosecuted its case with vigour while Golan maintained his innocence, defended by many of world's top archaeologists and epigraphers. Even Professor Ronny Reich, one of the founders of the IAA, who was called to argue that the plaque was a forgery, admitted,

> Finally, allow me to play devil's advocate and say the inscription appears to me to be authentic, because it's hard for me to believe that a forger (or group of forgers) could be so knowledgeable in all aspects of the inscription – that is, the physical, paleographic, linguistic and biblical ones – that they could produce such an object.[6]

Reich drew attention to the 'copper of Adam'. This was not, he said, a weak attempt to speak of 'copper of Edom' as one would speak of 'gold of Ophir'. On the contrary, the town of Adam, on the upper Jordan, was a copper-smelting centre in ancient Israel. But this was hardly common knowledge. What kind of forger, asked Reich, would know that? So the IAA prosecutors continued to press their claim, asserting that Golan was 'a forger of genius'.

Another remarkable fact about the stone was the crack in it, along which it split while in police custody. Hershel Shanks says:

> The plaque had a deep crack running through four lines of the inscription. After the police confiscated the plaque, it (accidentally) broke in two along the crack. The crack could then be seen from the side. Part of the crack had ancient patina in it, proving that the crack was ancient. Would a forger choose to work with a stone that had a crack in it, where a slip of his engraving tool might break the stone in two, ruining all his careful work? Hardly. But even if he decided to take the chance, how did he manage to engrave four lines *across the ancient crack*?[7]

Stranger still was the fact that the inscription has minute globules of gold, only one or two millionths of a meter across, embedded in the patina. Where did these globules come from? They are not available to buy. An article in the *Journal of Archaeological Science*, authored by five experts from Israel and the United States who defended the authenticity of the inscription, argues that the likeliest explanation would be an intense fire, in excess of 1000 degrees

---

[6] http://www.haaretz.com/weekend/magazine/faking-it-1.421463
[7] http://www.biblicalarchaeology.org/daily/news/israeli-court-return-the-jehoash-inscription

Celsius, in which gold would be vaporized and settle on the surroundings, a fire such as accompanied the destruction of the first temple.[8]

Nevertheless, despite this evidence, the trial wound on for years. In 2012, the judge declared that the case was not proven and Golan would not be convicted. The Israeli government (led by the IAA) appealed against the decision, still maintaining the plaque was a forgery. Finally, on 17 October 2013, in an extraordinary volta-face, the judge acquitted Golan of all forgery charges, and the Israeli government declared the plaque to be an antiquity and petitioned to keep it.

The plaque, having now passed the highest levels of verification, can be accepted for what it appears to be – the chronicle of King Jehoash's repairs in the ninth century BC. It tells how the son of Ahazyahu (that is, Jehoash) repaired the 'house' with holy offerings or *qedoshim*. Such *qedoshim* could only be used for repairing the temple, not for any lesser 'house'. This is corroborated exactly by the accounts of the offerings in 2 Kgs 12.4 and 2 Chr. 24.8–14. If a ninth-century BC plaque testifies that Jehoash repaired a holy 'house', then there must have been such a 'house' in ninth-century Jerusalem for him to repair.

Ivory pomegranate. During the course of his trial, Golan was charged with forging another article, an ivory pomegranate flower, made of hippopotamus tusk, bearing the inscription 'Holy to the priests of the house of Y[HV]H'. This ivory carving had surfaced in Jerusalem in the 1980s, had been recognized as coming from the temple, and displayed in the Israel Museum.[9] In the trial, there was no dispute about the function of the object. Such pomegranate carvings for ceremonial staffs are well-known in the ancient near east; some have been found with the staff still attached. Nor was there any issue about its possible origin in temple times. Carbon-dating showed the tusk to date from the late second millennium BC. Since ivory is an enduring material, the object could have been carved in temple times out of older ivory. Or an inscription could have been added in temple times to an older pomegranate decoration. Nor, despite the fact that the middle letters of the Tetragrammaton are missing, was there much doubt about the 'house' indicated in the inscription. The Israel Museum had already exhibited it as coming from the temple. After all, it is in paleo-Hebrew and was found in Jerusalem. If it was 'Holy to the priests of the house of Y . . H', then in which other house in Jerusalem did priests serve, if not the 'house of YHVH'?

The dispute centred on one thing only: Is the inscription itself ancient, or is it a modern forgery on a previously uninscribed pomegranate decoration. The matter was intensely debated during the Golan trial, both in and out of court. Distinguished epigraphers, notably André Lemaire of the Sorbonne, Nahman Avigad of the Hebrew University, and Robert Deutsch of Haifa University, upheld the authenticity of the inscription, but their view was consistently

---

[8] Ilani *et al.* 2008.
[9] Lemaire 1984: 24–29.

contested by the IAA authorities.[10] But when, in late 2013, Golan was cleared of all counts of forgery, the Israeli authorities implicitly recognized the authenticity of the pomegranate which he had formerly been accused of forging. Doubters of the temple must now debate whether the pomegranate was sacred to another 'house of Y . . H' in Jerusalem other than the one known to us.[11] Such suggestions have not elicited much assent.

Ninth century cedar beam on the Temple Mount. When the roof of the Al-Aqsa Mosque was restored in the 1940s, it was noticed that many of its roof beams showed signs of secondary use. In particular, they had notches not corresponding to other parts of the mosque roof which indicated that they had previously been used in another structure. When, more recently, the discarded beams were carbon-dated, many were found to date from Herodian times, with one from the ninth century BC.[12] Clearly, this beam is unlikely to have been in Solomon's (or Herod's) temple when it was burned down. But it testifies to a building project with a large cedar-wood structure in the Mount area at that date.

Walls from Solomon's temple. Laperrousaz proposes that much of the eastern retaining wall of the Temple Mount dates from Solomon's time.[13] Herod extended the Temple Mount enclosure on the north, south and west sides. However, he could not extend it to the east, for the eastern retaining wall was already built at the edge of the rock-scarp above the Kidron Valley. The joint of Herod's southern extension is still visible in the east wall today, a straight line running up the lowest ten courses, some 107 feet from the wall's southern end, from which the east wall was extended south. However, argues Laperrousaz, the northern part of the eastern wall, from Herod's joint to the northern end, is from Solomon's time. For the Babylonians could not have pulled it down. There was no advantage in expending labour on it; its rock-scarp base made the eastern side unassailable with or without a wall. And if the Babylonians had pulled it down, then the Temple Mount's huge platform would have collapsed, and the returning exiles could not have built the Second Temple on its old foundations, as they did. Laperrousaz then notes that the 'Phoenician' cut of the stones of the older part of the eastern wall resembles such stones from many other sites of the early first millennium BC, including Byblos, Sidon, Tel Dan, and Solomon-period Megiddo. This suggests Phoenician supervision of the temple's construction, as the Bible also testifies (1 Kgs 7.13–47; 2 Chr. 2.3–14).

---

[10] Ada Yardeni, of the Hebrew University, formerly ambivalent, endorsed the inscription's authenticity in summer 2015.
[11] As did Halpern 1992: 42–45.
[12] Reuven 2013: 40-47.
[13] Laperrousaz 1987: 34–44.

DATE, LOCATION, AND LAYOUT OF SOLOMON'S TEMPLE

Several factors surround the date of the dedication of Solomon's temple.[14] There is the matter of the Ephraimite and Judahite new years beginning in Nisan and Tishri respectively. There is also the matter of Judah and Israel counting the accession year differently, at least until the mid-ninth century. In Solomon's case, the uncertainty is compounded by the period of co-regency with his father. But Galil and Thiele suggest a date of 959 BC, which is the date I assume throughout.[15]

It was traditionally held that the sanctuary area of Israel's temples was beneath the *Kubbat es-Sakhra* or Dome of the Rock. But recently, other views have been proposed. In 1983, the Hebrew University physicist Asher Kaufman proposed that the temple was originally located some 100 metres (330 feet) north of the Dome of the Rock, at the northern end of the Temple Mount enclosure, where a small Islamic shrine, the Dome of the Spirits, now sits. More recently, Tuvia Sagiv, a Tel Aviv architect, proposed that the temple was located south of the Dome of the Rock, midway between the Dome and Al-Aqsa Mosque, with the Holy of Holies lying under the El-Kas Fountain.

The arguments for the three locations are detailed, involving issues of the location of the Antonia Fortress, the North Moat, the Hulda Gates, the availability of water supply to the Mount, discrepancies in height with Josephus' accounts, and evidence of ground-penetrating radar. However, the traditional location, beneath the Dome of the Rock, is supported by the uncontestable fact that the *es-sakhra* rock beneath the Dome is the highest projection of the bedrock of the Mount, and that this accords with the fact that the temple was built on the highest point of the Mount. The rock beneath the Dome also accords with the description of the *sh'tiyah* rock which was in the Holy of Holies, and its cut edges accord with the 20 cubit square area of the temple's *devir* or inner sanctuary.[16] It is presumably the 'pierced stone' over which the Bordeaux Pilgrim saw the Jews lament the temple's destruction in the fourth century, for, with its hole leading to the cave beneath, it is the only pierced stone on the Mount. For these reasons, and others, the traditional location is vigourously defended by Dan Bahat, former District Archaeologist for Jerusalem, and by Leen Ritmeyer, who proposes that the 500 cubit square enclosure which the Mishnah records around the temple can still be identified around the Dome of the Rock.[17] Therefore I have assumed the traditional location throughout.

The area of the temple court. The Bible gives no dimensions for the court of Solomon's temple. However, Josephus relates that Solomon built the court as a square of one stade on each side, which roughly agrees with the Mishnah's

---

[14] Galil 1996.
[15] 'Solomon's temple was probably dedicated ca. [the Judahite year] 960/959.' Personal correspondence from Professor Galil. Thiele (1983: 78) concurs.
[16] Ritmeyer 2006: 246-47.
[17] Ritmeyer 2006.162–63, discusses Kaufman's and other views in detail.

proportions of 500 cubits square.[18] A central area of 500 cubits square is still visible today, unaltered by the vast expansions of the Hasmoneans and Herod, but current restrictions on the site do not allow investigation as to when it was made.[19] However, as Ezekiel's visionary temple has an inner court of 500 cubits square, it is likely that these measurements reflect the first temple as Ezekiel knew it, before the Babylonian destruction of 586 BC.[20]

The ark's position in the inner sanctuary. The entry to the *heikhal* (or Holy Place) and to the *devir* (or Holy of Holies) faced east toward the rising sun. But did the ark within lie lengthwise north-south or east-west? And were its poles on its short or long sides?

The north-south orientation is supported by a talmudic tradition which relates:

> Our Rabbis taught: Every article that stood in the temple was placed with its length parallel with the length of the house, except the ark whose length was parallel with the breadth of the house. (B. *Men.* 98a)

Assuming then that the ark lay lengthwise north-south, how did its poles lie? We read that they were seen from the *heikhal*, outside the *devir* (1 Kgs 8.8). But they could not have been visible at the north and south sides of the entrance to the *devir*. For the poles would not have been longer than the ten cubits of the holy place in the desert Tabernacle, where the ark formerly was housed. And so they would not stretch the twenty-cubit width of the *devir*. Moreover, the wooden jambs on each side of the entrance to the *devir* allowed no visibility at the sides.[21] Therefore the poles must have been visible by protruding forward through the separating curtain (as explained more fully below). In that case, they must have run east-west, along the short sides of the ark. Such a layout, a north-south alignment of the ark with the poles running east-west, would allow a gap for the feet of the east-facing deity on the long west side of the footstool-ark, the *keruvim* wings being lowered on that side, as suggested in chapter five.

Others would like to place the ark lying lengthwise east-west with poles on the long sides, still protruding through the curtain. Ritmeyer has identified the east-west-aligned 1.3 by 1 metre oblong indentation visible today in the *sh'tiyah* rock as the ark's ancient emplacement.[22] It is true that this indentation lies in the exact centre of the marks which Ritmeyer identifies as the ancient foundation of the walls of the *devir*, and it conforms to the ark's measurements of 2.5 by 1.5 cubit, which, by the Royal Cubit, is 1.31 by 0.79 metres.[23]

---

[18] *Ant.* VIII.iii.9; XV.xi.3: M. *Mid.* 2.1.

[19] Ritmeyer 2006: 186–94.

[20] *War*, V.v.1. The dimensions of Ezekiel's inner court can be deduced from the sizes of the gates and inner courts in Ezek. 40-41; cf. Ritmeyer 2006: 193.

[21] Schatz 2007.118 assumes the poles to have been under 125 cm in length.

[22] Ritmeyer 2006: 247, 264–77.

[23] From 3000 BC on, Egypt used both the Royal Cubit (20.67"; 525 mm) and the Short Cubit (c. 18"; 450 mm). Both were in use in Israel throughout the kingdom period (2 Chr. 3.3; Ezek. 40.5; 43.13) (Ritmeyer 2006: 171).

Ritmeyer also adds that the 2.5-cubit-long ark, carried broadways, would not have passed between the pillars of the Tabernacle, which were less than two cubits apart.[24]

To decide between these two views is not easy. Ritmeyer's case seems plausible. Yet, on balance, the former view seems preferable. The Talmud's witness is important. The introductory rubric, *Our rabbis taught*, indicates a tradition of great antiquity, while its terse form of expression reads like a temple memorandum. And the ark's role as a footstool required a north-south orientation, to leave one long edge open for the feet of the invisible deity. Nor is the ark's removal from the Tabernacle a crucial matter. The Tabernacle was generally dismantled when the ark departed, but if the ark had to be removed while the Tabernacle was standing, it would require moving only one pillar.

That is not to say that Ritmeyer is wrong in identifying the oblong indentation in the *sh'tiyah* stone with the ark's emplacement. But it would require that the emplacement contained another structure which received the ark, something not unlikely, given the holiness of the ark. Or it would require the feet of the ark to be closer than the total length of the ark, or Moses' cubit to have been smaller than supposed. If the ark were built according to the Short Cubit, and the feet were indented 6 cm at either end, then such a 1.12 m long ark would fit into the one metre width of the indentation in the *sh'tiyah* stone.[25] The remainder of the space might have received the scroll of the law, as Ritmeyer suggests.[26]

The poles seen from the Holy Place. How the poles were seen depends on what separated the *heikhal* (Holy Place) from the *devir* (Holy of Holies) when the temple was first built. Both Kings and Chronicles speak of the two chambers being separated by wooden doors (1 Kgs 6.31; 2 Chr. 4.22), attached to a cedar-wood partition wall (1 Kgs 6.16). But Chronicles also speaks of an embroidered veil or curtain hung across the entrance to the *devir* (2 Chr 3.14). The apparent solution is that the first temple had both a door and a veil to ensure the sanctity of the Holy Place. This is confirmed by a talmudic discussion, which says that Herod's temple had two veils with a cubit's space between them, which were provided specifically because there was no 'partition' (i.e., partitioning doors) as in the first temple.[27] Therefore, in neither temple, when the *kohen ha-gadol* entered the *devir* on Yom Kippur, would those who opened the door or curtain for him see inside the hidden chamber. The Mishnah records the ritual of the *kohen ha-gadol's* approach to the ark through two curtains. (This may suggest that there were already two curtains in later first temple times, before the ark was removed from the *devir*.) The

---

[24] Ritmeyer 2006: 247–250, 268–277. Exod. 26.3; 36.38.
[25] Schatz (2007.116) calculated the cubit of Hezekiah's time to have been 17" (43.2 cm), based on the cubit of the Siloam tunnel (said in the extant Inscription to be 1200 cubits in length). By that measure, the ark was 108 cm long by 64.8 cm broad and high, closer still to the measurements of the indentation.
[26] Ritmeyer 2006: 27–74.
[27] M. *Yoma* 5.1; M. *Mid.* 4.5; 4.7; B. *Yoma* 51b; Y. *Yoma* 5a (1–2).

Kohen passed southward outside the curtain – 'between the incense altar and *menorah*' – and then entered behind the outer curtain, passed along, and entered behind the inner curtain, approaching the ark from the north.

> The outer curtain was looped up on the south side and the inner one on the north side. He went along between them [the curtains] until he reached the north side; when he reached the north he turned round to the south [inside the *devir*] and went on with the curtain on his left hand until he reached the ark. When he reached the ark he put the fire-pan between the two poles. (M. *Yoma* 5.1)

Note that there is no suggestion that the poles impeded the *Kohen's* entry to the *devir*; they were not running north-south. Instead, he reached the poles and the ark together, and placed his fire-pan between the poles, either behind or before the ark. Therefore the poles of the ark ran east-west, pressing against the curtain, and this was visible from the *heikhal*, either through both curtains, or when the partition doors were open. (The doors may have been open if, as in other ancient near eastern cults, they were shut by night and open by day.) The poles would have pressed visibly against the curtain if they were moved forward or *extended* in their rings (1 Kgs 8.8), so as not to obstruct the feet of the invisible deity. For although the poles of the ark might not be removed from their rings (Exod. 25.15), it was permitted to move them within the rings. This seems the best solution overall.[28] It is supported by the Talmud.

> Scripture says: *They* [the poles] *could not be seen outside* [the Holy Place] (1 Kgs 8.8). How then? They pressed forth and protruded as the two breasts of a woman, as it is said: *My beloved is unto me as a bag of myrrh, that lieth betwixt my breasts* (Song 1.13) (B. *Yoma* 54a).

How did the kohen ha-gadol stand to sprinkle blood on the ark on Yom Kippur? Lev. 16.14 says, *And he shall take of the blood of the bullock and sprinkle with his finger upon the* kaporet *eastward* (Heb.: *qedmah*; LXX: *kata anatolas*). The *kohen* would have sprinkled with his right hand. (The use of the left hand for ablutions would have made it unthinkable for this role.) He would therefore have stood on the north or northwest side of the ark, and sprinkled forward and eastward with his right hand onto the ark's long west side, where the gap in the surrounding *keruvim*, to allow for the feet of the deity, would allow his hand to move unimpeded.

---

[28] Another solution, if the doors were always shut, would be that the poles were visible under the door. The *heikhal* was some 10 cubits lower than the *devir* (Ritmeyer 2006: 288–91). Therefore, looking up the access slope from the lower to the higher chamber might allow a glimpse of the ark's poles, fastened low on the feet of the ark (Exod. 25.12), if there were a gap of several centimetres between the doors and the floor.

Appendix III

The Hebrew Calendar

Moses instructed the Israelites to go up to Jerusalem to celebrate three feasts a year, all of which began on the fifteenth day of the month. The Feast of Passover began on the fifteenth of Aviv (later called Nisan). Then after the ten days of Passover and Firstfruits, another fifty days were counted off until the fifteenth day of the third month when the Feast of Shavuot or Weeks began. Finally, the Feast of Sukkot began on the fifteenth day of the seventh month, Ethanim (later called Tishri). The number fifteen is, of course, the number of the name Yah. But there is another reason why all these feasts fall on the fifteenth of the month: they do so to coincide with the night of the full moon.

The Hebrew calendar is different from the Roman Gregorian calendar which governs the modern world. The Gregorian calendar is a solar calendar which counts off the 365.2425 days of the earth's annual progress round the sun. This it does quite accurately. The main solar events – solstices and equinoxes – fall on the same days each year. It achieves this accuracy by a system of leap years and centurial years to keep the calendar in phase with the solar year. However, the Gregorian calendar proceeds without any reference to the moon. The month, although its name derives from the moon, passes its allotted 28, 29, 30 or 31 days quite independently of the moon's phase cycle of 29.53 days. The first day of the year and of the month of January can occur at any point in the lunar cycle. Likewise, the days of the week have no reference whatsoever to month or year, moon or sun. The first of January or the full moon or solstice can fall on any day of the week.

THE RABBINIC LUNI-SOLAR CALENDAR

The rabbinic luni-solar calendar differs from this in several ways. First, it follows the phases of the moon. Each new month coincides with the new moon,[1] while the night between the fourteenth and fifteenth day of each month is the night of the full moon. The twelve months are irregular in length – some

---

[1] At least in theory. Since the Rabbinic new moon is now determined astronomically and not by observation, and since a seasonal drift has crept into the Rabbinic calendar, the result is that the night of the full moon may now fall between the thirteenth and fourteenth days of the month.

have 29 days and some 30 – reflecting the phases of the moon. Every few years, a thirteenth month is inserted to keep the calendar more or less in line with the solar year. Since the Hebrew calendar keeps time with the phases of the moon, it means that the beginning of the Feast of Unleavened Bread in the month of Aviv and the Feast of Sukkot in the month of Tishri always fall on the fifteenth night-day of the lunar cycle, the night of the full moon.

There is another major difference between the Hebrew and Gregorian calendars. Whereas the Gregorian calendar measures the day from midnight to midnight, the Hebrew calendar measures the day from sunset to sunset. As a result, the first days of Passover, Shavuot, and Sukkot, begin at sunset following the fourteenth day, as the full moon rises on the eastern horizon.[2] This made good sense in ancient times, before the invention of electric lights. Since the first days of feasts were preceded by night festivities, either in the home (at Passover) or in the temple (at Sukkot), it was essential to have the light of the full moon for night celebrations.[3]

In the same way that our western calendars have several new years – calendrical year, tax year, academic year, ecclesiastical year – so the Hebrew calendar recognizes four new years (M. *RH* 1.1). The most important ones are the ceremonial new year on the first of Aviv and the civil new year, Rosh ha-Shanah, on the first of Tishri. In ancient times, the first of Aviv, the beginning of the calendar year, was determined by the first new moon after the ripening of barley, a formula still followed by the Karaites. However, Rabbinic Judaism now sets the first of Aviv on the first new moon after the vernal equinox.

Yet, for all the alignment between the month and the moon in the rabbinic calendar, this calendar still proceeds quite independently of the days of the week. The high feasts, such as the fifteenth of Tishri, can fall on any day of the week.

---

[2] The Passover lamb was sacrificed *beyn ha'arbayim*, 'between the two evenings' (Ex. 12.6, Lev: 23.5, Num 9.3, 5, 11) on the afternoon of the fourteenth day of the month. This was the prescribed hour of the daily evening sacrifice (29.39, 41; Num. 28.4, 8), a time when one might see well enough to catch quail or prepare lamps (Exod. 16.12; 30.8). According to Rashi on Exod. 12.6, it is midway between the beginning of the sun's descent at the sixth hour or midday and its setting at the twelfth hour; that is, at the ninth hour or the third hour of the afternoon (3 pm). This concurs with Acts 3.1, Josephus, *War* VI.ix.3, and Mt 27.46–50; Mk 15.33–37; Lk 23.44-46, which highlight the ninth hour as the time of Jesus' sacrificial death. Thus the Passover sacrifice took place on the afternoon of the fourteenth day, but the eating of it began at sunset, the beginning of the fifteenth day.

[3] In the Matabele bush, I once set out to walk to the top of a distant *kopje* in the afternoon. But it was further than it looked, and the African sun falls fast. When we reached our goal, the sun reached the horizon. Without torches, a hundred miles from the nearest small town, we were worried about the long walk back in the dark. But as the sun vanished in the west, a white glow lightened the eastern sky and the moon appeared. We walked two hours back in silver moonlight, every *donga*, tree, stick, and pebble illuminated as by floodlight.

A LOST LUNAR CALENDAR?

However, there is a view that the rabbinic Hebrew calendar differs in one important matter from the calendar of ancient Israel. Rabbi Max Joseph wrote in the *Universal Jewish Encyclopedia* (1943) that, 'The New Moon is still, and the Sabbath originally was, dependent on the lunar cycle.'[4] He is alluding to a view that, in biblical times, the Hebrew calendar was based upon the Babylonian calendar, which reset the days of the week with every new moon. Rabbi Simon Cohen, the editor of the Encylopedia and librarian of the Hebrew Union College in Cincinnati explained the matter more fully:

> The idea of the week, as a subdivision of the month, seems to have arisen in Babylonia, where each lunar month was divided into four parts, corresponding to the four phases of the moon. The first week of each month began with the new moon, so that, as the lunar month was one or two days more than four periods of seven days, these additional days were not reckoned at all. Every seventh day (sabbatum) was regarded as an unlucky day. This method of reckoning time spread westward through Syria and Palestine, and was adopted by the Israelites, probably after they settled in Palestine. With the development of the importance of the Sabbath as a day of consecration and emphasis laid upon the significant number seven, the week became more and more divorced from its lunar connection, so that by the time of the second temple it was merely a period of seven days and no longer depended on the new moon.[5]

According to Friedrich Delitzsch, the Babylonian month consisted of three seven-day weeks, followed by a week of eight or nine days to complete the lunar cycle, then the next month began with the sighting of the new moon.[6] The day of the sighting was called Shabattu, a day of cessation and rest in honour of the gods. (This is not at odds with Cohen's 'unlucky day'; it was unlucky not to honour the gods.) It was the first day of the month, and other Shabattu days followed at seven-day intervals throughout the month.

The similarities to the Israelite calendar are obvious, and one must ask, with Joseph, Cohen, and Delitzsch, whether a similar calendar, with the week resetting every month, was not employed by the Hebrews? Biblical evidence suggests it might have been, and that, after the New Moon first day, Israel's Shabbat days fell on the eighth, fifteenth, twenty-second, and twenty-ninth days of every month.

The biblical evidence begins with the prologue to the law of the feasts in Leviticus, which reads as follows:

> The appointed feasts of the LORD, which you shall proclaim as holy convocations: my appointed feasts, are these. Six days shall work be done; but

---

[4] Joseph 1939-44: vol. V, p. 410.
[5] Cohen 1939044: vol. X, p. 482.
[6] Delitzsch 1903: 37–38; cf. Pinches 1908–27: X.889–891.

on the seventh day is a Shabbat of solemn rest, a holy convocation; you shall do no work (Lev. 23.2–3).

Note that this law is not about Shabbat observance in general, as in the Decalogue (Exod. 20.9; Deut. 5.13). Rather, it is about Shabbat observance during the appointed feasts, specifying that during the feasts, as at other times, they must work six days and rest the seventh. (For working six days was as much a command as resting on the seventh.) Thus the first day and octave of Passover and Sukkot, which were days of cessation, must have concurred with the weekly Shabbat. For if they did not, the Israelites would have to rest both on the holy days of the feasts on the fifteenth and twenty-second of the month and on the intervening Shabbat, hence breaking the command to work six days.

The legislation agrees with the account of the dedication of the temple in 2 Chronicles 7.8–10. Solomon's prayer on the first day of the Feast falls on the fifteenth of the month. They then hold a solemn convocation on the twenty-second day and depart on the twenty-third. There is no suggestion of an intervening Shabbat during the six working days in between.

The same idea finds support in the Exodus narrative. In the month after the Exodus, the manna began to fall on the sixteenth day (Exod. 16.1, 13–31). It fell for six days, then ceased for Shabbat, making Shabbat the twenty-second day of the month. Counting backward and forward, the other Shabbats of the month would fall on the first, eighth, fifteenth, and twenty-ninth days.

However, crucially, the same days were Shabbat in the preceding month also. For Israel sacrificed the Passover in the afternoon of the fourteenth of Aviv, kept the Feast of Unleavened Bread at sundown, on the fifteenth night, rested on the fifteenth day, and left Egypt after sundown of the fifteenth day, that is, on the sixteenth night.[7] Therefore the fifteenth day was Shabbat and the other Shabbats fell on the first, eighth, twenty-second, and twenty-ninth days of the month, just as in the month after. With a strictly recurring cycle of seven-day weeks, this would be impossible, for repeating seven-day weeks would not concur with the 29.5 day lunar cycle. Further, this pattern conforms to the perennial legislation for Shabbat in Lev. 23.4–16, where the Feast of Unleavened Bread on the full-moon fifteenth night-day is Shabbat, followed by seventh-day-of-the-week Shabbat (v. 8) on the twenty-second day.

Likewise, in the second year of the Exodus, Aaron and his sons were sanctified for seven days beginning on the New Moon, the first day of Aviv, and ending on the eighth day (Exod. 40.2–17; Lev. 8.1–9.1). Both days were days of convocation (Lev. 8.3; 9.5, 23–24) and so appear to have been Shabbat. The next Shabbat of that month would therefore have been the fifteenth, the day of Passover, in keeping with the Passover legislation. And so, crucially

---

[7] Israel ate the Passover on the fifteenth night (preceding the fifteenth day). During the fifteenth day, they rested, while the Egyptians lamented their dead and surrendered their treasures. Israel left their dwellings at the end of Shabbat, at sunset following the fifteenth day, and travelled by moonlight (Deut. 16.1).

again, the fifteenth day Passover would fall on Shabbat, as in the year before, something hard to reconcile with a strictly recurring seven-day cycle.

Similarly, the Jews of Shushan, in the time of Esther, who might have continued their slaughter for as many days as they chose (Est. 9.11-15), ceased on the fifteenth of the month to rest (Est. 9.18).[8]

If this is as it appears to be, then the ancient Israelite calendar reset the days of the week at the end of every lunar phase. On the afternoon of the twenty-ninth day Shabbat, they looked for the appearance of the new moon in the western sky. If the new moon appeared, the next day was the New Moon feast, the first Shabbat of the new month from which the other days were counted. But if the new moon did not appear until the thirtieth day, they had a long weekend – twenty-ninth day Shabbat, thirtieth intermission day, and then New Moon feast – before the first working day on the second day of the new month.

Such a scenario is confirmed by the biblical record that the New Moon day, the first day of the month, was a great Shabbat. Like Shabbat, it was a festal day of gathering, worship, and holiday which the Israelites were commanded to observe (Num. 10.2, 10; Ps. 81.3–4; Isa. 66.23; Ezek. 46.1; Judith 8.6). Like Shabbat, it was a day without buying or selling (Amos 8.5). Like Shabbat, its sacrifices exceeded those of the other days of the week; indeed its sacrifices exceeded those of the regular Shabbat (Num. 28.9–15), while those of the New Moon of Tishri exceeded those of other new Moons (Num. 29.1–6). The New Moon period offered a longer period of rest than the one-day Shabbat, sufficient time to travel to family and clan gatherings in other parts of the country (1 Sam. 20.5–6).

It therefore does look like the old Hebrew calendar did reset Shabbat at each New Moon, so that Shabbat fell on the same days each month. I advance this view with caution, for there are unresolved issues even in the Bible account, such as the seven consecutive Shabbats of the omer, which included two New Moon periods (Lev. 23.16). (Did they count the two or three cessation days of the New Moon period as one Shabbat?[9]) I am also aware that this view runs counter to the rabbinic idea of an unbroken chain of Shabbats since Creation. Nevertheless, the Mesopotamian origin of the Patriarchs makes it likely that the Hebrews knew a Babylonian-type calendar. And the Bible evidence is persuasive, both for the monthly recurrence of Shabbat on the same days and for the nature of the New Moon feast. Additionally, there would have

---

[8] Some Adventist groups who hold to the lunar Shabbat suggest that it continued until the time of Herod's temple. They note that Jesus preached at the last day of Sukkot (John 7.37). Since this was the seventh day of a feast beginning on the fifteenth of the month, it would have been the twenty-first of the month (Lev. 23.34–36, 39–41; Num. 29.12–34; Deut. 16.13–15; Neh. 8.13–18; Ezek. 45.21–25). Jesus returned to the temple the next day (John 8.1–2), the twenty-second, which was Shabbat (9.14). However, a lunar Shabbat at this period seems impossible to reconcile with the frequent rabbinic discussions of temple practice when Shabbat did or did not fall on feast days (M. *Suk.* 4.1; 5.1, 5; B. *Suk* 51a; 54b; 56a). After all, even after the lunar calendar fell into disuse, Shabbat still fell sometimes on the fifteenth and twenty-second days of the month.

[9] See the discussion on the New Moon of Sivan at B. *Shab.* 86b.

been the simple practicality of festal cessation days coinciding with the regular Shabbat. For, if the two types of cessation day were at variance, there would have been great disruption. For instance, if the full moon of Sukkot on 15 Tishri fell on the second day of the week, the two-day journey to Jerusalem could not be taken on the one day between Shabbat and the Feast. Therefore, to avoid an impermissible Shabbat journey, the traveller would need to travel on the fifth and sixth days of the preceding week, then wait two days in Jerusalem for the Feast to begin. Then, after the journey home, there would barely be time to resume work before another Shabbat intervened. With such a scenario, the one-week feast would render several weeks of the busy autumn season workless.

Quite when Shabbat was divorced from the phases of the moon is not clear, though it may be that the tale of Hillel's ousting the Sons of Bathyra from the Sanhedrin presidency because of their ignorance of the regulations for Passover falling on Shabbat may be the Pharisaic-Rabbinic memorial of the time when this change was introduced.[10]

To conclude, in Israel's ancient lunar calendar, the feasts began with the full moon of the fifteenth night, and celebrations continued on the following fifteenth day. Further, it seems likely that the seven days of the week reset with a New Moon Shabbat on the first day of the month, and so every fifteenth night-day of the month was Shabbat, as were the eighth, twenty-second, and twenty-ninth days.

---

[10] B. *Pes.* 66a; Y. *Pes.* 6.1 (33a); see chapter eleven above.

Appendix IV

Revia mugrash and *oleh ve-yored*

The two sign-pairs, *revia mugrash* and *oleh ve-yored*, are unique to the poetic books and appear frequently within them. Understanding them is therefore vital to deciphering the sound of the Psalms.

REVIA MUGRASH

The sign-pair *revia mugrash* is the most frequent sign-pair in the Psalms. Its name signifies *revia* 'from' (i.e., following) *geresh*. It is composed of two signs. Reading from right to left, these are: first, the oblique line *geresh*, sloping up to the right; second, the little black diamond *revia*.

מֵאַ֛יִן יָבֹ֥א עֶזְרִ֑י (Ps. 121.1)

Although these two signs occur individually throughout the Bible, it is in the *revia-mugrash* combination that they occur most frequently in the poetic books. The sign-pair habitually occurs after the *etnah* and *oleh ve-yored* cadences, and over the sublinear signs *etnah*, *silluq*, or *merkha*.[1] It is usually spread over two, three, or four syllables, with *geresh* on an unaccented syllable and *revia* falling on the next accented syllable. Occasionally, however, the two signs occur together on a single syllable.[2] In the best Masoretic codices, Aleppo and Leningrad, the sign-pair is always non-cadential (conjunctive).[3]

Cantoral tradition recognizes four forms of *revia*, differing in the way they are sung. Maintaining this terminology is helpful to the discussion.
- *revia*, in the prosodic books.
- *revia mugrash* sign-pair, in the poetic books.
- *revia gadol*, in the poetic books, standing alone and cadential.
- *revia qatan*, in the poetic books, preceding *oleh ve-yored*.

---

[1] Occasional exceptions in printed editions are not supported by the Aleppo text; *e.g.*, at Pss. 7.10b; 149.9, Ginsburg has *revia mugrash* over *tifha*, but Aleppo has only *revia*.

[2] More in the printed editions than in the Aleppo text; but cf. Pss. 35.14; probably 97.7.

[3] Ginsburg's sources sometimes use it cadentially, in headings (*e.g.*, Ps. 8.1), or elsewhere (*e.g.*, Ps. 99.3, 5; 127.1). But, in these instances, Aleppo and Leningrad have *revia gadol*.

REVIA MUGRASH AS READ BY HAÏK-VANTOURA

Haïk-Vantoura does not use the name *revia mugrash*, but simply treats the sign-pair as the sum of its parts, according to her understanding of *geresh* and *revia*. She sees *geresh* as a rising and falling third above the reciting tone, and *revia* as a drop of a second. Therefore, for Haïk-Vantoura, *revia mugrash*, over a reciting tone of sublinear *etnah* (A), takes the form: (A-) C-A-G (-A), as in Psalm 121.1 (set in E minor, as Haïk-Vantoura):

Example 13. *Revia mugrash* in Haïk-Vantoura's conception

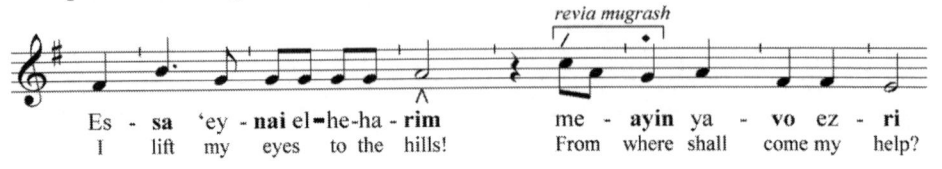

Es - sa ʿey - nai el-he-ha - rim   me - ayin ya - vo ez - ri
I   lift my   eyes to the hills!   From where shall come my help?

In the matter of rhythm, Haïk-Vantoura gives the falling third of *geresh* half the time value of the basic pulse.

But there are important riders. While she sees *revia* in the poetic books as a simple drop of one note on the *revia* syllable, she believes that, in the prosodic books, the *revia* syllable begins on the reciting tone and then falls to the note below.[4] Then she adds that *revia*, both in poetic and prosodic books, may sometimes resolve upward to rest on the reciting note.[5] In other words, she allows for both the initiation and resolution of *revia* to be on either the lower or upper note.

Further, she modified her view on the depth of the *revia* drop. In *La musique de la Bible révélée*, she saw the *revia* drop as within the tonality of the scale. That is, the voice would drop to the pitch of the lower harp string; say, a whole tone from A to G if the harp were tuned to the minor third. But in *Les 150 Psaumes*, she treats the *revia* drop as only a semitone; that is, to G♯ even when the harp is tuned to G. Her later view, therefore, is that *revia* is a vocal decoration of shallow pitch executed independently of the harp accompaniment.

Those who are familiar with music performance will observe that these two factors – the variable initiation and resolution and the small semitone drop – make *revia* look like a Baroque trill or shake. More of that later.

---

[4] Haïk-Vantoura 1991: 98, 99, 101, 38, 39.
[5] Haïk-Vantoura 1991: 459, 469–70, 148.

Appendix IV. Revia mugrash *and* oleh ve-yored

EVIDENCE FOR HAÏK-VANTOURA'S VIEW

Haïk-Vantoura's view that the rhythm of the *geresh* syllables are reduced to half-beats seems reasonable. Take Ps. 122.4, where *geresh* is over *l'ho-* and *revia* falls on the stressed syllable *-dot*.[6]

e-|**dut** l-|**yis**-ra-|**el** <u>l'ho-</u>|**dot** l'-|**shem** y'ho-|**vah**

The scansion requires that the three syllables of the *l'ho-* foot fit into the same time as the two syllables of the other metrical feet. This can be done only by giving the *geresh* pair, *l'ho*, half time-values. This rhythmic pattern works well with *revia mugrash* wherever it covers several syllables. As for those places where *revia mugrash* is on a single syllable, the sign-pair still works well with a reduced time value followed by a stressed note, to preserve the overall scansion and ensure the ornament's neat execution.

Example 14. The rhythmic execution of *revia mugrash*

Psalm 97.7

Hish-taḥ-a-**wu** lo ____ **kol** e-lo-**him**
Fall be-fore him ____ all gods

There is also support for Haïk-Vantoura's understanding of the broad melodic contour of *revia mugrash*. In the example above, the sign-pair is employed to depict prostration. The melodic contour perfectly depicts the bending and falling of the body. The same thing occurs in Psalm 95.6, where the melody bends just where the knee bends:

Example 15. Bowing *revia mugrash* in Psalm 95.6

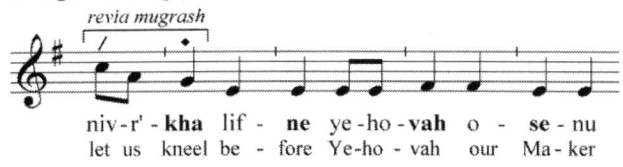

niv-r'-**kha** lif-**ne** ye-ho-**vah** o-**se**-nu
let us kneel be-fore Ye-ho-vah our Ma-ker

Or again, in Psalm 132.7, the bowing keeps going down until it reaches the feet of the deity.

---

[6] See the transcription of the psalm in chapter 13.

Example 16. Bowing *revia mugrash* in Psalm 132.7

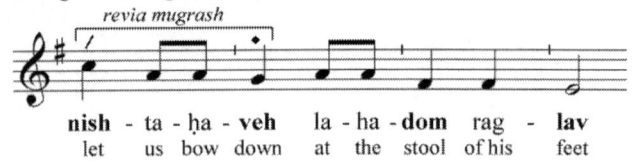

nish - ta - ha - veh la - ha - dom rag - lav
let us bow down at the stool of his feet

Or, in Psalm 29.2, the bowing takes place at the sacred name:

Example 17. Bowing *revia mugrash* in Psalm 29.2

hish - ta - ha - vu ii'y - ho - vah b - had - rat ko - desh
let us bow to Ye - ho - vah in splen - dour ho - ly

Or, in Psalm 72.9, the enemies first bow, then fall down to the dust.

Example 18. Bowing *revia mugrash* in Psalm 72.9

v - oy - vav a - far y - la - he - khu
and his ene - mies dust shall lick

Remarkably, the same phenomenon occurs just about every time bowing or mourning language occurs in the Psalms.[7] And the sign-pair is associated with other 'dropping down' language as well, such as in the 'descends' (*she-yored*) of Psalm 133.2. Since Haïk-Vantoura's interpretation paints the words well in such contexts, it suggests she may be on the right track.

Next, Haïk-Vantoura's proposal that *revia* is a one-step drop seems to be confirmed by Masoretic variants. At Psalm 91.13, for instance, after the *etnah* semi-cadence, the Aleppo and Leningrad codices give *tifha* on the second syllable of *tirmos*, while Ginsburg and Letteris give *revia mugrash*. Following Haïk-Vantoura's system the two readings would be:

---

[7] Pss. 5.7 [8]; 35.14; 45.11 [12] (*adonaikh*); 81.9 [10]; 95.6; and probably 97.7, where the *geresh* of *lo* has a dot above it, to avoid confusion with the *holam*. Interesting variants are Pss. 99.5; 99.9, which execute their bow with the dropping third of *tifha* and *silluq*; and Ps. 138.2, which executes its bow with a drop (?) to circular *galgal*.

Appendix IV. Revia mugrash *and* oleh ve-yored

Example 19. *Tifḥa* versus *revia mugrash* in Psalm 91:13

Aleppo, Leningrad

Ginsburg, Letteris

tir - mos k'- fir v'-ta-nin.
you will trample the li - on and serpent

tir - mos k'- fir v'-ta - nin.
you will trample the li - on and serpent

In each case, the stressed syllable *-mos* is the same note (G$^\sharp$), but is attained on the one hand by *tifḥa* and on the other by *revia* following *etnaḥ*. This suggests that *revia* may indeed force some kind of drop from *etnaḥ*, the fourth step of the scale, to *tifḥa*, the third step. The same thing is seen in Ascents Psalm 131, where the Letteris text is the odd man out.

Example 20. *Tifḥa* versus *revia mugrash* in Psalm 131.2

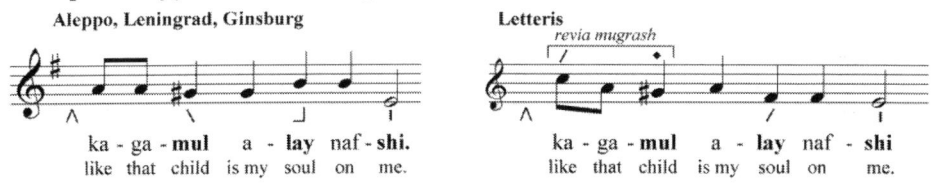

Aleppo, Leningrad, Ginsburg

Letteris

ka - ga - mul a - lay naf - shi.
like that child is my soul on me.

ka - ga - mul a - lay naf - shi
like that child is my soul on me.

Of course, this raises all kinds of questions about the origins of the variants in the printed Masoretic texts, from Soncino on. But, these issues aside, it is fair to say that Haïk-Vantoura's system makes sense even of the Masoretic variants, which is no small feat.

RETHINKING HAÏK-VANTOURA'S VIEW

Therefore Haïk-Vantoura's reading of *revia-mugrash* seems to agree with the evidence available. But can we improve on it?

We saw above how her interpretation of *revia mugrash* looks like a Baroque trill. Gerson-Kiwi points out that in the cantoral traditions of Cairo, *revia* is a 'trill-like ornament whose corresponding cheironomic sign is a trembling hand movement'.[8] (The shaking hand, she plausibly adds, may be a memory of the manipulated vibrato of ancient times.) Now the Cairo cantoral tradition is particularly ancient. Hickmann pointed out that some of its cheironomic signs seem to have the same meaning as in Pharaonic friezes. So, giving credence to the Cairo tradition, *revia* would be not simply a one-note drop, but instead a vocal shake. This would support Haïk-Vantoura's later tendency to make *revia* only a semitone drop, for shakes or trills work better with smaller intervals. Rather than invalidating her system, this proposal

[8] Gerson-Kiwi 2001: V.557.

modifies it in line with ancient cantoral tradition. Meanwhile, the change from a simple dropped note to a shake would make the *revia* syllable more emphatic and forceful, exactly as such trills are used for emphasis in oriental singing.

Example 21. Trilled *revia mugrash*

me - **ayin** ya - vo ez - **ri**
From where shall come my help?

Further, such a modification would explain Haïk-Vantoura's issues about whether *revia mugrash* initiates and resolves on the reciting note or the dropped note. For such issues surround every trill, as any musician knows. In different musical contexts, times and places, trills may begin on the note above – the upper auxiliary – or on the lower note, and the same complexities attend its resolution.

Reading *revia* as a vocal shake or trill has implications for the choice of mode. Since trills work better with smaller intervals, it follows that when *revia* is found over *silluq*, *merkha*, or *etnah*, then it is likely that there is only a semitone step to the notes below. This may help us in identifying the mode of each song.

In addition, if the *revia* trill were to begin on the upper auxiliary, then the descent from *geresh* might be not a dropping third, but a step progression. This would bring the interpretation of *revia mugrash* closer not only to the stepwise movement of synagogue cantillation, but also to the old Syrian cantoral tradition described in chapter twelve, and to Jeffrey Burns's reconstruction of *revia mugrash* from the Lithuanian cantoral tradition.[9]

Example 22. Three readings of *revia mugrash*

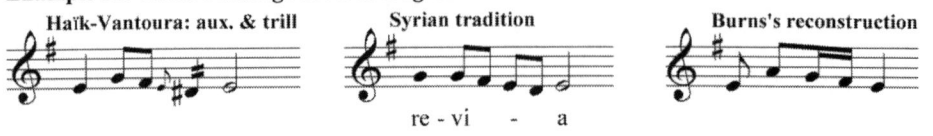

Haïk-Vantoura: aux. & trill   Syrian tradition   Burns's reconstruction

re - vi - a

However, it is simpler and clearer to notate this with the *revia* ornament on a single note with a lower shake, as follows:

---

[9] Burns 2011: 156.

Appendix IV. Revia mugrash *and* oleh ve-yored

Example 23. ***Revia mugrash*** **as a lower shake**

me - **ayin** ya - **vo** ez - **ri**
From where shall come my help?

It is therefore in this manner that *revia mugrash* has been notated in the transcriptions in this book.

OLEH VE-YORED

The sign-pair *oleh ve-yored* is the third strongest cadence in the poetic books, after the final pause *silluq* and the semi-pause *etnaḥ*. Its name signifies 'rising' (*oleh*) 'and falling' (*ve-yored*). It is composed of two signs: first, the supralinear arrowhead or *shofar* sign; second, the sublinear *merkha* sign.

שִׁיר הַֽמַּעֲלוֹת (Ps. 120.1)

Both signs occur individually throughout the Bible. The arrowhead sign, when placed below the text, is *mehuppakh*. And *merkha* occurs occurs frequently on its own. Yet the *oleh ve-yored* sign-pair evidently has a different role. Most importantly, it is always cadential, whereas simple *mehuppakh* and *merkha* never are.

In verses with an *etnaḥ* cadence, the *oleh ve-yored* sign-pair always precedes that cadence, as follows.

oleh-ve-yored → etnaḥ → silluq

However, it is also found in cadence-sequences without *etnaḥ*, such as:

oleh-ve-yored → silluq

revia → oleh-ve-yored → silluq

Just as *revia mugrash* occurs only over certain sublinear signs (*etnaḥ*, *silluq*, *merkha*), so *oleh ve-yored* occurs only on or after certain sublinear signs, namely *etnaḥ hafukh* (*galgal*), *silluq*, *merkha*, and *mehuppakh*.

מִפַּ֣ח י֭וֹקְשִׁים (Ps. 125.7; *etnaḥ hafukh*)

שִׁיר הַֽמַּעֲלוֹת (Ps. 120.1; *silluq*)

יַחֵ֣ל יִשְׂרָאֵ֣ל אֶל־יְהוָ֑ה (Ps. 130.7; *merkha*)

אִם־לֹ֣א שִׁוִּ֤יתִי ׀ וְדוֹמַ֗מְתִּי נַ֫פְשִׁ֥י (Ps. 131.2; *mehuppakh*)

The sign-pair covers two or three syllables, with the sublinear *merkha* sign on the accented syllable.

OLEH VE-YORED IN HAÏK-VANTOURA AND THE CANTORS

Haïk-Vantoura's interpretation of this sign-pair seems counter-intuitive.[10] Although she treats *revia mugrash* as the sum of its parts – *geresh* followed by *revia* – she does not do the same for the arrowhead sign of *oleh ve-yored*. True to her view of the upper signs as single jumps to another note, she sees the supralinear arrowhead as indicating an upward jump. Since in her system the sublinear arrowhead, *mehuppakh*, indicates the sixth step of the scale, one would expect an upper jump of a sixth. But this, in combination with a lower *mehuppakh* would make the jump stratospheric, as she realizes.

Example 24. *Oleh ve-yored* **as leap to the sixth above**

Silluq / Tonic   Mehuppakh   *oleh* jump after *Mehuppakh*

Her solution is that the supralinear arrowhead of *oleh ve-yored* causes a jump to the fourth above and then back down to its original tone, before resting on *merkha*, the second (or supertonic) step of the scale.

Example 25. *Oleh ve-yored* **as leap to the fourth above (Haïk-Vantoura)**

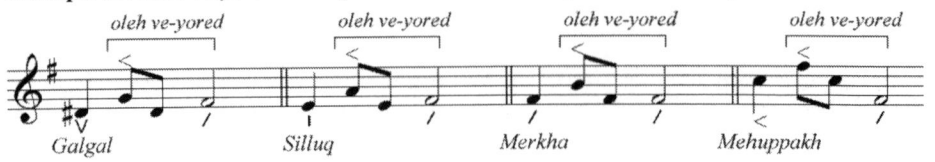

Galgal   Silluq   Merkha   Mehuppakh

The result is that, in Haïk-Vantoura's hands, *oleh ve-yored* becomes not a 'rising and falling', as its Hebrew name suggests, but instead a 'rising and falling and rising again'. The effect of this construction frequently seems unmusical, while its upward leaps of fourths and sudden falls, by as much as an octave, are quite untypical of the stepwise movement of synagogue chant.

Turning from Haïk-Vantoura to the oldest Sephardi cantoral traditions – those of Babylon, Djerba, and Yemen – we see that they take *oleh ve-yored* as

---

[10] Haik-Vantoura 1991: 34–42.

Appendix IV. Revia mugrash *and* oleh ve-yored

a rise or short jump to a higher note, followed by a descent to the supertonic or tonic, as follows.[11]

Example 26. Three readings of *oleh ve-yored*

Ps. 1:2. Babylon — ḥe - f - tso

Ps. 24:8. Djerba — ha - ka - vod

Ps. 104:3. Yemen — a - li - yo - tav

The rising and falling pattern is evident, while the fall to the supertonic (in the Babylonian and Yemeni examples) agrees well with Haïk-Vantoura's interpretation of *merkha*, the cadence tone of the *oleh ve-yored* sign-pair. A similar pattern, rising a third or so and cadencing on the supertonic or tonic, is preserved by the Syrian tradition of the Aderet Eliyahu School.[12]

Example 27. *Oleh ve-yored* in Syrian cantoral tradition

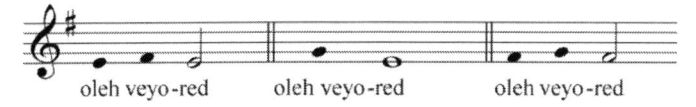

oleh veyo-red   oleh veyo-red   oleh veyo-red

And the most ancient poetic *te'amim* tradition of all – that of Finzi – shows a higher jump but a similar fall.

Example 28. *Oleh ve-yored* in Finzi's tradition

o - leh   ve-yo - red

Therefore the cantoral traditions, though diverse in pitch, agree on a rising and falling contour, frequently cadencing on the supertonic (F or F♯) in agreement with Haïk-Vantoura's hypothesis. If then the *oleh* arrowhead is taken as a simple jump to the sixth step of the scale, the very scale-step Haïk-Vantoura proposes for the sublinear arrowhead, *mehuppakh*, followed by a descent to the supertonic, something not unlike synagogue psalmody emerges.

Example 29. *Oleh ve-yored* of a rising sixth

Shir ha - ma - 'a - lot

---

[11] The extracts are from exs 4, 7, and 8 in the 'Music Examples' appendix to Flender 1992. They are transposed here to E minor.

[12] Jacobson 2014: 16. Here transposed from tonic D to tonic E.

Such a jump is wider than most cantoral traditions, though not unlike Finzi's leap of a fifth. Such a solution seems to be the best combination of cantoral tradition and Haïk-Vantoura's system. It is therefore in this manner that *oleh ve-yored* has been interpreted in the transcriptions in this book.

Finally, since *oleh ve-yored* is, as its name says, a 'rising and falling', it appears to be the counterpart to *revia mugrash* which is a 'falling and rising'. This parity between the two poetic sign-pairs holds promise of shedding further light on both.

Appendix V

Pietro Santi Bartoli's Arch of Titus

Glossary

anadiplosis or **step-parallelism**: a word at the end of one line repeated at the beginning of the next.
anaphora: repetition of the initial word(s) of succeeding lines or phrases.
azarah: the precincts immediately surrounding the temple, beyond the eastern gate.
bet-din: Jewish court of law.
bicolon: a line of poetry consisting of two *cola*.
Birkat kohanim: the Aaronic or Priestly Blessing of Num. 6.24–25.
cadence: a point of musical pause or resolution.
colon, pl. **cola**: the sub-unit of the Hebrew poetic verse, a phrase usually of no more than three words; also known as stich, hemistich, verset.
devir: the temple 'holy of holies', entered only by the *kohen ha-gadol* once a year on Yom Kippur.
diaphony: two-part polyphony, the lower part accompanying the upper *melos*.
diatonic: describing a musical scale with seven notes, excluding the top octave (= heptatonic).
dominant: the fifth step of a musical scale.
double-ison: a drone of tonic and dominant below a melody line.
enneatonic: describing a musical scale with nine notes.
first temple: Solomon's temple, dedicated in 959 BC and razed in 587 BC.
foot: the basic division of metrical verse, the distance between recurring stresses, equivalent to a musical measure or bar.
gematria: biblical interpretation based on the numerical value of Hebrew words.
heikhal: the 'holy place' of the temple, where the *kohanim* had daily access, outside the 'holy of holies' or *devir*.
Herod's temple: the last phase of the second temple, from 20 BC–AD 70.
heptatonic: describing a musical scale with seven notes, excluding the top octave (= diatonic).
ison: a tonic drone below a melody line.
LXX: see **Septuagint**.
kohen, pl. *kohanim*: an Aaronite 'priest' offering temple sacrifices.
kohen ha-gadol: the chief 'priest'.
mashiaḥ: 'anointed'; a divinely-appointed king or priest; the Messiah.
melos: the melodic line of a chant or song.
merism, merismus: a literary device where two opposites embrace all in between.
metre: the regular and predictable pattern of sound-stresses in a poetic text.
Mishnah: a collection of Israel's temple laws and oral traditions, compiled by R. Judah ha-Nasi in the latter 2nd century AD to save Israel's national memory from extinction, after the Roman conquest of AD 135. Much of its material dates from the time of the temple.

pentatonic: describing a musical scale with five notes, not including the top octave.

rhythm: the characteristic of a poetic text in terms of the recurrence of stressed syllables.

mediant: the third step of a musical scale.

metre: the regular and predictable pattern of sound in a poetic text. In Classical verse, metre is composed of the regular variation of short and long syllables according to a prescribed pattern. In Hebrew poetry, it is composed of the distribution of stressed syllables which may follow several different patterns within the one text.

nekudot (points): the vowel and pronunciation signs of the Masoretic codices.

second temple: the temple built in 516 BC by the exiles returned from Babylon. It was greatly expanded by the Maccabees and Herod the Great, but was razed during the Roman siege of Jerusalem in AD 70.

Septuagint (LXX): Greek translation of the Law, Prophets, and Writings (Old Testament), made in Alexandria before the mid-second century BC.

subdominant: the fourth step of a musical scale.

submediant: the sixth step of a musical scale.

subtonic (or **leading note**): the seventh step of a musical scale.

supertonic: the second step of a musical scale.

Talmud Bavli (Babylonian Talmud): a commentary on the **Mishnah** compiled in Babylonia in the 5th or early 6th century AD. It contains ancient traditions omitted from the **Mishnah** and **Tosefta**.

Talmud Yerushalmi (Jerusalem Talmud, Palestinian Talmud): a commentary on the **Mishnah** compiled in Galilee (not Jerusalem) in the 4th century. It too contains ancient traditions omitted from the **Mishnah** and **Tosefta**.

te'amim (tastings): the cantillational signs of the Masoretic codices.

tessitura: the compass or range of notes – whether high or low – in which the majority of notes of a piece of music lies.

tonic: the first step of a musical scale, the home-note or key-note.

Tosefta ('supplement'): other temple laws and oral traditions supplementary to R. Judah's **Mishnah**, compiled in the late 2nd century. Much of its material dates from the time of the temple.

tricolon: a line of poetry consisting of three *cola*.

Bibliography

Abou Mrad, N.,
    2012 'Noyaux distinctifs par tierces de l'articulation monodique modale', *Musurgia* XIX: 5–32.

Abou Mrad, N., Maatouk, T., Chédid, Y.
    2015 *Hymnes syriaques de l'office maronite, selon le Père Maroun Mrad* (Baabda: Éditions de l'Université Antonine).

Adler, I.
    1989 *Hebrew Notated Manuscript Sources up to circa 1840*. Vol. 1. (Répertoire Internationale des Sources Musicales IX[1]; Munich: Henle).

Adler, M.N.
    1907 *The Itinerary of Benjamin of Tudela* (London: Oxford University Press).

Aharon ben Asher
    c. 950 *Diqduqe ha-te'amim* (ed. A. Dotan) (Jerusalem: Academy of the Hebrew Language, 1967).

Aharon ben Asher
    c. 950 *Diqduqe ha-te'amim* (eds. and trans. S. Baer and H.L. Strack) (Leipzig, 1879).

Ahituv, S.
    1992 *Handbook of Ancient Hebrew Inscriptions* (Jerusalem: Bialik).

Albright, W.F.
    1924 'The Name Yahweh', *JBL* 42: 370–78.
    1925 'Further observations on the name YAHWEH and its modifications in proper names', *JBL* 44: 158–162.
    1961 'What were the Cherubim?' in G.E. Wright & D.N. Freedman (eds.), *The Biblical Archaeologist Reader, Volume 1* (Chicago: Quadrangle): 95–97.
    1968 *Yahweh and the Gods of Canaan* (Winona Lake: Eisenbrauns).

Aletti, J.-N. & J. Trublet
    1983 *Approche poétique et théologique des psaumes* (Paris: Cerf).

Alfrink, B.
    1948 "La prononciation 'Jehova' du tétragramme", *Old Testament Studies* 5:43–62.

Allen, L. C.
    1983 *Psalms 101–150* (Waco, TX: Word).

Alonso Schökel, L.
    1988 *A Manual of Hebrew Poetics,* (Subsidia Biblica 11; Rome: Pont. Inst. Biblico).

Alonso Schökel, L. & Strus, A.
    1980 'Salmo 122: Canto al nombre de Jerusalén', *Biblica* 61: 234–250.

Alter, R.
    1985 *The Art of Biblical Poetry* (New York: Basic Books).

Anderson, A. A.
    1972 *The Book of Psalms*. 2 vols. (New Century Bible; London: Oliphants).

Anderson, B. W.
    1983 *Out of the Depths* (Philadelphia: Westminster Press).

Arieh, E.
    1972 'Earthquake', *EJ* VI.340–42.

Astour, M.C.
    1979   'Yahweh in Egyptian Topographic Lists', in *Festschrift Elmar Edel in Ägypten und Altes Testament* (eds. M. Görg & E. Pusch) (Bamberg): 17–34.

Armfield, H. T.
    1874   *The Gradual Psalms* (London: J. T. Hayes).

Auffret, P.
    1982   *La sagesse a bâti sa maison: Etudes de structures littéraires dans l'Ancien Testament et specialment dans les Psaumes* (Fribourg: Editions Universaires).

Avenary, H.
    1963   'Formal Structure of Psalms and Canticles in Early Jewish and Christian Chant', *Musica Disciplina* 17: 1-13; repr. in Avenary, *Encounters of East and West in Music – Selected Writings* (Tel Aviv: Tel Aviv University, 1979): 105-111.
    1968   'A Geniza Find of Sa'adya's Psalm-Preface and its Musical Aspects', *Hebrew Union College Annual* 39: 145-162.
    1979   *Encounters of East and West in Music* (Tel Aviv: Tel Aviv University).

Baer, S. and H.L. Strack (eds. & trans.)
    1879   *Dikduke ha-te'amim* of Aharon ben Asher (Leipzig); with prefatory note and appendix, 'The Aleppo Codex or Diqduqe Hatte'amim?' by D.L. Loewinger.

Baker, J. and E.W. Nicholson (eds. and trans.)
    1973   *The Commentary of Rabbi David Kimḥi on Psalms CXX-CL* (Cambridge: University Press).

Barton, J.
    1986   *Oracles of God* (London: Darton, Longman, & Todd).
    2013   'Postscript' in Gillingham (ed.) 2013b: 259–61.

Beaucamp, E.
    1979   *Le Psautier*. 2 vols. (Paris: Gabalda).
    1979   'L'unité du recueil des montées, Psaumes 120–134', *Liber Annuus Studii Biblici Franciscani* 29:73–90.

Begbie, J.S.
    2011   'Faithful feelings' in Begbie & Guthrie 2011: 323–354.

Begbie, J.S. and S.R. Guthrie (eds.)
    2011   *Resonant Witness: Conversations between Music and Theology* (Grand Rapids, MI: Eerdmans).

Bellinger, W.H., Jr,
    1984   *Psalmody and Prophecy* (JSOTS 27; Sheffield: JSOT).
    1990   *Psalms: Reading and Studying the Book of Praises A Guide to Studying the Psalter* (2nd ed.; Grand Rapids, MI: Baker, 2012).

Berger, P.
    2012   *The Crescent on the Temple: The Dome of the Rock as Image of the Ancient Jewish Sanctuary* (Leiden: Brill).

Berlin, A.
    1987   'On the Interpretation of Psalm 133', in *Directions in Biblical Hebrew Poetry* (ed. E.R. Follis), Journal for the Study of the Old Testament Supplement Series 40 (Sheffield: Sheffield Academic Press): 141–48.

Beyerlin, W.
    1982 *We Are Like Dreamers: Studies in Psalm 126,* (trans. D. Livingstone) (Edinburgh: T. & T. Clark).

Biran, A. and J. Naveh
    1993 'An Aramaic Stele from Tel Dan', *IEJ* 43: 81–98.
    1995 'The Tel Dan Inscription: A New Fragment', *IEJ* 45: 1–18.

Bonhoeffer, D.
    1961 *The Psalms: Prayer Book of the Bible* (Oxford: SLG Press, 1982); tr. from *Das Bebetbuch der Bibel* (Bad Salzuflen: MBK-Verlag, 1961).

Booij, T.
    2010 'Psalms 120-136: Songs for a Great Festival', *Biblica* 91: 241–255.

Braun, J.
    2002 *Music in Ancient Israel/Palestine: Archaeological, Written, and Comparative Sources* (Eerdmans: Grand Rapids, MI–Cambridge).
    2006 *On Jewish Music: Past and Present* (Frankfurt am Main: Peter Lang).

Brennan, J. P.
    1976 'Some Hidden Harmonies in the Fifth Book of Psalms', in R. F. McNamara (ed.), *Essays in Honor of Joseph P. Brennan* (Rochester, NY: St Bernard's Seminary).

Breuer, M.
    1996 *Pentateuch, Prophets, and Writings According to the Text and Masorah of the Aleppo Codex and Related Manuscripts* (Jerusalem: 1998 [2nd ed.]). Hebrew.

Briggs, C.A. and E.G. Briggs
    1906–07 *A Critical and Exegetical Commentary on the Book of Psalms*, 2 vols. (Edinburgh: T. & T. Clark).

Bright, J.
    2000 *A History of Israel* (Louisville, KT: Westminster John Knox Press, 4th ed. [1st ed. 1959]).

Brown, W.P.
    2002 *Seeing the Psalms: A Theology of Metaphor* (Louisville: Westminster John Knox Press).

Brown, W.P. (ed.)
    2014 *The Oxford Handbook of the Psalms* (Oxford: Oxford University Press).

Broyles, C.C.
    2005 'The Psalms and Cult Symbolism: The Case of the Cherubim-Ark' in D. Firth & P. Johnston (eds.), *Interpreting The Psalms* (Downers Grove, IL: Inter-Varsity Press): 139-158.

Bruce, F.F.
    1997 *Israel and the Nations*, rev. D.F. Payne (Downer's Grove, IL: Inter-Varsity Press).

Brueggemann, W.
    1984 *The Message of the Psalms: A Theological Commentary* (Minneapolis: Augsburg).
    1988 *Israel's Praise: Doxology against Idolatry and Ideology* (Philadelphia: Fortress).
    1991 'Bounded by Obedience and Praise: The Psalms as Canon', *JSOT* 50: 63–92.

2007 *Praying the Psalms: Engaging Scripture and the Life of the Spirit* (2nd ed.; Eugene, OR: Cascade).

Burns, D. and J.W. Rogerson
2012 *Far From Minimal: Celebrating the Work and Influence of Philip R. Davies* (London: T. & T. Clark).

Burns, J.
2011 *The Music of Psalms, Proverbs and Job in the Hebrew Bible: A Revised Theory of Musical Accents in the Hebrew Bible* (eds. D. Bers and S. Tree) (Wiesbaden: Harrassowitz).

Burton, I.
1884 *The Inner Life of Syria, Palestine, and the Holy Land: From My Private Journal* (London: Kegan Paul, Trench and Company, 3rd edn.).

Busink, Th. A.
1970–80 *Der Tempel von Jerusalem von Salomo bis Herodes*. 2 vols. (Leiden: Brill).

Butin, R.F.
1906 *The Ten Nequdoth of the Torah* (Baltimore: Furst).

Buxtorf, J. (*père*)
1620 *Tiberias, sive Commentarius Masoreticus* (Basel: König).

Buxtorf, J. (*fils*)
1648 *Tractatus de punctorum vocalium et accentuum origine, antiquitate, et authoritate* (Basel: König).

Calvin, J.
1563 *Commentary on the Psalms* (Grand Rapids, MI: Eerdmans, 1949).

Campbell, D.G.
1997–2009 *The Mozart Effect* (New York: Avon/HarperCollins).

Ceresko, A. R.
1989 'Psalm 121: a prayer of a warrior?' *Biblica* 70: 496-510.

Chernoff, R.
1991 'Tehillim – the Psalms', *JBQ* 19: 191–94.

Chilton, B.
2011 'The Kabbalah of Rabbi Jesus', in Z. Garber (ed.), *The Jewish Jesus: Revelation, Reflection, Reclamation* (West Lafayette, IN: Purdue University Press): 20–34.

de Claissé-Walford, N.L.
2004 *Introduction to the Psalms* (Grand Rapids, MI: Eerdmans).
2014 'The Meta-Narrative of the Psalter', in Brown 2014: 363–376.
2014 *The Shape and Shaping of the Book of Psalms: The Current State of Scholarship*, Ancient Israel and Its Literature 20 (Atlanta: Society of Biblical Literature).

Clifford, R.J.
2014 'Psalms of the Temple', in Brown 2014: 326–337.

Cohen, A.
1945 *The Psalms* (Hindhead, Surrey: Soncino).

Cohen, S.
1939–44 'Week', in I. Landman (ed.), *The Universal Jewish Encyclopedia.* 10 vols. (New York): X.482.

Cole, R.L.
    2013   *Psalms 1–2: Gateway to the Psalter*, Hebrew Bible Monographs 37 (Sheffield: Phoenix).

Coogan, M.D.
    2013   *The Old Testament: A Historical and Literary Introduction to the Hebrew Scriptures* (Oxford–New York: Oxford University Press).

Cox, S.
    1885   *The Pilgrim Psalms* (Dickinson: London).

Craigie, P. C.
    1983   *Psalms 1–50*, Word Biblical Commentary 19 (Waco, TX: Word).

Crenshaw, J.L.
    2001   *The Psalms: An Introduction* (Grand Rapids, MI: Eerdmans).

Crickmore, L.
    2009   'The Tonal Systems of Mesopotamia and Ancient Greece', *ARANE* 1: 1–16.

Cross, F.M.
    1962   'Yahweh and the God of the Patriarchs', *Harvard Theological Revue* 55: 225–259.

Crow, L.D.
    1996   *The Songs of Ascents (Psalms 120-134): Their Place in Israelite History and Religion* (Atlanta: Scholars Press).

Dahood, M.
    1965–70   *Psalms*. 3 vols, Anchor Bible 16-17A (New York: Doubleday).

Davies, P.R.
    1992   *In Search Of 'Ancient Israel'* (London and New York: T. & T. Clark).
    2004   *Whose Bible Is It Anyway?* (London and New York: T. & T. Clark).

Delitzsch, Franz
    1887   *Biblical Commentary on the Psalms*. 3 vols. (tr. D. Eaton) (London: Hodder and Stoughton).

Delitzsch, Friedrich
    1903   *Babel and Bible: Two Lectures on the Significance of Assyriological Research for Religion* (trans. T.J. McCormack and W.H. Carruth) (Chicago: Open Court Publishing).

Derenbourg, J. (trans.)
    1870   'Manuel de Lecteur d'un auteur inconnu, publié d'après un manuscrit venu du Yémen et accompagné de notes', *Journal Asiatique,* 6th series: vol. 16 (Paris: Oct.–Dec. 1870): 309–550. (Bible no. 62 in the Jewish Theological Seminary).

Deurloo, K.
    1992   'Gedächtnis des Exils – Psalm 120-134', *T. & K.* 55.3.28–34.

Dobbs-Allsopp, F.W.
    2014   'Poetry of the Psalms', in Brown 2014: 79–99.

Dotan, A.
    1957   'Was Ben Asher Really a Karaite?' *Sinai* 41: 280–312. Hebrew.
    1967   *The Diqduqei Ha-Teamim of Aharon Ben Moshe Asher – With a Critical Edition of the Original Text from New Manuscripts* (Jerusalem: Academy of the Hebrew Language). Hebrew.
    1972   'Masorah', *EJ* XVI:1401–82.

1981 'The Relative Chronology of Hebrew Vocalization and Accentuation', *Proceedings of the American Academy for Jewish Research* 48: 87–99.

Duchesne-Guillemin, M.
1965 Appendix: 'Note complimentaire sur la découverte de la gamme babylonienne', in Kilmer 1965: 268–272.
1984 'A Hurrian Musical Score from Ugarit: The Discovery of Mesopotamian Music', *Sources from the Ancient Near East* 2 (Malibu, CA: Undena).

Driver, G.R.
1976 *Semitic Writing from Pictograph to Alphabet* (Oxford: Oxford University Press, 3rd ed.).

Duhm, B.
1899 *Die Psalmen* (Freiburg: Mohr–Siebeck).

Dumbrill, R.J.
2005 *The Archaeomusicology of the Ancient Near East* (Victoria, BC–Crewe, UK: Trafford).
2010 'Music Theorism in the Ancient World', in R. Dumbrill (ed.) 2009–10: 107–34.

Dumbrill, R.J. (ed.)
2009–10 *Iconea* (Proceedings of the International Conference of Near Eastern Archaeomusicology) 2009-10 (University of London–Gorgias Press).

Eaton, J. H.
1967 *Psalms* (London: SCM).
1976 *Kingship and the Psalms* (London: SCM).

Edersheim, A.
1874 *The Temple: Its Ministry and Services As They Were At the Time of Jesus Christ* (repr: Grand Rapids, MI: Kregel, 1997).

Ehrlich, T.F.
2012 'The Disappearance of the Ark of the Covenant', *JBQ* 40: 175–78.

Eldar, I.
1992 '*Mukhtaṣar* (an abridgement of) *Hidāyat al-Qāri* : a grammatical treatise discovered in the Geniza' in J. Blau and S.C. Reif (eds), *Genizah Research After Ninety Years* (Cambridge: Cambridge University Press, 1992).
1994 *The Art of Correct Reading of the Bible* (Jerusalem: Academy of the Hebrew Language). Hebrew.

Ettisch, E.
1987 *The Hebrew vowels and consonants as symbols of ancient astronomic concepts* (Brookline Village, MA: Branden). Tr. H. Zohn, from the unpublished German text.

Faulkner, Q.
1996 *Wiser Than Despair: The Evolution of Ideas in the Relationship of Music and the Christian Church* (Westport: Greenwood Press).

Fine, S.
2005 'The Temple Menorah—Where Is It?', *BAR* 30: 18–25, 62–63.

Finkelstein, I. and N.A. Silbermann
2002 *The Bible Unearthed: Archaeology's New Vision of Ancient Israel and the Origin of its Sacred Texts* (New York: Simon & Schuster–Touchstone).

2007   *David and Solomon: In Search of the Bible's Sacred Kings and the Roots of the Western Tradition* (New York: Free Press).
Firth, D. and P.S. Johnston (eds.)
    2005   *Interpreting the Psalms: Issues and Approaches* (Downers Grove, IL: Inter-Varsity Press).
Fleischer, O.
    1895   *Neumen-Studien* (Leipzig).
Flender, R.
    1992   *Hebrew Psalmody* (Jerusalem: Magnes).
Flint, P.W.
    2014   'Unrolling the Dead Sea Psalms Scroll', in Brown 2014: 229–250.
    2006   'Psalms and Psalters in the Dead Sea Scrolls', in J.H. Charlesworth (ed.), *The Bible and the Dead Sea Scrolls: Scripture and the Scrolls* (Waco, TX: Baylor University Press): 233–272.
Flint, P.W. and P.D. Miller (eds.)
    2005   *The Book of Psalms: Composition and Reception* (Leiden: Brill).
Florinus, C.
    1667   *Doctrina de accentuatione divina* (Sulzbach: Lichtentaler).
Forbes, J.
    1888   *Studies on the Book of Psalms* (Edinburgh: T. & T. Clark).
Freedman, D.N.
    1960   'The Name of the God of Moses', *JBL* 79: 151-156.
Friedman, M.
    2012   *The Aleppo Codex: In Pursuit of One of the World's Most Coveted, Sacred, and Mysterious Books* (Chapel Hill, NC: Algonquin).
Galil, G.
    1996   *Chronology of the Kings of Israel and Judah* (Leiden: Brill).
    2000   'The historical context of Joshua 19:40–48', *Biblische Notizen* 104: 11-15.
    2012   'Solomon's temple: Fiction or Reality?' in G. Galil *et al.* (eds.) 2012: 137-146.
Galil, G., A. Gilboa, A.M. Maeir, and D. Kahn (eds.)
    2012   *The Ancient Near East in the 12th–10th Centuries BCE: Culture and History* (Proceedings of the International Conference held at the University of Haifa, 2–5 May, 2010; *AOAT* 392; Münster: Ugarit Verlag).
Galpin, F.W.
    1937   *The music of the Sumerians and their immediate successors, the Babylonians & Assyrians* (Cambridge: University Press).
Garfinkel, Y.
    2012   'Another View: Christopher Rollston's Methodology of Caution', *BAR* 38:58–59.
Garsiel, M.
    1991   *Biblical Names: A Literary Study of Midrashic Derivations and Puns* (Ramat-Gan: Bar Ilan University Press).
Génébrard, G.
    1567   *Chronologia* (Paris, 1600).
Gerson-Kiwi, E. and D. Hiley
    2001   'Cheironomy', in *The New Grove Dictionary of Music and Musicians*, ed. S. Sadie (London: Macmillan), V.554–559.

Gesenius, W.
    1812 'Hallesche Literatur-Zeitung' Nr. 205.
    1834 *Hebräisches und Chaldäisches Handwörterbuch über das Alt Testament* (Leipzig: Vogel).
Gesenius, W., E. Kautzsch (ed.), & A. Cowley (tr.)
    1910 *Gesenius' Hebrew Grammar* (28th ed.; Oxford: Clarendon).
Geyer, P. and O. Kuntz
    1965 'Itinerarium Burdigalense' in *Itineraria et alia geographica* (*Corpus Christianorum Series Latina* 175; Turnhout: Brepols).
Gibson, S. and D.M. Jacobson
    1996 *Below the Temple Mount in Jerusalem: A Sourcebook on the Cisterns, Subterranean Chambers and Conduits of the Haram Al-Sharif* (British Archaeological Reports International Series 637; Oxford: Tempus Reparatum).
Gill, J.
    1767 *A Dissertation Concerning the Antiquity of the Hebrew-Language, Letters, Vowel-Points, and Accents* (London).
Gillingham, S.E.
    2008 *Psalms Through the Centuries* (Oxford: Blackwell).
    2013a 'The Reception of Psalm 137 in Jewish and Christian Traditions' in Gillingham (ed.) 2013b: 64–82.
    2013a *A Journey of Two Psalms: The Reception of Psalms 1 and 2 in Jewish and Christian Tradition* (Oxford: Oxford University Press).
    2014 'The Levites and the Editorial Composition of the Psalms' in Brown 2014: 201–213.
Gillingham, S.E. (ed.)
    2013b *Jewish & Christian Approaches to the Psalms: Conflict and Convergence* (Oxford: Oxford University Press).
Ginsburg, C.D.
    1861 *The Massoreth Ha-Massoreth of Elias Levita* (London).
    1871 *The Moabite Stone. A Fac-simile of the Original Inscription, with an English Translation, and a Historical and Critical Commentary* (London: 2nd ed.).
    1897 *Introduction to the Massoretico-Critical Edition of the Hebrew Bible* (London: Trinitarian Bible Society).
Glück, J.J.
    1970 'Paronomasia in Biblical Literature', *Semitica* 1: 50–78.
Goldingay, J.
    2006–08 *Psalms*. 3 vols. (Grand Rapids, MI: Baker Academic).
Goldwasser, O.
    2010 'How the Alphabet Was Born from Hieroglyphs', *BAR* 36: 40–53.
Gordon, N.
    2012 *Shattering the Conspiracy of Silence* (Grand Prairie, TX: Hilkiah).
Gorris, E. and W. Verhulst
    2010 'Summon the Gods and the People to the Sound of the Conch', in Dumbrill (ed.) 2009–10: 21–28.
Goulder, M.D.
    1997 'The Songs of Ascents and Nehemiah', *JSOT* 22:43–58.

Gradenwitz, P.
 1998 *The Psalms of the Return (Book V, Psalms 107-150): Studies in the Psalter IV*, Journal for the Study of the Old Testament Supplement Series 258; Sheffield: Sheffield Academic Press).

Gradenwitz, P.
 1996 *The Music of Israel* (2nd ed.; Portland, Oregon: Amadeus Press).

Graetz, H.
 1853–70 *History of the Jews.* 6 vols. (trans. P. Bloch) (Philadelphia: The Jewish Publication Society of America, 1902) from *Geschichte der Juden* (1853–70).

Grant, J.
 2005 'The Psalms and the King', in Firth and Johnston (eds.) 2005: 101–18.

Gravett, S.L., K.G. Bohmbach, F.G. Greifenhagen, and D.C. Polaski
 2008 *An Introduction to the Hebrew Bible: A Thematic Approach* (Louisville, KT: John Knox Westminster Press).

Grossberg, D.
 1989 *Centripetal and Centrifugal Structures in Biblical Poetry* (SBL Monograph Series 39: Atlanta: Scholars Press).

Grünhut, L.
 1905 סבוב הרב רבי פתחיה מרעגנשבורג [The Voyage of Rabbi Petahiah of Regensburg] (Frankfurt).

Gunkel, H. and J. Begrich
 1933 *Einleitung in die Psalmen: die Gattungen der religiösen Lyrik Israels*, Göttinger Handkommentar zum AT (Göttingen: Vandenhoeck & Ruprecht).

Güterbock, H.G. and T. Jacobsen
 1965 *Studies in Honor of Benno Landsberger on his Seventy-fifth Birthday, April 21, 1965* (Assyriological Studies 16; Chicago: University of Chicago Press).

Guthrie, S.R.
 2011 'The Wisdom of Song', in Begbie and Guthrie 2011: 382–407.

Habel, N.C.
 1972 '"Yahweh, Maker of Heaven and Earth': A study in tradition criticism," *JBL* 91: 321-337.

Haïk-Vantoura, S.
 1976 *La musique de la Bible révélée* (Robert Dumas: Paris), with a recording by Harmonia Mundi France. 2nd rev. ed.; Dessain et Tolra: Paris, 1978.
 1985 *Les 150 Psaumes dans leurs mélodies antiques* (Paris : Fondation Roi David).
 1991 *The Music of the Bible Revealed* (Tr. D. Weber; ed. J. Wheeler; Berkeley CA: Bibal Press).

Halpern, B.
 1992 'The Pomegranate Scepter Head – From the Temple of the Lord or from a Temple of Asherah?' *BAR* 18: 42–45.

Hayman, P.
 1976 'Rabbinic Judaism and the Problem of Evil', *Scottish Journal of Theology* 29: 461–476.

Hengstenberg, E.W.
  1845–48 *Commentary on the Psalms*. 3 vols. (trans. P. Fairbairn and J. Thompson). (Edinburgh: T. & T. Clark); from *Commentar über die Psalmen* (Berlin, 1842–1847).
Herzog, A.
  1963 *The Intonation of the Pentateuch in the Heder of Tunis* (Tel Aviv: Israel Music Institute).
  1972 'Psalms, Book of: Musical Rendition in Jewish Tradition', *EJ* XIII:1328-33.
Herzog, A. and A. Hajdu
  1968 'A la recherche du *tonus peregrinus* dans la tradition musicale juive', *Yuval* 1:194–203.
Hickmann, H.
  1956 *Musicologie Pharaonique. Études sur l'évolution de l'art musical dans l'Égypte ancienne* (Kehl am Rhein).
Hickmann, H and E. Hickmann
  1996 'Handzeichen' §1&2, in A Jaschinski *et al.* (eds.), *Die Musik in Geschichte und Gegenwart* (Kassel-Weimar: Bärenreiter, 1996), Sachteil IV: 6-14.
Hoffmeier, J.K.
  1996 *Israel in Egypt: The Evidence for the Authenticity of the Exodus Tradition* (Oxford: Oxford University Press).
  2005 *Ancient Israel in Sinai: The Evidence for the Authenticity of the Wilderness Tradition* (Oxford: Oxford University Press).
Hossfeld, F.-L. and E. Zenger
1993–2012 *Die Psalmen*. 3 vols. (Die Neue Echter Bibel 29; Würzburg: Echter).
Hossfeld, F.-L. and T.M. Steiner
  2013 'Problems and Prospects in Psalter Studies', in Gillingham (ed.) 2013b: 240–258.
Houwelingen, P.H.R., van
  2003 'Fleeing Forward: The Departure of Christians from Jerusalem to Pella', *Westminster Theological Journal* 65: 181–200.
Howard, D.M., Jr
  2005 'The Psalms and Current Study' in Firth and Johnston (eds.) 2005: 23–40.
Humbert, P.
  1946 *La «Terou'a». Analyse d'un rite biblique* (Neuchatel: Université de Neuchatel).
Hunter, A.G.
  2008 *An Introduction to the Psalms* (T&T Clark Approaches to Biblical Studies; London: Bloomsbury Academic, 2008).
Hurowitz, V.A.
  2012 'Yhwh's Exalted House Revisited: New Comparative Light on the Biblical Image of Solomon's temple', in G. Galil *et al.* (eds.) 2012: 137-146.

Huwiler, E. F.
    1987   'Patterns and Problems in Psalm 132', in K. Hoglund *et al.* (eds.), *The Listening Heart*, Journal for the Study of the Old Testament Supplement Series 58 (Sheffield: Sheffield Academic Press) 199-215.

Idelsohn, A.Z.
    1914   *Gesänge der jemenischen Juden* (Volume 1 of *Hebräisch-orientalischer Melodienschatz*. 10 volumes) (Berlin: Harz, 1914–32).
    1929   *Jewish Music in its Historical Development* (New York: Henry Holt & Co., 1929; repr. New York: Tudor, 1929).

Ilani, S., A. Rosenfeld, H.R. Feldman, W.E. Krumbein, and J. Kronfeld
    2008   'Archaeometric analysis of the Jehoash Inscription tablet', *Journal of Archaeological Science* 35: 2966–2972.

Irsigler, H.
    1987   '"Umsonst ist es, daß ihr früh aufsteh': Psalm 127 und die Kritik der Arbeit in Israels Weisheitsliteratur', *Biblische Notizen* 37: 48-72.

Ito, J.P.
    2011   'On Music, Mathematics and Theology', in Begbie and Guthrie 2011: 109–34.

Jacobson, J.
    2014   'The Cantillation of the Psalms', *Journal of Synagogue Music*.

Jenkins, J.S.
    2001   'The Mozart Effect', *Journal of the Royal Society of Medicine* 94: 170–72.

Joseph, M.
    1939–44   'Holidays', in I. Landman (ed.), *The Universal Jewish Encyclopedia*. 10 vols. (New York): V.410.

Jourdan-Hemmerdinger, D.
    1973   'Un nouveau papyrus musical d'Euripide', in *Comptes rendus des séances de l'Académie des Inscriptions et Belles-lettres* (Paris: Klinksieck): 292–302.
    1986   'Suzanne HAÏK-VANTOURA. Les 150 Psaumes dans leurs mélodies antiques', *Revue des études juives* 145: 127-131.

Kahle, P.
    1947   *The Schweich Lectures of the British Academy* (London, Oxford University Press, 1947.
    1953   'The Karaites and the Manuscripts from the Cave', *VT* 3.1: 82–84.
    1959   *The Cairo Geniza* (2nd ed.; Oxford: Blackwell).

Kallai, Z.
    1986   *Historical Geography of the Bible: The Tribal Territories of Israel* (Leiden: Brill).

Keet, C.C.
    1969   *A Study of the Psalms of Ascents: A Critical and Exegetical Commentary upon Psalms CXX-CXXXIV* (London: Mitre).

Kendall, R.T.
    1995   *Higher Ground: Insights From the Songs of Ascents* (Fearn, Ross-shire: Christian Focus).

Khan, G. *et al.* (eds.)
    2013   *Encyclopedia of Hebrew Language and Linguistics.* 4 vols. (Leiden: Brill).

Kidner, D.
    1975   *Psalms.* 2 vols. (London: Inter-Varsity Press).

Kilmer, A. Draffkorn
    1960   'Two New Lists of Key Numbers for Mathematical Operations', *Orientalia* 29: 273-308.
    1965   'The strings of musical instruments: their names, numbers and significance' in Güterbock 1965: 261–268.
    1971   The Discovery of an Ancient Mesopotamian Theory of Music. *Proceedings of the American Philosophical Society* 115: 131–49.
    1984   'A Music Tablet from Sippar(?): BM 65217 + 66616', *Iraq* 46: 69–80.

Kilmer, A.D. and M. Civil
    1986   'Old Babylonian Musical Instructions Relating to Hymnody', *Journal of Cuneiform Studies* 38.1: 94–98.

Kilmer, A.D., R.L. Crocker, and R.R. Brown
    1976   *Sounds from Silence: Recent Discoveries in Ancient Eastern Music* (LP with information booklet; Berkeley, CA: Bit Enki Publications).

Kimḥi, David
    1235   *Perush Radak al tehillim. Sepher ḥamishi.* J. Bosniak, ed., (Jewish Theological Seminary of America; New York: Bloch, 1954).

Kirkpatrick, A.F.
    1902   *The Book of Psalms* (Cambridge: Cambridge University Press).

Kitchen, K.
    1986   *The Third Intermediate Period in Egypt* (1100–650 B.C.) (2nd rev. ed. with supplement; Warminster, England: Aris & Phillips).
    2001   'Ancient Egypt and the Hebrew Monarchies', *Themelios* 26: 38–50.
    2003   *On the Reliability of the Old Testament* (Eerdmans: Grand Rapids-Cambridge).

Klar, B.
    1953   'Ben Asher', *Tarbiz* 14: 156-173.

Klein, I.
    1992   *A Guide to Jewish Religious Practice* (2nd ed.; Jewish Theological Seminary of America: Ktav).

Kleinig, J.W.
    1992   'The Divine Institution of the Lord's Song in Chronicles', *JSOT* 55: 75–83.
    1993   *Lord's Song: The Basis, Function and Significance of Choral Music in Chronicles* (Sheffield: JSOT).

Kraus, H.-J.
    1966   *Worship in Israel* (Richmond: John Knox Press).
    1978   *Psalms. 2 vols.* (tr.) H. C. Oswald (Minneapolis: Augsburg, 1988); from *Psalmen* (5th ed.; Neukirchen-Vleyn: Neukirchener Verlag, 1978).

Kugel, J.L.
    1981   *The Idea of Biblical Poetry: Parallelism and its History* (Baltimore: John Hopkins University Press).

Kuhn, M.
    2010   'Hand Position of Musicians Before and After the Hyksos Kings', in Dumbrill (ed.) 2009-10: 11-18.

Labuschagne, C.
    2010   'Significant Sub-Groups in the Book of Psalms: A New Approach to the Compositional Structure of the Psalter (Lezing Bijbelse Studiedagen te Leuven, 6-8-2008)' in *The Composition of the Book of Psalms* (BETL 238; Leuven 2010): 623–34.
    2009   'Significant Compositional Techniques in the Psalms: Evidence for the Use of Number as an Organizing Principle', *VT* 59: 583–605; erratum in VT 60.1 (2010): 1-4.

Lachmann, R.
    1940   *Jewish Cantillation and Song in the Isle of Djerba* (Jerusalem: Magnes).

de Lagarde, P.A.
    1858   *Hippolytus Romanus* (Leipzig-London: Teubner-Williams and Norgate).

Landels, J.G.
    1999   *Music in Ancient Greece and Rome* (London: Routledge).

Lane, W.
    1991   *Hebrews 1–8* (Word Biblical Commentary 47a; Dallas: Word).

Lane-Poole, S.
    1883   *Picturesque Palestine, Sinai and Egypt* (New York: Appleton).

Laperrousaz, E.-M.
    1987   'King Solomon's Wall Still Supports the Temple Mount', *BAR* 13: 34–44.

Leach. J.
    2011   *Thirty Ways to Use Music in Worship* (Cambridge: Grove Books).

Leaver, R.A.
    1976   'The Calov Bible from Bach's Library', *Bach* 7: 16–22.

Ledebuhr, C.
    1647   *Catena Scripturae. Tractatus novus, in quo ratio accentum, quibus Hebraeus S. Scripturae contextus interpungitur* (Leiden).

Lemaire, A.
    1984   'Probable Head of Priestly Scepter from Solomon's Temple Surfaces in Jerusalem', *BAR* 10: 24–29.
    1994   '"House of David" Restored in Moabite Inscription', *BAR* 20: 30–37.

Leonitius, J.
    1650   *Libellus effigiei templi Salomonis* (Amsterdam).

Leval, G.
    2012   'Ancient Inscription Refers to Birth of Israelite Monarchy', *BAR* 38: 41–43, 70.

Levin, S.
    1968   'The Traditional Chironomy of the Hebrew Scriptures', *JBL* 87: 59–70.
           'The Traditional Chironomy of the Hebrew Scriptures', video on Youtube.com [accessed June 2012].

Levin, Y.
    2010   'Sheshonq I and the Negev Ḥāṣērîm', *Maarav* 17: 189–215.
    2012   'Did Pharaoh Sheshonq Attack Jerusalem?' *BAR* 38: 42–52, 66.

Levita, Elias
    1538   *Sefer tuv ta'am* (Venice: Bomberg).

1538　*Massoret ha-Massoret* (Venice).
Lewis, C.S.
　　1961　*Reflections on the Psalms* (14th impression; Glasgow: Collins–Fount, 1979).
Liebermann, S.
　　1950　*Hellenism in Jewish Palestine* (New York: Jewish Theological Seminary of America).
Liebreich, L. J.
　　1955　'The Songs of Ascents and the Priestly Blessing', *JBL* 74: 33–36.
Liverani, M.
　　2003　*Israel's History and the History of Israel* (trans. C. Peri and P.R. Davies) (London; Equinox, 2005), from *Oltre la Bibbia: Storia Antica di Israele* (Roma-Bari: Laterza & Figli Spa, 2003).
Lyra, Nicholas de
　　1322–31　*Postillae perpetuae in universam S. Scripturam* (Rome: 1st printed ed., 1471).
McCann, J.C.
　　1993　*A Theological Introduction to the Book of Psalms* (Nashville: Abingdon).
　　1993　'Books I–III and the Editorial Purpose of the Hebrew Psalter', in McCann (ed.) 1993: 93–107.
　　2011　*Psalms* (Nashville TN: Abingdon Press).
　　2014　'The Shape and Shaping of the Psalter: Psalms in Their Literary Context', in Brown 2014: 350–362.
McCann, J.C. (ed.)
　　1993　*The Shape and Shaping of the Hebrew Psalter* (JSOTS 159; Sheffield: JSOT).
MacLaren, A.
1893-1904　*The Book of Psalms*. 3 vols. (The Expositor's Bible Series; London: Hodder and Stoughton).
Mannati, M.
　　1979　'Les psaumes graduels constituent-ils un genre littéraire distinct à l'interieur du psautier biblique?' *Semitica* 29: 85–100.
Mantel, H.
　　1961　*Studies in the History of the Sanhedrin* (Cambridge, MA: Harvard University Press).
Mattheson, J.
　　1713　*Das Neu-Eröffnete Orchestre, Oder Universelle und gründliche Anleitung/Wie ein Galant Homme einen vollkommenen Begriff von der Hoheit und Würde der edlen Music erlangen...möge* (Hamburg).
　　1721　*Das Forschende Orchestre, oder desselben Dritte Eröffnung* (Hamburg).
　　1739　*Der vollkommene Capellmeister* (Hamburg).
　　1747　*Behauptung der Himmlischen Musik aus den Gründen der Vernunft, Kirchen-Lehre und Heiliger Schrift* (Hamburg).
Mays, J.L.
　　1994　*Psalms* (Louisville, KT: Westminster John Knox Press).
Mazar, E.
　　2009　*The Palace of King David. Excavations at the Summit of the City of David. Preliminary Report of Seasons 2005–2007* (Jerusalem–New York: Shoham).

McKinnon, J.
    1987   *Music in Early Christian Literature* (Cambridge: Cambridge University Press).

Migne, J.-P.
    1857-1866   *Patrologia Graeca.* 162 vols. plus index (Lutetiæ Parisiorum).
    1844-1974   *Patrologia Latina.* 221 vols. plus indices and supplements (Lutetiæ Parisiorum).

Millard, A.
    1989   'Does the Bible Exaggerate King Solomon's Golden Wealth?' *BAR* 15: 20–29, 31, 34.
    2014   'The New Jerusalem Inscription – So What?' *BAR* 40: 49–53.

Miller, P.D.
    1986   *Interpreting the Psalms* (Philadelphia: Fortress Press).
    1993   'The Beginning of the Psalter', in McCann (ed.) 1993: 83–92.

Milstein, M.
    2010   'King Solomon's Wall Found—Proof of Bible Tale?' *National Geographic News.* 26 February 2010.

Mitchell, D.C.
    1997   *The Message of the Psalter. An Eschatological Programme in the Book of Psalms*, Journal for the Study of the Old Testament Supplement Series 252 (Sheffield: Sheffield Academic Press).
    2005   'Rabbi Dosa and the Rabbis Differ: Messiah ben Joseph in the Babylonian Talmud', *Review of Rabbinic Judaism* 8 (Brill: 2005): 77–90.
    2006a   '"God Will Redeem My Soul from Sheol": The Psalms of the Sons of Korah', *JSOT* 30: 365–384.
    2006b   'Firstborn Shor and Rem: A Sacrificial Josephite Messiah in 1 Enoch 90.37–38 & Deuteronomy 33.17.' *Journal for the Study of the Pseudepigrapha* 15: 211–28.
    2006c   '"Lord, Remember David": G.H. Wilson and the Message of the Psalter', *VT* 56: 526–48.
    2012   'Resinging the Temple Psalmody', *JSOT* 36.3: 355–78.
    2013   'How can we sing the Lord's song? Deciphering the Masoretic Cantillation', in Gillingham (ed.) 2013b: 119–133.

Mithen, S.
    2005   *The Singing Neanderthals: The Origins of Music, Language, Mind, and Body* (London: Weidenfeld and Nicolson).

Moltmann, J.
    1985   *God in Creation: A New Theology of Creation and the Spirit of God* (trans. M. Kohl) (Gifford Lectures, 1984–85; London: SCM).

Mowinckel, S.
    1962   *The Psalms in Israel's Worship.* 2 vols. (trans. D. R. Ap-Thomas (Oxford: Basil Blackwell).

Mykytiuk, L.J.
    2012   'Sixteen Strong Identifications of Biblical Persons (Plus Nine Other Identifications) in Authentic Northwest Semitic Inscriptions from before 539 B.C.E.', in M. Lubetski and E. Lubetski (eds.), *New Inscriptions and Seals Relating to the Biblical World* (Atlanta: Society of Biblical Literature): 35–58.

Na'aman, N.
    2010   'David's Sojourn in Keilah in Light of the Amarna Letters', *VT* 60: 87–97.

Nathan ha-Bavli
    10th cent. *Aḥbar Baghdad* [Chronicle of Baghdad] in A. Neubauer, *Medieval and Jewish Chronicles and Chronological Notes, Volume II.* (Oxford, 1895).

Nel, P.
    1988   'Psalm 132 and Covenant Theology', in W. Claassen (ed.), *Text and Context. Old Testament and Semitic Studies for F. C. Fensham*, Journal for the Study of the Old Testament Supplement Series 48 (Sheffield: Sheffield Academic Press).

O'Connor, M.
    2011   'The Singing of Jesus', in Begbie and Guthrie 2011: 434–53.

Ofer, Y.
    2002a 'The History and Authority of the Aleppo Codex', in M. Glatzer, *Jerusalem Crown Bible Companion Volume* (Jerusalem: Ben-Zvi): 25–50.
    2002b 'The *Jerusalem Crown* and Its Editorial Principles', in M. Glatzer, *Jerusalem Crown Bible Companion Volume* (Jerusalem: Ben-Zvi): 51–59.

Parfitt, T.
    2008   *The Lost Ark of the Covenant* (London: HarperCollins).

Parke-Taylor, G.H.
    1975   *Yahweh: The Divine Name in the Bible* (Waterloo, Ontario: Wilfrid Laurier University Press, 1975).

Peters, J.P.
    1894   'Notes on the Pilgrim Psalter', *JBL* 13: 31–39.
    1922   *The Psalms as Liturgies*, The Paddock Lectures for 1920 (London: Hodder & Stoughton).

Peterson, E.H.
    1989   Answering God: The Psalms as Tools for Prayer (San Francisco: Harper & Row).

Pinches, T.G.
    1908–27 'Sabbath (Babylonian)' in J. Hastings (ed.), *Encyclopedia of Religion and Ethics* (Edinburgh: T. & T. Clark): X.889–91.

Portaleone, Abraham ben David
    1612   *Shiltei ha-giborim* (Mantua).

Preuss, H. D.
    1959   'Die Psalmenüberschriften in Targum und Midrash', *ZAW* 71: 44–54.

Prinsloo, W. S.
    1986   'Psalm 131: Nie my wil nie, o Here', *Skrif en Kerk* 7: 74–82.

Prinsloo, G.T.M.
    2005   'The Role of Space in the שירי המעלות (Psalms 120–134)', *Biblica* 86: 457–477.

Pritchard, J.B. (ed.)
    1950   *Ancient Near Eastern Texts Relating to the Old Testament* (2nd ed. 1955; 3rd ed. 1969).

Provan, I., V.P. Long, and T. Longman
  2003 *A Biblical History of Israel* (Westminster John Knox: Louisville, KT).
Puech, E.
  2010 'L'ostracon de Khirbet Qeyafa et les débuts de la royauté en Israel', *Rev. Bib.* 117: 162–184.
Quasten, J.
  1983 *Music and Worship in Pagan and Christian Antiquity* (trans. B. Ramsey) (Washington, DC: National Association of Pastoral Musicians).
Raabe, P.R.
  1971 'Deliberate Ambiguity in the Psalter', *JBL* 110: 213–227.
Randhofer, R.
  2005 'Singing The Songs of Ancient Israel: *ta'ame 'emet* and Oral Models as Criteria for Layers Of Time In Jewish Psalmody', *Journal of Musicological Research* 24.3: 241–64.
Ratzinger, J.
  1981 *Feast of Faith* (San Francisco: Ignatius).
Redford, D.B.
  1993 *Egypt, Canaan, and Israel in Ancient Times* (Princeton, NJ: Princeton University Press).
Reuven, P.
  2013 'Wooden Beams from Herod's Temple Mount: Do They Still Exist?' *BAR* 39: 40–47.
Ritmeyer, L.
  2006 *The Quest: Revealing the Temple Mount in Jerusalem* (Jerusalem: Carta).
Römer, T.
  2007 *The So-Called Deuteronomistic History: A Sociological, Historical and Literary Introduction* (London–New York: T. & T. Clark).
Ross, A.P.
  2011–15 *A Commentary on the Psalms.* 3 vols. (Grand Rapids, MI: Kregel).
dei Rossi, Azariah
  1573–75 *Me'or enayim* (Mantua).
Rubenstein, J.L.
  1995 *The History of Sukkot in the Second Temple and Rabbinic Periods* (Brown Judaic Studies 302; Atlanta: Scholars Press).
Sa'adya ben Yosef al-Fayumi Gaon
  933 *The Book of Beliefs and Opinions* [*Kitab al-amanat wal-i'tiqadat*] (trans. S. Rosenblatt) (Yale Judaica Series 1; New Haven: Yale University Press, 1948).
        Psalms with a Translation and Commentary of the Gaon Rabbenu Sa'adya b. Joseph Fayumi, tr. into Hebrew by J. Kafih (Jerusalem, 1966).
Sachs, C.
  1929 'Zweiklänge in Altertum', in *Zeitschrift für Johannes Wolf* (Berlin).
  1943 *The Rise of Music in the Ancient World East and West* (New York: Norton).
Sacks, O.
  2007 *Musicophilia* (Toronto: Knopf).

Sáenz-Badillos, A.
   1993 *A History of the Hebrew Language* (Cambridge: Cambridge University Press) (trans. J. Elwold from *Historia de la Lengua Hebrea*) (Editorial AUSA, Sabadell, 1998).

Sagrillo, T.L.
   2012 'Šîšaq's [Shishak's] Army: 2 Chronicles 12:2–3 from an Egyptological Perspective', in G. Galil *et al.* (eds.) 2012: 137-146.

Sanders, E.P.
   1992 *Judaism: Practice and Belief, 63 BCE–66 CE* (London–Philadelphia; SCM–Trinity).

Sanders, P.
   2014 'The Ashkar-Gilson Manuscript: Remnant of a Proto-Masoretic Model Scroll of the Torah', *Journal of Hebrew Studies* 14, article 7 <DOI:10.5508/jhs.2014.v14.a7>: 1–22.

Sarna, N.M.
   1993 *Songs of the Heart: An Introduction to the Book of Psalms* (New York: Schocken).

Sawyer, J.F.A.
   2013 'The Psalms in Judaism and Christianity: A Reception History Perspective' in Gillingham, S.E. (ed.), 2013b: 134–146.

Seidel, H.
   1982 'Wallfahrtslieder', in H. Seidel and K.-H. Bieritz (eds.), *Das Lebendige Wort. Festgabe für G. Voigt* (Berlin: Evangelische Verlaganstalt) 26-40.

Sendrey, A.
   1969 *Music in Ancient Israel* (New York: Philosophical Library).

Seybold, K.
   1978 *Die Wallfahrtspsalmen* (Neukirchen-Vluyn: Neukirchener Verlag).
   1979 'Die Redaktion der Wallfahrtspsalmen', *ZAW* 91:247–268.
   1990 *Introducing the Psalms* (trans. R.G. Dunphy) (Edinburgh: T. & T. Clark).
   2013 'The Psalter as a Book', in Gillingham (ed.) 2013b: 168-181.

Schatz, E.
   2007 'The Weight of the Ark of the Covenant', *JBQ* 35.2: 115-118.

Schick, C.
   1887 *Beit el Makdas, oder der alte Tempelplatz zu Jerusalem: Wie er jetzt ist* (Jerusalem).
   1896 *Die Stiftshütte, der Tempel in Jerusalem, und der Tempelplatz der Jetztzeit* (Berlin).

Shanks, H.
   1994 '"David" Found at Dan', *BAR* 20: 26–39.
   1999 'Has David Been Found in Egypt?', *BAR* 25: 34–35.

Shiloah, A.
   1992 *Jewish Musical Traditions* (Detroit, MI: Wayne State University Press).

Shoemaker, H. S.
   1988 'Psalm 131', *RevExp* 85: 89-94.

Shragai, N.
   2006 'Raiders of the Lost Ark', *Haaretz*, Sunday, February 19, 2006.

Simon, U.
  1982 *Arba Gishot Le-Sefer Tehillim* (Ramat Gan: Bar Ilan University Press); ET: *Four Approaches to the Book of Psalms: From Saadiah Gaon to Ibn Ezra* (Albany, NY: State University of New York Press, 1991).

Smith, P.
  2014 'Infants Sacrificed? The Tale Teeth Tell', *BAR* 40: 54–56, 68.

Stapert, C.
  2007 *A New Song for an Old World: Musical Thought in the Early Church* (Grand Rapids, MI: Eerdmans).

Steindorff, G. and W. Wolf
  1936 *Die Thebanische Graberwelt* (Glückstadt und Hamburg: Augustin).

Stern, M.
  2010 'Reconstructing the Voice of King David's Harps' in Dumbrill (ed.) 2009-10: 161–74.

Stocks, S.
  2012 *The Form and Function of the Tricolon in the Psalms of Ascents: Introducing a New Paradigm for Hebrew Poetic Line-Form* (Eugene, OR: Wipf & Stock).

Talmon, S.
  1969 'Prolegomenon' to R. Butin, *The Ten Nequdoth of the Torah* (1906) (NY: Ktav): i-xxvii.

Tate, M. E.
  1990 *Psalms* 51-100 (Word Biblical Commentaries 20; Waco, TX; Word Books).

Taylor, J.G.
  1993 *Yahweh and the Sun: Biblical and Archaeological Evidence for Sun Worship in Ancient Israel*, Journal for the Study of the Old Testament Supplement Series 111 (Sheffield: Sheffield Academic Press).
  1994 'Was Yahweh Worshiped as the Sun?', *BAR* 20: 53–61, 90–91.

Thiele, E.R.
  1983 *The Mysterious Numbers of the Hebrew Kings* (3rd ed.; Grand Rapids, MI: Zondervan/Kregel; 1st ed. Chicago : University Press, 1951).

Thompson, T.L.
  1999 *The Mythic Past: Biblical Archaeology and the Myth Of Israel* (New York: Basic Books).

Tollinton, R.B.
  1929 *Selections from the Commentaries and Homilies of Origen* (London: SPCK).

Tournay, R.J.
  1982 *Quand Dieu Parle aux Hommes le Langage de l'Amour: Études sur le Cantique des Cantiques* (Cahiers de la Revue Biblique 21; Paris: Gabalda).
  1991 *Seeing and Hearing God with the Psalms*, Journal for the Study of the Old Testament Supplement Series (trans. J.E. Crowley) (Sheffield: Sheffield Academic Press).

Tov, E.
  2009 'The Many Forms of Hebrew Scripture: Reflections in Light of the LXX and 4QReworked Pentateuch', in A. Lange, M. Weigold, & J. Zsengeller (eds.), *From Qumran to Aleppo: A Discussion with Emanuel

Tov about the Textual History of Jewish Scriptures in Honor of his 65th Birthday (Göttingen: Vandenhoeck & Ruprecht).

Tromp, J.
    1989   'The text of Psalm 130:5–6', *VT* 39: 100–103.

De Vaux, R.
    1958–60   *Ancient Israel* (trans. J. McHugh) (London: Darton, Longman and Todd, 1961), from *Les institutions de l'Ancien Testament*. 2 vols. (Paris: Cerf, 1958–60).

VanGemeren, W. A.
    1982   'Ps 131:2 – *kegamul*. The Problems of Meaning and Metaphor', *Hebrew Studies* 23: 51–57.

Vesco, J.-L.
    2006   *Le Psautier de David* (Paris: Cerf).
    2012   *Le Psautier de Jésus* (Paris: Cerf).

Viviers, H.
    1992   'Trust and Lament in the *ma'alot* Psalms (Psalms 120–134)', *OTE* 5: 64–77.
    1994   'The Coherence of the *Ma'a lot* Psalms (Psalms 120–134)', *ZAW* 106: 275–89.

Wal, A. J. O. van der
    1988   'The structure of Ps 129', *VT* 38: 364-367.

Waldman, N.M.
    1989   *The Recent Study of Hebrew: A Survey of the Literature With Selected Bibliography* (Hebrew Union College–Jewish Institute of Religion)

Warker, M. (ed.)
    2012   *Ancient Israel in Egypt and the Exodus* (Washington, DC: Biblical Archaeology Society).

Warren, C. and C.R. Conder
    1884   *Survey of Western Palestine* (London).

Warren, C. and C.W. Wilson
    1871   *The Recovery of Jerusalem: A Narrative of Exploration and Discovery in the City and Holy Land* (London).

Weil, D.M.
    1996   *The Masoretic Chant of the Hebrew Bible* (Jerusalem: Rubin Mass).

Weil, G.E.
    1963   *Elie Levita* (Leiden: Brill).

Wenham, G.J.
    2012   *Psalms as Torah: Reading Biblical Song Ethically* (Grand Rapids, MI: Baker).
    2013   *The Psalter Reclaimed: Praying and Praising with the Psalms* (Wheaton, IL: Crossway).

Werner, E.
    1957   'Musical Aspects of the Dead Sea Scrolls', in *The Musical Quarterly*, 43: 21–37.
    1959   *The Sacred Bridge – The Interdependence of Liturgy and Music in Synagogue and Church during the First Millennium* (New York: Columbia University Press).

1962 'Der vorchristliche und frühchristliche Psalm', in *Die Musik in Geschichte und Gegenwart* (Kassel: Bärenreiter) X:1668-1676.
West, M.L.
1994 'The Babylonian Musical Notation and the Hurrian Melodic Texts', *Music & Letters* 75: 161-179.
Westermann, C.
1981 *Praise and Lament in the Psalms* (Atlanta: John Knox).
de Wette, W. M. L.
1811 *Commentar über die Psalmen* (ed. G. Baur) (5th edn.; Heidelberg: Mohr, 1856).
Whitelam, K.W.
1996 *The Invention of Ancient Israel: The Silencing of Palestinian History* (London: Routledge).
Wickes, W.
1881 טעמי אמ״ת *Taʻamey emet: A Treatise on the Accentuation of...Psalms, Proverbs and Job* (Oxford).
Williams, R.
1994 'Keeping Time', in *Open to Judgement: Sermons and Addresses* (London: Darton, Longman and Todd): 247–50.
Willis, J.T.
1990 'An attempt to decipher Psalm 121:1b', *CBQ* 52: 241–251.
Wilson, C.W.
1866 *Notes on the Survey, and on Some of the Most Remarkable Localities and Buildings in and about Jerusalem* (London).
Wilson, G.H.
1985 *The Editing of the Hebrew Psalter* (SBLDS 76; Chico, CA: Scholars Press).
1986 "The Use of Royal Psalms at the 'Seams' of the Hebrew Psalter", *JSOT* 35: 85–94.
1992 'The Shape of the Book of Psalms', *Interpretation* 46: 129–142.
1993 'Shaping the Psalter: A Consideration of Editorial Linkage in the Book of Psalms', in J. C. McCann (ed.) 1993: 72–82.
1993 'Understanding the Purposeful Arrangement of Psalms in the Psalter: Pitfalls and Promise', in McCann (ed.) 1993: 42–51.
2005 'King, Messiah, and the Reign of God: Revisiting the Royal Psalms and the Shape of the Psalter', in Flint and Miller (eds.) 2005: 391–406.
2005 'The Structure of the Psalter', in Firth and Johnston (eds.) 2005: 229–246.
Wilson, K.A.
2005 *The Campaign of Pharaoh Shoshenq I into Palestine* (Forschungen zum Alten Testament 2. Reihe 9; Tübingen: Mohr Siebeck).
Wilson, R.D.
1926a 'The Headings of the Psalms (1)', *PTR* 24: 1–37.
1926b 'The Headings of the Psalms (2)', *PTR* 24: 353–395.
1925 'Aramaisms in the Old Testament', *PTR* 23: 234–66.
Winer, G.B.
1833–38 *Biblisches Realwörterbuch* (Leipzig).

Yeivin, I.
    1968   *The Aleppo Codex of the Bible: A Study of its Vocalization and Accentuation*. The Hebrew University Bible Project Series, vol. 3, ed. M. Goshen-Gottstein (Jerusalem: Magnes). Hebrew.

Zenger, E.
    1998   'The Composition and Theology of the Fifth Book of Psalms, Psalms 107-145', *JSOT* 80:77–102.

Index of Extra-Biblical Names

Abd al-Malik, Caliph, 57, 187
Abou Mrad, N., 149
Abu al-Faraj Harun, 124, 127
Adler, I., 142, 150
Agrippa, King, 113
Aharon b. Asher, 130, 131, 133, 135, 195, 237, 267, 268, 271
Akiva, 100, 230
Albright, W.F., 46, 79, 113, 238, 267
Aletti, J.-N., 176
Alexander Jannaeus, 121
Alfrink, B., 235
Allegri, G., 228
Allen, L.C., 4, 36, 267
Alter, R., 153
Ambrose of Milan, 124, 225, 226
Amenhotep III, 50
Ammianus Marcellinus, 185
Antiochus Epiphanes, 55
Arends, L., 140
Arieh, E., 179
Aristoxenos, 145
Auffret, P., 4, 12, 268
Augustine of Hippo, 212
Avenary, H., 101, 109, 130, 268
Avigad, N., 243
Bach, J.S., 4, 221
Baer, S., 123, 135, 267, 268
Bahat, D., 245
Baḥya ben Asher of Saragossa, 15
Baker, J. & Nicholson, E.W., 33
Barton, J., 212
Bathyra, sons of, 128, 129, 134, 254
Beaucamp, E., 4, 12, 268
Beaulieu, S., 68
Bede, 15
Beethoven, L., 75
Benjamin of Tudela, 131
Ben-Zvi, I. President, 133
Berl, H., 140
Berlin, A., 206
Bernstein, L., 97
Biran, A., 72
Boethius, 218

Bonhoeffer, D., 188, 228, 269
Booij, T., 3
Bordeaux Pilgrim, 58, 245
Boyce, W., 4
Brahms, J., 182
Breuer, M., 133, 269
Briggs, C.A. & E.G., 33, 36, 269
Bright, J., 36
Brown, R.L., 123, 146, 269, 270, 271, 273, 274, 278, 280
Browning, R., 10
Bruce, F.F., 36, 41, 269
Buonaparte, Napoleon, 73
Burns, D., 240
Burns, J., 260
Burton, Lady Isabel, 60
Burton, Sir Richard, 60
Caedmon, 223
Calov, A., 221
Calvin, J., 225, 270
Campbell, D.G., 220
Cassuto, M.D., 132
Champollion, J.-F., 140, 142
Chédid, Y., 149
Churchill, W.S., 73
Civil, M., 95
Claissé-Walford, N. de, 212, 270
Clement of Alexandria, 155, 156
Cohen, A., 189, 197
Cohen, M., 133
Cohen, S., 251
Cole, R.L., 212
Coogan, M.D., 240
Crassus, 55
Crickmore, L., 109, 143, 271
Cristiani, P., 235
Crocker, R.L., 123, 146, 278
Cross, F.M., 238
Crow, L.D., 4, 12, 271
Ctesibius, 88, 89
Curwen, J., 100
Dahood, M., 9, 36, 203, 238, 271
Dallán Forgaill, 223
Darius, 46

Davies, P.R., 240
Dayan, M., 61
de Bergerac, Cyrano, 73
De Wette, W.M.L., 34
Delitzsch, Franz, 33, 34, 132, 138
Delitzsch, Friedrich, 7, 251
Derenbourg, J., 124, 135, 271
Deutsch, R., 243
Diodorus Siculus, 188
Disney, W., 183
Dobbs-Allsopp, F.W., 152
Dotan, A., 127, 132, 134, 135, 267, 271
Driver, G.R., 70, 74
Duchesne-Guillemin, M., 142, 272
Duhm, B., 181, 182
Dumas, A., 73
Dumbrill, R.J., xiv, 86, 144, 145, 146, 219, 272, 274, 279, 285
Dupré, M., 141, 142
Duruflé, M., 142
Dutilleux, H., 142
Edersheim, A., 30
Ehrlich, T.F., 55
Eleazar b. Zemaḥ, 131
Eliezer b. Jacob, 106
Elizabeth II, 49
Ephrem of Nisibe, Saint, 149
Euripides, 136
Eusebius, xvi, 57, 124
Ewald, G.H.A., 231
Finkelstein, I., 85, 240, 272
Finzi, J.L., 150
Fleischer, O., 123, 273
Flender, R., 123, 124, 138, 263, 273
Fletcher, A., 170
Flint, P.W., 70, 273, 287
Forbes, J., 12, 211, 212, 273
Freedman, D.S., 238
Friedman, M., 133
Galil, G., xiv, 73, 79, 241, 245, 273, 276, 284
Gamaliel, Rabban, 118
Gamliel I, 58
Garfinkel, Y., 72
Garsiel, M., 34

Génébrard, G., 231, 273
Gerson-Kiwi, E., 100, 101, 123, 139, 259, 273
Gesenius, W., xvi, 34, 74, 231, 232, 233, 274
Getz, Rabbi Y., 61
Geyer, P. & Kuntz, O., 58
Gibb, R., 101
Gibran, K., 4, 187
Gibson, S., 57
Gikatilla, Joseph b. Abraham, 15
Gikatilla, Moshe ha-Kohen, 78
Gillingham, S., 4, 132, 268, 274, 276, 281, 284
Ginsburg, C.D., 127, 134, 135, 151, 169, 182, 195, 255, 258, 274
Glareanus, H., 145
Glaser, O., 140
Glover, S., 100
Glück, J.J., 34
Golan, O., 242, 243, 244
Goldingay, J., 4, 36, 75, 164, 176, 274
Goldwasser, O., 72
Goren, Rabbi S., 61, 171
Gorris, E., 89
Gould, G., 97
Goulder, M.D., 36, 274
Graetz, H., 127, 135, 275
Graziano, A.J.S., 150
Grossberg, D., 4
Gunkel, H., 79
Haïk-Vantoura, S., 123, 134, 140, 141, 142, 146, 147, 148, 150, 151, 152, 154, 155, 156, 159, 176, 256, 257, 258, 259, 260, 262, 263, 264, 275, 277
Hajdu, A., 146
Halpern, B., 244
Hananiah, Rabbi, 58
Handel, G.F., 4, 220, 222
Hanina b. Teradion, 230
Hattusil, 49
Haupt, L., 140
Hayman, P., 6
Hengstenberg, E.W., 8, 12, 18, 19, 113, 209, 276

Henry V, King, 73
Henry VIII, King, 73
Herodotus, 123, 162
Herzog, A., 132, 146, 276
Hickmann, H., 95, 109, 145, 146, 259, 276
Hilary of Poitiers, 223
Hiley, D., 100, 101, 123, 273
Hillel, 125, 129, 254
Hippolytus, 32, 279
Hisda, Rabbi, 33
Hoffmeier, J.K., 36, 276
Hossfeld, F.-L., 36
Houwelingen, P.H.R. van, 124
Hygros the Levite, 101, 125
Ibn Ezra, Avraham b. Meir, 77, 78, 185, 285
Idelsohn, A.Z., 138, 146, 155, 277
Ilani, S., 243
Jacobson, D.M., 57
Jacobson, J., 148, 263
Jenkins, J.S., 220
Jerome, 5, 33, 226
John Chrysostom, 124, 225
Joseph, M., 251
Josephus, Flavius, xvi, 32, 52, 54, 57, 61, 85, 86, 93, 105, 112, 113, 115, 121, 124, 152, 240, 245, 250
Joshua b. Hananiah, 104, 112
Josquin des Prez, 4
Jourdan-Hemmerdinger, D., 142
Judah Maccabee, 129
Judah, Rabbi, 118
Julianus Caesar, 185
Kahle, P., 127, 129, 277
Kallai, Z., 79
Kaufman, A., 245
Keet, C.C., 27, 189
Khan, G., 76
Kilmer, A. Draffkorn–, 95, 109, 123, 142, 143, 146, 278
Kimḥi, David, 33, 78, 79, 94, 183, 185, 198, 206, 214, 268, 278
Kirkpatrick, A.F., 33, 161, 278
Kitchen, K.A., 36, 41, 71, 72, 241, 278
Klein, 4

Kleinig, J.W., 84, 98, 221, 278
Kodaly, Z., 100
Lachmann, R., 138, 279
Landels, J.G., 95
Lane-Poole, S., 60
Laperrousaz, E.-M., 244, 279
Lassus, O., 4
Leaver, R.A., 221
Lemaire, A., 72, 243, 279
Leonitius, J., 33
Leval, G., 72
Levin, Y., 41, 79
Levita, E., 134, 231, 274, 279, 286
Lewis, C.S., 164
Liebermann, S., 136
Liverani, M., 240, 280
Long, V.P., 36
Longman, T., 36
Luther, M., 218, 221
Lyra, N., 33, 280
Maatouk, T., 149
Maimonides. *See* Rambam
Mannati, M., 4, 12, 189, 280
Mantel, H., 129
Martini, R., 235
Mattenah, Rabbi, 88
Matheson, J., 220, 221, 228, 280
Mazar, E., 37, 73, 79, 280
McCann, J.C., 212
McCorkle. D., 150, 151
Meiri, Menachem, 198
Mendelssohn, F., 4
Menelik I, 55
Messiaen, O., 142
Midrash on Psalms, 6
Millard, A., 73, 241, 281
Miller, P.D., 189
Mitchell, D.C., 3, 6, 8, 11, 31, 51, 71, 80, 91, 106, 148, 150, 211, 212, 215, 216, 226
Mithen, S., 219
Moltmann, J., 224
Monteverdi, C., 4, 97
Moses de Leon, 15
Mosheh b. Asher, 128, 129, 130, 134, 135

Mowinckel, S., 65
Mozart, W.A., 4
Murray, J., 220
Mykytiuk, L.J., 72, 281
Na'aman, N., 42
Nathan b. Isaac ha-Kohen, 125
Natronai b. Ḥilai, 130, 135
Naveh, J., 72
Nebuchadnezzar, 241
Newman, M., 73
Nicetas, 223
O'Connor, M., 226
Ofer, Y., xiv, 132, 133, 141, 282
Origen, 5, 11, 285
Parfitt, T., 56
Parke-Taylor, G.H., 231, 238, 282
Pesikta de-Rav Kahana, 6
Petaḥiah of Regensburg, 130
Petrie, F., 72
Philo Judaeus, xvi, 105, 240
Plato, 156, 218
Pliny, 218, 223
Plutarch, 183, 188
Pompey, 55
Portaleone, A. ben David, 140, 282
Prinsloo, 13, 282
Provan, I., 36
Prudentius, 223
Puech, E., 72
Purcell, H., 4
Pythagoras, 142, 145, 218
Quasten, J., 103, 283
Raabe, P.R., 34
Rabbah b. Shela, 88
Rachmaninov, S., 228
Radak. *See* Kimḥi
Ralegh, Sir Walter, 73
Rambam (Moshe b. Maimon), 56, 130
Randhofer, R., 139
Rashi (R. Shlomo b. Yitzhak), 77, 78, 88, 100, 124, 126, 161, 185, 188, 190, 198, 250
Ratzinger, J. (Pope Benedict XIV), 224
Reich, R., 242
Reuven, P., 244

Rhau, G., 218
Rhodes, C.J., 171
Ritmeyer, L., xiv, 57, 58, 59, 111, 115, 245, 246, 247, 248, 283
Rogerson, J.W., 240
Römer, T., 240
Ross, A.P., 74
Saʻadya Gaon, 130, 132, 135, 216, 268, 283
Sachs, C., 92, 95, 141, 155, 156, 283
Sachs–Hornbostel, 92
Sacks, O., 220
Sáenz-Badillos, A., 76, 203, 239, 284
Sagiv, T., 245
Sagrillo, T.L., 41
Samuel Ha-Nagid, 73
Sanders, P., 130, 135
Sargon II, 46
Saul, Abba, 230
Schatz, E., 246, 247, 284
Schick, C., 57
Schiller, H., 142
Segre, A., 150
Seidel, H., 12, 36, 284
Sendrey, A., 86, 91, 96, 101, 104, 111, 123, 140, 152, 284
Seybold, K., 3, 4, 12, 284
Shakespeare, W., 75
Shanks, H., 72, 242, 284
Shishak, Pharaoh, 40, 41, 42, 54, 55, 72, 73, 188, 211, 241, 284
Shlomo b. Buya'a, 131
Shragai, N., 61, 284
Silbermann, N.A., 240
Silverman, J., 148
Simeon b. Gamaliel, 88, 115
Simon bar Kokhba, 85, 230
Smith, P., 188
Sozomen of Gaza, 186
Stapert, C., 225
Steindorff, G. & Wolf, W., 50
Steiner, T.M., 36
Stern, M., 159
Stocks, S., 152, 153, 285
Strack, H.L., 123, 135, 268
Stravinsky, I., 228

Sulgi, King, 142
Suso, H., 223
Sydney, Sir Philip, 73
Talmon, S., 136
Taylor, J.G., 68
Theodoret, 187, 231, 232
Thiele, E.R., 245
Thomas of Celano, 223
Thompson, T.L., 240
Timotheus, Patriarch, 129
Tisserand, J., 223
Titus, 54, 55, 90, 113
Tollinton, R.B., 5
Tolstoy, L., 24
Tournay, R.J., 34, 285
Trajan Caesar, 223
Trublet, J., 176
Tut-ankh-amun, 45, 47, 49
Varro, Marcus Terentius, 95
Verhulst, W., 89
Vesco, J.-L., 12, 286
Viviers, M., 4
Viviers, X., 12, 286
Waldman, N.M., 154
Warker, M., 85
Warren, C., 57

Weil, D.M., 134
Weil, G.E., 130, 151
Weil. D.M., 150
Wenham, G., 170
Werner, E., 123, 124, 139, 140, 146, 149, 157, 286
Wesley, J., 227
Whitelam, K., 240
Whitman, W., 10
Wickes, W., 132, 134, 138, 287
Willaert, A., 97
Williams, R., 220
Wilson, C.W., 57
Wilson, G.H., 5, 71, 212
Wilson, R.D., 9, 27, 75
Winer, G.B., 34, 287
Winnington-Ingram, R.P., 142
Yardeni, A., 244
Yasser, J., 140
Yehudah ha-Levi, 238
Yeivin, I., 133, 141, 148, 150, 151
Yoḥanan ben Zakkai, 124, 125, 126
Zalzal, M., 149
Zelenka, J., 4
Zenger, E., 4, 12, 276

Printed in Great Britain
by Amazon